Efficacy of Sound

Efficacy of Sound

Power, Potency, and Promise in the
Translocal Ritual Music of Cuban Ifá-Òrìṣà

RUTHIE MEADOWS

The University of Chicago Press
Chicago and London

The University of Chicago Press, Chicago 60637
The University of Chicago Press, Ltd., London
Published 2023
Printed in the United States of America

32 31 30 29 28 27 26 25 24 23   1 2 3 4 5

ISBN-13: 978-0-226-83022-3 (cloth)
ISBN-13: 978-0-226-82895-4 (paper)
ISBN-13: 978-0-226-82894-7 (e-book)
DOI: https://doi.org/10.7208/chicago/9780226828947.001.0001

Library of Congress Cataloging-in-Publication Data

LCCN: 2023005944

Contents

Examples and Transcriptions

All audio and video examples are available on this book's companion website, https://press.uchicago.edu/sites/meadows/index.html.

Audio Examples

Audio Example 1: Olóyè

Audio Example 2: Ẹnu olóyè

Audio Example 3: Calle Infanta

Audio Example 4: Eni rere

Audio Example 5: Excerpt of opening incantation

Audio Example 6: Ìyánífá wring the herbs and plants

Audio Example 7: Ìyánífá give the ikin Ifá their bath

Audio Example 8: Egúngún masquerade in Baracoa

Audio Example 9: Egúngún masquerade in Havana

Transcriptions

Example 1. Nagybe Madariaga Pouymiró plays the toque obanlá on all three consecrated batá drums while ìyánífá Fonseca and ìyánífá López Rubio join her in singing the chorus of a praise song to Ifá. As performed on June 22, 2015. Transcription by the author.

Example 2. Sketch of Michael Spiro and Justin Hill's transcription of the Havana-style approach to the fourth road of Osain as played by Regino Jiménez, Fermin Naní, and José Pilar Suárez in the mid-1990s. Transcription adapted by the author from Spiro and Hill (2017, 34).

Video Example

Abbreviations

ACYC   Yoruba Cultural Association of Cuba
ICFIR   International Council for Ifá Religion
OIATYR Odùgbemi International Association for Traditional Yoruba Religion
YTR   Yorùbá traditional religion

Preface

In 2016, I sat in the open-air dining room of Enrique Orozco Rubio's home in the Cuban city of Santiago de Cuba, facing a table covered with laptops, microphones, electronic cables, and flash drives. Adjacent to an outdoor courtyard that provided an intermittent breeze, we—and our electronic equipment—mercifully evaded direct contact with the sun, if not the pervasive summer heat. Seated and facing his laptop, Orozco Rubio played the final cut of a documentary he cowrote and edited that summer with one of his *ahijados* (ritual godchildren), the young Santiago de Cuba filmmaker Noel Rodríguez Portuondo. Entitled *Ìyánifá: The Necessary Evolution*, the documentary opens with a striking scene (Rodríguez Portuondo 2016). In it, a young woman, Yadira Flamand Rodríguez, sits on a tan, palm-frond mat, her legs outstretched on the ground and flanking a carved, circular divination tray made of thick mahogany wood and covered with yellow powder. In her hands, she rubs together a set of sacred *ikin* (palm tree nuts) while breathing a prayer through her fingers.[1] On the ground across from her sits her client, the film's director, Portuondo, dressed casually in dark pants and a light-blue T-shirt and patiently awaiting his divination reading. Suddenly, Rodríguez breaks into powerful song, rubbing the sacred ikin together in her palms. Expertly, she lifts as many nuts as she can out of her left hand swiftly with her right, instantaneously registering the number that are left behind before forcefully bringing her hands—and the sacred ikin—back together. The ikin strike one another loudly, creating a distinctive, repetitive sound in her palms that punctuates the rich cadence of her voice. The camera traces downward from the silk ceremonial cap that Rodríguez wears on her head, briefly lingering on a tattoo on her upper arm long enough for the viewer to register its image: a silhouette of palm trees emerging from a three-pronged crown, with

FIGURE P.1. Still of the documentary *Ìyánífá: The Necessary Evolution* (2016). Yadira Flamand Rodríguez uses the *ikin* (palm tree nuts) to reveal a sign for her client, the filmmaker Noel Rodríguez Portuondo. Photo by the author.

the words *Ifá Ìranlówo* inked beneath.[2] The camera finally rests on a close-up of Rodríguez's hands, juxtaposing her hot pink–painted fingernails with the expert maneuvering of the black, clattering ikin. With the middle finger of her right hand, Rodríguez methodically "cuts" the powder of the divining tray in front of her with a series of single and double lines, gradually form-ing the distinctive ideogrammatic figure of an *odù*, or divinatory "sign" (see Bascom 1969a, 7, 8). This sign forms the basis of her client's reading and the foundation of the divinatory practice of Ifá in Cuba (see fig. P.1).

   The exquisite details of this enrapturing, opening filmic scene break forcefully with a foundational taboo in Cuban Ifá: the strict and passionately enforced prohibition against female use of Ifá's implements—including its ca-pacious ritual sonority—for divination. Through on-screen text, Rodríguez is revealed to be an *iyánífá*, or priestess of the divining practice of Ifá. This controversial and recently introduced designation is modeled on the gender norms of female initiation in contemporary Yorùbáland, Nigeria, where Cu-ban Ifá traces its roots. On-screen, Rodríguez's forceful voice, the striking sound of the sacred ikin crashing between her palms, and her commanding use of Ifá's instruments of divination offer powerful demonstrations of fe-male presence and ritual authority. Behind her, a chorus of ìyánífá erupt into song, strengthening Rodríguez's verse in call-and-response and animating the manifesting force (*àṣẹ*) of her reading.[3] For many Cuban viewers, includ-ing those who first witnessed the film's premier at the Almacén de Imagen film festival in Camagüey in 2016, these shocking images provide their first glimpse into the controversial gendered and ritual transformations wrought through the burgeoning "African traditionalist" movement (*el tradicionalismo africano*) in Cuba.

Across the Americas and Europe, women and men are transforming the landscape of Ifá divination and *oricha* (deity) worship through transatlantic travel and reconnection with Yorùbáland, Nigeria.[4] Mobile Ifá missionaries hailing from Cuba, Latin America, the Caribbean, Europe, and Nigeria itself traverse the reaches of the Yorùbá-inspired ritual diaspora, instigating revisionist ideologies in Ifá and oricha practice (see Barnet 1997; Fernández Olmos 2007). In Cuba, where oricha worship and Ifá divination—collectively, Regla de Ocha-Ifá—emerged as a ritual complex in the wake of transatlantic slavery, women and men are driven to Nigerian-style Ifá by its promise of efficacy—in other words, because they find Yorùbá approaches more useful, more efficacious.[5] Through efficacy, African traditionalists reshape Cubans' relationships with West Africa, providing new opportunities for gendered participation and transatlantic ritual authority.

As I watched Orozco Rubio and Portuondo's documentary, I was struck by the ways that this logic of efficacy drives ruptures in Cuban ritual. On-screen, priestesses and priests actively resculpt sound—from music to the sonority of voice and language—to heighten the power, potency, and success of Ifá ritual. Women wield the fate-transformative sonority and instruments of Ifá divination—a form of gendered use unthinkable in Cuban-style Ifá—through their participation in "Nigerian-style" ritual communities. These revisionists look beyond Cuba and toward contemporary Yorùbáland as a source of heightened ritual efficacy and, more broadly, life-altering potentiality. As I viewed this opening scene, several of the key questions informing this book coalesced. How does the perception of efficacy in Nigerian-style Ifá serve as a driver of engagement and authority in a local yet profoundly globally oriented ritual movement? How is the efficacy of ritual intimately bound with the efficacy of sound? And how do women in particular harness the efficacy of "Nigerian-style" Ifá to create novel forms of access and potentiality?

In *Efficacy of Sound: Power, Potency, and Promise in the Translocal Ritual Music of Cuban Ifá-Òrìṣà*, I explore the "Nigerian-style" ritual movement in Cuban Ifá divination.[6] Drawing on thirty-two months of extensive, multisited ethnographic research in Cuba (2014–16) and follow-up trips to Cuba (2020) and Nigeria (2018), I examine what I term *efficacy*—the perceived power, potency, and capacity of a given approach or thing to enact a desired change— in the revisionist African traditionalist movement in Cuba. Proposing an alternative lens through which to view engagement in ritual movements across the Global South, this book uses feminist and queer theory along with critical studies of Africanity to explore the relation between utility and affect within translocal ritual music circulations. In it, I take seriously the role of usefulness and problem-solving in transatlantic practices rooted in solutions-oriented interventions and life-altering transformations of fate. I point to the ways in which the perceived efficacy of distant "Yorùbá" versus proximate "Cuban" approaches to ritual sonority builds on and recrafts transatlantic sensibilities and global affective ties. I trace the ways in which Ifá priestesses (ìyánífá), priests (babaláwo), and female batá drummers (bataleras) harness Yorùbá-centric approaches to ritual music and sound to heighten efficacy and achieve desired ritual outcomes. Additionally, I expand the notion of efficacy to explore the ways that African traditionalists creatively mobilize contemporary Yorùbá models of gender and institution-building as a potent, powerful, and capacity-filled means to achieve specific goals and personal desires some 5,800 miles away. Within a contentious religious landscape marked by the idiosyncrasies of revolutionary state policy, women and men mobilize the efficacy of Nigerian-style Ifá-Òrìṣà to reshape ritual femininity and masculinity, state religious policy, and transatlantic ritual authority in Cuba.

In a broad sense, *Efficacy of Sound* journeys through the ways in which the local exists in complex interplay with the global, providing a specific yet broadly relevant case study on the intricate dynamics of use and influence between the far and the close, the proximate and the distant. In it, I explore the logic of efficacy as a central driver of engagement and authority in a globally oriented ritual movement, underscoring the perception and predication of efficacy—and the efficacy of sound—on a richly translocal scale. In this way, the book brings a renewed focus on use and usefulness to the study of music, ritual sonority, and, more broadly, transnational ritual movements. Additionally, it brings a renewed interest in the imbrication of usefulness and promise to transnational studies of gender, particularly as these relate to the refashioning of femininity and masculinity through transnational forms of engagement and reenvisioning.

On Terminology and Orthographic Choice

"Nigerian-style" revisionists in Cuba use the terms "African traditionalism" (*el tradicionalismo africano*) and "Nigerian-style Ifá-Òrìṣà" (*Ifá-Òrìṣà nigeriano*) to distinguish themselves and their practices from "Cuban-style" Regla de Ocha-Ifá.[7] Additionally, revisionists use the terms "traditional African Ifá" (*Ifá tradicional africano*), "African-style Ifá" (*Ifá africano*), "Nigerian-style Ifá" (*Ifá estilo nigeriano, Ifá nigeriano*), "traditional Nigerian Ifá" (*Ifá tradicional nigeriano*), and, often, simply "traditionalism" (*el tradicionalismo*) to make this distinction.

In reference to Cuban-style Ifá, revisionists use the terms "Cuban Ifá" (*Ifá cubano*), "traditional Cuban Ifá" (*Ifá tradicional cubano*), or *Ifá criollo* (Creole, or Cuban-engendered, *Ifá*). To reference Cuban-style oricha worship specifically, practitioners use the terms *Regla de Ocha* (Rule of the Oricha) (see Barnet 1997) and *Santería* (see Cabrera 1993; De La Torres 2004; Hagedorn 2001).

In this book, I use the aforementioned terms interchangeably to reference "Nigerian-style" and "Cuban-style" Ifá and oricha/*òrìṣà* practice, following the language and terms used contextually by revisionists themselves.

The use of specific spellings and diacritics (e.g., *babalao* vs. *babaláwo*) can also be indicative of the linguistic and ideological split between Cuban-style Regla de Ocha-Ifá and Nigerian-style Ifá-Òrìṣà.[8] Thus, orthography often conforms to Lucumí (Cuban ritual lexicon) spellings in the case of Regla de Ocha-Ifá (e.g., *babalao, Yoruba, oricha/Ocha*),[9] or, more recently and in preference for the contemporary Yorùbá language in African traditionalism, to Standard Yorùbá orthography and diacritics as established in Nigeria (*babaláwo, Yorùbá, òrìṣà*).[10] These demarcations, however, are often blurred on both sides of the fence. African traditionalists and Regla de Ocha-Ifá practitioners, for example, regularly make idiosyncratic orthographic and diacritic choices that conform neither to traditional Lucumí spellings nor to Standard Yorùbá. This dynamic reflects the creative and flexible spelling choices made across the long history of Lucumí "denotation" in Cuba (Wirtz 2007a, 250); the variegated and contested nature of orthography and diacritics among Yorùbá speakers in Nigeria itself (Olúmúyìwá 2013, 40);[11] and, subsequently, the idiosyncratic spelling and translation choices made by Nigerian-style and Yorùbá traditional religion practitioners globally (chapter 1).

In this book, I've chosen to uphold orthographic preference according to whether the signified falls within the domain of Cuban Regla de Ocha-Ifá (e.g., *babalao* [Lucumí]) or African traditionalism (*babaláwo* [Standard Yorùbá]). Any orthographic choices made in writing by practitioners are repeated verbatim and indicated in the text. Any idiosyncratic spellings conforming to neither Lucumí nor Standard Yorùbá (a common occurrence) are also reproduced verbatim and indicated.

INTRODUCTION

I first traveled to Havana in August 2012, a time of electrifying change and socioeconomic transformation in Cuba's capital city. After completing my PhD coursework in ethnomusicology at the University of Pennsylvania, I took a semester-long position as the resident director for Penn Global's study abroad program at the University of Havana and the Fundación del Nuevo Cine Latinoamericano, Cuba's renowned Latin American film institute. Unbeknownst to me at the time, I would continue to work and conduct research in Cuba year-round from 2012 to 2016, serving both as a foreign ethnomusicology researcher affiliated with the Cuban Ministry of Culture's Juan Marinello Cultural Research Institute (El Instituto Cubano de Investigaciones Culturales Juan Marinello [ICIC], 2014–2016) and as resident director for Penn Global's study abroad program during fall semesters (2012–2015). As a US American woman living full-time in Havana, this unusually extended stay in Cuba—and my dual and often vastly discrete professional capacities as an ethnographic researcher and director of a US-affiliated university program—afforded invaluable opportunities to engage with academic and state cultural institutions, researchers and ethnographers, ritual practitioners, and musicians in Havana and throughout Cuba's regional provinces. Notably, these four years in Cuba also offered a deep and prolonged lens into a sociopolitical and economic landscape that was rapidly shifting. Shortly before my arrival, President Raúl Castro introduced sweeping economic reforms to expand Cuba's private and entrepreneurial sector, announcing the impending elimination of 500,000 state sector jobs and a promised "parallel increase in the non-state sector" that included licenses for 181 types of private-sector and entrepreneurial (*cuentapropismo*) work.[1] The facades of the buildings of the neighborhoods I most frequented in my initial years—Centro Habana,

Vedado, Playa, and La Habana Vieja—seemingly transformed before my eyes as hundreds of thousands of Cubans obtained licensed, private-sector work, opening *paladares* (private restaurants), *cafeterías*, barbershops, clothing stands, pirated DVD and CD stores, and other businesses out of their homes (A. Hamilton 2011; P. Peters 2012).

Globally, these years also marked worldwide media coverage of Cuba born from the reestablishment of relations between Cuba and the United States. As would later become starkly apparent, these four years in Cuba overlapped directly with the second US president Barack Obama administration, a period of unprecedented opening in US-Cuba relations that would soon be reversed, aggressively and abruptly, by President Donald Trump.[2] Long before the reality TV star and future White nationalist instigator was on the radar as a serious contender for the US presidency, however, President Obama enacted historic and unprecedented changes to US-Cuban relations that significantly reversed decades of hostility between the two nations. These, in turn, significantly impacted my own capacity as a US American citizen to conduct multiyear, multisited, and relatively unfettered research there. On December 17, 2014, presidents Castro and Obama bilaterally announced the reestablishment of diplomatic ties between Cuba and the United States. President Obama proclaimed "the most significant changes in our policy in more than fifty years" and the end to "an outdated approach that, for decades, has failed to advance our interests" (White House 2014). The next morning, my study abroad students rushed to nearby kiosks and street vendors to buy up copies of the *Granma* newspaper with the historic headline "Aplauso mundial por acercamiento entre Cuba y Estados Unidos" (Global applause over the closening [of relations] between Cuba and the United States) before their flights home that day (Redacción Internacional 2014). The US embassy in Havana, officially shuttered since 1961 due to the severing of diplomatic ties between both nations, reopened officially in tandem with the Cuban embassy in Washington, DC, in 2015.[3] A month later, John Kerry became the first US secretary of state to travel to Cuba in seven decades, and the following March 2016, President Barack Obama visited with his entire family—the first active US president to do so since 1928. With a rise in global media coverage of Cuba, tourism to the island skyrocketed, with a 77 percent increase from US citizens alone (Bouchet 2016). As commercial flights, cruise ship travel, and mail delivery resumed between both nations, residents of Habana Vieja and Centro Habana witnessed daily hordes of cruise ship tourists from all over the world walking through their densely populated, urban streets.[4]

Despite these changes with the United States, however, the lives of those I most deeply engaged with during my four years in Cuba were profoundly reshaped by a very different reconnection: not that of Cuba and the United States, but of Cuba and Nigeria. My first encounter with Nigerian-style Ifá occurred a month into my first visit in the fall of 2012. At the time, the visual artist and cultural promoter Ruddy Fernández García asked me to coproduce a music video for an amateur rumba group, Los Caballeros de la Rumba, in Santiago de las Vegas, a small ward on the outskirts of Havana.[5] During one of many consecutive weekends spent shooting the film, Fernández, the group's artistic director, introduced me to a close friend, Julio Martínez Betancourt, an African traditionalist *babaláwo*, ethnographer, and ethnobotanist at the University of Havana–affiliated National Botanical Garden of Cuba (Jardín Botánico Nacional). Over the course of the next four years, Martínez Betancourt would become a major player in the academic study of African traditionalism in Cuba, tracing a genealogy of the approximately forty-six *egbé*, or African traditionalist brother- and sisterhoods,[6] that have emerged in Cuba since the 1990s.[7] In his role as both an academic researcher and practitioner of Nigerian-style Ifá-Òrìṣà, Martínez Betancourt laid the foundation for the academic study of African traditionalism in Cuba while also—through his own status as a babaláwo—serving as a messenger between (and, to a degree, organizer of) the varied African traditionalist egbé located throughout Cuba's regional provinces. Martínez Betancourt's dual academic and ritual approaches to *Ifá nigeriano*—and the ways that his academically minded approaches to Ifá and his ritually minded approaches to academic ethnography inform one another—offered a profound glimpse into what anthropologist Stephen Palmié (2013, 9) theorizes as the "ethnographic interface" at the heart of Afro-Cuban religion since its inception as such in the early twentieth century. As I encountered in my fieldwork throughout Cuba's provinces, this dynamic is heightened in Nigerian-style Ifá-Òrìṣà by notable and influential scholars-turned-practitioners and practitioners-turned-scholars, an aspect of African traditionalism that I explore in detail in chapter 3 (see fig. I.1).

Slightly over a year after meeting Martínez Betancourt, I initiated ethnographic fieldwork as a foreign ethnomusicologist affiliated with the ICIC (January 2014–August 2016). During this time, I conducted extensive, multisited research on Nigerian-style Ifá-Òrìṣà in eastern, central, and western Cuba, including the urban centers of Havana and Santiago de Cuba and the regional provinces of Holguín, Ciego de Ávila, and Guantánamo. Martínez Betancourt was one of my principal, ongoing interlocutors and friends during my four years in Cuba and almost three years of ICIC-affiliated research. He also generously provided the initial contacts with members of the fifteen egbé with whom I later conducted research (at the time, twenty-two egbé were active across Cuba's regional provinces, a number that more than

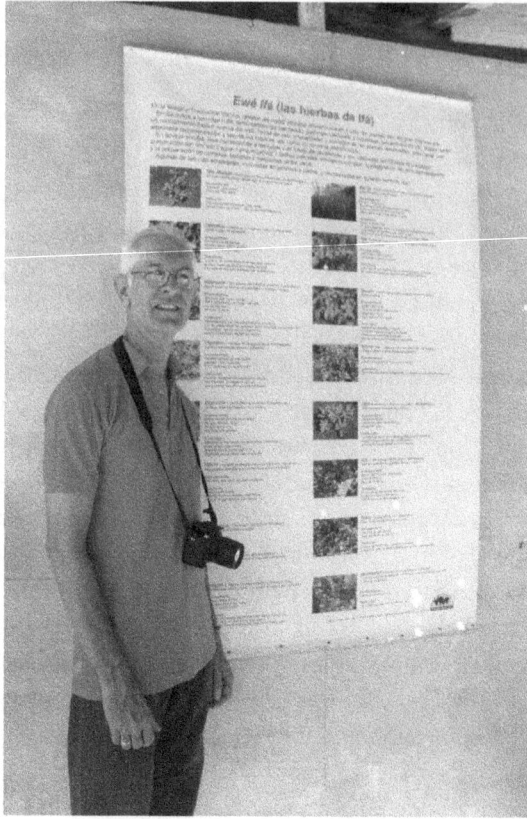

FIGURE I.1. Ethnobotanist and babaláwo Julio Martínez Betancourt, who has traced a genealogy of the forty-six ẹgbẹ́ in Cuba. Santiago de las Vegas, Cuba, 2015. Photo by the author.

doubled between when I left Cuba in 2016 and my last visit to Havana in March 2020) (Martínez Betancourt, pers. comm., 2020).

As I initiated research with ẹgbẹ́ in western Havana, eastern Santiago de Cuba, and throughout Cuba's regional provinces, I witnessed how the interventions of African traditionalist practitioners and ritual musicians present a microcosm of polemical debates in Cuba surrounding Africanity, traditionality, and ritual femininity, particularly in relation to a given individuals' ability (ever gendered and racialized) to audibly wield African-inspired, fate-transformative efficacy. Additionally, I found that musicians' and ritual practitioners' creative adaptations of contemporary Yorùbá approaches to ritual respond to—and locally shape—larger shifts in the processes of state religious mediation that have occurred since the postatheist "Special Period" of the 1990s. I encountered women and men who actively craft sound, language, and listening as a means to articulate a Yorùbá-centric orientation to "true"

African traditionality in Ifá divination and òrìṣà worship. I became intrigued by the relation of efficacy to affect and orientation in a translocal, globally oriented ritual movement.

I came to understand that in Ifá divination, sounds carry use. Through this usefulness, sounds potentiate possibilities. And through possibility, sounds enable novel forms of orientation and affect, transformation and change. In Ifá divination and òrìṣà worship in Cuba, ritual practices center on efficacy—in other words, on the transformative potential of the òrìṣà to aid in solving real-world problems within conditions of human precarity. Beyond necessity, women and men work with Ifá and the òrìṣà to create optimal conditions for the fulfillment of deep personal desires (health, success, love, wealth, etc.), in turn improving and sculpting the circumstances of life. Central to this fulfillment is the perceived usefulness of particular approaches to ritual sonority, including ritual music and the sonority of language. In Nigerian-style Ifá, practitioners harness the generative potential of sounds, materials, and Yorùbá-centric approaches to the actionable ritual knowledge of Ifá—grounded in the sacred verses of the *odù*—to enact powerful transformations and refashion the trajectories of their lives (see fig. I.2).[8]

The individuals I engaged with in Cuba are also infinitely complex and diverse women and men of heterogeneous ethnicities, backgrounds, religious upbringings, sexualities, perspectives, and careers, all enmeshed in the

FIGURE I.2. Members of the Ẽgbë Íran Àtelé Ilôgbôn Baracoa (*sic*), during the initiation of five babalá-wos, and myself (*bottom row, second from right*). Baracoa, Cuba, May 2016. Photo by the author.

ever-shifting sociocultural and political environments of contemporary Cuba. Practitioners of Nigerian-style Ifá are university professors and bread makers (*panaderos*), ethnobotanists and all-night emcees at local cabarets and nightclubs. Given Cuba's inverted economy, several work simultaneously as medical doctors and babaláwo, academic writers and musicians; they hustle multiple gigs to meet the demands of Cuba's abundantly precarious economy.[9] Like others in and outside of Cuba, these are individuals of divergent socioeconomic and ethnic backgrounds who navigate complex environments not isolated from but intimately connected with the sociocultural and political vicissitudes of other nations, including my own (the United States). As ethnomusicologist Melvin L. Butler (2019, xiii) states in reference to his research with Pentecostal communities in Jamaica, "[they] are not frozen in place and time. The musical world they inhabit . . . likewise abounds with conflict and ambiguity." Like Butler, I wish to emphasize that practitioners of Nigerian-style Ifá "are every bit as complicated" as individuals elsewhere, and the worlds they navigate are as dynamic, ever transforming, and ever transformative as those anywhere. As Butler succinctly states, "They modify their beliefs and musical practices, they adapt to varying local and global circumstances, and they change their minds about things" (xiii). Practitioners of Nigerian-style Ifá likewise modify their beliefs and approaches to ritual, reevaluate their positions in response to local and global shifts, and, ultimately, change their minds in light of novel transformations in themselves and the worlds around them.

Ifá and Ritual Sound

This book is the first book-length study on music and Ifá. As such, it intervenes into a vast body of scholarship privileging Santería and òrìṣà practice in studies on ritual music and sound in Cuba, Nigeria, and their attendant ritual diasporas while sidelining Ifá divination (see Vaughan and Aldama 2012; Hagedorn 2001; Klein 2007; Moore 2004, 2006; Omojola 2014; Ortiz 1954; Schweitzer 2013; Villepastour 2010, 2015b; Vélez 2000). English-language monographs on African-inspired Cuban ritual music focus overwhelmingly on Santería in relation to its African-inspired ritual peers, particularly Ifá (see, e.g., Vaughan and Aldama 2012; Hagedorn 2001; Schweitzer 2013; Vélez 2000; Villepastour 2015b). In twentieth-century US American scholarship in particular, Cold War–era divisions of the Global South along axes of US American political anxieties tied Cuba to the frame of the Latin American left, influencing an ongoing fascination with revolutionary socialism and Cuba's involvement in leftist social movements that continues to influence ritual music studies. In this vein, US American–authored studies focus overwhelmingly on Santería, often analyzing ritual music for the oricha in relation to revolutionary socialism and socialist-inflected processes of folklorization (see Berry 2010; Hagedorn 2001; Moore 2004, 2006).[10] On the island itself, Spanish-language, Cuban-authored monographs treat a wide array of African-inspired ritual music practices in addition to Regla de Ocha (Santería), often analyzing these traditions in relation to Cuba's rich African-inspired cultural heritage. Unlike their foreign, English-language peers, Cuban studies elide discussions of African-inspired ritual music's imbrication with the revolutionary socialist state and its religious policies. While these studies engage Abakuá, Palo, Arará, and other African-inspired ritual variants in addition to Santería (see Betancourt [2004] 2014; Eli Rodríguez 1997; Esquenazi Pérez 2001; Ortiz 1954, [1920] 1960), they nonetheless also exclude discussions of Ifá. This lack of scholarly attention to music and sound in Ifá ritual is likely due to the absence of a set of drums specific to Ifá ritual in Cuba (and in distinction with Nigeria, see chapter 2), which inspires more attention toward the rich *batá* ritual drum repertoire of Regla de Ocha (termed *bàtá* in Yorùbáland).[11] Other aspects of the sonority of Ifá divination in Cuba, including its recitative traditions tied to the odù Ifá and its repertoire of songs dedicated to Ifá and Orula/Orunmila (the *oricha* of divination), however, likewise receive little, and often no, scholarly attention.[12] As a key intervention into previous scholarship, *Efficacy of Sound* centers the sonority and music of Ifá divination at the core of Yorùbá-centric ritual revisionism, pointing to the centrality of Ifá and its sonority to a global, Nigerian-style ritual movement in Cuba and across the Global South.

As an additional intervention, this book reconceives our understanding of West Africa as a historical—and static—legacy, reframing the African continent (and its actors) as a contemporary, and active, force in Cuba and the Americas. Studies on African-inspired ritual and music in Cuba (in anthropology, linguistics, musicology, folklore, and other fields) overwhelmingly frame the African continent in terms of the past, where Africa operates as a spatio-temporal, originary chronotope tied to—and frozen in—Cuba's nineteenth-century colonial history of slavery (Wirtz 2016, 343; see Guanche 1983; Hagedorn 2001; Holbraad 2012; Figarola 2006; Lachatañeré 1939, 1992; López Valdés 1980, 1998, 2002; Moore 1997, 2006; Ochoa 2010; Ortiz 1921, 1954, [1950] 2001). Few studies address the immense impact of the contemporary African continent in reshaping ritual, gender, and state religious policy in Cuba.[13] By mapping the spaces of possibility and practices of potentiality engendered through dialogue with contemporary Nigeria, this project calls attention to the ways in which engagement between actors on both sides of the Atlantic reformulates ritual practice—and its relationship to the state—in Cuba's present. Accordingly, this project presents the relationship between Cuba and the contemporary African continent as a dynamic, ongoing, and creative one rather than as a static, historical one bound to—and suspended in—Cuba's colonial, slave-era past.

Languaging Sound

In this book, I treat ritual sonority and the efficacy of sound as inextricable, first, from language and, second, from conceptions of the sensorial that inform and embed fate-transformative moments of ritual. Rather than analyze ritual music or sound as a disembodied object separate from the realm of language, I aim to present sound as a capacious, transformative force intricately linked to embodied forms of relationality and the entanglements of language, materiality, and visuality that inform Ifá-Òrìṣà practice. As ethnomusicologist Deborah Wong (2019, 26) succinctly states, "languaging about sound constructs what we hear." Following Wong, I privilege analysis of language and the linguistic as key sites for understanding the capacity, power, and resonance of ritual sonority in Nigerian-style Ifá.[14] I consider everyday ritual talk surrounding Ifá (hablar Ifá, or "speaking Ifá," chapter 4) and approaches to ritual language as crucial sites for examining predications of efficacy and the efficacy of sound. Like Wong, who privileges analysis of material objects and the affective orientations toward these objects as valid sites of inquiry in ethnomusicology (i.e., their capacity to invoke pleasure, power, comfort, pain, and/or profound senses of personal transformation), I also analyze the materiality and visuality of Nigerian-style Ifá (plants, clothing, beads, powders, snails, animate materials, instruments, and icons) as valid sites of ethnomusicological analysis.

Everyday ritual talk surrounding Ifá is central to the understanding, predication, and force of efficacy in Nigerian-style ritual. It is also a forceful and reverberant form of sonority in and of itself (and marker of gender, race, age, geographical provenance, and authority).[15] The ìyánífá and babaláwo with whom I most deeply engaged repeatedly emphasize Ifá divination's "effectiveness" (efectividad), "efficacy" (eficacia), and "functional power" (poder funcional) in transforming the circumstances of life.[16] In everyday talk, women and men draw heavily on the widespread, quotidian discourse surrounding the Cuban Spanish verb resolver, roughly translated as "to get by" (literally to "solve" or "work out"), to highlight this logic. Practitioners emphasize Ifá's "resolutive power" (poder resolutivo) in solving problems and creating solutions within conditions of precarity, need, and desire (Torres Hurtado, interview). As Orozco Rubio states from his home in Santiago de Cuba, "If you ask, 'Why do you believe in Ifá?' The whole world will tell you, 'Because it resolves'" (*porque resuelve*).[17] Beyond the imperative to "get by," the verb *resolver* connotes a nationally inflected spirit of resourcefulness and "working around the rules" prized in the everyday hustle for survival and dignity (*dignidad*) (Serazio 2016; Leslie Santana 2020).[18] The verb inflects everyday speech to such an extent that the term is said to invoke a "way of life in Cuba" tied to "[operating] at the edges of legality and inventiveness" (Serazio 2016). As I explore throughout, this spirit of resourcefulness, hustle, inventiveness, and breaking the rules deeply inflects Nigerian-style Ifá ritual and approaches. The frequent use of the verb *resolver* in relation to Ifá's potency and power also points to the imbrication of African-inspired ritual with the racialized economic conditions of precarity in (post-)revolutionary Cuba, particularly following the capitalist market reforms introduced since the 1990s that disproportionately affect Cubans of color (Bastian Martínez 2018; Roland 2011). The rhetorical framing of Ifá as a powerful resource for resolution within the everyday fight (*la lucha*) for dignity and survival conjoins the coconstitutive domains of functionality, use, and promise at the core of Ifá ritual. The discursive framing of Ifá in relation to *resolver* also underscores individual resourcefulness, power, and potency—what I explore as personal efficacy or *being eficaz* (see chapter 2)—as key to efficacious resolution.

Ritual Efficacy

While the logic of efficacy emerged primarily as a grounded theory through ethnographic engagement with practitioners of Ifá-Òrìṣà in Cuba, my formulation of efficacy is also deeply indebted to Todd Ramón Ochoa's (2010) ethnography of the Kongo-inspired practices of Palo Briyumba in western Cuba. As Ochoa richly describes, Palo constitutes an African-inspired ritual society rooted in the intricate, lifelong care of "collections of healing-harming substances," in the form of urns or cauldrons (*ngangas*), that allow practitioners to work with and phenomenologically experience "the dead" in the pursuit of specific goals and aims. Pointing to the centrality of *trabajos*, or "works," to craft and worldmaking in Palo, Ochoa underscores "claims to efficacy in fate-transforming works" as central to the materiality, phenomenology, and narrative arts of Palo practice (131). For me, Ochoa's approach to framing fate-transformative efficacy at the heart of Palo generatively distills previous scholarship that grapples with the centrality of function and instrumentality in African-inspired ritual, both on and off the African continent. British anthropologist and scholar of Yorùbá ritual in Nigeria J. D. Y. Peel

(2016, 230–31), for example, framed this as the preeminent "instrumental" dimension of Yorùbá ritual in colonial-era West Africa and its twentieth- and twenty-first-century ritual diasporas. In his formulation, Peel differentiates this instrumental driver of ritual participation in Yorùbáland from what he terms "expressive" motivations in the African-inspired ritual diaspora (i.e., identitarian expression, or the restorative force of twentieth- and twenty-first-century Black racial consciousness on Yorùbá-inspired ritual participation, particularly among Black practitioners in the United States). While Peel's distinction fruitfully points to discrepant ontologies of racial and ethnic belonging between the Yorùbá traditional religion (YTR) of Nigeria—which promotes an explicitly universalizing racial approach to YTR as "world religion" (Frigerio 2004; Olupona and Rey 2008)—and US American, post–Black Power ritual communities' racialized boundaries of inclusion in aptly termed "racist America" (see Clarke 2004, xiv), this binary distinction often collapses in Nigerian-style Ifá-Òrìṣà at the tension point between Afro-Cuban racial and ethnic consciousness and the movement's explicitly universalizing aims (chapter 1).

On the island itself, Cuban academics and ethnographers point to the force of instrumentality in African-inspired ritual while simultaneously recognizing Afro-Cuban religion as a powerful form of "resistance, safeguarding, and conservation" of Yorùbá (and subsequently, Afro-Cubans') "cultural and cultual values," as described in wordplay by ethnographer, *palero*, and *santero* Abelardo Larduet Luaces (2014, 20).[19] Like Ochoa, these scholars generatively point to the role of instrumentality in practices of African inspiration without reducing these practices to mere functionalism. Cuban practitioner-ethnographers, joining Larduet Luaces, likewise frame ritual in Cuba and in West Africa as an influential form of "philosophical thought" (Millet 2018) and "philosophical richness" (Larduet Luaces 2014, 15) rooted in actionable, utilitarian forms of knowledge making and potentiality. In eastern Cuba, poet, researcher, and palero José Millet Batista succinctly summarizes the functionality at the core of Palo Mayombe by describing it as a religion whose "basic objective is to control the forces of nature," without reducing it to such (Millet 1998, 118, in Sublette 2004, 182). In western Cuba, Julio Martínez Betancourt's extensive ethnography of *yerberos*, or commercial plant sellers in Havana, likewise points to the importance of plant-based materiality and its specific conditions (leaves, sticks, roots, seeds, flowers, honey, and fruits; fresh or dry, robust or wilted) to the capacity to potentiate favorable outcomes for ritual clients of Regla de Ocha, Ifá, Palo, Espiritismo, and other African-inspired ritual practices in the capital city. Like Larduet Luaces and Millet, Martínez Betancourt (2013, 196) underscores the ways yerberos empower clients to "obtain specific plants in order to satisfy material and spiritual needs" while simultaneously maintaining the rich knowledge—or "herbalist Cuban cultural patrimony"—of the nation.

In *Efficacy of Sound*, I recenter the sonority of ritual at the core of such "claims to efficacy" in Nigerian-style Ifá. Following Ochoa (2010, 16), who describes how the manipulation of potency-filled, material objects in Palo Briyumba "can transfer forces that solidify one version of reality" or, alternately, "create a tear in the screens of petrified, fated thought and for an instant make fluid thinking possible," I engage the ways predications of sonorous efficacy create the possibility for tears in stagnant ways of thinking and doing, in turn engendering novel—and transformative—possibilities.

Use, Affect, and Orientation: Queer of Color and Feminist Critique

In *Efficacy of Sound*, I mobilize queer of color and feminist theorization on use and affect with an eye toward extending this generative work to the realm of global, African-inspired ritual sound. I argue that queer and feminist critical theory offers a fruitful reservoir from which to engage the ways efficacy in Ifá—and the perceived capacity, usefulness, and potentiality of sound— lies at the core of emergent, translocal dynamics of affect and orientation. Here, I draw on queer and critical race theorist Sara Ahmed's (2006, 2010a, 2010b, 2019) writings to explore the links between use, affect, and orientation on a translocal scale. In *Queer Phenomenology: Orientations, Objects, Others* (2006, 3), Ahmed points to how our orientations toward objects and things—indeed, the "orientation *of* phenomenology" itself—is racialized, sexualized, gendered, and inextricable from labor and ability, thus differentially impacting the experiences of individuals in relation to the objects and things around them. This work instantiates an intersectional concern with the affective and orienting force of objects that Ahmed subsequently explores in relation to broader entities—e.g., feeling states—and the affect(ings) and promises these engender (Ahmed 2010a). In *What's the Use? On the Uses of Use* (2019), Ahmed extends this concern with the affective and orienting force of objects and things to the domain of "use," highlighting the ways in which the perceived usefulness of an entity can engender *forness*, in other words, an orientation toward that weds the actionable potential of something *for* something else (its utility) with a judgment of "positive value" (or even a feeling of "affection") (7). When something is perceived to affect us "in a good way," Ahmed (2010a, 32) writes, we can become oriented toward that thing "as being good." This form of intentionality (in the phenomenological sense) offers a promise and orientation that "directs us toward certain objects" and even to the larger environment beyond those objects (33) that are perceived as affecting us in profound (and, presumably, positive) ways (29).[20] "To be affected by something is to evaluate that thing," says Ahmed. "Evaluations are expressed in how bodies turn toward things" (31).

In Cuba, ìyánífá, babaláwo, and *bataleras* repeatedly reiterate this amalgamative force of being-affected, evaluation, and turning toward in ritual practice and in everyday talk surrounding Nigerian-style Ifá. Practitioners point to the resolutive potency of contemporary Yorùbá ritual sonority—in music, language, and sound—while highlighting the generative possibilities offered to them by way of contemporary Yorùbáland. In eastern Santiago de Cuba, Orozco Rubio pointed to this expansive potential in one of our conversations, underscoring, first, the importance of use in Ifá divination: "A babaláwo can be reciting any verse for you in Africa, and he knows: 'In what moment do I use this? Why am I using it? Why this one and not the other?' But, also, he's capable of saying, 'No, no, I don't use that one because that one doesn't give me what I want.' . . . In other words, he is conscious of what he says" (Orozco Rubio, interview, June 23, 2015). Here, Orozco Rubio points to the mandate of properly utilizing the sacred verses of the odù in Ifá ritual, a capacity to use he attributes to the intelligibility that the odù hold for African babaláwo who use their own spoken language—Yorùbá—as a ritual tongue (chapters 2, 4, and 5). Tying this linguistic efficacy to broader horizons of potentiality,[21] Orozco Rubio continues: "In Africa, I come across a babaláwo [who is] completely unprejudiced, open-minded. Who doesn't question who it is that sits there for a consultation. A babaláwo who gives the same treatment to all human beings. A babaláwo who, yes, knows what he's saying, who, yes, knows what he sings, because it is his language, it is his culture. A babaláwo who wraps me in infinite possibilities for understanding Ifá."

Here, Orozco Rubio, like other African traditionalists in Cuba, highlights the vast possibilities offered by babaláwo in Africa, wedding the capacious promise of their sonorous and linguistic ritual knowledge to personal judgments of positive value and esteem. Orozco Rubio's statement also demonstrates how African traditionalists sculpt "remote intimacies" (Tongson 2011, 23; Marcus et al. 2021) with their African counterparts, or what queer theorist Karen Tongson describes as affective relations of affinity and communion among actors disjunct across space and time. Despite never having traveled to Africa (or having encountered a Nigerian babaláwo on the continent itself),[22] Orozco Rubio asserts the deep knowledgeability and "open-minded[ness]" of a symbolic, even utopic and prototypic, babaláwo in Africa, one whose command and use of the ritual sonority, language, and knowledge of the odù Ifá inspires "infinite possibilities" for him, an ocean away.

Relational Ontologies of Sound

In pointing to the efficacy of sound as a core logic of engagement, potentiality, and actionability in Nigerian-style Ifá-Òrìṣà, this book also theorizes efficacy as a relational ontology of sound that entangles the epistemic and the ontological (Ochoa Gautier 2014, 26).[23] This position builds, first, on critical work in posthumanist critique, queer of color theory, and the work of Latinx and Caribbean decolonial scholars who point to the relational nature of the human and of sound itself. Such scholars underscore human relationality to, with, and across entities and objects (Ahmed 2006, 2010a, 2010b, 2019; Ochoa 2010; Ochoa Gautier 2014; Seremetakis 1994), cross-species sociality and non-human interaction (Haraway 2003; Stoller 1989; Viveiros de Castro [2004] 2019), environment and ecology (Feld 1996, [1982] 2012, 2017; Gómez-Barris 2017), and media and technologies (Martín Barbero 1993; Wolfe 2009). In music and sound studies, Steven Feld (2017, 84) influentially grounds his formulation of acoustemology (a combining of "acoustics" and "epistemology") in the field of relational ontology. Drawing on decades-long ethnographic research on sound and listening with inhabitants of the Bosavi rainforest of Papua New Guinea, Feld (1996, [1982] 2012, 2017) advocates "the position that substantive existence never operates anterior to relationality" (Feld 2017, 85). Feld theorizes what I view as a relational ontology of sound that imbricates the nature of the human, conjoining "substantive" human existence and experience to "sonic knowing" (86). "Knowing in and through sound" emerges in humans' relationality to, with, and across environments and entities (birds, watercourses, flight paths, ancestors, the living, plants, and trees) (88, 94).

Contemporary Caribbean, Latin American, and Latinx decolonial perspectives also generatively engage theories of relationality as a means to hear, see, and perceive the region beyond colonial matrices. As Gómez-Barris (2017, 2) notes, Édouard Glissant's *Poetics of Relation* (1997) became "one touchstone for perceiving the modes of difference that emerge within the spaces of potential of other Américas." Glissant's poetics offered a means of envisioning the relation between humans, animate and inanimate materiality, animals, and "visible and invisible forces" as a foundational principle in Américan and Caribbean knowledge making and self-conceptualization (Diawara 2018, 22, in Gómez-Barris 2017, 2).[24] Gómez-Barris's decolonial queer and femme scholarship on the "extractive zones" of indigenous regions of Colombia, Ecuador, and southern Chile likewise mobilizes Glissant's theory of relationality to underscore the relation of knowledge to "social ecologies," or "the visible and invisible forces between the human and nonhuman, between animate and inanimate life" (2, 9). In Gómez-Barris's analysis, such social ecologies privilege human relations to the nonhuman and to animate and inanimate materiality as crucial nodes of knowing. In the emergent domain of archipelagic studies, likewise, ethnomusicologist Jessica Swanston Baker's (2020, 397) formulation of "archipelagic listening" across the small island Caribbean draws on Glissant's poetics of the oceanic and oceanic and island studies to underscore relationality and "intertraversibility" as foundational to contemporary "Caribbeanity."

Drawing on decolonial Caribbean, Latin American, and Latinx scholarly formulations of relationality that implicate the sonic, the material, and the nonhuman, I argue here that efficacy in Ifá nigeriano operates as a relational ontology of sound—a locus of contested "ontologies and epistemologies of the acoustic" (Ochoa Gautier 2014, 2)—that mediate notions of ritual potency and power within the social ecologies of contemporary Cuba. As a core logic of potentiality and actionability, the efficacy of sound operates multiply within Nigerian-style Ifá-Òrìṣà as a perceived means of heightened communication between humans and Ifá/òrìṣà; as a source of heightened ritual authority, power, and prestige; and as a generative domain for the reformulation of ritual femininity and female ritual and epistemic access. Within contexts of state-linked and actively monitored Afro-Cuban religion, such "claims to efficacy" (Ochoa 2010, 131) in Nigerian-style sound additionally challenge the boundaries of Cuban religion within a nationalized and state-monitored institutional environment (chapter 2). Here, African traditionalists' "Yorubizing" project underlines the multiple ways that listening, sound, and the sensorial are bound in contested "regimes of truth" (Clarke 2004, 8). In Nigerian-style Ifá, practitioners mobilize these regimes of truth in the service of heterogeneous projects and desires.

Overview of the Book

In this book, I consider efficacy as a potent form of African-inspired usefulness grounded in the fate-transformative capacity of ritual to enact changes in the lives of practitioners of Ifá-Òrìṣà. The case studies in this book accumulatively draw out the force and complexity of efficacy in Nigerian-style Ifá, elaborating and deepening the exploration of the book's core themes through resonant, yet discrete, examples. As such, several thematic threads emerge in and across multiple case studies. I have organized the chapters to allow for these themes to resonate across distinct environments and historical periods. In chapter 1, I interrogate the global history of Nigerian-style Ifá-Òrìṣà as it emerged between Cuba, the Americas, Europe, and Nigeria between the 1970s and 1990s. In it, I trace the at times bizarre history of Nigerian-style Ifá's

mobile, globally oriented priests. In traversing the Global South, these babaláwo instigated a movement to re-Yorubize Ifá divination across the Americas while creating a polemical ritual movement in Cuba itself. This chapter
examines efficacy as a central tenet of Yorùbá revisionism, connecting the
promise of heightened efficacy to the contentious politics of sound and gender in Nigerian-style Ifá-Òrìṣà. Chapter 2 offers the first case study. In it, I
trace the introduction of the *dùndún* "talking" drums of Yorùbáland into a
prominent African traditionalist lineage in Havana, describing how members
of the Ilé-Ifẹ̀-rooted Aworeni lineage mobilize the dùndún ensemble as a
means to "re-Yorubize" the sonority of Cuban Ifá and promote the spread of
Nigerian-rooted institutions in Cuba. This chapter also expands the notion
of efficacy to engage the ways in which a given approach or thing "works"
or offers a desired "result" in and beyond ritual. I trace the ways that babaláwo mobilize Nigerian models of institution-building and hierarchical male
councils of "chiefs" as a means to achieve ritual autonomy, religious legitimacy, and personal efficacy within Cuba's restrictive state religious landscape.

Chapter 3 explores the first instance in Cuba or internationally that a
group of women (ìyánífá Caridad Rubio Fonseca, ìyánífá Anais López Rubio, and percussionist Nagybe Madariaga Pouymiró) achieved a decades-
long goal of playing the previously prohibited consecrated bátá drum set of
Santería through their involvement in Nigerian-style Ifá. This chapter con-
siders how women in eastern Cuba creatively animate the gendered norms
of Yorùbáland, Nigeria, to realize deep-seated personal desires for female access to sacred instruments within the restrictive gendered landscape of Regla
de Ocha-Ifá. In it, I also trace the impact of Cuban revolutionary, socialist-
egalitarian feminism and Yorùbá-inspired, transatlantic gendered reimagining on the first instance of women playing the consecrated bátá set in Cuba. I
highlight the ways in which women mobilize the transformative, futurist potential of Yorùbá gendered norms to enact a desired change in another hemisphere from Nigeria itself. Finally, this chapter interrogates the ways that female bataleras mobilize discrete logics of efficacy in evaluating the perceived
utility of proximate Cuban-style versus distant Nigerian-style approaches to
ritual instrumentation, playing techniques, and language. Ultimately, I consider how this indicates a selective Yorùbá-centrism in African traditionalist
approaches to ritual sound.

Chapter 4 traces the emergence of ìyánífá, or priestesses who "speak Ifá,"
lead ritual ceremonies, and wield the sacred implements of Ifá divination. In
it, I analyze the ways in which ìyánífá break forcefully with a foundational
taboo in Regla de Ocha-Ifá: the strict and passionately enforced prohibition
against female initiation into the Ifá priesthood. This chapter explores the

relationship between philosophies of gendered polarity and logics of efficacy, foregrounding the ways in which ìyánífá are centered in ceremonies as
a means to heighten ritual success through intoned and sung presence. Here,
I additionally frame gendered debates on ìyánífá in relation to debates on
sexuality in Nigerian-style Ifá-Òrìṣà, exploring the ways in which mandates
of heterosexuality in Ifá versus tendencies toward homosexual and queer
inclusivity in òrìṣà practice mirror and reinscribe the sexual boundaries of
Regla de Ocha-Ifá on the island.

Chapter 5 details the introduction of egúngún masquerade as an all-
male, Yorùbá-inspired means of "working with" the dead in the eastern city
of Baracoa and the western city of Havana. In it, I analyze the dynamic interplay of heterogeneity, regionalism, and masculinity in African traditionalism through the lens of localized adaptations of egúngún (ancestor worship) throughout Cuba's provinces. I explore the centrality of an aesthetics of
pleasure to efficacy in egúngún masquerade, indicating how regional ritual
music styles (e.g., bembé in eastern Cuba and batá in western Cuba) are mobilized according to their ability to effectively animate, and give pleasure to,
human and nonhuman listeners. This chapter also underscores how Yorùbá-
centric revisionism in Cuba—including egúngún practices drawn from ancestor and òrìṣà worship in Yorùbáland—ultimately arrives in Cuba through
Nigerian-style Ifá (see also chapter 3). In so doing, this chapter points to African traditionalism as the overwhelming dominion of male babaláwo and
their Ifá-centric ritual houses, even in instances in which novel YTR societies
dedicated to the ancestors and the òrìṣà are introduced.

Finally, the book ends with reflections on a research trip to Ọ̀yọ́ in Yorùbáland, Nigeria. In it, I explore the broader dynamics of transatlantic travel
and ritual tourism that prove useful to practitioners on the opposite side of
the Atlantic: in Nigeria itself. While diverse aspects of YTR prove useful to
women and men in Cuba, Yorùbá priestesses and priests also mobilize their
own efficacious engagements with African-inspired ritual diasporas abroad—
in Cuba, the Caribbean, the Americas, the United States, and Europe—to revitalize a declining and even "endangered" religious tradition in Nigeria that
falls in inverse proportion to the heightened practice of YTR globally. In
pointing to the ways that efficacy works in a multiplicity of directions, this epi-
logue reflects on the ways that efficacy may serve as a lens through which to
explore dynamics of utility, effectiveness, and transformative capacity more
broadly—in other words, to engage the ways that individuals "work out" and
"accomplish" specific desires and outcomes within translocal spheres of influence and engagement.

The Global Ifá Missionary:
Revisionism and Nigerian-Style Ifá-Òrìṣà in Cuba

On October 28, 1990, a Cuban counterintelligence officer, Juan Manuel Rodríguez Camejo, was arrested by US Border Patrol after crossing the US-Mexico
border at Tijuana without authorization with his young wife and five-year-
old daughter. A self-proclaimed "double-agent," the forty-year-old Rodríguez
claimed in court to have worked for the Central Intelligence Agency (CIA)
and the Cuban equivalent (Dirección General de Inteligencia) simultaneously
at the height of the Cold War in the 1980s (McDonnell 1990b). Rodríguez
alleged to US immigration officials that he worked both sides, using his connections with the CIA to contribute to the "embarrassing" exposure of over
two dozen US intelligence agents in Cuba in 1987.[1] Now, in a surprising turn,
Rodríguez sought political asylum in the United States. Lobbying the Cold
War–era rhetoric of the time, Rodríguez professed to be a "[convert] to capi-
talism and democracy"; a "sworn enemy" of Fidel Castro, the revolutionary
leader and then president; and a political refugee who faced "certain death"
if returned to Cuba, according to reporters (McDonnell 1990a, 1990b; UPI
Archives 1990). Adding to the incredible details of the story, Rodríguez professed involvement in a conspiracy plot to overthrow Fidel Castro the year
prior, one that he claimed culminated in a cover-up by the Cuban government via the executions of four high-ranking army officers by firing squad in
the highly publicized drug-trafficking scandal of 1989.[2] Standing in an orange
jumpsuit after a judge's temporary decision to release Rodríguez on bail, Rodríguez proclaimed, "Fidel must go. . . . We are seeing the collapse of commu-
nism everywhere . . . [and] I am part of this movement" (McDonnell 1990b).

Over the coming weeks, the *Los Angeles Times* reported on the "perplex-
ing" case of the Cuban counterintelligence officer being denied asylum in the
United States (McDonnell 1990b). Earlier that year, Rodríguez attempted to

seek asylum at the US Consulate in Hamburg, Germany, and, when denied, later flew with his family to Mexico to seek asylum at the San Ysidro border crossing in San Diego. When denied again, Rodríguez crossed with his family at Tijuana without US authorization and was ordered to be deported the day after his arrest by the INS (the former Immigration and Naturalization Service). This apparently came as a surprise to Rodríguez, if, perhaps less so, to those reporting on his case. At the time, Cuban defectors were overwhelmingly granted political asylum once they reached US soil, a legacy of the decades-long "wet foot, dry foot" policy that emerged at the height of the political vitriol between both nations in the 1960s. In comparison with their Latin American and Caribbean counterparts, Cuban immigrants were fast-tracked for permanent residency and, ultimately, US citizenship.[3] Rodríguez, however, was not a typical case. "We are dealing with a master of deception who has been in the business for the past 24 years," an investigator for the INS, Robert McCowan, argued in an interview with the *San Diego Union* (UPI Archives 1990). Rodríguez's lawyer countered, contending that Rodríguez was not hiding his identity and truly sought political asylum as a deemed "traitor" to the Cuban government. "I am not a lion. I am not a danger to this country," Rodríguez pleaded. "There is no reason to put me behind bars" (McDonnell 1990a). In fact, the former, and White, counterintelligence agent planned to stay with his wife and daughter at his wealthy, Cuban-born father-in-law's upscale residence in Beverly Hills upon receiving asylum.[4] There, he explained, he would write a tell-all book about his involvement in the attempted coup against Castro. "I want all the world to know that I am here because I want to keep on fighting for the freedom of my people," he pontificated to the *Los Angeles Times* (McDonnell 1990a). The Board of Immigration Appeals disagreed, deeming Rodríguez a threat to US security and placing him in custody. As Patrick McDonnell of the *Los Angeles Times* summarized: "Now residing in a federal cell here, he is a man without a country, his tale a bewildering account enmeshed in intrigue and three decades of hostility between Washington and the island nation."

In a fortuitous turn of fate, Spain granted Rodríguez a visa two months later, and the exiled agent chose to go to Europe rather than continue appealing his US deportation order from prison in San Diego. On January 17, 1991, Rodríguez was released from US custody—not to be deported to Cuba, where he faced potentially dire retribution, but to board a flight from Los Angeles to Zürich, Switzerland, with a connecting flight to Madrid. In Spain, the former double agent and charismatic counterintelligence officer—whom a reporter for the *Los Angeles Times* described as "an energetic, fast-talking man"—continued his "bewildering" path in new, unanticipated directions

(McDonnell 1990a). Rodríguez established a home base in the city of Valencia, on the southeastern coast of Spain, and founded several businesses there: a real estate venture, a book publishing press, and an exports company. During two decades as a Cuban counterintelligence officer, Rodríguez had traveled extensively "under the cover of business" to Latin America, Europe, and Africa, forging personal and business connections between and across continents. Now, in 1992, Rodríguez began traveling on repeated, extended stays to Nigeria—specifically, to the ethnic, linguistic, and cultural region known as Yorùbáland.

Nigeria—the most populous Black nation in the world and the most populous country on the African continent—bore witness to profound transformations between Rodríguez's first travels there in 1992 and his death in 2019. After gaining independence from Britain in 1960, Nigeria witnessed a postcolonial history marked by the paradox of profound regional and continental influence and a fractured, even kaleidoscopic, internal landscape. With one of the highest population growth rates globally, the West African nation would double its population to over 200 million people between 1990 and 2020 (according to UN projections, Nigeria will be the third-most-populous nation in the world by 2050, behind India and China) (Adegoke 2017; UN DESA 2017). In tandem with this staggering population growth, Nigeria ascended as an economic juggernaut in the postcolonial era, wielding the largest economy on the continent and making the nation, in the words of Tanzanian scholar Godfrey Mwakikagile (2002, 17), "unquestionably the richest and most powerful black country on Earth."[5] Nigeria furthermore assumed a leadership role as a decolonizing force in Africa following its independence struggles, contributing significantly to the anti-Apartheid movement in South Africa as well as to conflict resolution and economic integration efforts in Liberia, Sierra Leone, Côte d'Ivoire, and other nations (Nwosu 1993; Adebajo 2002; Dauda, Zaki Bin Ahmad, and Faisol Keling 2017). Despite its continental vision and influence, however, Nigeria witnessed a tempestuous and economically fractured experience of postcolonialism internally. Numerous military coups, a bloody civil war, and the "resource curse" of an oil-dependent economy created an environment ripe for corruption, political instability, and inequity (Sachs 2012). Nigeria's staggering ethnic diversity—unparalleled on the African continent in size and scope with over 250 ethnic groups and some four hundred spoken languages, according to estimates[6]—further contributed to a fractured socioeconomic landscape compounded by occasional fissures between competing Christian and Muslim majority religions.[7] Nonetheless, the nation's global influence and so-called soft power boomed. Nigeria's film industry, "Nollywood," emerged as the second-largest film industry on earth in the 1990s (Bright 2015), and Nigeria's fashion, literature, and popular music industries garnered global influence and acclaim (Adedeji 2016; Offiah 2017). The "New African Diaspora" of millions of Nigerian immigrants to Europe and the United States continued to reshape the demographic and cultural landscapes of the Global North anew.[8] Into the twenty-first century, the expansion of telecommunications industries and a multibillion-dollar energy deal with China also propelled speculation of Nigeria's emergence as "Africa's First Superpower."[9] All the while, however, a jihadist, violent insurgency group, Boko Haram (Islamic State in West Africa), emerged in the north, contributing to an ongoing regional crisis and displacing millions (Adesoji 2010; Nichols 2015).

Within the complexity of this postcolonial landscape, the cultural and linguistic region known as Yorùbáland long exerted its own profound influence on the global stage. Stretching across southwestern Nigeria, bridging into southeastern Benin and the north-central region of Togo, Yorùbáland is home to a diverse array of ethnic groups that came to be anachronistically known as the Yorùbá through the creative interventions of nineteenth-century Christian Yorùbá nationalists and priests (Peel 2000). Now the second-largest ethnic and linguistic group in Nigeria, the Yorùbá are one of the largest ethnic groups in Africa and, arguably, one of the most influential to shape the Americas from the continent. Through their prominence in the transatlantic slave trade, the Yorùbá sculpted the cultural and religious terrains of the New World in inexorable ways. Radiating outward via the trafficking of human beings, the epistemic, ritual, and philosophical practices of the Yorùbá flourished and transformed in locations throughout the Americas: Brazil, Haiti, Trinidad and Tobago, St. Lucia, Jamaica, the United States, and, with impactful force, Cuba.

One form of Yorùbá divination and knowledge making, Ifá, took hold forcefully in Cuba. An actionable tool for navigating treacherous terrains and personal horizons of possibility and desire, the intricate oral literature of Ifá provided a practical means to recraft the conditions of life for the Yorùbá— and, later, Cubans of diverse ethnic backgrounds—within situations of precarity and need. A complex system of divination, Ifá combines the scholarly interpretation of a vast oral literature with prescriptive action, mobilizing an epistemic view of ritual knowledge grounded in the actionability of Ifá's poetic verses. Through intricate rituals of sound and sacrifice, Ifá priests and priestesses skillfully excavate the verses of a divinatory sign (odù) drawn from 256 possibilities, unearthing ritual mandates that marshal sound and language to "revalue" materiality and transform "fates and lives" (Ochoa 2010, 14, 18).[10] In Cuba, this powerful tool flourished as a ritual branch parallel to, and interconnected with, the practices of oricha worship known as Regla de Ocha (or Santería). The Yorùbá-inspired "Regla de Ocha-Ifá religious complex," as it is called, also transmuted rapidly from a practice exclusive to the ethnically Yorùbá into a tool mobilized by Cubans of diverse ethnic and racial backgrounds. Despite the racial diversification of practitioners themselves, Ifá nonetheless remained grounded in richly ecological, African-inspired "submerged perspectives" (Gómez-Barris 2017, 11), or alternative forms of perception that linked the odù with the vitality, materiality, and livability of "local terrains" (1). As such, Ifá operated at once within and beyond the epistemic matrices of Spanish coloniality and its racialized ontologies of environment, meaning, and self, proffering alternative forms of knowledge making rooted in African-inspired forms of divination and craft.[11]

Following the Cuban Revolution of 1959, Ifá took a second leap internationally, traveling from Cuba to the United States, Europe, and the Spanish-speaking Americas in tandem with the exodus of the island's "secondary diasporas" abroad (Frigerio 2004; Menéndez 2002). There, Cuban immigrants and others soon forged a heterogeneous landscape of ritual lineages beholden, in key ways, to the hierarchies, ritual mores, and gendered strictures of Regla de Ocha-Ifá on the island. By the late 1970s, these transnational, Cuban-inspired lineages came into dispute with an incipient, revisionist, and Yorùbá-centric ritual movement in the United States. Driven in part by conflicts over ritual authority between practitioners on and off the island (see Palmié 2013), *babalaos* in Cuban American lineages in Miami began turning in earnest to Nigeria as a source of heightened ritual authority and transnational legitimation, creating long-standing breaches with the lineages (*ramas*) of Regla de Ocha-Ifá on the island itself.

In 1992, Rodríguez found a new calling as a protagonist within this competing global landscape of Yorùbá- and Cuba-centric ritual lineages.[12] Rodríguez, in yet another, chameleonic turn of resourceful reinvention, transformed himself in exile from a double agent engaged in Cuban counterintelligence and US-backed espionage into a global missionary-entrepreneur for Yorùbá-centric ritual revisionism. That year, Rodríguez traveled to the Nigerian city of Ikire to be initiated as a "Nigerian-style" priest of Ifá, the first of many consecrations he would receive in Nigeria over the coming years. Cultivating a rising social and economic status in Yorùbáland through extensive travels, consecrations, and monetary investments in local schools and clinics in the 1990s and early 2000s, the exiled Rodríguez gained permission from Yorùbá ritual elders to establish his own global organization of Nigerian-style Ifá-Òrìṣà in Yorùbáland. In 2004, Rodríguez founded the Odùgbemi International Association for Traditional Yoruba Religion (OIATYR) in the town of

Iragbiji in the state of Ọ̀sun, becoming the first non-Yorùbá foreigner (literally, "Westerner") to establish a traditional religious lineage in Yorùbáland
itself.[13] In 2006, the Ọ̀ọ̀ni of Ilé-Ifẹ̀, considered the "king" of the Yorùbá
people, proffered OIATYR with an "international character" and tasked the
organization with a mission: "to disseminate the Yoruba Religion throughout
the world."[14] For the next fifteen years Rodríguez did precisely that, crafting
the Nigerian-rooted OIATYR into a global organization with some 3,500 *babaláwo*, ìyánífá, and òrìṣà priests initiated (and reinitiated) as representatives
and leaders in numerous Ifá-Òrìṣà communities globally. With OIATYR,
Rodríguez distanced himself from his given, Spanish-language name and became known internationally by his name in Ifá, "Ifáshade Odùgbemi." Without ever stepping foot in Cuba again, Ifáshade Odùgbemi served as head of a
worldwide lineage of his own creation that, by the time of his death in Spain
in 2019, extended from Nigeria to Spain, Italy, Argentina, Chile, Venezuela,
Colombia, the United States, and Cuba itself.

The Odùgbemi Lineage

In 2015, when I first encountered members of the Odùgbemi lineage in eastern
Cuba, Ifáshade Odùgbemi towered in many Cubans' imaginations as an infamous yet powerful figure who—despite his controversial and even dubious
past—served as a forceful bridge between practitioners on the island and the
contemporary practice of the Yorùbá traditional religion (YTR) in Yorùbáland,
Nigeria. Despite his inability to return to the island himself, Ifáshade (as he is
called in Cuba) wielded active influence in the burgeoning African traditionalist ritual movement from abroad, sending mobile Ifá missionaries—often
Cuban immigrants like himself—to the island to found new, and highly controversial, African traditionalist ritual communities (*ẹgbẹ́*) there. Through
mobile Ifá missionaries, Ifáshade established three branches of the Odùgbemi
lineage across the breadth of the island, serving somewhat extraordinarily as
OIATYR's absent and exiled Spiritual Leader of the World ("Arabá Awò Ag-
bayè"). From exile in Spain and Nigeria, Ifáshade also published books, informal essays, and blog posts detailing a Yorùbá-centric vision of Ifá-Òrìṣà
practice for global followers. Linguistically, these publications bridge the
Yorùbá- and English-language domains of YTR practice in Nigeria with the
Spanish-language domain of ritual practice among Caribbean, Latin American, Latinx, and other Spanish-speaking followers across the Américas and
Europe, providing Yorùbá-to-Spanish-language translations of the odù and
notes on interpretation, philosophy, and ritual. Through his writings, Ifáshade
elaborated an influential, revisionist, and often inflammatory discourse that

decried the "syncretizing and disintegrating pressure" he viewed as diluting the "transformative magic" of the traditional Yorùbá religion in its peregrinations to the New World (Odùgbemi 2007). Proclaiming an antidote to "the liturgical improvisation so fashionable" throughout the diaspora, Ifáshade provided Spanish-speaking readers with a brand of "African traditionalist Ifá" rooted in his knowledge of contemporary Yorùbáland and legitimated through extensive travel and accolades (Odùgbemi 2007). In mobilizing Nigerian-style Ifá as a means to achieve global influence (and infamy) and a radical revaluation of individual fate, Ifáshade also became emblazoned in many practitioners' imaginations as an emblem of personal efficacy in Ifá (chapter 2), in other words, as a powerful, resourceful babaláwo with an astounding capacity to manifest and achieve intended results.

Ifáshade Odùgbemi's emergence in the 2000s as a White, globally renowned babaláwo leading a racially heterogeneous, West African–rooted organization tasked with global Yorùbá ritual revisionism points to the complexities of race—and racial leadership and affiliation—in the burgeoning African traditionalist movement. Nigerian-style Ifá-Òrìṣà ritual communities in Cuba promote a universalizing racial approach to ritual belonging, participation, and leadership that often fuels racial heterogeneity in the membership of individual ẹgbẹ́ (especially the recently founded ones, as discussed in this chapter) and includes, and even privileges, non-Black membership and leadership. This universalizing approach to African-inspired ritual belonging and efficacy-wielding, personal legitimacy occurs even as "Africa" as a chronotope continues to constitute a "vital point of reference for any construction (or contestation) of 'authenticity' and 'legitimacy' in contemporary Afro-Cuban ritual practice" (Palmié 2013, 28). Notably, this universalizing logic in Nigerian-style Ifá-Òrìṣà diverges significantly from the racial logics of inclusion and belonging that govern Yorùbá-inspired ritual communities elsewhere, particularly among US Black American ritual communities in the United States (Clarke 2004).

In key ways, this universalist logic builds on the complexities of racialization and racial affiliation in the history of Cuban-style Regla de Ocha-Ifá on the island itself. As anthropologist, transnational feminist, and queer theorist Aisha Beliso-De Jesús (2015b) deftly shows, the phenomenological experience of Regla de Ocha-Ifá is at once diasporic, temporally agile, and racially interpolative, with practices grounded in "copresences," or "the sensing of a multiplicity of being (in beings joined together) that are felt on the body" (9). These "presences" (las presencias) include transatlantic òrìṣà, slaves, ancestors, and indigenous persons (6). In Santería, "practitioners, regardless of racial identification, are understood to be able to hail the racial codas of enslavement and be transformed into African Diaspora bodies" (4). This phenomenological ontology of sentient copresence—accelerated in recent years by digital connectivity and the traveling of the oricha onto bodies through screens (1)—collapses temporal, spatial, and, often, racialized, bodily distance through the corporealization of African slaves and oricha in and on the body. As anthropologist Kristina Wirtz (2014; 2016, 343) adds, these healing, excavating practices draw on the gravitational, weighty chronotopes (space-times) of slavery and its figures in Cuba as etched in oral history and the larger imaginary of the nation. Since the nineteenth century, in other words, White and non-Black Cubans have engaged in the phenomenological practices of racially interpolative copresence, transforming into "African Diaspora bodies" through sentient ritual. Notably, this separation of one's ritual ability to hail Africanity and fate-transformative efficacy from the necessity of one's self-identification as Black, Afro-Cuban, and/or of African descent in Regla de Ocha-Ifá also characterizes much Cuban scholarship on "Afro-" "Cuban" "Religion," which is now officially labeled by the Cuban government and numerous Cuban scholars alike as "Cuban religions of African origins (*religiones cubanas de orígen africano*)," a subtle but telling distinction (Palmié 2013, 25).

The histories of non-Black racial inclusivity—and, at times, privileging—in Cuban-style Regla de Ocha-Ifá undoubtedly serve as a template for Ifáshade and other White and non-Black babaláwo in their ascendent leadership roles in Nigerian-style Ifá. At the same time, racial affiliation and particularly leadership in Nigerian-style Ifá is influenced by recent changes in access to international travel, internet and IT equipment (computers, hard drives), and the economic capital necessary to engage directly with foreign, Nigerian-style babaláwo, all of which disproportionately disadvantage Black and dark-skinned Cubans.[15] The early pioneers of African traditionalism in Cuba itself in the 1990s (Victor Betancourt Estrada, Filiberto O'Farrill, and Frank Cabrera Suárez, discussed later in this chapter) emerged from a deep history of protagonism in Regla de Ocha-Ifá and self-identify (or have been identified) as Afro-Cuban and/or of African descent.[16] Since the 2000s, and with the marked growth of Nigerian-style Ifá across the island, White and non-Black Cubans have increasingly assumed leadership roles in African traditionalist ẹgbẹ́ (even from abroad, as in the case of Ifáshade Odùgbemi), at times initiating directly into Nigerian-style Ifá-Òrìṣà without previous initiations in Regla de Ocha-Ifá. These newer ẹgbẹ́, formed in the 2000s and 2010s, exhibit more racial heterogeneity and diversity than their 1990s-founded antecedents and younger membership. Professor, babaláwo, and African traditionalist practitioner-scholar Manuel de Jesús Rabaza Torres of the University of Havana attributes this phenomenon to the racially inflected "digital divide" (*brecha digital*) that has developed in Cuba since the 2000s, which disproportionately advantages young, university-educated, White and light-skinned babaláwo with access to computers, internet, hard drives, and travel in relation to their Afro-Cuban peers.[17] Increasingly, such access and digital literacy provides a key advantage within a domain of digitally distributed audiovisual files, multilingual text documents, and access to blogs, social media sites, email, and digital correspondence that enable practitioners to access and ultimately forge knowledge about YTR abroad.

Ifáshade's prominence as a male and internationally mobile babaláwo also points to the intersectional gendered dynamics of race and gendered (im)mobility that impact leadership roles in Nigerian-style Ifá. Amid the variegated cartography of African traditionalist Ifá missionaries traveling across the Americas, Europe, Nigeria, and, ultimately, Cuba itself, those I encountered who embarked on international travels (and even the grand majority I heard about secondhand) were exclusively male. In contrast, the women and ìyánífá I encountered in Cuba never traveled to Nigeria directly themselves, never traveled internationally to oversee the founding of foreign temples and ritual lineages, and never directly oversaw or organized the visits of foreign babaláwo to Cuban ẹgbẹ́ (a noticeable difference from their male counterparts). While leadership roles may be racially heterogeneous in Nigerian-style Ifá-Òrìṣà, in other words, these positions are profoundly gendered. Nonetheless, women such as *batalera* Nagybe Madariaga Pouymiró directly participate in generative forms of transnational dialogue through academic scholarship and musical engagement, contributing to a transnational, feminist-informed politics of ritual inclusion and transnational solidarity that exceed the boundaries of the island (chapter 3).

These racial, gendered, and intersectional complexities underscore how African traditionalists increasingly envision and mobilize YTR as a racially universalized, globally oriented "world religion" ostensibly more inclusive of women (chapters 3, 4). This universalizing racial and gendered vision, in turn, capacitates Black, African-descendant, and non-Black women and men to hail Africanity, wield fate-transformative efficacy, and, to divergent degrees, shape and lead a transnational, South-South ritual movement. As I highlight throughout, one's capacity to wield efficacy and assume leadership positions is overwhelmingly determined by one's intersectional status as male, cisgender, heterosexual, university-educated, digitally literate, computer-owning, and mobile. While the personal relationship of individual practitioners to the imbrication of race, ancestral heritage, and ritual in Cuba is heterogeneous and, in innumerable cases, unquestionably profoundly meaningful, I argue here that the logic of efficacy nonetheless serves as a central driver of personal legitimation and actionability in Nigerian-style Ifá. As such, one's gendered, economic, and social ability to access and wield efficacy often subsumes race in Nigerian-style Ifá-Òrìṣà as a core logic of ritual inclusion, belonging, and leadership, ultimately determining a given individual's ability to "use" (Ahmed 2019).

In tracing Ifáshade Odùgbemi's story from defection and exile to global Ifá-Òrìṣà leadership, I offer but one notorious example—and not the first—of the heterogeneous, transoceanic landscape of mobile, globally minded, and overwhelmingly male Ifá missionary-entrepreneurs who transform Ifá divination and òrìṣà/oricha worship through voyages of mobility and influence. While Ifáshade would come to play a forceful, protagonistic role in African traditionalism in Cuba from exile in the 2000s and 2010s, key practitioners of Regla de Ocha-Ifá on the island itself felt the incipient waves of global Yorùbá ritual revisionism much earlier, in the late 1980s. At precisely the time that Rodríguez found himself embroiled in a drug-trafficking scandal that would ultimately push him to defection, Cubans experienced their first encounters with contemporary Nigerian babaláwo on the island itself.

The Emergence of Nigerian-Style Ifá: 1987–Present

In Cuba, the Yorùbá-inspired ritual complex of Ifá divination and Regla de Ocha emerged on the western side of the island in the nineteenth and early twentieth centuries in the midst and aftermath of the transatlantic slave trade (Bolívar Aróstegui 1990; D. Brown 2003; Cabrera 1993; De La Torres 2004; Guanche 1983; Martínez Betancourt 2013; Ortiz 1921; Palmié 2002).[18] As a wealth of scholarly literature delineates, Regla de Ocha-Ifá came to be designated as Lucumí or Regla Lucumí (the Lucumí law or religion) within the "religious-*cum*-ethnic" typology of African-inspired *naciones* in colonial-era Cuba (D. Brown 2003, 67; Holbraad 2012, 12). This rich institutional landscape of African (and Afro-Cuban) ritual-and-ethnic "nations" organized themselves within colonially sanctioned, fraternal religious institutions called *cabildos de nación* (D. Brown 2003, 25, 26). These naciones included the Congo nation (associated with the Palo ritual complex and inspired by BaKongo and other central African peoples),[19] the Caràbàlí (associated with the Abakuá ritual fraternity and inspired by the Èfik Ékpè and Ejagham Úgbè peoples of southwestern Cameroon and southeastern Nigeria),[20] and the Arará (inspired by the Dahomey kingdom of contemporary Benin), among others.[21] Within this varied landscape of naciones, the Lucumí nation came to occupy

a "pre-eminent position" (Holbraad 2012, 12), and their cabildos de nación included slaves believed to be descendants of (or direct transplants from) the
Yorùbá.[22] As David Brown meticulously demonstrates, the Lucumí religion
that consolidated in early twentieth-century Cuba emerged within a turn-
of-the-century environment of coexisting Lucumí institutions that "bridged
the era of the old-style cabildos de nación and the period of modern *casa-
templos*" (or house-temples, through which ritual lineages are now organized
and practiced) (D. Brown 2003, 65).[23] Within the processes of transplantation
and creative reformulation of Yorùbá-inspired, lineage-based descent in nine-
teenth- and twentieth-century Cuba, the Lucumí ritual *ramas*, or branches,
underwent significant changes in relation to the parallel—and equally historically contingent—evolution of their counterparts in Yorùbáland. Separated by
the impenetrable vastness of the Atlantic Ocean, the two coeval "Yorùbá" and
"Lucumí" ritual complexes of Nigeria and Cuba[24]—both with common roots
in nineteenth-century Yorùbáland—developed in relative isolation from one
another for over a century between the nineteenth century and the late 1980s.[25]

In Cuba, like in Nigeria itself, the century between the 1880s and 1980s
encompassed sweeping historical and political changes. These included the
emergence of Cuba as an "independent" nation (though bound to the political
and military interventions of the United States),[26] the ensuing dictatorships
of Gerardo Machado (1925–1933) and Fulgencia Batista (1940–1944, 1952–
1959),[27] and the triumph of the Cuban Revolution in 1959 (Lievesley 2004;
Joaquín Roy 2009). Over the course of this volatile century, state policies toward religious practice—and Afro-Cuban religion, specifically—ranged from
the persecution of African-inspired ritual practice in the early republican era
(see Moore 1997, 2004) to the militant, socialist-inspired atheism of the Cuban revolutionary government (Delgado 2009; Romeu 2013). The "Lucumí
religion" necessarily developed, transformed, and adapted within the over-
arching context of these political vicissitudes (D. Brown 2003; Palmié 2013),
evolving within an alternate sociocultural and political reality from that of
contemporary Yorùbáland.

The question of whether African-inspired ritual practices in Cuba constitute "religions" forms a matter of debate among practitioners and scholars
(and practitioner-scholars) alike. Stephen Palmié (2013, 17–20) argues that
within the changing judicial landscape of republican-era Cuba (and its attendant policies of racialized, African-inspired ritual oppression), practitioners of Regla de Ocha-Ifá in the early and mid-twentieth century discursively
adapted the presentation of their practices to the legal landscape of the republic in an effort to practice openly and without persecution. In the second

decade of the twentieth century, for example, and in the midst of "violent antiwitchcraft campaigns on the part of a vocal republican elite of 'scientific modernizers,'" Palmié argues that "adherents of what they cleverly called the 'Christian Lucumi morality' were actively trying to inscribe themselves into the republican legal system" (18). This self-framing as "Christian Lucumi morality" mobilized Christianity as the basis for a simultaneously "Christian" and African-inspired "morality," reflecting an attempt by adherents to practice openly within the contemporary juridical and institutional landscape of the nation. By the 1940s and 1950s, practitioners of the Lucumí "morality" now referred to their ritual practices as "regla de ocha, that is, the rule of the oricha" and as a "religion" (18). By the time of the atheist, scientific modernizing experiment of the Cuban Revolution, however, this framing as "religion" became less valuable within a state institutional landscape of religious persecution, only reemerging decades later with the "religious liberalization" of "Afro-Cuban religions" in 1991 (20).

While Palmié generatively traces the shifting (self-)framings of practitioners under the different institutional and "religious" vicissitudes of the nation, others argue against the use of the term *religion* to describe African-inspired ritual practices in Cuba. Todd Ochoa (2010, 16) influentially uses "inspiration" rather than "religion" to refer to Palo and Regla de Ocha-Ifá. For Ochoa, "religion" is "overladen with European assumptions of form, doctrine, and homogeneity, in short, with a static sense of belief and practice" (16). As Ochoa states, "inspiration," on the other hand, acknowledges "the new" that is often absent in formulations of "African-derived" Creole culture:

> "Inspiration," as I use it here, functions as a hinge between the past and the future, inspiration being the active, forward-looking, creative spark linking past forms with objects, powers, and rules born anew. Inspiration implies a playful attitude toward past and future, as opposed to a perspective marked only by the trauma of dislocation and impossible recovery. Inspiration is a force of the moment that arrives unannounced and has little time to recognize its debts before being swept up in the currents of its own prodigious, and often unexpected, creation. . . . Inspiration seems less defined [than *religion*]; it is a more mobile term that has nonreligious usages important to my description of Palo's overflowing creativity. (16)

Building on both Ochoa and Palmié's formulations, I use the term *religion* in this book to specifically index the imbrication of African-inspired ritual practices in Cuba with the institutional and discursive framings of the state (chapter 2). Outside of this context, I describe Regla de Ocha-Ifá and Nigerian-style Ifá-Òrìṣà as sets of ritual, epistemic, and ontological practices of African "inspiration," pointing to the generative, creative force of African-inspired ritual in Cuba.

After some one hundred years of isolation between the two domains of Yoruba/Yorùbá practice in Cuba and Nigeria, Cuban *santeros* and babalaos and practitioners of YTR in Yorùbáland were afforded their first official reencounter in 1987. That year, the Cuban Institute of Friendship with the Peoples invited the Ọọ̀ni, or "king" (traditional ruler), of Ilé-Ifẹ̀ Ọba Síjúwadé Okùnadé Olúbùse II (1930–2015) to visit the island,[28] an event that inaugurated a new era of exchange between Cuba and Yorùbáland and catalyzed the emergence of Nigerian-style Ifá-Òrìṣà in Cuba. The Ọọ̀ni of Ilé-Ifẹ̀—considered the "father of the Yorùbá" and one of the supreme spiritual leaders of the Traditional Yorùbá Religion of Yorùbáland (Abímbọ́lá 1997, 111)—stayed in Cuba for a five-day visit and was personally received by Fidel Castro (Baloyra and Morris 1993). Although the Ọọ̀ni was officially hosted as an African cultural ambassador rather than as a religious leader per se, the historic visit nevertheless indicated a significant shift on the part of the Cuban socialist state in its policy toward religion—and toward Afro-Cuban religion specifically—which had been effectively banned since the early years of the revolution (see Castro Figueroa 2012; Moore 2004). Beginning in the mid-1960s, the Cuban revolutionary government moved toward a state-sponsored policy of militant socialist atheism based on Marxist principles, adopting a "hostile and paternalistic attitude" toward religion (Delgado 2009, 55; Romeu 2013).[29] Adopting an atheist approach to revolutionary socialism, the Cuban revolutionary government tolerated—and at times lauded—Afro-Cuban music and dance as popular culture and folklore at the same time that the ritual practices from which these practices were based were ridiculed as "superstitious" and "antithetical to scientific truth" (Castro Figueroa 2012, 90; Delgado 2009, 55). Organizers of the First Congress of the Communist Party in 1975, for example, dictated that Afro-Cuban "music, dance, and musical instrumentation" could be "assimilated" into revolutionary socialism as long as the "mystical elements" of these practices were eliminated (Partido Comunista de Cuba 1976, in Castro Figueroa 2012, 90, my translation). For Cuban practitioners of Regla de Ocha-Ifá, the historic 1987 visit of the Ọọ̀ni of Ilé-Ifẹ̀ marked a symbolic step away from the state-sponsored, militant atheism of the previous twenty-five years and toward a potential future of open religious tolerance and freedoms. Equally significantly, however, the visit of the Ọọ̀ni of Ilé-Ifẹ̀ marked the first documented encounter that practitioners of Ifá and oricha had with the contemporary Yorùbá homeland—the heir to the originary, historico-mythical chronotope to which Ifá and Regla de Ocha also trace their roots (Wirtz 2014, 18; see also Abímbọ́lá 1997, 111).

Revolution and South-South Solidarity

From the perspective of the Cuban socialist state, the extension of an invitation to the Ọọ̀ni of Ilé-Ifẹ̀ aligned with a politics of solidarity with the Global South that the Cuban revolutionary state actively cultivated globally, and in Africa specifically, beginning in the 1960s and 1970s. During these years, Cuba's foreign policy shifted away from one of reactivity to the Cold War dynamics of the United States and the Soviet Union and toward a proactive stance of engagement with countries in the Caribbean basin and Africa (Kirk and Erisman 2009). This vision of global "South-South" solidarity took the form of increasing diplomatic ties with Caribbean and African nations (Fiddian-Qasmiyeh 2015); cultivating a central role in expanding global medical internationalism in Africa and the Americas (Cassells 2016; Fiddian-Qasmiyeh 2015; Huish 2013; Kirk and Erisman 2009); and volunteering military support for leftist revolutionary causes, culminating in Cuba's extensive, decades-long military intervention in the war in Angola (see Bridgland 2017; George 2005; C. Peters 2012; Polack 2013).[30] In addition to internationalist medical and military missions across the Cold War–era "Third World" (Salehi-Nejad 2011), Cuba cultivated diplomatic, artistic, and cultural ties with African nations, hosting visits from renowned African personalities in the arts and politics.[31] Even more significantly, the Cuban government extended full scholarships—including room, board, books, transportation, and uniforms—to between thirteen thousand and fifteen thousand students from sub-Saharan Africa for tertiary degrees in Cuba throughout the 1980s (Fiddian-Qasmiyeh 2015; Hatzky 2015; López Segrera 1988; Entralgo and González 1991). This brought students from Angola, Ethiopia, Mozambique, Namibia, Sudan, and other nations directly to Cuba's Isla de la Juventud, or "Island of Youth," to study between the late 1970s and early 1990s (Salehi-Nejad 2011).[32] Additionally, the Cuban government set up schools for foreign children and teenagers from war-torn and infrastructurally challenged regions in Africa, including primary and secondary schools for thousands of children from Mozambique and child refugees and orphans from the civil war in Angola (Hatzky 2012, 151; Richmond 1991). For the revolutionary government, these efforts reflected a core value of universal education and healthcare as a "human right" and as a means to build "commitment and economic production capacity" between Cuba and nations across the Global South (Hickling-Hudson et al. 2012, 15, in Fiddian-Qasmiyeh 2015). Additionally, military internationalist missions reflected an anticolonialist vision that crafted Cuba as a global player in socialist and leftist liberation movements abroad (Fiddian-Qasmiyeh 2015; Salehi-Nejad 2011).[33]

For Cubans, this direct engagement with Africa through military, medical, and diplomatic missions "simultaneously demystified" Africa as an originary chronotope tied to Cuba's colonial slave past and "elevated [Africa] in Cuban discourse" as a site of solidarity and shared anticolonialist and liberationist vision (C. Peters 2012, 157). In relation to Cuba's bond with Angola, for example, Fidel Castro stated: "Many things link us to Angola: the common goal, shared interests, politics and ideology. But we are also connected by blood, blood in its double meaning: the blood of our ancestors and the blood that we've spilled together on the battlefields" (Fiddian-Qasmiyeh 2015, citing Hatzky 2012, 144). Here, Fidel Castro succinctly bridges Cuba's Afro-Cuban ancestral heritage with race-blind ideologies of shared political struggles and liberationist goals as the basis for transatlantic solidarity. For Cubans of all backgrounds, these political and anticolonialist discourses of solidarity with Africa—as well as personal experience with the contemporary African continent through military service, medical missions, and encounters with sub-Saharan students studying at La Isla de la Juventud and other locales—served to universalize a Cuba-Africa transatlantic bond rooted in revolutionary socialist and liberationist ideals of South-South solidarity. For many Black Cubans in particular, these ties also contributed to "powerful feelings of identification" rooted in a deep-seated consciousness of pan-African racial solidarity, common ancestry, and shared cultural and ritual heritage (C. Peters 2012, 157). As Christabelle Peters (2012, 157) outlines, Cuba's revolutionary involvement with Africa in the 1970s and 1980s created a "collective sense of dignity" for Black Cubans—or, as described to her by Rogelio Martínez Furé, "self-esteem in every sense."

Despite discourses of solidarity and extensive military, medical, and diplomatic engagement with Angola, Mozambique, Sudan, and other sub-Saharan nations in the 1970s and 1980s, however, the Cuban revolutionary government did not facilitate exchange with Yorùbáland, Nigeria. Cuba's ritual ties to West Africa fell explicitly outside of the purview of the revolutionary government's socialist-atheist and Global South–liberationist vision for engagement with the African continent. While practitioners of Congo-inspired ritual practices in Cuba, such as Palo Mayombe, may have benefited secondarily from contact with contemporary Angolan and Congolese soldier and student practitioners during this period, practitioners of Regla de Ocha-Ifá remained effectively isolated from the contemporary Yorùbá homeland and its ritual practices. Even so, military and medical internationalism with sub-Saharan Africa brought Africa "out of the past" for many Cubans, for whom it "came to represent 'una fuente viva'" (literally, a "living source") (C. Peters 2012, 157, my translation).[34]

The Ọ̀ọ̀ni of Ilé-Ifẹ̀'s historic 1987 visit as an African cultural ambassador, then, fell in line with the Cuban revolutionary government's vision of anticolonial and liberationist solidarity with the Global South—and the African continent, specifically—through military, medical, and diplomatic engagement. At the same time, the extension of an invitation to the leading religious figure of the Yorùbá traditional religion of Nigeria—a ritual tradition that held a common point of origin with the Afro-Cuban ritual complex of Regla de Ocha-Ifá—reflected a shift away from the staunch, militant atheism that characterized revolutionary policy toward religious practice in the late 1960s and early 1970s.[35] This shift—which began in the mid-1970s—was instigated, at least in part, by Cuba's military missions in Africa, which "helped develop greater sensitivity on the part of the leadership to sub-Saharan culture" (Moore 2006, 214). Additionally, the role of the Catholic Church and Liberation Theology in liberationist movements in Latin America—and the struggles of Oscar Romero and Camilo Torres in movements in El Salvador and Colombia, respectively—indicated that a "belief in God was not inherently opposed to Marxism" and could even serve as a "tool of insurgents" (Moore 2006, 214, citing Cardenal 1974 and Cox 1987).

Although leading Cuban social scientists and government officials of the period continued to frame Afro-Cuban religion as antithetical to revolutionary socialism and scientific rationalism (e.g., Guanche 1983; Ministerio de Educación 1971, in McGarrity 1992; see also Moore 2006; Palmié 2013), the government's militant stance began to thaw in the mid-1970s (Delgado 2009; Moore 2006). In 1976, a group of leading babalaos created a national organization entitled Ifá Ayer, Ifá Hoy, Ifá Mannana (Ifá Yesterday, Ifá Today, and Ifá Tomorrow) that, although not formally recognized by the Cuban government, was unofficially tolerated.[36] In 1984, a symbolic step toward reconciliation with the Catholic Church occurred when Castro met with the US American Baptist minister and Black civil rights activist the Reverend Jesse Jackson, during which both leaders "publicly visited a Methodist Church" (Cox 1987, in Moore 2006, 215). In 1986, the revolutionary government unofficially permitted the reinstitution of the annual Letra del Año (Letter of the Year) ceremony—a seminal Ifá divination tradition eliminated in Cuba following the 1959 revolution (Castro Figueroa 2012, 91). This ceremony, which offers guidelines for the well-being and prosperity of ritual communities and individuals for the coming year (chapter 4), was reinstituted by a group of babalaos led by Miguel Febles and included future African traditionalist pioneers Frank Cabrera Suárez and Victor Betancourt Estrada (D. Brown 2003; Castro Figueroa 2012). While the Cuban government "permitted" the formation of these groups, government agents from the Cuban Ministry of the Interior reportedly made repeated efforts to infiltrate the organizations (Castro Figueroa 2012, 91–92).

Within this environment of gradually increasing religious tolerance, the Cuban state took steps toward the reestablishment of official contact with Yorùbáland. A few months before the Ọ̀ọni's visit in June, the vice-chancellor of the University of Ife in Nigeria, Wándé Abímbọ́lá, arranged a visit to Cuba on a "cultural mission" in order to initiate a Spanish-Yorùbá language exchange program between the University of Ife and Havana.[37] In addition to his academic position as vice-chancellor (University of Ife, now Obafemi Awolowo University, 1982–1989), Abímbọ́lá serves as an internationally renowned Nigerian babaláwo who was designated in 1981 as the "Àwíṣẹ Awo Ní Àgbáyé," or the "messenger and ambassador of the Yorùbá religion for the world," by the Ọ̀ọni of Ilé-Ifẹ̀ (Konen 2013, my translation). Although the Yorùbá language instruction program never came to fruition, Abímbọ́lá's visit marked one of the first documented points of contact between Cuba and Yorùbáland since the abolition of the slave trade in 1886, if not significantly earlier (Abímbọ́lá 1997, 111). For Cuban practitioners of Regla de Ocha-Ifá, the visit of the Ọ̀ọni of Ilé-Ifẹ̀—or the "father of the Yorùbá"—in 1987 marked the landmark reestablishment of contact with the contemporary Yorùbá homeland. The Ọ̀ọni, who reportedly "kissed the ground and declared 'I arrive at home away from home'" when he arrived on Cuban soil, left a profound impact on Cuban babalaos (Olorunnisola and Akinbami 1992, 66).[38] In a period still characterized by the long shadow of militant, socialist atheism and a state context of official nonrecognition, the Ọ̀ọni's visit came as a revelation to many Cuban practitioners, who had been unaware of the complexity of Nigeria's traditional Yorùbá religious institutions or the possibilities they offered for transatlantic validation (Ayorinde 2004). During his visit, the Ọ̀ọni made proposals that resonated with Cubans' desires for state recognition and institutional validation, including voicing a call for the establishment of a Yorùbá temple in Havana and the future hosting of an international Yorùbá Congress (224).[39] From the perspective of the Ọ̀ọni, the establishment of a Yorùbá temple and the hosting of a Yorùbá Congress fell within a global vision of Cuban Regla de Ocha-Ifá as an extension of a transcontinental domain of YTR as world religion, with its homeland located in contemporary Yorùbáland. In other words, these goals reflected the Ọ̀ọni's vision of Cuba as a "constituency" of the ritual authority and religious jurisdiction of contemporary Ilé-Ifẹ̀ (Ayorinde 2004; Olorunnisola and Akinbami 1992, 65).

Although the Yoruba Cultural Association of Cuba (ACYC) would develop a decidedly antagonistic stance toward Nigerian-style Ifá-Òrìṣà and African traditionalism in the 1990s and 2000s, the Ọ̀ọni's 1987 visit—and the landmark reestablishment of official contact with Yorùbáland that it signified—served as one of the principal catalysts for the establishment of the ACYC itself in 1991 (Ayorinde 2004; Palmié 2013). In certain respects a manifestation of the Ọ̀ọ̀ni's envisioned "Yoruba Temple" (Ayorinde 2004, 224), the ACYC was founded in the wake of the collapse of the Soviet Union and the subsequent landmark announcement of the freedom of open religious practice by the Cuban state at the Fourth Congress of the Communist Party in 1991 (Argyriadis and Capone 2004; Fernández Robaina 1994, 36, in Moore 2006, 208). The ACYC's membership and leadership were drawn from the group of babalaos known as Ifá Ayer, Ifá Hoy, Ifá Mañana, who were chosen by the Office of Religious Affairs of the Central Committee of the Communist Party of Cuba for what Castro Figueroa (2012) describes as their "political reliability" (92, my translation). Originally founded in the home of the institution's first president, José Manuel "Monolo" Ibañez González, in the densely populated Centro Habana neighborhood of Havana, the ACYC subsequently moved to the home of Antonio Castañeda Márquez in Centro Habana following the death of Ibañez shortly thereafter (Fernández 2003).

In 1992, Castañeda helped organize the first International Workshop on the "Influence of Yoruba and Other African Cultures in Cuba" in conjunction with the Cuban Academy of Sciences (Palmié 2013, 74). This controversial workshop marked one of the first major fissures in Cuban Regla de Ocha-Ifá between advocates of the "Yorubization" of the Cuban religion and those who vehemently opposed it. As Ayorinde outlines, multiple presenters at the workshop proposed "a structured *yorubización* (Yorubization) of santería" that entailed ridding Regla de Ocha-Ifá of its syncretic elements, "recovering ritual orthodoxy by returning to the liturgy of the Nigerian oricha cults and the Ifá corpus," replacing Cuban ritual terminology with Yorùbá-centric wording, and reorienting Regla de Ocha-Ifá as a set of ritual practices falling "under the jurisdiction of Ile Ife" (Ayorinde 2004, 224, in Palmié 2013, 74). These proposals sparked an outcry among Cuban practitioners who valued Regla de Ocha-Ifá as an autonomous—and even superior—set of ritual practices in relation to its counterpart in Nigeria. Lázara Menéndez's (1995) oft-cited essay in response to the workshop in 1995, titled "¡¿Un cake para Obatalá?!," argued against the "indiscriminate and uncritical substantivation of the Yoruba component" in Regla de Ocha-Ifá and against a Yorubizing perspective that denied the value of Cuban Regla de Ocha-Ifá as a historically enriched and positively transformed system unique to the sociocultural realities of Cuba itself. For Menéndez, a perspective that only valued Regla de Ocha-Ifá in terms of its "conservation of its African antecedents" was both ahistorical and "naïve" (Menéndez 1995, in Palmié 2013, 75). The second president of the ACYC, Castañeda, ultimately followed this line of argumentation himself, developing an increasingly militant stance against the Yorubization of Regla de Ocha-Ifá in the 1990s and 2000s.

The long-standing isolation between Regla de Ocha-Ifá and the YTR of contemporary Nigeria had, however, been breached, and notable Cuban babalaos became early pioneers of the Yorubizing turn in the 1990s. The Cuban babalao Victor Betancourt Omolófaoló Estrada, considered by many to be the first pioneer of African traditionalism in Cuba (Larduet Luaces 2014, 163), used international contacts with his foreign *ahijados*, or ritual "godchildren," to obtain information about the contemporary Yorùbá religion of Nigeria following the Ọ̀ọ̀ni of Ilé-Ifẹ̀'s visit in 1987. Through the efforts of one of Betancourt's Italian ahijados who frequently traveled to Nigeria, Betancourt established contact with Nigerian babaláwo through letters and mailed correspondence, also obtaining books and written materials on the Yorùbá traditional religion during that period (Betancourt, pers. comm., 2016).[40] Increasingly aware of the discrepancies between the Nigerian YTR and Cuban Regla de Ocha-Ifá, Betancourt became driven by the purpose of what he terms "filling the gaps" between the two domains of ritual practice (Betancourt, pers. comm., 2016).

In 1991, Betancourt founded what is considered by many to be the first African traditionalist lineage in Cuba, Ifá Ìranlówo (salvation is in Ifá)[41] in Havana, with the explicit purpose of "rescuing those deities, rescuing those ceremonies, and rescuing those rituals that didn't arrive in Cuba" and putting them "into practice" (Betancourt, interview). As part of his Yorubizing vision for ritual transformation, Betancourt advocated for the "pie y cabeza" (foot and head) style of oricha initiation, which is "thought to be of African provenance" (D. Brown 2003, 10, 137–38). In this style of initiation, neophytes receive only one òrìṣà (the owner of the head, or *dueño de la cabeza*) and the deity Elegguá/Èṣù rather than the five or six additional oricha that Cuban practitioners receive in Cuban-style initiations (D. Brown 2003, 10, 137–38; Rauhut 2014).[42] Additionally, Betancourt adopted West African styles of dress and, idiosyncratically, openly practiced polygamy, citing a multiplicity of wives as traditional practice in Yorùbáland (Larduet Luaces 2014, 163). Most controversially, however, Betancourt pioneered the initiation of ìyánífá, or female high priestesses of Ifá, in Cuba—a practice strictly prohibited in Regla de Ocha-Ifá—initiating the first two ìyánífá in Cuba in the year 2000 (Fernández 2010).[43] The initiation of women into the Ifá priesthood by Betancourt and the Ifá Ìranlówo lineage ultimately led to the "Iyanifa debate" of 2004, a polemic uproar in which the ACYC issued a "worldwide proclamation to oricha practitioners condemning the practices of Iyanifa" and demanding that the "criminal" priests involved be "blacklisted, have their priesthood titles revoked, and be excluded from their religious communities" (Beliso-De Jesús 2015a, 820–21; see chapter 4). Ultimately, this event fueled a deepening rift between practitioners of Regla de Ocha-Ifá and proponents of Nigerian-style Ifá-Òrìṣà centered on gender and, specifically, female partici- pation and ritual authority in Ifá.

In the mid-1990s, two pioneering babalaos of Nigerian-style Ifá-Òrìṣà in Cuba, Filiberto O'Farrill and Frank Cabrera Suárez, also made direct con- tact with YTR through extensive study with the Nigerian babaláwo Táíwò Abímbọ́lá, son of the renowned Wándé Abímbọ́lá. Following his father's visits to Cuba beginning in the late 1980s, Táíwò Abímbọ́lá received a full scholarship from the Cuban government to study medicine, and he moved to the island for several years in the mid-1990s (Argyriadis and Capone 2004; Konen 2013; Larduet Luaces 2014).[44] Upon learning that Táíwò Abímbọ́lá was residing in Cuba to study, Filiberto O'Farrill and Frank Cabrera made con- tact with Abímbọ́lá through the Nigerian embassy. Abímbọ́lá subsequently became their ritual and religious superior in their study of Nigerian-style Ifá- Òrìṣà.[45] After a period of study with the Nigerian babaláwo, O'Farrill and Cabrera cofounded the Nigerian-rooted religious and cultural organization Ilé Tuntún in Havana in conjunction with Abímbọ́lá in 1997.[46] Significantly, the establishment of Ilé Tuntún marked the first case of the transcontinental founding of a cultural-religious organization recognized by the Nigerian gov- ernment's Corporate Affairs Commission but not by the Cuban government. This pan-African, transcontinental recognition from Nigeria stands, to this day, in stark contrast to the Cuban government's continued denial of official recognition and state legitimization to African traditionalist institutions (see chapter 2).[47]

For Cabrera, who succeeded O'Farrill as the leader of Ilé Tuntún follow- ing his death in 1999, Táíwò Abímbọ́lá's tenure in Cuba and the unusually extensive contact that both Cuban babalaos were able to have with the Ni- gerian babaláwo fulfilled a prophecy that Cabrera had been given through his odù as a young man. Through the divinatory prophecy of Ifá, Cabrera learned from his ritual superiors in Cuban-style Ifá that he was to become a "chosen one" in life, a revelation set forth in one of the caminos, or paths, of his divinatory sign, Ogbe Ché.[48] Upon the Ọọ̀ni of Ilé-Ifẹ̀ Síjúwadé's visit in 1987, Cabrera explains that he became aware of the nature of his sign's prophecy, which he interprets as a call upon him to bring the YTR of con- temporary Nigeria to Cuba (Cabrera, interview, April 4, 2016). For him, the patronage of the first International Congress of Òrìṣà Tradition and Culture in Nigeria in 1981 and subsequently in Brazil (1983, 1989) by Ọọ̀ni of Ilé-Ifẹ̀

Síjúwadé—whose name Cabrera translates from Yorùbá as "the crown that opens to the world"—and his historic visit to Cuba in 1987 marked the beginning of a Nigerian-rooted evangelical movement prophesized to carry YTR to the "world."[49] Following his cofounding of the Nigerian-rooted Ilé Tuntún institution in Cuba, Cabrera worked to fulfill an African traditionalist vision of global evangelism in Ifá-Òrìṣà worship. This included the establishment of a Yorùbá calendar of Ifá and òrìṣà festivals in Cuba that would replace the Catholic-oriented, syncretic calendar of Regla de Ocha-Ifá saints and oricha days (Konen 2013). Through extensive contact and collaboration with Abímbólá following his return to Nigeria in 1998, Cabrera continued to enrich his Yorùbá-centric practices by incorporating novel Yorùbá rituals, deities, praise songs, and ceremonies into the temple's practices.

Together, Victor Betancourt's Ifá Ìranlówo (1991) and Frank Cabrera's Ilé Tuntún (1997) constitute the two African traditionalist ẹgbẹ́ established in Cuba in the 1990s (Martínez Betancourt 2014). During that same decade, broad economic and sociopolitical trends altered Cubans' possibilities for establishing relationships with foreigners, ultimately amplifying opportunities for other Cuban babalaos to establish communication with contemporary Yorùbáland in the 2000s. The collapse of the Soviet Union and the inauguration of the euphemistic "Special Period in Times of Peace" in Cuba in 1990 precipitated drastic measures by the Cuban revolutionary government to curtail conditions of economic collapse, fuel and food shortages, and extreme scarcity—a dire situation brought on by the loss of the Soviet Union as Cuba's primary economic and trade partner (Hernandez-Reguant 2009). On the brink of economic disintegration, the revolutionary government decriminalized the US dollar in 1994 and, in 1995, released the National Plan for the Development of International Tourism, outlining a drastic shift in national policy that reoriented the Cuban economy toward foreign tourism (Colantonio and Potter 2006, 122; C. Hamilton 2012; Simoni 2016). In Cuba, which had been "previously isolated and closed to tourism in fear of its damaging influence" (Morad 2014, 103), the shift toward tourism as a primary means of economic development marked a drastic change in revolutionary policy and enabled Cubans unprecedented access to contact with foreign visitors. During the 1990s and 2000s, this opening of Cuba to foreign travel and tourism led to heightened communication with Cuba's "secondary diasporas" in the United States, Latin America, Europe, and elsewhere (Frigerio 2004; Menéndez 2002) and to the initiation of frequent visits to the island by babaláwo of YTR abroad (both Nigerian and non-Nigerian). Additionally, in the mid-2000s, selective—and often illegal—internet access enabled a select number of Cuban babalaos to forge contacts with practitioners of Nigerian-style

Ifá-Òrìṣà abroad through Spanish-language online websites and forums. Together, these changes in (post-)revolutionary policy—and the opening of Cuba to heightened international contact—potentiated the growth of the African traditionalist movement in Cuba in the 2000s. Despite attempts to police the boundaries of correct Cuban-style Regla de Ocha-Ifá by the state-linked ACYC, novel ẹgbẹ́ dedicated to *Ifá nigeriano* proliferated across the island, reflecting the snowballing growth of the African traditionalist movement in Cuba (Martínez Betancourt 2014). By the time I completed my fieldwork in Cuba in June 2016, Nigerian-style Ifá-Òrìṣà extended from Havana to seven of Cuba's fifteen provinces, including the provinces of Matanzas, Ciego de Ávila, Villa Clara, Holguín, Guantánamo, and Santiago de Cuba (Martínez Betancourt 2014; Martínez Betancourt, pers. comm., 2016). When I returned to Cuba in March 2020, the number of ẹgbẹ́ had nearly doubled in just four years (Martínez Betancourt, pers. comm., 2020).

Efficacy and Africa

When I initiated fieldwork with African traditionalist ẹgbẹ́ throughout Cuba's provinces, I encountered a heterogeneous landscape of individuals and communities who forged connections with the YTR of contemporary Nigeria in discrete ways. While three of the ẹgbẹ́ founded in regional provinces outside of Havana were extensions of Victor Betancourt's Ifá Ìranlówo, the remaining nineteen ẹgbẹ́, including Frank Cabrera's Ilé Tuntún, emerged within a heterogeneous and variegated network of exchange between Cuban babalaos and practitioners of YTR abroad. Accordingly, African traditionalists (*los tradicionalistas africanas*) exhibit a wide array of ritual approaches to Ifá-Òrìṣà practice, each elaborated in and through the specificity of their personal contacts with discrete foreign babaláwo; the translocal, Nigerian-style ritual lineages with which they engage; and the idiosyncrasies of individual approaches to Ifá and òrìṣà worship among practitioners themselves. Despite this heterogeneity, however, I encountered a landscape of Nigerian-style ẹgbẹ́ firmly oriented toward the promise of efficacy of Nigerian-style Ifá-Òrìṣà, with women and men discursively and epistemically grounded in efficacy as a key acting principle.

The logic of efficacy in Nigerian-style Ifá-Òrìṣà is intimately tied to the ontological weight that "Africa" carries in the historical imagination of the nation, the larger Caribbean, and the Americas. As Robin D. G. Kelley (2002, 15–24) beautifully explores in his historiography of transnational Black social movements, Africa has long operated as a site of "radical imagination" and a "place of freedom" for Afro-diasporic peoples, ranging from nineteenth-century Ethiopianism, Black Zionism, and the "Back-to-Africa proposals" of activists and writers such as Marcus Garvey to the historical revisionism and future visions of US American jazz musicians Sun Ra and Duke Ellington or Jamaican reggae legend Bob Marley (Lewis 2008; Lock 1999; Weinstein 1993). Temporally, ancient Africa likewise offered a "utopian dreamscape" through which to "imagine what we desired and what was possible" through generative and restorative recourse to the past (Kelley 2002, 30).[50] In *Listening for Africa: Freedom, Modernity, and the Logic of Black Music's African Origins* (2017), David F. Garcia provocatively extends the imaginative potential of this geotemporal logic of ancient Africanity to sound, pointing to the weight of ancient Africa in a diverse array of listening and musical practices in Cuba, the United States, and throughout the Americas. In an opening vignette, Garcia points to a 1940 write-up in a New York City newspaper to highlight a "logic" that allows three "jungle drums" played atop a skyscraper in Manhattan in celebration of a Nigerian couple's wedding "to not simply sound as such but to bring sound from the historical past to the modern present" (2). This geotemporal channeling of ancient Africanity through sound has long influenced African-inspired music making and listening across the African diaspora (Díaz 2021).[51] In Cuba, this logic foundationally influences the way people listen to and for "Africa" in sonic practices ranging from secular rumba, *songo*, and *timba* to ritual *bembé*. Crucially, the logic by which the sounds of ancient Africa are channeled into the necessities and desires of the present forms a cornerstone of African-inspired ritual in Cuba, particularly in Ifá and òrìṣà/oricha worship.

In Nigerian-style Ifá-Òrìṣà and Regla de Ocha-Ifá, the channeling of ancient Africanity through sound is intimately bound with the notion of ritual efficacy, in other words, with the potency and transformative capacity of ritual acts. Notably, however, divergences in when and where individuals locate the "true" geotemporality of ancient Africanity forms a key, fraught distinction between Cuban- and Nigerian-style Ifá. As a set of fate-transformative practices tracing its roots to nineteenth-century Yorùbáland, Cuban-style Regla de Ocha-Ifá offers its own claims to African traditionality as rooted in historical—rather than contemporary—Yorùbáland. Cuban practitioners of Regla de Ocha-Ifá and members of the ACYC often discursively frame the diasporic Cuban tradition as more unchanged (and therefore "traditional") than the contemporary YTR of Yorùbáland itself, which has declined significantly in influence in Nigeria in the face of Islam and Christianity (Beliso-De Jesús 2015a; Clarke 2004; Omojola 2011; Villepastour 2015a). Practitioners of Ifá nigeriano, meanwhile, mobilize discourses of loss, "lacunas," and *invenciones* (inventions) in Regla de Ocha-Ifá, which many frame as a diluted practice ravaged by the legacy of slavery and the vagaries of Catholic syncretism in the New World (see, e.g., Odùgbemi 2007; Orozco Rubio 2015a).

Despite these discursive divides, the task of parsing out objective distinctions between the two traditions and communities—"Cuban-style" and "Nigerian-style"—is, inevitably, a considerably complex methodological and analytical endeavor. On the one hand, self-evident differences abound. Central deities crucial to òrìṣà worship in Yorùbáland, including, for example, the òrìṣà Ẹgbẹ́, did not survive (or, perhaps, thrive) as such within the pantheon of deities in Cuba (Bolívar Aróstegui 1990; D. Brown 2003; Martínez Betancourt 2014; Sublette 2004; Villepastour 2015b) and have been reintroduced through Nigerian-style Ifá-Òrìṣà.[52] Beyond distinctions in the core deities worshiped in Cuba and Yorùbáland, the number of deities that a practitioner receives during initiation also differs. Since the 1990s, African traditionalists have returned to a "pie y cabeza" (foot and head) style of initiation rather than the "modern," multideity style of Regla de Ocha-Ifá initiations, as mentioned previously (D. Brown 2003, 10, 137–38; Rauhut 2014). Additionally, in Nigeria, the concept of reincarnation forms a core principle in Ifá and òrìṣà worship (Bascom 1969a; McClelland 1982). As Castro Figueroa (2012, 93) states, this "eschatological concern" is "practically void" in the Cuban tradition, which generally concerns itself with more "concrete and immediate problems."[53] Emerging within the lived catastrophes of the transatlantic slave trade, Regla de Ocha-Ifá also emphasizes rituals and rites related to "protection and divination" with a diminished emphasis on rites of fertility (Castro Figueroa 2012, 93). Other differences also abound: the preferred use of the contemporary Yorùbá language in Yorùbá-style ritual versus the vestige, nonsyntactical ritual lexicon of Lucumí in Regla de Ocha-Ifá;[54] a discrete yearly calendar of òrìṣà days and festivals; distinct weekly and monthly cycles of rituals; and myriad differences in the musical, linguistic, and sonorous approaches to Ifá divination and communication with the òrìṣà.

Despite these self-evident differences, however, the question of what is "African," "Cuban," "Yorùbá/Yoruba," or "Afro-Cuban" about individual ritual practices remained a lingering epistemological and methodological concern, ultimately pointing to the emergent, contested nature of such descriptors. On both sides of the Atlantic, Cuban-style and Nigerian-style practitioners lay claim to "true" African traditionality and fate-transformative efficacy as rooted in a pre-twentieth-century and often mythical Yorùbáland—one inevitably separated from the present by the vagaries of each country's respective colonial and postcolonial histories and by the dynamism of living traditions that inevitably transform and adapt through time. Furthermore, as

J. Lorand Matory (1999, [1994] 2005) has shown, the very emergence of the concept of "Yorùbáland" and of a "Yorùbá tradition" itself is inexorably linked to the coeval dialogue that occurred between Africa and the Americas in the nineteenth and early twentieth centuries. Matory's dialogic—rather than linear—formulation of the relation between Africa and its diasporas complicates notions of a purportedly "true" Yorùbá traditionality that often characterize discursive mobilizations of a Yorùbá "baseline" (Matory 1999, 74). Matory ([1994] 2005, 70) states:

> What came to be classified as "Yorùbá" tradition [in the nineteenth and early twentieth centuries] fed on cultural precedents in the hinterland of Lagos, but its overall name, shape, contents, standards of membership, meaning, means of transmission, and degree of prestige would have been radically different—if they had come into existence at all—were it not for the intervention of a set of transnational financial, professional, and ideological interests that converged on the West African Coast. Returnees from Brazil, Cuba, Jamaica, North America, the Virgin Islands, and Sierra Leone converged on Lagos during the 19th century and not only composed a novel African ethnic identity but, through a literate and politicized struggle, guaranteed that it would be respected in a unique way by generations of students of Africa and its diaspora.

The influence of Brazilian, Cuban, and other returnees to Lagos in the nineteenth century on shaping the formation and prestige of a "'Yorùbá' tradition"— which, in turn, influenced the writings of the pioneering Cuban scholar of Afro-Cuban culture and religion Fernando Ortiz in the early twentieth century (112–13)—points to the emergence of "Yorùbá traditionality" as fundamentally dialogic and coeval both on and off the African continent. The mobilization of contemporary formulations of Yorùbá traditionality, then, rests not only in the "story of Africa in the Americas" but on the story of "the Americas in Africa," as Matory succinctly states (1).[55]

Matory's approach to addressing Yorùbá traditionality as an emergent, dialogic, and historically contingent ascription offers a productive lens through which to examine the ways in which Nigerian-style Ifá-Òrìṣà and Cuban-style Regla de Ocha-Ifá practitioners mobilize divergent predications of African traditionality in the service of contemporary—and historically situated— projects.[56] Here, I build on scholars who generatively examine circulating logics of ancient Africanity and traditionality in transatlantic Ifá and òrìṣà ritual as "fundamentally emergent" in nature (Palmié 2008, 32; Palmié 2013; Clarke 2004; Matory [1994] 2005), a view of African-inspired ritual that pushes against linear, twentieth-century Herskovitsian models of African cultural "retentions" in the New World (Herskovits 1958; Price and Price 2003). Such attributions of Africanity in the Americas are "ill-understood as mere transcontinental and transtemporal reflexes, residues, or memories of an originary set of dispositions or essences," as numerous scholars have demonstrated (Palmié 2008, 32; see also Clarke 2004; Larduet Luaces 2014; Ochoa 2010; Wirtz 2014). Even so, the mobilization of discourses of purity in Nigerian-style Ifá and, concomitantly, discourses of *barbaridades* (barbarities), loss, and lacunas in *Ifá criollo* forms a foundational aspect of African traditionalism, a discursive posturing that mirrors the Herskovitsian logics of retention/dilution that emerged in the twentieth-century anthropology of Black cultural forms in the New World (Herskovits 1958; Price and Price 2003). Rather than undertake the fraught methodological and epistemological task of parsing out "true" historical authenticity vis-à-vis a historiography of New and Old World comparisons, I interrogate predications of Yorùbá traditionality that ground "claims to efficacy" (Ochoa 2010, 131) in Nigerian-style Ifá as foundationally emergent, historically constituted ascriptions mobilized by contemporary Cuban women and men in the service of heterogeneous aims.

South-South Translations: Sonorous *Décalage*

As historically emergent ascriptions, the predications of Yorùbá ritual efficacy that ground Nigerian-style Ifá-Òrìṣà in Cuba manifest through intricate acts of translation and creative adaptation within and across South-South contexts of encounter and exchange. At once a revisionist and generative movement aiming to revitalize fate-transformative ritual, Nigerian-style Ifá-Òrìṣà emerges precisely at the juncture of translative acts that, in turn, engender complex polarities of opposites: affirmation and deaffirmation, genesis and erasure, sounding and silencing. These translative polarities—and the "new" engendered in and through them (Ochoa 2010, 16)—manifest in concert with the affective intricacies of use and disuse. Indeed, the selective forms of use attendant to such acts of revitalization necessarily occur concomitantly with the slippage (intentional or unintentional) of other elements—ritual, linguistic, epistemic, sonorous—into obscurity.

At the intersection of translation studies, African diaspora studies, and Black radical historiography, Brent Hayes Edwards's (2003) formulation of "décalage" as central to the articulation (following Hall 1980) of Black diasporic forms, discourses, and practices offers a fruitful framework through which to explore the myriad translative acts inherent to Nigerian-style Ifá-Òrìṣà and its South-South forms of exchange. The unequal, heterogeneous, and imperfect means by which information surrounding YTR travels to Cuba and other locales across the Global South underscores Edwards's (2003, 13) formulation of *décalage,* which emphasizes "gap[s]," "discrepanc[ies]," and "lag." In the realm of language, linguistic translations between Yorùbá, English, and Spanish circulate unevenly between Nigeria, the Americas, Europe, and Cuba itself, generating a variegated, traveling archive—itself a "generative system" (Scott 1999 and Foucault 1972, in B. Edwards 2003, 7)—of information, correspondences, and print and digital media. This generative, mobile archive instantiates proliferating iterations of difference that, as I argue here, ultimately potentiate the practices of Nigerian-style Ifá-Òrìṣà on the island.

Notably, practitioners of Ifá nigeriano in Cuba rarely speak English or Yorùbá. As such, African traditionalists rely heavily on amateur Spanish-language translations of Yorùbá- and English-language publications, including both popular and academic publications in the fields of religious studies, anthropology, history, linguistics, art history, and Africana studies, among others.[57] Often, documents that circulate the sacred verses of the odù of the Ifá corpus or specific instructions for ritual are passed digitally and authored anonymously. Many of these documents arrive in the hands of Cuban practitioners via unofficial Spanish translations of English-language texts originally translated from Yorùbá, a labor undertaken by Spanish-speaking practitioners throughout the Americas and Europe with varying degrees of direct contact with and knowledge of contemporary Yorùbáland. Spanish-language blogs, forums, and websites based out of Mexico, Venezuela, Ecuador, Spain, Colombia, and other countries in Latin America provide further means of digital exchange, a novel phenomenon afforded through the recent, and painfully gradual, changes to the infrastructural and state-mandated impediments to Cubans' internet accessibility (Brooklyn 2021; Rodriguez 2017).

Beyond the linguistic dimensions of the Yorùbá-English to English-Spanish translations that enable access to information on YTR in Cuba, the décalage inherent to diasporic articulations of Ifá nigeriano encompasses broader ideological and cultural (mis)translations. As Edwards (2003, 14) notes, décalage transcends the merely linguistic, constituting "the kernel of precisely that which cannot be transferred or exchanged" and "the received biases that refuse to pass over when one crosses the water." Décalage thus encompasses a far-reaching and ever-transformative "changing core of difference" inherent to points of differentiated, and unequal, contact at different scales. In Nigerian-style Ifá-Òrìṣà, we witness décalage at work in exchanges between Yorùbá-speaking Nigerian babaláwo and Spanish-speaking Cuban babaláwo and ìyánífá; at varied points of encounter between Cuban, Cuban

expat, US American, Latin American, and other European Ifá-Òrìṣà revisionists and YTR practitioners; and even (trans)locally in Cuba between women
practitioners who mobilize radical feminist positionings toward the potentiality of Yorùbá-inspired revisionism and those who resist them (chapter 3).

In a South-South ritual movement centrally concerned with the efficacy
of sound as a technique, technology, and driver of Yorùbá-inspired ritual revisionism, the realm of sonority acts as a central locus for such discrepancies,
gaps, and (mis)hearings: in other words, for sonorous décalage. Here, I turn
to ethnomusicologist Ana María Ochoa Gautier's (2014) decolonial historiography of listening and the voice in nineteenth-century Colombia as a fruitful
lens through which to explore the (mis)hearings and ontological-epistemic
reconfigurations that occur in and through sites of multi-entity, sonorous encounter. Drawing on Brazilian anthropologist Eduardo Viveiros de Castro,
Ochoa Gautier points to the "cycle[s] of transduction" that differentially situ-
ate the interrelationship between discrete entities at sites of encounter: that is,
a "sound producing entity," "sound objects," and "listening entities" (human
and nonhuman) (26). These points of contact between extant things and beings generate "different perspectives in the conceptualization of an entity"
and "contested understandings and uses of 'ways of making' with sound that
entangle the ontological and epistemological" (26). Extending Ochoa Gautier's and Edwards's formulations at the intersections of global ritual sonority
and use, I argue that sites of sonorous décalage in Nigerian-style Ifá-Òrìṣà
generate novel ontological and epistemic entanglements that also formu-
late new horizons of potentiality. Notably, Edwards (2003, 15) foregrounds
the "unhappy" dimensions of décalage as a foundational aspect of the act of
translation—or what he refers to as the "necessary haunting" attendant to its
proliferation of misunderstandings and difference. Ochoa Gautier likewise
underscores de Castro's formulation of "equivocations," or ontological discrepancies, as inherent to sites of unequal, intercultural encounter. In this
project, I engage these equivocations and mishearings while also proposing
that African traditionalists mobilize such sites of disjuncture precisely as
fields of use, of generative potentiality. If décalage (and the act of translation itself) is a metaphorical two-sided coin, its iterability as a "gap," "discrep-
ancy," or "lag" (Edwards 2003, 13) provides both the possibility for negative
proliferations of difference while, simultaneously, enabling generative sites
of creative possibility. Décalage, as a site of disjuncture, enables interstitial
spaces of potentiality that provide the grounds for acts of reconfiguration. In
Nigerian-style Ifá-Òrìṣà in Cuba, African traditionalists continually harness
the generative potentialities of décalage to creatively adapt aspects of YTR
ritual practice to suit their own objectives and needs. Rather than merely

copying Nigerian forms of Ifá and òrìṣà worship wholesale (a practical—and undesired—impossibility), practitioners creatively refashion and selectively fuse tenets of Nigerian-style Ifá-Òrìṣà and Cuban-style Regla de Ocha-Ifá to suit their own uses, creating novel forms of worship and "ways of making" with sound that enable the realization of specific projects and desires.

2

Yorùbá Geographies and the Efficacy of the Far: The *Dùndún* "Talking Drums" and Transatlantic Institutions in Havana

On June 14, 2016, a group of thirty men and women paraded through the most densely populated neighborhood of Havana, engulfing the streets with a novel sound. At the heart of the procession, percussionist Francisco Mario Delgado Iglesias played an unusual series of gliding pitches on the ìyáàlù "talking" drum, resonorizing the streets of Centro Habana with a recently imported Yorùbá instrument. Delgado alternately squeezed and released the cords of the lead "mother drum" with his left hand, increasing and decreasing the tension of the drumhead while playing the instrument with a curved, wooden stick (*kòngó*).[1] As he did, the ìyáàlù slid effortlessly between pitches, approximating the onomatopoeic *dùn* (low tone) and *dún* (high tone) characteristic of Yorùbá speech (see A. Euba 1990, 34).[2] The ìyáàlù resounded loudly above the crowd, sounding melodic glides largely unfamiliar to the fixed-pitched instrumentation characteristic of African-inspired Cuban percussion.[3] Surrounding Delgado, men and women punctuated the glides of the ìyáàlù with a shouted phrase in call-and-response: "¡Olóyè, Olóyè, Olóyè!" A contemporary Yorùbá term meaning "titleholder" or "chief," *olóyè* referenced the six newly coronated lineage chiefs who mingled among the procession, clearly distinguished from their casually dressed peers by West African–inspired, chiefly regalia.[4] The chiefs donned body-length, multicolored robes and carried powerful emblems, including intricate, hand-beaded bracelets, necklaces, and royal staffs. Enveloping the busy thoroughfares of the capital, the *babaláwo*, ìyánífá, and other members of the procession proclaimed the arrival of African traditionalism in Cuba to the sounding of the *dùndún*, a "talking drum" percussion ensemble from Yorùbáland that has arrived in tandem with the Nigerian-style ritual movement in Cuban Ifá (Audio Example 1: Olóyè) (see fig. 2.1).

FIGURE 2.1. Francisco Mario Delgado Iglesias (left, *iyáàlù* drum), Hugo Máximo Mendoza Marín (middle, *gángan* drum), and Osniel González (right, *gúdúgúdú* drum) head a procession announcing the coronation of six new lineage chiefs. Centro Habana, June 2016. Photo by the author.

In this chapter, I explore how male members of the Nigerian-rooted Aworeni lineage mobilize the dùndún as a means to promote contemporary Yorùbá titles that confer transatlantic ritual authority—and personal efficacy—to their holders. I explore how African traditionalist men harness what I term the efficacy of the far—in this case, the usefulness of Nigerian-rooted models of institution-building and hierarchical councils of chiefs—to achieve heightened personal efficacy and ritual authority in Cuba itself. Through contemporary Yorùbá titles, these newly crowned chiefs craft forms of institutional autonomy and legitimacy otherwise inconceivable within Cuba's state religious landscape. Through the foundation of temples, the forging of novel geographical constituencies, and the establishment of hierarchical titled councils, members of the Nigerian-rooted Aworeni lineage build a network of pan-African, Yorùbá-rooted institutions on the island. These institutions, in turn, challenge the religious and juridical monopoly of the state-linked Yoruba Cultural Association of Cuba (ACYC), contesting the Cuban state's relationship with African-inspired religion and challenging the constraints of its burgeoning civil society.

Novel Geographical Constituencies: The Àràbà of Havana

In December 2013, the Nigerian news network TVC interviewed Cuban medical doctor Ángel William Viera Bravo on-site in Òṣogbo, Nigeria. The interview

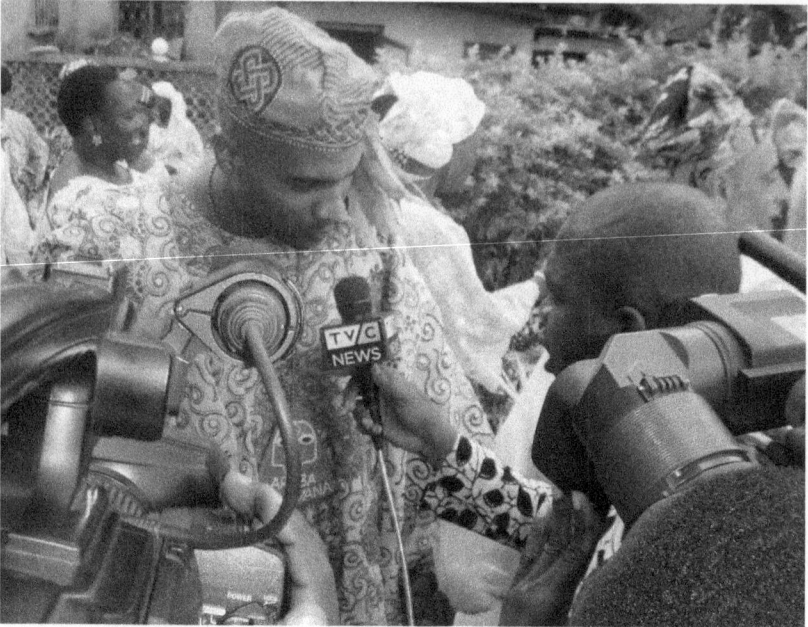

FIGURE 2.2. Cuban babaláwo Ángel William Viera Bravo is crowned "Àràbà of Havana." Òṣogbo, Nigeria, December 2013. Photo courtesy of Ángel William Viera Bravo.

followed Viera's coronation as Àràbà of Havana by the esteemed Nigerian babaláwo, musician, and playwright Ifáyẹmí Ẹlẹ́buìbọn (b. 1940). In Yorùbáland, the title Àràbà designates a position of spiritual authority and leadership over a given geographical region, indicating the wearer of the title (or "crown") as the "head diviner" of a town or region (Bascom 1969a, 91). Additionally, the title of Àràbà converts the "chief" into a living reincarnation of the òrìṣà Ọ̀rúnmìlà, the deity of wisdom and divination (Omidire 2014). Named after the towering silk cotton tree (*Ceiba pentandra*, commonly referred to as "Araba, father of trees") in Yorùbáland, the title of Àràbà emerged in the Òkè Ìtàṣẹ Ifá lineage based out of the World Ifá Temple of Òkè Ìtàṣẹ in Ilé-Ifẹ̀ (Bascom 1969a, 91). As Àràbà of Havana, Dr. Viera now held the status of supreme spiritual leader for all followers of the Yorùbá religion in Havana, Cuba—a newly minted geographical constituency an ocean away. Significantly, the crowning of Viera as the Àràbà of Havana marked the first documented case of a Nigerian Àràbà crowning a non-Nigerian babaláwo as the Àràbà of a geographical region located outside of Yorùbáland—in this case, Cuba's capital city of Havana (see fig. 2.2).[5]

For the gathered Nigerian priests in Òṣogbo and members of Dr. Viera's Aworeni lineage in Cuba, the crowning of Chief Viera as the Àràbà of Havana marked the readoption of Cuban worshipers of Regla de Ocha-Ifá into the religious authority and hierarchies of contemporary Yorùbáland, including Yorùbá traditional religion's (YTR) complex network of institutions and titles. In Cuba, however, the president of the ACYC responded by labeling the Nigerian-rooted title an "African thing," pointing to Nigerian-rooted titles and institutions as legally unrecognized and invalidated on the island itself.[6] The crowning of the Àràbà of Havana in Nigeria instigated a polemical debate surrounding African traditionalism in Cuba, pointing to contested claims of Yoruba/Yorùbá traditionality, Africanity, and authority on the island and across a broad transnational landscape of competing ritual lineages.

From Ilè Ìfè to Havana: The Aworeni Lineage

Babaláwo Ángel William Viera Bravo's ritual house in Havana, the Àràbà Aworeni Ilè Ìfè Ifá Temple of Cuba, serves as the headquarters for one of the most prominent, and controversial, African traditionalist lineages in Cuba. Dr. Viera was born in 1978 in the dense Centro Habana neighborhood of Havana. Flanked on one side by the neoclassical mansions and eclectic art deco architecture of the historically wealthy Vedado neighborhood and on the other by the beautifully restored colonial and touristic areas of Old Havana, Centro Habana, by comparison, offers a striking contrast in urban decay and decline (see Scarpaci 2005). With the highest population density in the city, Centro Habana's residents have long suffered from state-directed efforts to steer tourists away from their streets and toward adjacent neighborhoods, isolating residents from the tourist industry so crucial to revitalizing Cuba's economy since the fall of the Soviet Union (Anguelovski 2014; Colantonio and Potter 2006). A neighborhood with a strong Black and mixed-race presence, Centro Habana is also well-known for its thriving Afro-Cuban traditions (De la Fuente 2001). Viera entered this Afro-Cuban religious milieu as a young teenager, receiving his *mano de Orula*, an initial step of initiation into Cuban-style Ifá, at age thirteen. As a young adult, he was initiated into numerous Afro-Cuban ritual traditions, including Ifá, Regla de Ocha and the Congo-inspired practice of Palo Mayombe. During this period, Viera also pursued a career in medicine, graduating and working as a medical doctor in Havana with a specialization in general comprehensive medicine and psychiatry.[7]

Viera first came into contact with Nigerian-style Ifá in 2008–9 through contact with a global Ifá missionary of YTR: the Mexican babaláwo Eli Torres Gongora. Torres was himself first introduced to Cuban-style Regla de Ocha-Ifá in Mexico by means of contact with Cuba's ritual diasporas abroad. Torres traveled to Cuba to be initiated into Ifá in 1996, and, in subsequent years, traveled frequently to Cuba for ritual purposes. As the influence of the YTR of Nigeria increased globally in the 1990s and 2000s, Torres ultimately established direct contact with Yorùbáland. In 2006, Torres traveled to Nigeria to receive his *itenifa*, or Nigerian-style initiation into Ifá, at the Odewale Village of Alakuko in Lagos, Nigeria.[8] By traveling directly to Nigeria to (re-)initiate into Nigerian-style Ifá, Torres enacted a reconfiguration of the concept of "homeland" in Ifá-Òrìsà worship from Cuba to contemporary Nigeria, a move reflective of the trajectory of other babaláwo across the Spanish- and English-speaking Americas. Like Torres, Ifá and òrìsà practitioners throughout Latin America, the Caribbean, and the United States often first come into contact with Ifá-Òrìsà/Ocha religion through Cuba's secondary diasporas abroad (Frigerio 2004), subsequently connecting directly with Yorùbáland itself (Clarke 2004; Martínez Betancourt 2015; Ovalle 2014). For many Cuban *babalaos*, this turn to contemporary Yorùbáland as the "homeland" comes as a potent threat. The transmutation of Yorùbá traditionality from Cuba—as rooted in the colonial-era history of slavery on the island—to present-day Yorùbáland is seen as compromising the authority of Regla de Ocha-Ifá on the island itself.

Following Torres's first visit to Nigeria in 2006, the International Council for Ifá Religion (ICFIR), a globally focused Yorùbá religious organization based in the Nigerian city of Ilé-Ifè, named Torres its national coordinator of Mexico and its regional coordinator of Latin America (Torres 2016). As the ICFIR's Latin American regional coordinator, Torres began his evangelizing role as a "transatlantic messenger" of YTR between the African continent and the Americas, spreading information about contemporary Yorùbáland and proselytizing Yorùbá-style Ifá and òrìsà practice through repeated visits to Cuba and other Latin American nations.[9] Torres organized academic conferences and religious encounters on YTR in Mexico, Venezuela, Colombia, and Cuba (Torres 2016). In 2015, Torres helped organize the "First Hispanophone Encounter of the Ifá-Òrìsà Tradition" (Primer Encuentro Hispanoparlante de la Tradición Ifá-Òrìsà) at the Casa de la Poesía in Old Havana, marking the first formal attempt to unite the heterogeneous array of African traditionalist egbé throughout Cuba's provinces in a formal meeting.

In his role as ICFIR's Latin American regional coordinator, Torres traveled extensively throughout the Americas with his Nigerian ritual and religious superior, the babaláwo Chief Sólágbadé Pópóolá. Pópóolá is the author of numerous books on YTR and serves as chairman of the Ethics and Scripture Committee of ICFIR (Omidire 2014). A transatlantic messenger himself, Pópóolá established numerous chapters of his own Nigerian-rooted religious organization, the International Ifá Training Institute, in various Latin American and Caribbean countries (including Mexico, Venezuela, Colombia, and Trinidad). During one of Pópóọlá's visits to Cuba in late 2008 and early 2009, Dr. Viera, the future Àràbà of Havana, was introduced to Nigerian-style Ifá-Òrìṣà through Pópóọlá and Torres. Dr. Viera was impressed with the Nigerian babaláwo and the claims of the other African traditionalists he met during Pópóọlá's visit. These babaláwo held contemporary Yorùbáland as the true homeland for ritual purity and fate-changing efficacy, and they controversially viewed Cuban Regla de Ocha-Ifá as a diluted tradition damaged by the legacies of slavery, the loss of the Yorùbá language, and the syncretic influence of Catholicism (Orozco Rubio 2015a).[10] After meeting Torres and Pópóọlá, Viera turned resolutely toward African traditionalism. In 2011, he received his first Nigerian consecrations from Pópóọlá, including material vessels for the òrìṣà Ṣàngó, Ọbàtálá, and Orí imported directly from Yorùbáland.[11] The following year, Dr. Viera moved beyond his connections with Pópóọlá and made contact with the Aworeni Ifá lineage of the World Ifá Temple of Òkè Ìtasè in Ilé-Ifè, a connection that would ultimately lead to his coronation as Àràbà of Havana.

For the Yorùbá, the Nigerian city of Ilé-Ifè represents the cradle of the Yorùbá civilization and the birthplace of humankind (Ogunleye 2007; Abímbọ́lá 1997). Ilé-Ifè is home to the World Ifá Temple of Òkè Ìtasè, one of the most important pilgrimage sites in southwestern Nigeria (Olupona 2011). There, the Àràbà Àgbáyé—literally, the "Àràbà for the whole world" and a purported direct blood descendant of the deity Ọ̀rúnmìlà (Omidire 2014)—presides. The Àràbà Àgbáyé also serves as the spiritual head of the Aworeni lineage, one of the most prominent Ifá lineages in Yorùbáland and a ritual line based out of the temple of Òkè Ìtasè. Through the connections of two foreign babaláwo, Dr. Viera made contact with the Àràbà Àgbáyé and the Aworeni lineage in 2012.[12] That same year, the Àràbà Àgbáyé, Chief Adisa Makoranwale Aworeni (d. 2018), sent one of his sons, Babaláwo Owólabí (Owólabí Awódòtun Awóreni Mákòránwálé II), from Ilé-Ifè to Havana to establish the first Nigerian-rooted Aworeni temple there.[13] In Dr. Viera's home in Centro Habana, Babaláwo Owólabí founded the Àràbà Aworeni Ilé-Ifè Ifá Temple of Cuba (Ilé Ijuba Ifá Àràbà Aworeni Ilẹ̀ Ìfẹ̀) with Dr. Viera as its Chief *Olúwo*, or spiritual leader, notably, only twenty-five blocks away from the ACYC.

After the temple's founding, Dr. Viera hosted a visit in 2012 from the Àràbà of the city of Òṣogbo, Nigeria, the renowned babaláwo and transatlantic òrìṣà entrepreneur Ifáyẹmí Ẹlẹ́buìbọn. Hailed by historian Peter Probst (2004, 352) as "by far the most successful religious entrepreneur of *oriṣa* worship in Oṣogbo," Ẹlẹ́buìbọn established a successful career as an authority on Ifá

worship and YTR in Nigeria beginning in the late 1960s. At the turn of the
decade, Ẹlẹ́buìbọn began producing radio programs, audio cassettes, films,
and books examining Ifá and YTR practice. By the mid-1970s, Ẹlẹ́buìbọn
had also traveled to France, Brazil, and the United States in his capacity as a
poet and playwright as part of Nigerian dramatist Duro Lapiddo's National
Theater (Probst 2011). In the 1980s, Ẹlẹ́buìbọn "expanded his business ventures in the U.S. and Latin America," where he "established himself as a poet,
filmmaker, and authority on Ifá divination" (89).

Ifáyẹmí Ẹlẹ́buìbọn also played a crucial role in the fierce controversy surrounding the Yorubizing turn among Cuba's diasporic lineages in Miami in
the late 1970s (Palmié 2013, 68–72). During these years, the Cuban American
babalao José Miguel Gómez Barberas instigated a transnational uproar by turning toward Yorùbáland as a source of consecrations and ritual authority from
his home base in Miami. After being denied access to the "crucial reproductive resource of the olofin" by the infamous Cuban babalao Miguel Febles y
Padrón (67)—an indispensable "sacrum" that allows babalaos to initiate others
and build their own ritual lineages—Barberas took matters into his own hands.
In 1977, he contacted the exiled Cuban ethnographer Lydia Cabrera about the
possibility of becoming reinitiated into Ifá in Nigeria (68). This move effectively
sidestepped Miguel Febles's tight control over babalaos' ability to initiate new
priests of Ifá and establish new ritual descent lines in Cuba and in the United
States. Now, Barberas adeptly turned toward Nigeria as a source for the coveted
Olofin (Odù in Nigeria).[14] Through Cabrera's contact with the French ethnographer Pierre Verger, Barberas ultimately succeeded in breaking with the tradition of descent-based ritual lines in Cuban-style Ifá, traveling to Òṣogbo in 1978
to be (re-)initiated into Ifá by Ifáyẹmí Ẹlẹ́buìbọn. As Palmié notes, Ẹlẹ́buìbọn
"bestowed upon his Cuban-American colleague the crucial consecrations" that
enabled Barberas to initiate others into Ifá in Miami, and Barberas's new Olo-
fin/Odù "went viral almost immediately after" (71). By providing Barberas with
the crucial reproductive mechanism of Odù, Ẹlẹ́buìbọn emerged as a central
player in one of the earliest turns toward Nigerian-style Ifá-Òrìṣà in the Cuban
American ritual community in Miami. This radical break from the descent-
based *ramas* of Cuban Ifá would serve as an important catalyst in the development of a rift between practitioners of Cuban-style Regla de Ocha-Ifá and
Nigerian-style Ifá-Òrìṣà on and off the island in subsequent decades.

Over thirty years after the reconsecration of the Cuban American babalao
Barberas in Nigeria in the late 1970s, Ẹlẹ́buìbọn continued his protagonistic
role as a major instigator of Nigerian-style Ifá-Òrìṣà internationally by facilitating and overseeing the crowning of Dr. Ángel William Viera Bravo as the
Àràbà of Havana in Òṣogbo, Nigeria, in 2013. Adding to the multinational and

polyglot complexity of this crowning, Dr. Viera's connection with Ẹlẹ́buìbọn was made through a US American clinical psychologist and professor at Loyola Marymount University in Los Angeles, Cheryl Tawede Grills, a ritual godchild of Ẹlẹ́buìbọn. According to Viera, Grills put Ẹlẹ́buìbọn in touch with Viera after meeting the Cuban doctor during one of Grills's visits to Cuba. Through their shared professional interests in community psychology and psychiatry, Viera and Grills became friends and colleagues, collaborating together on an academic publication exploring drug addiction and personal and community health in Havana (see Aguilar Amaya et al. 2014).[15] In 2012, Grills facilitated an informal, two-day conference in Viera's temple with Ẹlẹ́buìbọn as the primary speaker (Ovalle 2014). As Ẹlẹ́buìbọn would later relate, the Nigerian babaláwo was impressed by how Viera and other members of the Aworeni lineage took great interest in the extensive knowledge that the elderly priest held of YTR and of the practices of Ifá and òrìṣà in Yorùbáland. To him, the attitudes of these African traditionalists stood in stark contrast to the positions of other Cuban babalaos and practitioners of Regla de Ocha whom he met during his travels, who struck Ẹlẹ́buìbọn as "arrogant" and unwilling to "pay respect to the homeland."[16]

After the conference, Ẹlẹ́buìbọn reciprocated the visit by inviting Viera to stay with him in Òṣogbo, Nigeria, the following year. Crucially, Ẹlẹ́buìbọn's invitation to Òṣogbo coincided with a key policy change in Cuba's international travel laws. In 2013, President Raúl Castro lifted the restriction requiring Cubans to obtain exit visas prior to international travel (Cave 2012; De Ferrari 2014; Gupta 2013). For the first time in decades, Cubans with financial means were granted unprecedented opportunity to travel abroad.[17] That same year, Viera became one of the first two African traditionalist babaláwo residing permanently in Cuba to take advantage of the new law and travel directly to Nigeria for the first time, effectively ending a prolonged period of physical isolation between Cuban practitioners of Nigerian-style Ifá-Òrìṣà residing on the island and contemporary Yorùbáland.[18] During this first trip to Yorùbáland, Ẹlẹ́buìbọn hosted Viera in his home, escorting Viera to sites of importance in and around Òṣogbo and preparing him for his upcoming coronation. In a ceremony covered by Nigerian national news and by the Cuban American press in Miami, Florida (see Oshisada 2014; Ovalle 2014), Ẹlẹ́buìbọn crowned Viera as the Àràbà of Havana in Òṣogbo, Nigeria, in 2013.

Dùndún "Talking Drums" in Havana Ẹgbẹ́

With the title of Àràbà, Viera became an official representative of YTR in Havana. From the perspective of Ẹlẹ́buìbọn and his ritual superiors in Yorùbáland,

Àràbà Viera now served as the leader and religious authority for "all" practitioners of Ifá and òrìṣà/oricha in Cuba's capital city (Viera, interview, June 17,
2016).[19] Viera was now responsible for spreading the Yorùbá traditional religion of contemporary Nigeria—including its complex system of Nigerian-
rooted institutions, titles, and hierarchies—throughout the capital city. Notably, Dr. Viera's crowning by Ẹlẹ́buìbọn reflects a heightening transatlantic
effort on the part of Nigerian babaláwo to carve out global geographic constituencies of YTR ritual practice across the Americas. To aid in his new,
proselytizing mission of spreading YTR and its institutions in Cuba, the new
Àràbà of Havana purchased a set of Yorùbá dùndún talking drums in Òṣogbo
to introduce to the Àràbà Aworeni Ilé-Ifẹ̀ Ifá Temple of Cuba (Martínez Betancourt 2015; Martínez Betancourt and Barrero 2017).[20] For Chief Viera, the
dùndún drums would reintroduce contemporary Yorùbá percussion into Ifá
ritual—which does not have its own set of drums in the Cuban tradition—
heightening the efficacy of communication with Ifá and the òrìṣà and rean-
imating Ifá ceremonies. Furthermore, the sounding of the dùndún drums
in the temple and in street processions throughout Havana would promote
and legitimize the arrival of YTR's transatlantic, Nigerian-rooted geographical constituencies and institutions in Cuba. Framing himself as a pioneer in
bringing YTR and its efficacious sonority to the island, Dr. Viera proclaimed
the dùndún as "the first Ifá drums to be used to play for Ọ̀rúnmìlà [in
Cuba]."[21] Upon his return, Àràbà Viera integrated the "talking" instruments
into Aworeni rituals and public processions.

In Nigeria, the dùndún comprise the most widely used percussion ensemble in Yorùbáland, followed in popularity by the sacred bàtá set of Ọ̀yọ́
state (A. Euba 1990; Omojola 2014; Villepastour 2010). In Yorùbáland, the
term dùndún in fact designates a range of ensembles made of drums that
are collectively considered a "family" of instruments (Samuel 2008/2009, 50;
A. Euba 1990; Omojola 2014). These, in turn, vary considerably in instrumentation, with ensembles often named after their lead instruments (most
commonly the ìyáàlù) (Euba 1990, 19).[22] Nigerian musicologists Akin Euba
(1990, 109) and Kayode Samuel (2008/2009, 49) classify the dùndún into
"four sub-families," including the ìyáàlù subfamily (consisting of the ìyáàlù,
isááju, ìkẹhìn, and kẹríkẹrì drums), the gángan subfamily (including the gángan, kànàngo, and àdàmọ drums), and the kósó and gúdúgúdú. Of these, the
ìyáàlù and gángan subfamilies feature double-headed, hourglass-shaped tension drums; the kósó, a single-headed, open-ended hourglass-shaped drum;
and the gúdúgúdú, a nontension kettledrum.[23]

Of these, the lead ìyáàlù—the "most 'talkative'" of the dùndún instruments—is the principal drum to "speak" (Samuel 2008/2009, 56; A. Euba 1990).

By tightening or releasing the tension on the cords of the instrument, ìyáàlù drummers mimic the tonal characteristics of Yorùbá speech (Carter-Ényì 2018; Durojaye et al. 2021; A. Euba 1990; Omojola 2014; Samuel 2008/2009, 2021). Specifically, dùndún drummers reproduce the three tone levels and tonal contours of what is considered to be the Ọ̀yọ́ dialect of the Yorùbá language, using specific techniques on the principal talking instruments of the ensembles, including the ìyáàlù (or, alternatively, the gángan) (Durojaye et al. 2021; Samuel 2021).[24] Yorùbá drummers, for example, use "tight compression" on the cords to reproduce the high tone of the Yorùbá language, "light compression" for the mid tone, and "no or minimal compression" for the low tone, also often "obligatorily" striking the drum membrane to indicate the beginning of syllables (Samuel 2021, 5).[25] With impressive fidelity, drummers are able to reproduce "the lexical tones, the grammatical tones and the phonetic details of the tones" of Yorùbá (11). Together with other instruments of the ensemble, these "talking" drums also create rich, contrasting polyrhythms, playfully alternating narrative phrases with nonsemantic rhythmic improvisations (Omojola 2014; Oyelami 1989).[26]

The Yorùbá language is especially well-suited to this type of "speech surrogacy" because it is a tonal language (A. Euba 1990; Omojola 2014; Villepastour 2010, 2015b, 3).[27] Like Mandarin Chinese, Vietnamese, or Punjabi, semantic meaning in the Yorùbá language depends not only on vowels and consonants—as in stress languages such as Spanish and English—but on relative tone level and pitch contour (Akinlabi and Liberman 2000; Eme and Uba 2016; Laniran and Clements 2003). As Nigerian linguist Túndé Adégbọlá explains: "Drum language [in Yorùbá music] is the sounding of the melody that is inherent in Yorùbá speech . . . because Yorùbá is a tone language, there is inherent melody in the language" (Sublette 2016). Unlike African-inspired percussion traditions in Cuba that rely on fixed-pitched construction and techniques and hold only a vestigial relationship with the tonal nature of everyday speech in African languages,[28] Yorùbá ritual and secular drumming is intimately tied to the tonal properties of Yorùbá speech.

While Àràbà Viera and other members of the Aworeni lineage view the dùndún and its particular speech-imitative and tonal capacities as central to sounding a more pure and efficacious form of contemporary YTR ritual sound, numerous Nigerian and foreign scholars view the dùndún as an exogenous instrument of relatively recent arrival in Yorùbáland.[29] Estimates on the timeline of the dùndún's arrival vary. As Amanda Villepastour outlines, Nigerian musicologist Euba (1990, 60) dates the appearance of the dùndún to as early as the fifteenth century, while other estimates range from the late sixteenth century (King 1961, 3) to the mid-nineteenth century onward (Kubik

1999, 131, in Villepastour 2010, 77). In addition to being exogenous to Yorùbáland and of indeterminate arrival in YTR ceremonies, the dùndún differ markedly from other drum ensembles in the region in key regards. For one, they are "tied to no particular context" (A. Euba 1990, 33). Unlike drum ensembles restricted to the worship of specific òrìṣà, the dùndún are free "to participate in all kinds" of secular and religious festivities and rituals (33). This freedom of use differs, for example, from the ìpèsè drums associated with Ifá; the àgèrè associated with the òrìṣà Ògún; or the ìgbìn associated with the òrìṣà Ọbàtálá; among other instruments (33).[30] Due in part to this flexibility, the dùndún talking tension drums proliferated widely in Yorùbáland throughout the twentieth century.

The dùndún proliferated to such an extent that the instruments became the most ubiquitous drum ensemble in Yorùbáland, gradually displacing other sacred ensembles linked to specific òrìṣà (A. Euba 1990; Omojola 2014). The popularity of the dùndún ensemble draws from a variety of factors; however, undeniably, the dùndún owes its spread in large part to the ìyáàlù's uncanny capacity to mimic the tonal properties of Yorùbá speech (A. Euba 1990; Omojola 2014). As Euba (1990, 34) states, the tension drums are particularly well-suited to simulating speech sounds because "they can not only reproduce level tones but also the various glides between level tones which are characteristic of Yorùbá speech." Players easily manipulate the cords and ropes on the side of the instruments while playing to alter the pitch (and tension) of the drumheads. The ability to glide seamlessly between tones by stretching or releasing the ropes after hitting the drumhead distinguishes the dùndún ensemble from other talking drums in Yorùbáland, such as the bàtá drums associated with the òrìṣà Ṣàngó (Villepastour 2010).[31] Unlike the dùndún, the bàtá are fixed-pitch, nontension drums. As such, bàtá drummers have developed a coded language known as ẹnà bàtá that serves as the basis for surrogate speech on the instruments. This spoken code consists of a repertoire of drum vocables "spoken" only by bàtá drummers (and the lineage of Ọ̀jẹ̀ masqueraders with whom they intermarry); for this and other reasons, the bàtá's surrogate speech is difficult to understand for outsiders (Villepastour 2010; Villepastour, pers. comm., 2017). The dùndún drums, on the other hand, are generally intelligible to the common Yorùbá speaker (Túndé Adégbọlá in Sublette 2016). In addition to their enhanced capability to serve as speech surrogates for the common Yorùbá listener, the dùndún owe their ubiquity to their portability, a quality that differentiates them from other drumming ensembles linked to specific òrìṣà, such as the larger ìpèsè drums associated with Ifá (A. Euba 1990, 34). Additionally, the dùndún do not suffer from the same stigmatization as the bàtá, which are more directly associated with the òrìṣà in Yorùbáland (Villepastour, pers. comm., 2017). With these advantages, the dùndún are widely used within secular celebrations to communicate praise poetry, or oríkì, for guests at events such as house parties, weddings, or child-naming ceremonies (A. Euba 1990; Omojola 2014; Sublette 2016). Increasingly, the dùndún have entered ritual spaces in Yorùbáland, paradoxically aided by their destigmatized association with secular festivities. This has occurred to such an extent that the dùndún are replacing drum ensembles traditionally linked to specific òrìṣà, creating alarm for members of what Villepastour terms the "endangered" òrìṣà drumming traditions of Yorùbáland (Villepastour 2010, 15; Omojola 2014).

The "endangered" status of the òrìṣà drumming traditions is inexorably tied to the endangerment of YTR itself, which has declined steeply in significance in Nigeria in the face of the spread of Islam and Christianity (Clarke 2004; Villepastour 2010). As Villepastour (2010, 15) notes, "Most Yorùbá people are now Muslim or Christian (said to be fifty per cent and forty-five per cent respectively)." Accordingly, the vast majority of Àyàn drummers dedicated to bàtá drumming and dùndún "talking" drummers are Muslim (A. Euba 1990; Klein 2015; Villepastour 2010). This is true to such an extent that Euba, in 1990, stated: "I have not yet come across a dùndún drummer who is a devotee of Yorùbá òrìṣà, although such drummers may exist" (95–96). While the dùndún have spread as a ubiquitous, pan-Yorùbá instrument increasingly used within ritual contexts dedicated to the òrìṣà, many of the dùndún drummers hired for such rituals are not practitioners of these traditions themselves. "Though the roots of Yorùbá traditions are seen as emerging from Africa," Clarke (2004, 6) states, "Nigerian òrìṣà practitioners are few in number." The declining significance of YTR in Yorùbáland itself, however, inversely correlates with an increased interest in it abroad (Clarke 2004, 2006; Villepastour 2010). In the United States, Europe, and Latin America, interest in the Yorùbá homeland has continually increased as the number of practitioners of YTR globally grows (Clarke 2004, 2006; De La Torres 2004). As Ọlábíyí Babalọlá Yáì succinctly states, "The òrìṣà tradition has its foot in Africa and its head in the Americas" (Yáì 2001, 6, in Clarke 2004, 6–7).

Despite a drastic decline in hired ritual drummers who practice YTR themselves, Àràbà Viera became greatly impressed by the ubiquity of the percussion used in Ifá processions and ceremonies when he first visited Yorùbáland in 2013, including the dùndún, agogo Ifá bells, ṣèkèrè shakers, and ìpèsè.[32] In Nigeria, he marveled, "everything" is accompanied with instruments (Viera, interview, April 22, 2016). The use of percussion in ceremonies and processions related to Ifá marks a key distinction between Nigerian-style Ifá and Cuban-style Ifá. In Cuba, Ifá does not have its own specific

instrumental ensembles as in the case of Ifá in Yorùbáland (e.g., the ìpèsè and
the agogo Ifá) (A. Euba 1990). The repertoire of songs associated with Cuban-
style Ifá rituals are generally sung a cappella,[33] and the only sound that joins
the practitioners' voices is often the distinctive, percussive rattle of the *irofá*,
a thin, carved, wooden ideophone sounded to invoke the deity Orunmila
(*ìróké* in Yorùbá) (Martínez Betancourt 2014; Bascom 1969, 36).[34] In Cuba, the
batá ensemble most strongly associated with the òrìṣà Ṣàngó and Egúngún
in the Ọ̀yọ́ region of Yorùbáland came to stand in for a wide variety of the
orichas in the Cuban pantheon, and the specific drumming traditions associated with individual òrìṣà in Yorùbáland (e.g., the ìpèsè/agogo Ifá for Ifá, the
àgèrè for Ògún, the ìgbìn/agogo for Ọbàtálá) were lost or marginalized
(see Marcuzzi 2005). In Regla de Ocha, the consecrated batá, or *tambores
de Añá*, are used within ceremonies related to a multiplicity of orichas, such
as "presentations" of new initiates of oricha to Añá,[35] anniversaries of santeros' initiations (*cumpleaños de santo*), or *toques de santo* marked through Ifá
or *dilogún* divination (Schweitzer 2013, 48). While Ifá does not have its own
specific drum ensemble or drumming traditions in Cuba, the sacred Yorùbá-
inspired batá drums are directly associated with Ifá's intersecting, yet divergent, branch of oricha-centric worship: Regla de Ocha.

In order to re-Yorubize the sonority of Ifá ritual, the Àràbà of Havana
purchased two principal instruments of the dùndún ensemble in Òṣogbo to
integrate into the Àràbà Aworeni Ilè Ìfè Ifá Temple of Cuba. These included
the ìyáàlù and the gúdúgúdú, two instruments considered the "mother" and
"father" of the dùndún family and often played together in dùndún ensembles
in Yorùbáland (Samuel 2008/2009, 49–50). The Àràbà of Havana's choice to
import dùndún instruments rather than the ìpèsè drums traditionally associated with Ifá speaks to the rise of the dùndún as a quintessential pan-Yorùbá
drum ensemble and to its displacement of traditional òrìṣà ensembles in Yorùbáland. By wielding the dùndún, Àràbà Viera asserted a novel orientation
toward Yorùbá traditionality and sounded his mission to build a transatlantic
system of Nigerian-rooted YTR institutions in Cuba.

This creative reformulation of "true" Yorùbá traditionality and fate-
transformative efficacy as rooted in the ritual sonority of present-day Yorùbáland—including exogenous instruments that Nigerian scholars and òrìṣà
drummers alike deem *not* "traditional," and even invasive, to Yorùbá òrìṣà
worship (A. Euba 1990; Omojola 2014)—is reflected in the name that Viera
gives to the dùndún themselves. Viera and other members of the Aworeni
lineage in Cuba call the instruments *ilú Ifá*, or, literally, "drums of Ifá" (Martínez Betancourt and Barrero 2017, 52). While the individual instruments
are referred to by their Yorùbá language correlates (i.e., ìyáàlù, gángan, or

gúdúgúdú), the instruments are consistently collectively termed ilú Ifá or, alternatively, *tambores de Ọ̀rúnmìlà* (drums of Ọ̀rúnmìlà). Indeed, the term *dùndún* was one that I never encountered during my three years of fieldwork with the Aworeni lineage.[36] On the one hand, the renaming of the instruments as ilú Ifá speaks to the survival and prevalence in Cuban Lucumí of the Yorùbá-inspired word *ilú* ("drum" or "percussion"), which has been used in phrases such as "Obá-Ilú" (king of the drum) to signal exceptionally skilled batá players and drum makers of the Havana batá tradition (Abímbọ́lá 1997, 133).[37] At the same time, this adaptive renaming of the dùndún ensemble in African traditionalist temples in Cuba reontologizes the essence of the instruments themselves, which, as ilú Ifá, transform from instruments exogenous to Yorùbá traditionality to specifically Yorùbá—and, in their link to speech, ritually efficacious—"talking drums" dedicated to Ifá. In reontologizing the dùndún ensemble as "drums of Ọ̀rúnmìlà" in their importation to Cuba, Àràbà Viera and the Aworeni percussionists draw the instruments into African traditionalist logics of heightened linguistic and ritual efficacy, locating the efficacy of sound in contemporary forms of YTR practice and instrumentation.

Contentious (Il)Legality

When I first met Dr. Viera in January 2014, the newly coronated Àràbà of Havana had just returned from his first trip to Òṣogbo, Nigeria, with two dùndún drums, the lead ìyáàlù and the smaller gúdúgúdú. Not a drummer himself, Viera assembled a group of percussionists from among the temple's members, assigning them the task of learning to play the ìyáàlù and gúdúgúdú themselves. To assist, Viera provided the drummers with videos and recordings of dùndún drumming in Yorùbáland. These included the recent òrìṣà praise albums of well-known Nigerian babaláwo and ìyánífá, such as *Orin Orisa: Yoruba Traditional Songs of Praises for Orisa* (2009) by the Nigerian babaláwo Adedayo Ologundudu (who, notably, was crowned as the first Àràbà of the United States a year after Dr. Viera, in 2014) and *Ìṣẹ̀ṣe Làgbà (Tradition and Culture Is the Best)* by ìyánífá Asabioje Afenapa (2007).[38] Both of these albums offer praise songs to Ifá and òrìṣà recorded over traditional Yorùbá instrumentation, including the dùndún and bàtá ensembles. Through autodidactic approximations of the Yorùbá rhythms and songs, the percussionists began incorporating the dùndún into the temple's Ifá rituals and ceremonies (see figs. 2.3 and 2.4).[39]

In 2015, Àràbà Viera traveled to Nigeria for a second time, where he was promoted from Àràbà of Havana to Àràbà of Cuba by an even more formidable

FIGURES 2.3 and 2.4. The lead ìyáàlù drum (*above*) and the supporting gúdúgúdú drum (*below*). Havana, Cuba, 2016. Photo by the author.

Nigerian babaláwo, the Àràbà Àgbáyé himself, Chief Adisa Makoranwale Aworeni (Abímbọ́lá 1997, 63). Considered the supreme ritual leader of Ifá for the Yorùbá and "the representative of Orúnmila on earth" (Alarcón 2008, 138), the Àràbà Àgbáyé serves as the head of the Aworeni lineage in Nigeria and presides over the World Ifá Temple of Òkè Ìtasẹ̀ in Ilé-Ifẹ̀ (Alarcón 2008, 138; Omidire 2014). From the perspective of his Nigerian superiors in Ilé-Ifẹ̀, Viera now held the status of supreme spiritual leader for all worshipers of the òrìṣà and Ifá in all of Cuba, not just the nation's capital. During this second trip, Viera purchased three additional dùndún instruments to bring back to Havana from Ilé-Ifẹ̀, including the gángan. When he returned from Nigeria as Àràbà of the nation, Àràbà Viera began a concerted effort to spread Nigerian-rooted Aworeni institutions in Cuba and to establish a council of titled male chiefs that would mirror and transatlantically extend the institutional hierarchies of YTR in contemporary Yorùbáland. In September 2015, Viera founded the first subsidiary temple of the national Àràbà Aworeni Ilè Ìfẹ̀ Ifá Temple of Cuba in the Havana neighborhood of Alamar. Titled the Aworeni Temple of Havana, the subsidiary temple functions under the guidance of the national temple and serves the inhabitants of the city of Havana, specifically. In June 2016, Viera founded yet another subsidiary temple in the beachside town of Guanabo, located about thirty kilometers east of the city, designating it as the Aworeni Temple of Eastern Havana. By carving out novel geographical constituencies legitimized through the authority of the Àràbà Àgbáyé and the World Ifá Temple of Òkè Ìtasẹ̀ in Ilé-Ifẹ̀, Viera used his status as Àràbà of Cuba to chart a new cartography of Yorùbá religious jurisdiction, masculine titled authority, and institutional hierarchies throughout western Cuba (see fig. 2.5).

For members of the Aworeni lineage in Cuba, the founding of a national African traditionalist temple and its subsidiaries in Havana, legitimated by the authority of the Àràbà Àgbáyé and ICFIR, indicates a radical, transatlantically inspired rupture from the official state institutional landscape of Afro-Cuban religion in Cuba itself. Notably, each Aworeni temple in Cuba is officially registered with ICFIR in Ilé-Ifẹ̀, Nigeria. The ICFIR, in turn, is registered with the Nigerian government's Corporate Affairs Commission of the Federal Ministry of Commerce and Tourism (see Corporate Affairs Commission 2016). For Viera and other African traditionalists in Cuba, this Nigerian legal affiliation and institutional recognition stands in stark contrast to the Cuban government's official stance of nonrecognition. In Cuba, the Ministry of Justice and the Communist Party's Office of Religious Affairs recognize only one organization, the ACYC, to represent the Yoruba religion on the island (Argyriadis and Capone 2004).[40] Since the ACYC's founding in

FIGURE 2.5. Àràbà Viera and the former Àràbà Àgbáyé, the Àràbà for the "whole world," Chief Adisa Makoranwale Aworeni, outside of the World Ifá Temple of Òkè Ìtasè in Ilé-Ifè, Nigeria, 2015. Photo courtesy of Ángel William Viera Bravo.

1991—the same year that the Fourth Congress of the Communist Party an-nounced a new, postatheist era of religious freedoms in Cuba (Argyriadis and Capone 2004; Fernández Robaina 1994, 36; Moore 2006)—the organization has wielded the juridical right to delineate the boundaries of Yoruba religious practice and to enforce a religious politics of delegitimization, and tacit crim-inalization, of Nigerian-style Ifá-Òrìṣà. In practice, this has taken the form of barring the entry of African traditionalists into the organization, dissemi-nating pamphlets aimed at discrediting African traditionalism, and, on oc-casion, sending representatives to harass religious practitioners (particularly women) who are seen as falling out of line (see chapter 3). In February 2015, for example, the ACYC's official bulletin included an essay labeling Ṣọlágbadé Pópóọlá—the influential Nigerian babaláwo who provided Viera with his first Nigerian consecrations—as a "fraud," a falsifier of the sacred verses of Ifá, and a "liar" (Águila de Ifá 2015, 16–17).[41] Framed acerbically as a "response to the mafia heads and religious hitmen of the Nigerian tradition"—a discursive posturing associating Nigerian-style Ifá-Òrìṣà with criminality and base immorality—the essay also declares the initiation of women into Ifá as ìyánífá a "cruel scam" (20). To battle what the author frames as the fraudulent "invention" of ìyánífá in the Yorùbá ritual traditions of Nigeria, the essay goes on to proclaim that the twenty-seven thousand members of the ACYC "will not accept in any of our homes—making this extensive call to the entire . . . Regla de Ocha and Ifá [community]—the presence of these women who claim to be Iyanifá . . . and much less . . . those babalawos who have lent themselves to this farce" (32). This statement effectively bars African traditionalist women and men not only from the ACYC itself but also from the private domain of its members' homes (casas). This banishment of Nigerian-style ìyánífá and babaláwo from ACYC members' homes also implicitly proclaims their banishment from Cuban-style temples (called casa-templos, or "house-temples"), which are located in Cuban practitioners' private residences (see fig. 2.6).

Beyond a heated campaign to discredit and ostracize African traditionalists, their exclusion from the ACYC also carries legal consequences. The

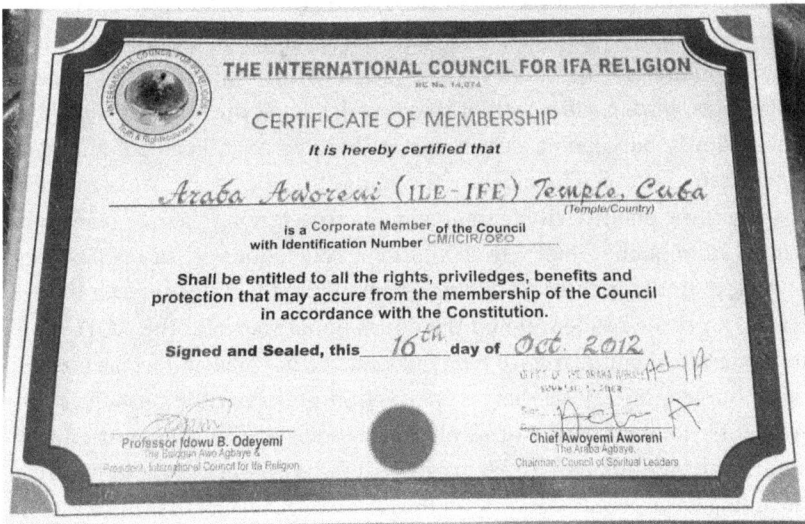

FIGURE 2.6. The Aworeni Temple of Cuba's official certificate of membership to the ICFIR in Ilé-Ifẹ̀, Nigeria, which is registered with the Nigerian government's Corporate Affairs Commission of the Federal Ministry of Commerce and Tourism. Photo by the author.

ACYC holds the exclusive right to grant foreign visas for religious tourism in conjunction with the Department of Immigration, and one must be a member of the ACYC to apply for this visa (Pérez Andino, interview; see also Beliso-De Jesús 2015b, Hagedorn 2014, and Hearn 2008). This policy effectively criminalizes African traditionalists who host foreigners for religious purposes, a common occurrence that serves as a vital source of income for Cuban babaláwo overseeing initiations. The withholding of foreign visas for religious tourism additionally complicates opportunities for African traditionalists to legally hold spaces of dialogue and encounter with religious figures from abroad. Accordingly, African traditionalist priests and ìyánífá are vulnerable to harassment from immigration officials or, worse to exorbitant fines for illegally hosting foreigners.

After founding the Aworeni Temple of Cuba, Viera petitioned the Cuban government to receive legal incorporation and official licensure as an association through the Ministry of Justice. Cuban law, however, "prohibits two or more legally inscribed bodies to execute the same functions," so "the recognition of the ACYC legally preempts all further claims" by alternative Yoruba institutions (Palmié 2013, 74). Following the rejection of the petition, the Aworeni Temple placed a trilingual banner on the outside of the house-temple—in Yorùbá, English, and Spanish—that listed the temple's name, its registration number with the ICFIR, Viera's accreditation and contact information, and a picture of the Aworeni lineage's religious superiors in Ilé-Ifè. Shortly thereafter, a representative from the Cuban Institute of Physical Planning (Instituto de planificación física), which grants permits to restaurants, *casas particulares* (private hostels),[42] and other businesses within Cuba's slowly burgeoning private sector (EcuRed 2017; Feinberg and New-famer 2016), informed members of the temple that the banner violated Cuban law regarding publicly visible signs and placards, forcing them to remove the banner from public view.[43] The institutional restrictions on the open practice of African traditionalism (including a banner placed, in this case, on the outside of a private residence) and the oppositional stance of the ACYC point to the juridical boundaries of religious practice in Cuba and to the confines of its burgeoning civil society—even within an ostensibly postatheist and religiously tolerant period of revolutionary socialism. In this restrictive institutional environment, the recognition of the Aworeni lineage in Nigeria—including its legal registration with the Nigerian government's Corporate Affairs Commission and the ICFIR—serves as a potent symbol of nationally transcendent legitimacy and pan-African affiliative authority in the face of a national, revolutionary context of nonrecognition and delegitimation.

Sounding Yorùbá Institutions

Within this environment of legal restriction, Àràbà Viera mobilizes the dùndún ensemble as a tool in legitimating and promoting the spread of Yorùbá temples and institutions in western Cuba. The instruments feature prominently in ceremonies for the coronation of new chiefs, in rituals for the consecration of new temples and geographic constituencies, and in public processions announcing the arrival of African traditionalism and its institutions in Havana. Since the establishment of the Àràbà Aworeni Ilè Ìfè Ifá Temple of Cuba in 2012, Àràbà Viera has worked to establish subsidiary temples of the national temple in eastern and western Havana and to establish hierarchical, male councils of chiefs for the national and subsidiary temples. As I outline in this chapter, members of the Aworeni lineage promote the establishment of subsidiary temples and the foundation of temples' "staffs"—or councils of titled chiefs—through the sounding of the dùndún in public processions in Havana's streets. Through the use of dùndún, Àràbà Viera and other members of the temple affirm the spread of Nigerian-rooted institutions in Cuba, also animating novel, and highly contentious, relational ontologies of ritual sound in Nigerian-style Ifá.

The coronation of a council of sixteen chiefs marks an indispensable component of the establishment of new Aworeni temples in Cuba and mirrors the council of elders that exist in the Òkè Ìtasè compound in Ilé-Ifè.[44] Known as the Awoolodumeringidolgun, the sixteen-member group of religious leaders in the World Ifá Temple of Òkè Ìtasè encompasses the "highest ranking babaláwos" of Yorùbáland and is presided over by the Àràbà Àgbáyé, the highest-ranked babaláwo in the world (Abímbọlá 1997; Orishada 2013). The sixteen members of the council of elders are considered to be living reincarnations of the sixteen *méjì*, or sixteen principal odù (divinatory signs) of the divining system of Ifá (Viera 2015). Each individual member of the council of elder babaláwo receives a specific title indicative of occupational responsibility and rank. These include designations such as Àgbọngbòn, the "immediate deputy of the Àràbà" (Abímbọlá 1997, 71); Àwísẹ, the "messenger" or "ambassador" of the temple (Viera 2015; Konen 2013); and Akọda, the "sword-bearer" and "one who arrives first" (Bascom 1969a, 92).[45] In addition to this first set of sixteen highest-ranking babaláwo, an additional set of sixteen "chieftaincy titles"—thought to be "born" out of the higher-ranking first set—follows (Orishada 2013). Beyond these initial two sets of sixteen chiefs, additional lower-ranked chieftaincy titles follow, including the titles Olúwo, Lodagba, Olori Eledgan, and others (Orishada 2013).

The complex organizational hierarchy of male titles, chieftancies, and rank in the Aworeni lineage indicates what William Bascom (1950, 68) frames as the "wealth" of "institutional detail" within the Yorùbá traditional religion of Nigeria. This "wealth" differs markedly from Cuban Ifá (Bascom 1950; D. Brown 2003, 282). In Yorùbáland, the complex system of ritual lineages grew out of the politico-religious "royal dynasties" of traditional Yorùbáland, which are often mythologically framed as extensions of the royal, descent-based lineages established by the ancient "deified grandsons of [the òrìṣà] Oduduwa" (Sklar 1963, 10). As J. D. Y. Peel (2003, 30) outlines, these politico-theological lineages formed the political centers of the traditional Yorùbá ìlú ("town" or "community") and were presided over by an ọba, or semidivine "king," and a council of chiefs or titleholders ("ijoye or oloye, from oye, 'title'") (31). As Peel notes, in the "title system" an ìlú "achieved a two-way flow of control, resources, and information between its center (the ọba) and its periphery (the household heads, or bale). . . . Power and dependents, title and power, were reciprocally linked. Titles might be conferred as a recognition, and serve as an expression, of power otherwise attained (as by a successful hunter, farmer, or warrior); but an established title also conferred power, since it gave his holder the presumptive support of a given constituency, and, by virtue of its place in the title system, a certain access to resources distributed from the center" (32–33). In the most prominent lineages of Yorùbáland, such as that of the Aláàfin (the traditional ruler of Ọ̀yọ́), the ọba's power was complemented and counterbalanced by the council of titled chiefs (Sklar 1963, 11). Although many of the highest-ranked positions within discrete lineages are hereditary (e.g., the titles of Àràbà Àgbáyé and Àgbọngbọ̀n in the council of elders of Ilé-Ifẹ̀), other chieftaincy titles are awarded according to merit and prestige (Abímbọ́lá 1997, 72). In contemporary Yorùbáland, the lineages of the traditional "principal royal dynasties" such as those of the Aláàfin of Ọ̀yọ́ or the Ọọ̀ni of Ilé-Ifẹ̀ are supplemented by innumerable minor, and often offshoot, religious lineages, compounds, and temples dedicated to specific òrìṣà or to Ifá. Many of these, in turn, hold their own individualized systems of chieftaincy titles and hierarchies (Olajubu 2003; Sklar 1963, 10; Bascom 1969a).[46] As Bascom and Viera note, the titles' names—and even the number of titles that constitute the council of elders—vary from lineage to lineage and inevitably shift over time (Bascom 1969a; Viera 2015). For example, the title of Àràbà itself may have originated in Ọ̀yọ́ before traveling to the Aworeni lineage of Ilé-Ifẹ̀ in "fairly recent times" (Bascom 1969a, 93). A number of Bascom's informants also maintained that there were originally seventeen titles in the council of elders rather than sixteen "in accordance with the 17 palm nuts" of Ifá divination (93).

The complexly hierarchical political and religious systems of the Yorùbá were effectively dismantled in Cuba (Bascom 1950; D. Brown 2003). As David Brown (2003, 282) notes, the Lucumí religion flourished within the "niches provided by the stratified colonial society and early Republic, particularly the networks of *cabildos* and houses of Ocha." In Cuba, these cabildos and casa-templos replaced the complexity of the politico-religious structures of the kings and councils of the Yorùbá ìlú (282). As Jorge and Isabela Castellanos outline, the hierarchy of Cuban babalaos shifted from the structure of chief-taincy titles and councils of rank to a specifically Cuban system of rank recon-textualized within the framework of casa-templos. In their study, Castellanos and Castellanos outline the Cuban hierarchy, from lowest- to highest-ranked, as follows: "Omofá (Hand of Orula), Awó (a *babalawo* initiated in Ocha first), Oluo (a *babalawo* of rank), Adofín—next after Oluo, Aró—third in rank at this high level" (D. Brown 2003, 343, citing Castellanos and Castellanos 1992, 84–86). The Cuban ranks outlined by Castellanos and Castellanos bear di-rect linguistic resemblance to prominent Yorùbá titles. These include Olúwo (from *olu awo*, meaning "chief or master of secrets") and *awo* (meaning "se-crets or mysteries") (Bascom 1969a, 83). The latter, *awo*, forms a foundational term within YTR and is widely used within Yorùbá terms and titles, including *babaláwo* ("expert [or master] in the realm of *awo*") (Oyěwùmí 2006, 20);[47] *awo egan*, or "secret of *egan*," considered the lowest rank of Ifá diviners in Yor-ùbáland; and *awǫni/awo ǫni*, the highest-ranking category of the counsel of Ifá diviners of the Ǫòni, or the king of Ilé-Ifè (Bascom 1969a, 81, 83).[48] Accordingly, Cuban Ifá differs markedly from the level of institutionalization of hierarchies and the complexity of systems of rank in Yorùbáland, including its structures of formalized councils and chieftaincy titles (Bascom 1950; D. Brown 2003).

The president of the ACYC, José Manuel Pérez Andino (Babalao Manolo Ogbeyao) succinctly summarized this difference in 2016: "The greatest title a [Cuban] babalao has is being *Olofista* [a possessor of Olofin]" (Pérez Andino, interview). Rejecting the importation of African titles in Nigerian-style Ifá and their institutional or ritual bearing on the island, Pérez Andino main-tains: "'Àràbà of Cuba' is an African title. . . . He [Viera] is not 'Àràbà of Cuba' because Africa is Africa. That's African; it's not Cuban. . . . [The title] is not [part of] the Afro-Cuban transcendence." To President Pérez Andino's point, the extension of contemporary Yorùbá titles and hierarchical councils of chiefs from Nigeria to the Americas—a system itself rooted in the shifting complexity of relations between colonial and postcolonial politico-religious towns (ìlús), kings (ǫbas), hereditary dynasties, and nonhereditary, merit-based councils in Yorùbáland—appears to have arrived, or at least ampli-fied, precisely in 2013 with the crowning of Dr. Viera as Àràbà of Havana by

68   CHAPTER TWO

Ẹ̀lẹ́buìbọn. This globalizing, evangelical maneuver catalyzed a novel form
of transatlantic, juridico-religious "Yoruba ecclesiogenesis" (Palmié 2013, 41),
one involving the creative extension of the hierarchies, titles, and constituencies of Yorùbáland across the newly proselytized ritual geographies of the
Global South.[49] Following Viera's original coronation as Àràbà of Havana in
2013, the former Àràbà Àgbáyé, Chief Adisa Makoranwale Aworeni, upped
the ante, crafting two extraterritorial, national geographical constituencies
outside of Yorùbáland. In 2014, the Nigerian-born babaláwo Adedayo Ologundudu was crowned Àràbà of the United States (ChiefDayo 2014), institut-
ing the first nation-level geographical constituency of YTR in the Americas.
In 2015, Dr. Viera himself was crowned the Àràbà of Cuba, up-leveling his
previous coronation as Àràbà of Havana two years prior and making him
only the second Àràbà of an entire nation outside of Nigeria.

For the Àràbà Àgbáyé, meanwhile, this globalizing, evangelical crowning
of two transnational Àràbà constituted one of the most important achievements of his life and career. Upon his death in 2018, the obituaries of the
former highest-ranking Yorùbá babaláwo in the world honored Chief Adisa
Makoranwale Aworeni by stating that, among his greatest life achievements,
the Àràbà Àgbáyé contributed to the crowning of the first two Àràbà of nations outside of Yorùbáland (see Adelaja 2018). This achievement, in turn,
points to the creative, and recent, global extension of YTR and its hierarchies
and constituencies across the Americas.

For their part, Àràbà Viera and members of the Aworeni lineage view the
establishment of YTR-rooted temples and councils of titled chiefs as indispensable to correct, Nigerian-style Ifá practice. This is so despite the rejec-
tions of such titles and institutions by the president of the ACYC, other practitioners of Regla de Ocha-Ifá, and even certain African traditionalists across
the island. This vision reflects, in part, the specificity of the Aworeni lineage's
connection to the World Ifá Temple of Òkè Ìtasè, where the Aworeni lineage
is rooted, and the complex hierarchies that govern Ifá diviners in Ilé-Ifẹ̀.
As Bascom noted in 1969, "organizations of comparable complexity" are not
found in other parts of Yorùbáland, even though "other Yoruba kings have
their special diviners" (Bascom 1969a, 91). As Àràbà of Cuba, Viera promotes
the spread of Aworeni institutions and the establishment of hierarchical, male
councils of chiefs as an ordained duty, one that links Nigerian-style Ifá-Òrìṣà
practice directly to the institutional authority of Ilé-Ifẹ̀.

Crucially, the chieftaincy titles ritually bestowed on babaláwo through the
Aworeni lineage are viewed as conferring a heightened degree of ritual power
and potency to the divining chief holders themselves, heightening their per-

sonal efficacy for life. For members of the Àràbà Aworeni Ilè Ìfè Ifá Temple of Cuba and its subsidiary temples, receiving the coveted title of chief bestows a babaláwo with not only a position of rank within a temple and the prestige of transatlantic, Yorùbá-rooted ritual authority but, importantly, heightened personal efficacy in the achievement of individual (and collective) desires. Becoming a "chief" ritually transforms the titleholder into a "king," guaranteeing spiritual elevation and prosperity in life. The chieftaincy title is also thought to elevate one's àṣẹ, or "vital force" (Hallgren 1995), a Yorùbá philosophical and ritual concept denoting the power to "effect change" and engender "the materialization of a given desire" (Afolabi 2005, 108).[50] Through the heightening of one's àṣẹ, the chieftaincy title heightens one's personal efficacy, offering a means to strengthen one's capacity to enact change, manifest desires, and realize one's highest, most aligned self. The chieftaincy title also guarantees titleholders ire, or "blessings" in life. These include the blessings of "money (ire ajé)," "long life (ire àìkú)," "wives (ire obìnrin)," "children (ire ọmọ)," and "defeat of one's enemy" (Bascom [1980] 1993, 8; Viera, interview, June 17, 2016; Rondon Ocaña, interview).

Chieftaincy titles are lifelong, and, accordingly, chiefs are carefully selected (Viera 2015). This makes chieftaincy titles highly prized—and, at times, coveted—because they are difficult to obtain. To attain a chieftaincy title, one must first consult with Ifá to determine if receiving a title is part of one's orí, a Yorùbá ritual concept denoting an individual's "inner or spiritual head," "personal divinity," and "essence of luck" that "governs" an individual's life (Abímbọlá 1996, 98).[51] If divination confirms that receiving the title is part of one's orí, a prospective chief must additionally pass a vote among the temple's staff, or council of chiefs, who decide if the individual is worthy of the rank and responsibility (Viera, interview, June 17, 2016). Finally, a prospective chief must possess the money to pay for the coronation, a largely prohibitive cost in Cuba.[52] Chieftaincy titles cost hundreds and even thousands of dollars, an exorbitant price in a country where the official average state wage during my fieldwork years was 687 pesos, about US$29 per month (Rose Marketing 2016; Whitefield 2016). Receiving the title of king or chief therefore inherently denotes a position of economic prosperity far out of reach for the average Cuban—a show of wealth that members of the Aworeni lineage often discursively link to notions of Yorùbá royalty.

Notably, titles in the Aworeni lineage are also gender-specific, with Aworeni chieftaincy titles in Cuba reserved, during my fieldwork years, exclusively for men. Through masculine hierarchies of wealth, influence, and preordained prophecy, male chiefs of the Aworeni lineage mobilize Nigerian-rooted titles as a means of heightening their own personal efficacy, in other words, their "vital force" (àṣẹ) and the ire they are to expect in life.[53] Through an efficacy of the far, African traditionalist men harness the usefulness of Nigerian-rooted institutions and titles geographically removed from and hierarchically beyond the boundaries of Cuba's state institutional environment.[54] In so doing, these babaláwo-chiefs transcend the juridical confines of the Cuban nation-state and the ritual strictures of Regla de Ocha-Ifá itself, accessing novel forms of personal and ritual efficacy legitimated through the translocal authority of Yorùbáland.

Gendered Titles and Personal Efficacy

The absence of female chieftaincy titles in the Aworeni lineage in Cuba diverges in key ways from the presence—and even historical abundance—of female chieftaincy titles across YTR institutions and lineages in Yorùbáland itself, an issue to which I now turn (see Denzer 1994; Familusi 2012; Olajubu 2004). Historically, women held some of the highest ritual and politico-religious leadership positions in Yorùbáland, including the position of Ọ̀ọ̀ni of Ilé-Ifẹ̀ (Fabunmi 1969, 23–24, in Denzer 1994, 8) and Aláàfin of Ọ̀yọ́ (R. Smith 1988, in Denzer 1994, 8). Historical documents additionally point to the common practice of titled councils of male chiefs consulting female chiefs on matters thought to be the domain of women, including "trade, markets, female support for community projects, marriage, divorce, their use of land, their rights of inheritance, and religious rites" (Denzer 1994, 29). In the contemporary, globally oriented YTR ritual movement, likewise, prominent female chiefs such as the Nigerian ìyánífá Chief FAMA now serve as vital "transatlantic messengers" and Ifá and òrìṣà ritual entrepreneurs (see chapter 4). In the Aworeni lineage of Ilé-Ifẹ̀, specifically, chieftaincy titles are likewise conferred to women, although the highest-ranking council of chiefs at the Òkè Ìtasẹ̀ temple consists of male babaláwo (Abímbọ́lá 1997, 72).[55]

On the broad gendered discrepancies between the presence of women in the Aworeni lineage in Cuba and in Yorùbáland, Àràbà Viera, for his part, pointed in our conversations to the problem of attracting women to the Aworeni Temple of Cuba in Centro Habana, particularly due to the temple's proximity to the ACYC: "Look, we have a lot of pressure from the Yoruba Society [the ACYC]. And so, since we have the Yoruba Society so close, women don't come close to the temple. . . . It's not that we don't admit women, it's that they simply don't come. That's why the ìyánífá that we have live in other provinces [and municipalities]. They're not really from Havana. . . . Up to this moment, in the ìtàdógún [ceremony] that we do, it's very rare for a woman to come, unfortunately" (Viera, interview, April 22, 2016).[56] Here, Viera frames the scarcity of women (including ìyánífá) in the Aworeni Temple of Cuba as a direct result of the towering, fear-inducing presence of the ACYC, located only blocks away from the temple on the opposite edge of Centro Habana. To his point, Viera adds that other Aworeni subsidiary temples located further away from the ACYC, including the Aworeni Temple of Havana (located in the neighborhood of Alamar, across the port of Havana in the municipality of Habana del Este), regularly include women in temple consecrations and ceremonies and have initiated ìyánífá as members of their ẹgbẹ́.

Other members of the Aworeni lineage offer a different take on this gendered imbalance. Babaláwo and gúdúgúdú player Osniel González, for example, noted that during Owólabí's visit to the Aworeni lineage from Nigeria months prior, the future Àràbà Àgbáyé critiqued the lack of women in Aworeni temples and implored its members to include the women in their lives in their temple activities and membership: "[Owólabí] told us that . . . we can't discriminate against women because they are women, because women have to be there . . . so that there's equilibrium, so that the energy of women is there, so that [the temple and its ceremonies] are complete. . . . Owólabí explained to us when he came to our activities that there were a lot of men, that he wanted there to be more women, that he wanted our women to be here, the children, he wanted our spouses to be here."[57] Continuing, González attributes the lack of women in the Temple of Cuba (and other Aworeni temples) to a larger "cultural problem" of machismo in Cuba: "It's a cultural problem. [Owólabí] says that in our culture, if we want things to work, we have to do things like they do them [in Yorùbáland]. We have to introduce women [into the temple]. The thing is that in Cuba we are too *machistas* [macho]. . . . Women are part of life, women are essential, it's women who give light . . . and if it's not that way, it doesn't flow. So, here in Cuba, our culture, its idiosyncrasy, [is that] we are very *machistas*" (González, interview). González suggests here that practitioners of Nigerian-style Ifá suffer from a larger "cultural" issue of machismo and gendered discrimination in Cuba, one that impacts the presence of women (including ìyánífá and, potentially, titled chiefs) in the lineage. Indeed, in a Nigerian-style ritual movement historically rooted in the masculinist (and heterosexual) edicts of Cuban-style Ifá, male babaláwo still control access to initiations, consecrations, and chieftancy titles in African traditionalism (see chapters 3 and 4).[58] In turn, male babaláwo control women's ability to access and harness the heightened personal efficacy that such initiations and titles confer, impacting women's capacity to "use" (Ahmed 2019) within the fate-transformative practices of Ifá.[59]

Ethnographic Encounters: The Crowning of Chiefs

In June 2016, the national Aworeni Temple of Cuba culminated its annual Ifá festival with a ceremony marking the foundation of the Aworeni Temple of Eastern Havana and the coronation of six new lineage chiefs. Throughout the event, I witnessed how members of the Aworeni lineage use the dùndún to announce and promote the establishment of new temples and councils of titled, all-male chiefs through public processions in Havana's streets. The celebration marked the close of the two-week annual Ifá festival, which, mirroring the calendar of contemporary Yorùbáland, occurs at the beginning of June. During the Ifá festival, the Aworeni Ifá Temple of Cuba holds daily ceremonies dedicated to specific òrìṣà to mark the festival's cycle, including ceremonies for the òrìṣà Ògún, Ifá, Ẹgbẹ́, Orí, and others. During the culminating ceremony on June 16, members of the Aworeni Temple of Cuba and the Aworeni Temple of Havana gathered to mark the foundation of the Aworeni Temple of Eastern Havana and the coronation of six new lineage chiefs. The new titles included three chiefs for the national Aworeni Temple of Cuba (Chief Aseda, Chief Lori, and Chief Balogún), one chief for the Aworeni Temple of Havana (Chief Aseda), and two chiefs for the newly founded Aworeni Temple of Eastern Havana (Chief Olúwo and Chief Àgbọngbòn). The dùndún featured prominently throughout the ceremony, including during the coronation rituals inside of the Aworeni Temple of Cuba and in the public procession of newly coronated chiefs through Centro Habana's streets.

The Aworeni Temple's annual Ifá festival is modeled after the extensive and intricate Ifá Festival of Yorùbáland, which begins in the first week of June (Abímbọ́lá 1997, 118). As Jacob Olupona outlines, this "complex ritual" in Ilé-Ifẹ̀ involves ceremonies and festivities that span the course of three months (Olupona 2011). In Yorùbáland, the Ifá festival "renews the communal life of the sacred city," ensuring "the community's personal, collective, and agricultural well-being" by "bestowing the blessings of Ifá's abundance upon the diviners and the sacred king" (Olupona 2011, 184). The festival includes the principal events of the King's Ifá festival (Ọdun Ifá-Àgbọnnìrègun festival) in Ilé-Ifẹ̀, which marks the beginning of the Yorùbá calendar in the first week of June, as well as the King's New Yam Ceremony (Ègbodò Ọ̀ọni), which takes place toward the end of the month (Abímbọ́lá 1997, 118; Olupona 2011, 184). As Wándé Abímbọ́lá (1997, 118) describes, the King's Festival encompasses divination ceremonies as well as all-night "chanting, dancing, and drumming" on the top of sacred Òkè Ìtasẹ̀ mountain. During the celebration, the festivities focus on the Àràbà Àgbáyé as the spiritual head of the Òkè Ìtasẹ̀ lineage and his role as custodian of the Yorùbá's "central Ifá shrine" and temple (Olupona 2011, 184).

In Cuba, Ilé Tuntún's cofounder Frank Cabrera Suárez is credited with first introducing the Yorùbá Ifá Festival and, accordingly, the Yorùbá ritual calendar, to the island in 1999 (Konen 2013). In subsequent years, numerous Nigerian-style ẹgbẹ́ throughout Cuba's provinces incorporated the annual Ifá festival into their yearly calendar, including, during the course of my field-work, Frank Cabrera's Ilé Tuntún in Havana, babaláwo Yunieski González Ramírez's (Ifáṣe Abodunde) Ẹgbé Ifá Olodu in Santiago de las Vegas, and babaláwo Enrique Orozco Rubio's Ẹgbé Irán Átele Ilogbon Odugbemi in Santiago de Cuba, among others. This shift toward a Yorùbá calendar of òrìṣà and Ifá festivals marks a temporal break from Cuban Regla de Ocha-Ifá, whose calendar of oricha "feast days" and festivals became linked with the Catholic calendar of saints' days and festivals during the colonial period (e.g., Changó's celebration on December 4, the day dedicated to Saint Barbara in the Catholic Church) (Azorena 1961; Deschamps Chapeaux 1968; O'Brien 2004; Ortiz [1920] 1960). This reorientation toward the Yorùbá calendar of òrìṣà and Ifá festivals in Nigerian-style Ifá-Òrìṣà mirrors a broader turn toward the Nigerian calendar within the Yorùbá revivalist movement across the Americas, including in the United States.[60]

On a hot summer day in mid-June 2016, I arrived at the Àràbà Aworeni Ilè Ìfè Ifá Temple of Cuba in Centro Habana to find members of all three Aworeni temples—the national Temple of Cuba, the Temple of Havana, and the Temple of Eastern Havana—in attendance at the culminating ceremony of the annual Ifá festival. Each temple's council of chiefs was dressed in Yorùbá-centric regalia indicative of stature and rank. The temple's designated "chief of the drums" (jefe de los tambores) began the ceremony by leading the dùndún ensemble in a medium-tempo polyrhythm built over the agogo Ifá, a metal bell imported from Nigeria and used, in Yorùbáland, as part of an ensemble of bells when reciting divination chants for Ọrúnmìlà (ìyèrè Ifá) (Ẹlẹbuìbọn 1999; Ológundúdú 2009).[61] Over the agogo Ifá, the dùndún drummers sounded the ìyáàlù, the gángan, and the gúdúgúdú instruments as the six new chiefs proceeded from a private ritual room into the public patio of the Temple of Cuba. Standing in the cramped patio space and overflowing onto the street, approximately one hundred people waited in attendance, including babaláwo, ìyánífá, and friends and family of the temple's members. Àràbà Viera coronated each chief individually in a formal ceremony, first outlining the babaláwo's educational and professional achievements before detailing the spiritual and moral demands of each title. After reciting verses and prayers in Yorùbá drawn from the odù Ifá, Viera offered the babaláwo their chiefly regalia. The regalia included intricately detailed, beaded necklaces with a double-sided, triangular emblem displaying the title and rank,

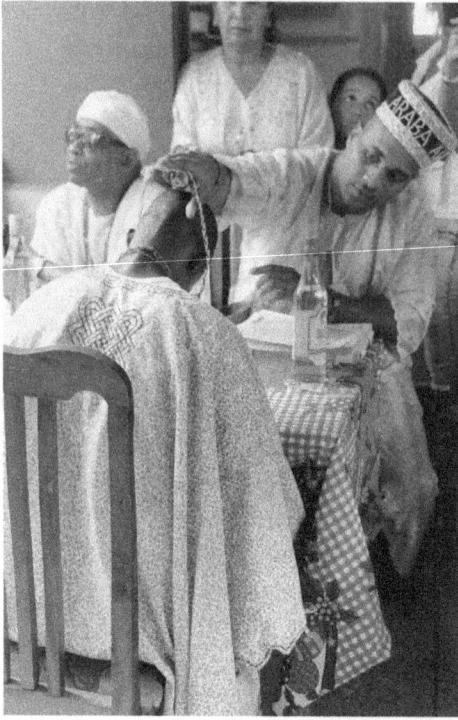

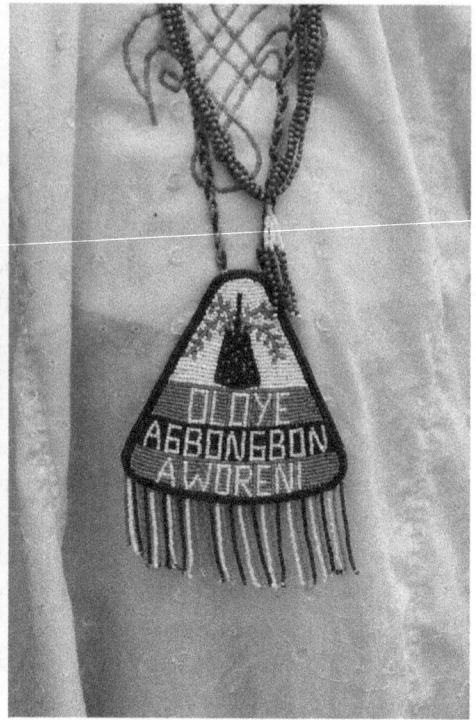

FIGURES 2.7 and 2.8. Àràbà Viera coronates Ernesto del Río Caraballo as Chief Aseda of the Aworeni Temple of Havana (*left*). A hand-beaded Àgbọngbọ̀n Title (*right*). Photos by the author.

hand-beaded beaded royal staffs, and brightly colored bracelets and neck-laces made of precious and semiprecious coral, jade, and fire agate stones. The intricate beadwork reflects the aesthetics of beadworking used to craft the crowns, staffs, caps, necklaces, and bracelets of the Yorùbá kings and ba-baláwo of Nigeria itself (see figs. 2.7 and 2.8).[62] As Àràbà Viera handed each new chief his regalia, he explained that the "expensive" stones of the necklaces and bracelets serve as symbols of royalty—and economic prosperity—for the chiefs as newly coronated "kings." Àràbà Viera's presentation weds the mate-riality of Yorùbá-style regal dress with the perception of heightened ritual and personal efficacy for the newly titled chiefs, whose titles carry the promise of economic prosperity for their holders.

To end the coronation ceremony, the dùndún ensemble and the six new chiefs poured into the streets of Centro Habana, announcing the foundation of the temple and the coronation of the chiefs. Heading the procession, the gúdúgúdú player, Osniel González, led a vocal call-and-response with other members of the ẹgbẹ́ while playing the gúdúgúdú. In it, he alternated varia-tions on the call *olóyè*, or titleholder/chief, prompting the crowd's response,

"Ẹnu olóyè," "from the mouth of the titleholder" (Audio Example 2: Ẹnu olóyè).[63] González varied the call with the title names of newly coronated chiefs: "Àgbọngbọ̀n Olóyè," the "immediate deputy" (Abímbọ́lá 1997, 71); "Olúwo Olóyè," the "principal religious leader and high priest" of a temple (Viera 2015); and "Oyugbona Olóyè," the temple's "messenger" and head of sacrifice (Viera, interview, June 17, 2016).[64] Weaving through the crowd, the newly coronated chiefs passed out Cuban bills, placing the money on the foreheads of the dùndún players as a symbol of their economic prosperity and generosity as newly coronated "kings" (González, interview). This "dash," or monetary offering to the forehead of itinerant dùndún drummers and procession leaders, mirrors the process of offering dùndún and bàtá players small monetary offerings in contemporary Yorùbá ritual processions and festivals (Ruskin 2010) (see fig. 2.9).

Throughout the procession, the particularities of the dùndún drummers' playing and performance techniques point to the creative adaptations—and sonorous décalage—attendant to the adoption of the instruments to Nigerian-style Ifá. One notable innovation is the use of a *clave*, played on the agogo Ifá bell, to set the tempo and orient the ensemble, marking a key divergence from dùndún performance in Yorùbáland. To kick off the procession, an agogo Ifá player cues the other percussionists by playing what members of the Aworeni lineage repeatedly referred to as "the clave."[65] In Cuba, the clave serves as an unvarying rhythmic backbone, or "timeline" (Nketia 1963, 78),

FIGURE 2.9. The newly coronated Chief Aseda of the Aworeni Temple of Havana, Ernesto del Río Caraballo, "dashes" the leader of the procession with a Cuban bill. Centro Habana, Havana, 2016. Photo by the author.

for polyrhythmic music in a wide range of African-inspired ritual and secular styles, from *bembé* and Palo to *son* and *timba*.[66] A central organizing principle in West African music (from which the Cuban clave derives), the timeline provides a rhythmic compass "by which the phrase structure of a song as well as the linear metrical organisation of phrases are guided" (Nketia 1963, 78, in Paulding 2017, 62). In West Africa and Cuba alike, the timeline often alternates between a more syncopated and a less syncopated measure in a two-bar pattern (Chor 2016, in Bøhler 2021, 200). In West Africa, the timeline is often sounded on a bell pattern, making the bell "one of the single most important instruments in many west African drum ensembles" (Paulding 2017, 62). In Cuba, meanwhile, the timeline/clave is often (though not always) explicitly sounded on claves (cylindrical hardwood sticks), a metal *güataca* hoe blade, or another metal implement, dependent on context.[67]

Despite the prevalence of bell patterns that mark the timeline in West African percussion ensembles, drummers in Yorùbáland notably play the dùndún without the accompaniment of a bell sounding the timeline. Instead, the rhythm and tempo of the ensemble is set by the lead ìyáàlù (Samuel 2008/2009, 57).[68] In Cuba, the use of the imported, Nigerian agogo Ifá to mark the clave is a novel adaptation of Yorùbá percussion to the context of Cuban ritual. While the use of the agogo Ifá to mark the clave is highly consistent with the use of a single güataca or other metal implement to sound the clave in numerous African-inspired ritual styles (e.g., bembé, cajón al muerto, Palo), it notably diverges from the use of the agogo Ifá in Yorùbáland itself, where the agogo Ifá bells are used as part of a larger, interlocking bell ensemble played for Ọ̀rúnmìlà (Ẹlẹ́buìbọn 1999; Ológundúdú 2009).

This novel adaptation of the imported agogo Ifá in Cuba points to the proliferating—and yet potentiality-filled—gaps and discrepancies inherent to acts of sonorous *décalage* in Nigerian-style Ifá, where difference forms a core aspect of transatlantic and translative acts (N. Edwards 2005, 120–21; see chapter 1). The novel use of a single agogo Ifá also refunctionalizes (and Cubanizes) the instrument, transforming the bell from one member of a larger ensemble of bells dedicated to Ọ̀rúnmìlà to a stand-alone instrumental marker of the clave. In the case of the Aworeni lineage, African traditionalists redeploy the agogo Ifá—notably, the first instrument Viera ever received directly from Nigeria (Viera, interview, April 22, 2016)—within already-extant logics of African-inspired ritual performance on the island.[69]

Despite divergences with their Yorùbá counterparts, the sonic and spatial takeover of the streets of Havana's most densely populated Centro Habana neighborhood by the Aworeni lineage, the dùndún ensemble, and the agogo Ifá powerfully asserts the arrival of African traditionalism in Cuba.

The gliding pitches and unique, roped design of the dùndún "talking" ìyáàlù serve as aural and visual emblems of contemporary Yorùbáland, announcing a Yorùbá-centric sensorial orientation to African traditionality and fate-changing efficacy that audibly contrasts with that of Cuban Regla de Ocha-Ifá. The use of the contemporary Yorùbá language and the chiefs' adornment with traditional Yorùbá dress and beadwork likewise contributes to a Yorùbá-centric sonority and materiality, one that temporarily engulfs Havana's streets in a potent ritual and political statement of presence and authority.

In Cuba, this public religious procession holds a specific resonance. The babaláwo, ìyánífá, friends, family members, and neighbors who join in or film the procession on their cell phones momentarily violate Cuban law, which requires authorization for public assemblies of three or more persons and which has prohibited processions since 1961 (Boyle and Sheen [1997] 2003, 125). The Aworeni lineage's choice to parade through Centro Habana with the dùndún ensemble—a mere twenty-five blocks from the ACYC's headquarters—exhibits a bold instance of self-legitimization of the presence of Nigerian-style Ifá-Òrìṣà and its institutions in the face of a state environment of delegitimization and official nonrecognition.[70] As the procession pours onto Calle Infanta, one of the principal thoroughfares of Havana, the gliding pitches of the dùndún and the shouts, claps, and singing of the participants mix with the honking of cars and motorcycles, whose agitated drivers are forced into the oncoming lane to get past the marchers (Audio Example 3: Calle Infanta). For a few minutes, the members of the Aworeni lineage temporarily circumvent state mandates on legal and civic order, inhabiting Havana's public streets and spaces as their own.

"Good People": "Eni rere"

In May 2016, the Aworeni Temple of Havana also held a street procession as a means to announce the future establishment of a temple in the west Havana neighborhood of Playa. This procession began several blocks away from the home of Santiago Ariosa Hercey, the Chief Akọda of the Aworeni Temple of Havana, who planned to establish and oversee the future (and fourth) Aworeni temple there. To begin the procession, Damián Francisco Paula Valdés, the Chief Oyugbona of the Temple of Cuba, made an offering to the ancestors with a series of Yorùbá prayers: "Today we make an offering to the ancestors of this community so that they allow our ìṣẹ̀ṣe practice, our traditional Nigerian practice, to be accepted [and] prolific here in this territory, with the temple that will later be founded here, and so that the Ifá-oricha community accepts it. In whatever way Ifá is practiced, we all come from the same place: Ilé-Ifẹ̀." Surrounding Chief Oyugbona Valdés, the temple's babaláwo and ìyánífá each rattled an ìróké, creating the constant, distinctive percussive sound of invocation for Ọ̀rúnmìlà. As they did, they punctuated Chief Valdés's phrases with the shout of "Àṣẹ!" manifesting the force of change and transformation (M. Drewal 1992, 27). Through his words, Chief Valdés expressed an evangelical calling to spread ìṣẹ̀ṣe, a Yorùbá term indexing the Yorùbá traditional religion of Nigeria and used throughout Cuba to denote YTR (Video Example: Ìṣẹ̀ṣe).[71]

Valdés then kicked off the procession with the Yorùbá song "Eni rere," accompanied by the ìyáàlù and the gúdúgúdú of the dùndún ensemble along with chékere and agogo Ifá (Audio Example 4: Eni rere).[72] Exuberantly, babaláwo and ìyánífá of the Temple of Havana followed Chief Valdés and the dùndún ensemble, with two ìyánífá of the Temple of Havana helming the first line of the procession. Together, members of the Aworeni Temple of Havana paraded, clapping, shaking the ìróké, and singing en route to the home of Chief Akọda:

eni rere la nwa o	We're looking for good people
eniyan rere la npe	It's only good people we need
ogunda meji ba wa se	Ogunda Meji come and help me
ba wa se o eni rere la nwa o [sic]	Help me to find them[73]

This contemporary Yorùbá praise song is a contraction of the sacred verses of the odù Osa Ika.[74] In Yorùbáland, "Eni rere" is widely used in ritual and festive contexts, including during key moments of initiation into Ifá as well as during public processions and festivals. Thematically, the song calls out in search of "good people," expressing a longing for others to join in the ritual community. It's a fitting theme for the day's procession, which, as Valdés expressed, aims to promote the future acceptance of African traditionalism in the Playa neighborhood of Havana and its "prolific" spread throughout Cuba's geographical territories. One by one, the song calls out for the sixteen méjì (e.g., Ogunda Méjì) to offer assistance in attracting "good people" to the community.

The members of the Aworeni lineage first learned this contemporary Yorùbá praise song through an informal voice recording of a Nigerian babaláwo that was passed to them—along with its amateur translation into Spanish as a text file—through digital exchanges with visitors from abroad. Notably, the original audio recording presents an informal recording of the Nigerian babaláwo singing the melody and lyrics of "Eni rere," as if into a mobile phone, without underlying percussion.

When the former Àràbà Àgbáyẹ́'s son, Babaláwo Owólabí (Owólabí Awódòtun Awóreni Mákòránwálé II), later visited the Aworeni Temple of Cuba in

April 2016, Owólabí also spent time teaching and explaining the meaning of the song "Eni rere" to members of the Aworeni lineage. In videos taken by the members of the Aworeni Temple of Havana in the neighborhood of Alamar, Owólabí communicates with Cuban practitioners by speaking in English as Àràbà Viera—who has a limited understanding of English—roughly translates the Nigerian babaláwo's explanations of the Yorùbá language song to other temple members and guests. This double act of translation—Owólabí's own translation from Yorùbá to English and Viera's rough translation from English to Spanish—exemplifies the complex processes of sonorous décalage through which African traditionalists gain access to knowledge surrounding the songs and verses of YTR, even in instances of direct encounter with Nigerian babaláwo. Owólabí's status as an esteemed Nigerian babaláwo and son of the Àràbà Àgbáyé (and, upon his passing, the future Àràbà Àgbáyé himself)—yet also *not* as a ritual percussionist—additionally speaks to the uneven ways in which knowledge about contemporary YTR ritual sonority reaches practitioners in Cuba.

Only a month after Owólabí's visit, Chief Oyugbona Valdés and other babaláwo and ìyánífá paraded through the streets of Playa singing "Eni rere" over the Yorùbá-centric sonorous tapestry of the dùndún ensemble. As Spanish speakers not fluent in the Yorùbá language, these babaláwo's and Ìyánífá's voices necessarily level the relative pitch contrasts and vocal glissandi characteristic of Owólabí's Yorùbá language vocal techniques, eliding the tonal intricacies present in the original voice and video recordings. Accordingly, the melody of the Yorùbá praise song necessarily adapts to Spanish-language—and, particularly, Cuban—modes of vocalization, slipping into a stress-based style that discards the tonal intricacies of the Yorùbá language (which are crucial to rendering semantic intelligibility to Yorùbá listeners) (see fig. 2.10).[75]

The practical limitations on Cubans' ability to mobilize the tonal characteristics of the Yorùbá language—which African traditionalists consider to be a sacred and more efficacious ritual language than the Lucumí ritual lexicon—reveals the contradictions inherent to logics of heightened ritual efficacy in Nigerian-style Ifá-Òrìṣà, particularly as these relate to the use of the Yorùbá language. Notably, these limitations apply to the dùndún "talking drums," which are mobilized as powerful speech surrogates capable of communicating oríkì and *owe* (proverbs) to the òrìṣà and human practitioner-listeners. Indeed, how do drummers communicate the oríkì, or the sacred verses of the odù, through speech surrogacy when they do not themselves speak Yorùbá or wield its complex tonal characteristics? The Aworeni dùndún drummers in Havana are limited not only by their lack of fluency in Yorùbá but also, pedagogically, by their physical isolation from the Nigerian lineages

FIGURE 2.10. Dùndún procession announcing the establishment of a temple in Playa. Havana, Cuba, May 2016. Photo by the author.

of dùndún drummers who might teach them how to play. As Villepastour notes, heightened exchange between Nigerian and Cuban babaláwo/ba-balaos since the 1990s has not, as of yet, translated into heightened exchange between ritual drummers, "primarily because most Nigerian Àyàn [bàtá] drummers are Muslims" (Villepastour 2015b, 7), as is the case with the vast majority of dùndún drummers as well (Omojola 2011).[76] Those Nigerian babaláwo who have traveled to Cuba to spread the Yorùbá traditional religion—including Owólabí, Pópóọlá, Ẹlẹ́buìbọn, and others—overwhelmingly specialize in the esoteric verses and divinatory practices of Ifá, specifically, and not in dùndún or bàtá ritual drumming. This pedagogical isolation from Yorùbá dùndún drummers curtails Cuban percussionists' ability to sound the dùndún as speech surrogates of the Yorùbá language in ritual (Villepastour 2010, 2015a, 2015b). In the absence of Nigerian mentors, the Aworeni dùndún drummers are left to approximating rhythms gleaned from an assortment of digital videos and recordings. Often, the drummers improvise the rhythms played in rituals and processions over the rhythmic foundation of the *agogo Ifá*, discarding the link between the dùndún as "talking drums" and the Yorùbá language altogether (Francisco Mario Delgado Iglesias, interview by the author, Havana, 2016; González, interview; Viera, interview, June 17, 2016). Nonetheless, the dùndún are mobilized by African traditionalists as sonic emblems of heightened ritual efficacy in Nigerian-style Ifá, a claim bolstered by the instruments' roles as speech surrogates for the sacred Yorùbá language and by African traditionalists' ability to glean certain rhythms from videos and recordings.

Conclusion

In Cuba, the dùndún "talking drums" of Yorùbáland have arrived in tandem with a new ritual movement—African traditionalism—that aims to validate the Yorùbá traditional religion of contemporary Nigeria as the reigning authority in Cuban Ifá-Òrìṣà worship. Through the crafting of novel geographical constituencies, the foundation of temples, and the establishment of hierarchical councils of all-male chiefs, the Aworeni lineage builds a network of transnationally legitimated Yorùbá institutions that stand in opposition to the juridical and religious monopoly of the state-linked ACYC. As potent sonic and visual emblems of contemporary Yorùbáland, the dùndún ensemble—a pan-Yorùbá instrument used for speech surrogacy in Nigeria—are employed to promote the foundation of Aworeni temples and the coronation of chiefs through public processions through Havana's neighborhoods. For male babaláwo, the Yorùbá-inspired titles further offer a means to achieve heightened personal efficacy and àṣẹ in the manifestation of life's desires and blessings. Given the gendered nature of the ability to self-manifest as personally *eficaz* (efficacious), the arrival of titled "chiefs" and hierarchies through the Aworeni lineage underscores the imbrication of masculinity and personal efficacy in Nigerian-style Ifá. Despite the limitations on the communicative capacity of Cubans' use of the Yorùbá language and on the instruments' potential as speech surrogates, the dùndún drums are nevertheless viewed as a key tool in "re-Yorubizing" Cuban Ifá through the reintroduction of Yorùbá percussion and sound into Ifá ceremonies and processions.

Revolutionary Feminism and Gendered Translocality: Women and Consecrated *Batá*

On June 22, 2015, Nagybe Madariaga Pouymiró, a professional percussionist and lifelong proponent for women's right to play consecrated *batá* in Cuba, organized the first group of women authorized to play the sacred batá in the eastern city of Santiago de Cuba. Marking the first documented instance in which three women played the consecrated batá set of Regla de Ocha (Santería) in Cuba or internationally, this event was authorized and overseen by Ifá priest, *omo Añá* (initiated ritual drummer), and *olubatá* (owner of a consecrated batá set) Enrique Orozco Rubio. A key figure in the revisionist, African traditionalist movement of the practices of Regla de Ocha-Ifá in Cuba, Orozco Rubio justified the breaking of this taboo by looking toward the gender norms of *òrìṣà* worship in contemporary Yorùbáland, Nigeria, from where the practices trace their roots. In Nigeria, unlike in Cuba, no strict prohibition against women playing the *bàtá* exists, and this newly acquired transatlantic knowledge has, in turn, potentiated enormous gendered break within the landscape of ritual music in Cuba.

Here, I interrogate this transatlantically inspired rupture, pointing to the African continent's contemporary—as opposed to historical—impact on gender and ritual music in Cuba and to the significance of transatlantic forms of reimagining for women in ritual music settings more broadly (see Hellier 2013; Koskoff 2014; Solie 1993). While studies on music and ritual in Cuba examine the African continent in copious reference to the past—where Africa exists as a colonial-era origin point for the immense impact of transatlantic slavery on Afro-Cuban culture (see, e.g., Guanche 1983; Hagedorn 2001; Holbraad 2012; James Figarola 2006; Lachatañeré 1939, 1992; López Valdés 1980, 1998, 2002; Moore 1997, 2006; Ochoa 2010; Ortiz 1921, [1950] 2001, 1954; Wirtz 2016)—the case of women and batá points to the ongoing ways in which interactions with Nigeria continue to reshape gender and ritual music in Cuba. As an inquiry into these contemporary dynamics, I delineate key aspects of the burgeoning African traditionalist movement in Cuba (*el tradicionalismo africano*), including the reconnections of male Nigerian-style Ifá priests with Yorùbáland and their academically minded approaches to Ifá-Òrìṣà worship. By means of a parallel and ultimately convergent history, I additionally trace Nagybe Madariaga Pouymiró's decades-long efforts to intervene into gendered batá performance, charting the route by which Pouymiró ultimately achieved male authorization for female access to the consecrated batá through African traditionalism. Using African traditionalism as an avenue for carving out novel forms of access to the consecrated batá, Pouymiró circumvented both Cuban prohibitions against women playing the sacred batá and Regla de Ocha orthodoxy regarding the batá set's ritual use. In drawing on Yorùbá-centric, revisionist ideologies born from emergent circulations between Cuba, the Americas, and Nigeria, Pouymiró mobilized novel forms of transatlantic potentiality to create spaces of gendered possibility in Regla de Ocha-Ifá. Finally, I outline the musical and ritual ruptures of the first instance of three women playing the consecrated batá set, detailing the ways in which Nagybe Madariaga Pouymiró, ìyánífá Caridad Rubio Fonseca, and ìyánífá Anais López Rubio creatively adapted rhythms (*toques*) from the Regla de Ocha ritual corpus to contemporary, Yorùbá-language praise songs. As I argue here, these women's interventions into batá performance—and their selective Yorùbá-centrism in approaching African traditionalist ritual sound—offer a rich, contextually grounded instantiation of the lived negotiation of gender for women in ritual music contexts, one that contributes to our understanding of the efficacy of translocal forms of engagement and reimagining for women globally.

Nigerian-Style Ifá and Gender in Eastern Cuba

In Cuba, the most heated and passionate outcries against Nigerian-style Ifá-Òrìṣà by babalaos and members of the state-linked Yoruba Cultural Association of Cuba (ACYC) center on gender. Reconnections with contemporary Yorùbáland now offer practitioners alternative models of òrìṣà/oricha worship that in many cases conflict with established rules of practice at home, and several key gendered prohibitions in Regla de Ocha-Ifá have been threatened by the turn to Nigeria as an acting model (Beliso-De Jesús 2015a, 2015b; Fernández 2010; Padilla 2006). In one of the most controversial examples, women are initiated into the priesthood of Ifá in African traditionalism and

FIGURE 3.1. Ìyánífá Noerlinda Burgal Hechevarría at the Ẹgbé Irán Átele Ilogbon Odugbemi's annual Letra del Año yearly divination ceremony. June 2015. Photo by the author.

can achieve status as Ìyánífá, a participation strictly and passionately prohibited in Cuban Ifá (Beliso-De Jesús 2015a; Fernández 2010; Olajubu 2003; Padilla 2006) (see fig. 3.1).

In eastern Cuba, specifically, African traditionalist babaláwo Enrique Orozco Rubio has spearheaded many of these gendered ruptures. Orozco Rubio's ritual house in Santiago de Cuba (Ẹgbé Irán Átele Ilogbon Odugbemi)[1] serves as a principal nexus for the African traditionalist movement in eastern Cuba. Attracting initiates from Santiago de Cuba and the surrounding provinces of Holguín and Guantánamo, since 2007,[2] the ẹgbé has served as a sacred space for Ifá divination and practice and as a pedagogical school with a semiformalized training center (*centro de entrenamiento*) dedicated to Ifá-Òrìṣà and Yorùbá language study. In line with other African traditionalists, Orozco Rubio established ties with the Yorùbá traditional religion abroad through contact with Cuba's diasporas in Venezuela and other locations in the Americas; the visits of Nigerian babaláwos to the island; and even through limited (and often illegal) internet access and communication. Open to babaláwos (priests), ìyánífá (priestesses), lower-ranked initiates, and even, in certain cases, noninitiates, the ẹgbé circumvents Cuban prohibitions regarding female initiation into the priesthood of Ifá and general norms regarding access to ritual and liturgy, justifying each by looking toward the norms of contemporary Yorùbáland. In the ẹgbé, as in contemporary Nigeria, women are initiated as ìyánífá, or Ifá priestesses, breaking the strictly enforced prohibition against female initiation in Cuba. Furthermore, the study of Ifá and participation in rituals and rites is encouraged prior to initiations, reflecting a more open didactic model in Nigeria whereby would-be initiates study Ifá for years or even decades before being initiated (Abímbọ́lá 1979, 1997). This Nigeria-centric didactic approach to Ifá circumvents, to a degree, Cuban strictures regarding the chronology of initiation and subsequent access to the guarded secrecy of liturgical knowledge.[3]

Born in 1975, Orozco Rubio's childhood home was a renowned house-temple of Espiritismo (Spiritism) in Santiago de Cuba, although, notably, he deliberately avoided Spiritism and other Cuban religions as a young man. Following military service, Orozco Rubio received academic training as a psychologist in 2003 at the University of Oriente (Universidad de Oriente), working for a decade after graduating as a professor of psychology at the University of Oriente and the Superior Institute of Medical Sciences (Instituto Superior de Ciencias Médicas) in Santiago de Cuba. Through contact with a fellow psychology student, Orozco Rubio was introduced to a community of Cuban-style babalaos in the city of Holguín, who stood out to Orozco for being intellectuals, wealthy,[4] and, importantly, White—traits that he previously disassociated with Ifá as an "Afro-" religion of the (presumably Black) lower classes.[5] Furthermore, their academic formation and skin color stood out to him in even sharper relief in Holguín, a province stereotypically known throughout Cuba as being the "most racist."[6] Curious, Orozco Rubio received the initiatory "hand of Orula"[7] and began regular travel to Holguín to visit with the Ifá priests from his home in Santiago de Cuba. In February 2004, Orozco Rubio was initiated into Cuban-style Ifá by Babalao Félix Arsenio Fuentes Cáceres, who officiated as his *padrino* (godfather), and Yanier Torres Tamayo, who officiated as *oyugbona* (second initiating godparent). That same month, he was initiated into Ocha (with Yemayá as his titular deity) by Kirenia del Carmen Mejías.[8]

That Orozco Rubio was initiated into Regla de Ocha-Ifá in Holguín, rather than Santiago de Cuba, proved to be both a source of great autonomy for him and a major "stumbling block" upon his return home. In Santiago de Cuba, local babalaos and *santeros* viewed the complete circumventing of local ritual hierarchies through initiation in another province as a "betrayal" and "lack of respect"[9] for local networks of authority by the locally born-and-raised Orozco Rubio. However, the lack of entanglement in local hierarchies of Ifá divination and oricha worship granted Orozco Rubio a level of autonomy and ritual freedom necessary to craft his own ẹgbẹ́ in Santiago de Cuba in 2007. There, and without the need to answer or justify his practices to local spiritual authorities, he was able to break from traditional Cuban Ocha-Ifá and turn toward the African traditionalist movement in his ritual philosophy, teachings, and practice.

Orozco Rubio's first contact with *Ifá nigeriano* occurred through his pa-drino, Félix Arsenio Fuentes Cáceres, who had illegally acquired access to dial-up internet in his Holguín home.[10] During Orozco Rubio's frequent trav-els to Holguín, Fuentes Cáceres often searched for information about Ifá on websites, blogs, and international forums. There, he began to come across information in Spanish about "Traditional Nigerian Ifá" and its incipient growth in Cuban-rooted Ifá lineages in Venezuela and other locations across the Americas, where babalaos had established contact with—and generally had increased access to information on—Ifá as practiced in contemporary Nigeria. Orozco Rubio became fascinated by Nigerian-style Ifá's claims to authority over the Cuban style, constantly arguing with his padrino—who Orozco Rubio maintains had a "very, very, *very* open mind"—over the pos-sibilities of incorporating *obras* (works) and other ritual criteria into their Cuban-style practice. Utilizing "tinkering" as a means of confronting the opacity of the unknown at the crossroads between contested domains of truth and logics of fate-transforming efficacy (Taleb 2012), Orozco Rubio faced the conundrum of novel, Nigerian-style ritual on a practical level. Quite simply, he convinced his padrino to test out the claims of Ifá nigeriano by putting them into action. "We're going to put this into practice," Orozco argued, "and we're going to see what happens. If it doesn't work, we turn away."

The works worked. After obtaining initial information on Nigerian-style Ifá through the internet, books, and whatever other reference materials they could find, the two babalaos made their first substantial contact with Nigerian-style Ifá abroad by initiating a dialogue with Venezuelan babaláwo and African traditionalist José Hidalgo Edibere Gamés. As Félix Ayoh' Omi-dire relates in his study of the "re-Africanization" of Cuban-style Regla de Ocha-Ifá in Venezuela (Omidire 2014), santero and babalao José Hidalgo Edi-bere is known for initiating the trend of re-Yorubizing ritual lineages there. Originally a direct descendant of ritual lineages of Ocha and Ifá rooted in Cuba, Edibere initiated the re-Yorubization of Ocha-Ifá in Venezuela after a visit to Yorùbáland, Nigeria, with his wife in 2006–7 (Omidire 2014). There, Edibere attended the annual Ọdun Ifá-Àgbọnnìrègun Ifá festival and met the Àràbà Àgbáyé Chief Adisa Mókòrànálé Awóreni, considered "the high-est priest of Ifá worldwide" and a direct descendant of the "mystical founder of Ifá religion," Òrúnmìlà-Bara-Àgbọnnìrègun (210). As Omidere elaborates, after inviting the Àràbà Àgbáyé to Venezuela for a monthlong visit in 2007, Edibere broke with the traditional hierarchy of Cuban-rooted Ifá lineages in the diaspora, deriving his authority as a priest of Ifá and òrìṣà from the Àràbà Àgbáyé instead of from his original Cuban-born lineage. With an African traditionalist approach to Ifá legitimated through contact with contemporary

Yorùbáland, Edibere established his Ẹgbẹ́ Òrìsà-Oko as a highly proliferative community of African-style babaláwo in Venezuela and throughout the
Americas (210).

Through a continued dialogue with Fuentes Cáceres, Edibere volunteered
to travel from Venezuela to Holguín to initiate Fuentes Cáceres's wife, Kirenia del Carmen Mejías (also Orozco Rubio's *madrina de santo*), as ìyánífá,
marking the first instance in which a woman would be initiated into Ifá
in an eastern Cuban province.[11] Edibere's visit with a delegation from his
Ẹgbẹ́ Òrìsà-Oko marked a turning point for Fuentes Cáceres and Orozco
Rubio in their turn toward traditional Nigerian Ifá. As Orozco Rubio recalls,
Edibere introduced Fuentes Cáceres and Orozco Rubio to the deity Igba
Odù, the divinity with which practitioners are initiated in Yorùbáland (Olofin in Cuban-style Ifá), in addition to Yorùbá-style *oríkì* (praise poetry), *orin*
(songs), and obras (works). Orozco Rubio notes that following the delegation's visit, he and Fuentes Cáceres "began to want to pray the same way that
the Africans do," "make African 'works' [obras]," and use the same "traditional [African] praise poetry [oríkì]."[12] Slowly, both men integrated these elements into their respective Holguín and Santiago de Cuba ẹgbé. Following
Edibere's visit, Fuentes Cáceres and Orozco Rubio continued to seek information on Nigerian-style Ifá through any means possible: internet forums and
websites, books passed digitally among other African-style Cuban babaláwo
or Cuban academics, and, crucially, direct contact with African-style delegations visiting Cuba from abroad. Since 2007, these visits have included delegations representing eight distinct lineages of Ifá rooted in contemporary
Yorùbáland,[13] visiting either directly from Nigeria or from other Latin American countries (e.g., Venezuela, Mexico, and Argentina). The heterogeneity of
Ifá lineages represented by these discrete delegations provided Fuentes Cáceres and Orozco Rubio with a wider scope of the richness and diversity of the
contemporary lineages of Ifá as practiced in Yorùbáland.

Fuentes Cáceres and Orozco Rubio's transition from Cuban Ifá to traditional Nigerian Ifá was not painless. Fuentes Cáceres in particular suffered
such polemical opposition to the turn to African traditionalism and to the
initiation of his wife as ìyánífá from Cuban babalaos in Holguín—including
the defection of many from his own ẹgbé—that Orozco Rubio attributes the
uproar to contributing to Fuentes Cáceres's subsequent emigration to Colombia. Meanwhile, in Santiago de Cuba, Orozco Rubio continued his own path
toward traditional Nigerian Ifá within his ẹgbé, losing certain membership
while also steadily building a following within African traditionalism.

In 2014, Orozco Rubio officially legitimized his authority as a babaláwo of
direct African lineage by (re-)initiating into the Nigerian-rooted Odùgbemi

lineage, the Ifá-Òrìṣà lineage founded by the exiled, former Cuban counter-intelligence officer Juan Manuel Rodríguez Camejo (Ifáshade Odùgbemi, see chapter 1), an initiation overseen by Cuban babaláwo Baba Àràbà Ifalere Odùgbemi. In so doing, Orozco Rubio—like Edibere before him—broke with the traditional hierarchies and ritual lineages of Cuban-style Ifá, deriving his authority as babaláwo instead from the Odùgbemi lineage founded in contemporary Nigeria. This move temporally transformed the African traditionality so crucial to claims of authority in Ifá and Afro-Cuban religions from a chronotope of Africa as rooted in Cuba's colonial-era slave past to an African traditionality rooted in the continent's contemporary present. Furthermore, the circumventing of Cuban hierarchies and ritual lineages through (re-)-initiation into the Odùgbemi lineage provided its own form of authoritative efficacy, granting Orozco Rubio an even larger degree of autonomy as babaláwo and leader of the African traditionalist movement in Santiago de Cuba (and eastern Cuba more broadly). As the ẹgbẹ́'s mission statement clarifies, "We do not surrender explanations or accounts of our actions to anyone who is not a religious elder of the Odugbemi lineage" (Orozco Rubio 2015a). This discursive and, more broadly, ecclesiastical move effectively eliminated the ẹgbẹ́'s embroilment in the local networks of indebtedness, responsibility, and deference attendant to the hierarchies of Cuban Ifá on the island itself.

Female "Emancipation" at the Ethnographic Interface

As a university-trained professor of psychology turned Ocha-Ifá practitioner, Orozco Rubio pushes forward an academically minded approach to Ifá, promoting the academic study of Yorùbá traditional religion (YTR) (including publications in the fields of anthropology, religious studies, sociology, gender and sexuality, and language) among his ẹgbẹ́ members as a key tool in the formulation of "correct" Ifá practice. Boasting an overwhelmingly professional and academically trained ẹgbẹ́ membership, in which "90 percent of our members are professionals of the distinct branches of the sciences, with a large representation from the social sciences and humanities, medicine, and engineering" (Orozco Rubio 2015a, my translation), Orozco Rubio promotes research, publication, and participation in regional, national, and international academic conferences among ẹgbẹ́ members as a means to strengthen and promote the tenets of his Nigerian-style Ifá practice. This academically minded epistemological approach to Ifá demonstrates a heightening of what anthropologist Stephen Palmié (2013, 32) terms the "ethnographic interface" at the heart of the crafting of Afro-Cuban religion since its inception as such in the early twentieth century. Noting the centrality of anthropological, sociological, or other studies of Afro-Cuban religion as indispensable ingredients in the "confection" of the religion itself, Palmié frames Afro-Cuban religion as an entity forged at the intersection between two operative fields: (1) the field of Afro-Cuban religion as an objectified entity and (2) the field of its study (9–10). Like many *santeros, paleros,* and babalaos before him, Orozco Rubio integrates mid-twentieth-century ethnographies on Afro-Cuban religion into his Ocha-Ifá practice (such as those by Fernando Ortiz, Lydia Cabrera, Rómulo Lachatañeré, and Teodoro Díaz Fabelo), transforming these ethnographic texts into ritual guidebooks that draw on descriptions of practices from the 1930s to 1950s as sources of closer-to-the-root Yorùbá traditionality. Through the incorporation of these studies and through direct academic engagement, Orozco Rubio and other members of the ẹgbẹ́ blur easy demarcations between the purported first-order and second-order discourses of Afro-Cuban religion and its study (Palmié 2013, 7) and also problematize the purportedly separate ontological and epistemological realms of academic scholarship and ritual praxis (see fig. 3.2).

Since 2013, Orozco Rubio's academic research has focused specifically on what he frames as the "emancipation of women" in Cuban Ifá-Òrìṣà and includes a thesis and academic conference presentations on gender, Ifá, and òrìṣà worship in contemporary Nigeria (see Orozco Rubio 2015b, 2022). Despite this rhetoric, however, it should be noted that discourses of female "emancipation" in Nigerian-style Ifá belie the ways in which the polemics surrounding female ìyánífá initiations serve to naturalize notions of appropriate femininity in a purportedly African traditional sense, that is, as explicitly heterosexual, with heightened emphasis on women's power to conceive children and to be good wives and mothers (Beliso-De Jesús 2015a, 833). As Aisha Beliso-De Jesús (2015a, 819) demonstrates, these discourses often serve more to "circumscribe nationalized gendered normativities between competing African and Cuban diasporic assemblages" than to domesticate so-called (North) American imperialist feminisms, such as liberated (homo)sexualities or other (White) feminist ideologies concerned with female emancipation from gender norms. Furthermore, the rhetoric of "total inclusion" mobilized by Orozco Rubio and others elides the fact that ìyánífá are denied access to the deity òrìṣà Odù, effectively disabling them from initiating other priests and forming their own ritual lineages, as babaláwos are able to do. Despite these caveats, Orozco Rubio's academically minded and idiosyncratic epistemological and practical approaches to Ifá-Òrìṣà mark a radical departure from Cuban gendered strictures and prohibitions. Accordingly, Orozco Rubio's interventions have provided women in Cuba with opportunities to achieve wider, if still limited, participation in Ifá and oricha worship. In the

FIGURE 3.2. Babaláwo Enrique Orozco Rubio presents "Ìyámi Òṣòròngá: Myth and Reality" (Ìyámi Òṣòròngá: Mito y realiad [sic]) at the Casa del Caribe's annual Festival de Caribe academic conference. July 7, 2015. Photo by the author.

case of consecrated batá, percussionist Nagybe Madariaga Pouymiró encountered one such opportunity through Orozco Rubio and his African traditionalist vision, achieving her decades-long mission of gaining women's access to the sacred instruments of Regla de Ocha through the Nigerian-style Ifá-Òrìṣà movement.

Nagybe Madariaga Pouymiró: Ritual Prohibition and Batá

Nagybe Madariaga Pouymiró was born in Czechoslovakia in 1958 to Cuban parents completing their university studies abroad, and she grew up in Santiago de Cuba after coming to Cuba as a young child. She first became interested in percussion in her early twenties when, while working as an actress in a theater troupe, one of the troupe's percussionists broke his arm the day before an opening performance, and Pouymiró stepped in to fill the role (Pryor 1999, 6). Shortly thereafter, the Conjunto Folclórico de Oriente opened a school for Afro-Cuban percussion, song, and dance in Santiago de Cuba (Pryor 1999), and Pouymiró auditioned and was accepted. Despite her merit-based entrance, she claims to have been subjected to virulent machismo while playing conga, bongó, and other Afro-Cuban folkloric instruments, and she was initially prohibited entirely from approaching the batá in the Conjunto (Pryor 1999). "They told me, 'No,' that I could not have access to this type of percussion because it was prohibited for women. I asked, 'Why?' They said, 'Because it is prohibited.'"[14] The shallowness of the explanation proved to be what Pouymiró terms a "propitious negation," an auspicious and even favorable exclusion that instilled in her the drive to use her status as a professional percussionist to break the barriers surrounding female access to the batá in both its unconsecrated (*aberinkulá*) and, eventually, consecrated forms.[15]

In the 1980s, like today, the consecrated batá (*tambores de Añá*) differed from the aberinkulá (unconsecrated batá) in that they are ritually "born" from another consecrated set and contain a sacred packet inside (the consecration), known in Cuba as "la carga, el secreto, el añá, or afowobo" (see Villepastour 2015a, 140). The aberinkulá drums also exhibit metal tuning keys and can be played on stands, both of which the consecrated tambores de Añá "never have" (Jassey 2019, 182). Most centrally, the consecrated batá are preferred in rituals to invoke the oricha while the unconsecrated aberinkulá are commonly used in nonritual, folkloric, or secular presentations of the batá in Cuba.[16] In the Conjunto Folclórico de Oriente in Santiago de Cuba, however, Pouymiró found herself prohibited from both.

Originally, it seems that Pouymiró's indignation concerning her prohibition from the batá arose from a secular rather than theological sense that the Conjunto Folclórico de Oriente, as a state-paid cultural arm of the revolutionary government, was violating the constitutional guarantee of women to full equality within "economic, political, social, and familiar" spheres as written in the 1976 Cuban Constitution, including their right to equal access to employment (see República de Cuba 1976, chap. 5, "Equality," article 43). "Imagine, I was raised in a society where women's right to equality within society is a constitutional law. In other words, I was formed, and I have learned to think, under the canons of feminism, because Cuban society allows you [women] to freely elect your destiny." Grounding feminism as a socialist-egalitarian Cuban revolutionary value rather than as an "American imperialism" (Beliso-De Jesús 2015a), Pouymiró asserts her conviction in women's right to play batá within a Cuban-inspired feminist lens of gendered equity. The Conjunto's negation of her playing batá constituted for her "an inexplicable prohibition. And since they prohibited me and let me know in such a grotesque way that [the answer was] no, well, I swore to myself, yes."

Pouymiró encountered her first opportunity to approach the unconsecrated aberinkulá batá set in the 1980s through Buenaventura Bell Morales (b. 1942), a percussionist, dancer, singer, and instructor at the Conjunto Folclórico de Oriente. Upon learning that santeros in Havana were imparting batá classes to foreign women in exchange for hard currency, Bell Morales became sympathetic to Pouymiró and began giving her private lessons on batá in secret.[17] Additionally, he helped her purchase her first unconsecrated set, which as Pouymiró notes, would never have been sold to her directly if the artisan knew that she was a woman. After three years of study with Bell Morales, Pouymiró continued her studies with Milián Galí (b. 1939), a respected olubatá, omo Añá, and santero known for bringing the first consecrated set of batá from Matanzas to Santiago de Cuba (Chatelain 2003; Larduet Luaces 2014). Pouymiró spent three years learning technique and ritual singing over the toques (rhythmic "archetypes") with Galí (Vaughan and Aldama 2012, 24), supplementing their lessons autodidactically by imitating the recordings of well-known ritual singers of Regla de Ocha (akpwones) Lázaro Ros and Merceditas Valdés (see fig. 3.3).

Playing the unconsecrated batá set in her house did come with costs. As word traveled that the sounds of the batá were emanating from Pouymiró's home, Pouymiró was visited by a member of Santiago de Cuba's cultural research institute, Casa del Caribe, demanding answers as to "what she was doing and why she was doing it." As Pouymiró claims, this apparent attempt at intimidation followed a visit to Santiago de Cuba by representatives of the ACYC in Havana who, as institutional arbiters of Regla de Ocha-Ifá since the association's establishment in 1991, had become increasingly concerned over the fact that women were beginning to play the unconsecrated batá in eastern Cuba.[18] Pouymiró continued playing, however, and following one of her public performances on the batá she was assaulted, physically beaten, and hospitalized, an event she directly attributes to her continued batá playing in the face of male intimidation and scorn. Undeterred, she continued playing batá publicly. However, in seeing that her performances were continually rejected by Regla de Ocha practitioners, Pouymiró turned toward academic and theological publications and presentations as a stage for voicing arguments—of both secular and ritual impetus—for the right of women to play consecrated batá in Regla de Ocha.

Pouymiró's writings on gender and batá include numerous self-published books and research papers dating from shortly after her "propitious negation" from playing in the mid-1980s. The titles include El derecho de igualdad de la

FIGURE 3.3. Nagybe Madariaga Pouymiró on *chékere* and Buenaventura Bell Morales (seated in white) on *tumbadora* at Ẹgbé Irán Átele Ilogbon Odugbemi. June 2015. Photo by the author.

mujer en la Santería afrocubana (The right to female equality in Afro-Cuban Santería, 1985), *Las mujeres y los tambores bata* (Women and the batá drums, 1992), *Mujeres vs mito* (Women vs. myth, 2011), *Ilú Ni Ochún: Tambor para mujeres dedicado a la diosa ochún* (Ilú Ni Ochún: Ritual rhythms for women dedicated to the deity Ochún, 2012), *Mujeres vs mito 2da parte* (Women vs. myth, part two, 2012), *Ritmos para los bata, por y para las mujeres* (Rhythms for batá by and for women, 2015), and, drawing on her training as a physicist, *El fenómeno físico acústico en los tambores bata* (The physical-acoustic phenomenon of the batá, 2010). Within these writings, Pouymiró uses a variety of discursive techniques to ground her argument, blending ritual, socialist-egalitarian, nationalist, and historical argumentation to make her case for "women's right to equality" in playing the consecrated batá.

Pouymiró's self-published treatise *Ritmos Nuevos para los Tambores Bata: Por el derecho de igualdad de género* (New rhythms for the batá drums: For the right to gender equality, 2015b) is indicative of this trend. In the introduction, Pouymiró discursively aligns her project of fighting for gender equality in batá to the freedom fighting of nineteenth-century national heroines Mariana Grajales Coello, an icon in Cuba's fight for independence, and enslaved women Fermina "Lucumí" and Carlota, known as architects of the Triumvirato slave rebellion in Matanzas in 1843 (Stoner 1991; Shepherd 2006; Godfried 2006).[19] Nationalizing her struggle within the lineage of these valiant nineteenth-century Cuban women who fought and died for freedom, Pouymiró then confronts theological arguments against women playing batá in Regla de Ocha, including the claim that women are prohibited from playing batá due to their menstruation.[20] For Pouymiró (2015b), this "strange and anything but noble argument" serves to reinforce the hierarchical nature of a male-dominated religious system, one that creates "a liturgical caste against women that confines her to a lower stature" and "consolidat[es] norms and criteria that contribute to the male sex obtaining more money, power, and personal triumph within the religion" (17, 13, 20–21). In response to this "plainly patriarchal and masculine interpretation," Pouymiró then proposes a novel and quite radical project: "[the creation of] new rhythms that demonstrate a renewing, feminine interpretation and perception" (37).

Pouymiró's radical project as outlined in this treatise claims access to the consecrated batá as a female right and puts forward a vision for the creation of novel ritual toques inspired by an explicitly feminine (and feminist) interpretation of Regla de Ocha-Ifá.[21] Demonstrating the breadth of her personal and spiritual commitment to breaking the patriarchal hierarchies and prohibitions of Regla de Ocha-Ifá, this treatise shows the consolidation of Pouymiró's thought in the years and, in this case, months preceding her initial meeting with Orozco Rubio. Orozco Rubio and other African traditionalist babaláwos, meanwhile, were themselves dedicated to breaking gender norms in Cuban Regla de Ocha-Ifá, initiating women as ìyánífá and creating novel spaces for female participation based on the gendered norms of contemporary Yorùbáland. It would be through Orozco Rubio and his Ẹgbé Irán Átele Ilogbon Odugbemi, with its theological dedication to strengthening the polemical gendered tenets of African traditionalism, that Pouymiró would encounter an avenue toward the realization of a decades-long goal of establishing female access to the consecrated batá.

Pouymiró and Orozco Rubio: Renewal and Rupture

Nagybe Madariaga Pouymiró learned of African traditionalist babaláwo and olubatá Orozco Rubio through a mutual friend and percussionist in Santiago de Cuba and, curious to learn more about the role of women in traditional Yorùbáland and in his ẹgbẹ́, approached him in 2014. Impressed with Orozco Rubio's mission to reinstate the role of women in YTR within the contexts of Nigerian-style Ifá-Òrìṣà, Pouymiró outlined her own research, publications, and creative vision for female access to the consecrated batá in the hopes that the ẹgbẹ́ might serve as an avenue for the realization of these projects. Orozco Rubio agreed that female access to the consecrated batá would be permitted within African traditionalism, having learned through contact with African traditionalist babaláwos in the Americas, visiting Nigerian babaláwos, and videos of contemporary sacred drumming in Yorùbáland that although female sacred percussionists were rare, there was no theological impediment or prohibition to their playing.

Together, Pouymiró and Orozco Rubio came to a mutual agreement, outlining objectives that would satisfy key elements of Pouymiró's vision and simultaneously elevate women's stature within the aural and theological configurations of òrìṣà worship in Cuba in accordance with Orozco Rubio's African traditionalist vision. Upon initiation in the ẹgbẹ́, Pouymiró founded a didactic and generative project with the future objectives of (1) enabling initiated women and ìyánífá access to the consecrated batá, (2) instructing ẹgbẹ́ members, both male and female, in batá performance, and (3) composing novel toques for the batá inspired in part by a feminist interpretation of the Ifá corpus to be used in future ẹgbẹ́ ritual ceremonies. Immediately, Pouymiró began working to fulfill the second and third objectives, initiating instruction for women and ìyánífá in the ẹgbẹ́ on how to play the unconsecrated aberinkulá batá and, additionally, continuing to compose toques inspired by ìyánífá and other references to feminine authority and power in the odù (signs) of Ifá (see fig. 3.4).

It's worth noting here the degree to which these objectives within the ẹgbẹ́ mark a radical departure from orthodoxy regarding batá performance as it has developed for generations in Cuban Regla de Ocha. First, the use of consecrated batá within Ifá recontextualizes and refunctionalizes the instruments. The tambores de Añá (consecrated batá) are traditionally reserved for specific ceremonies in Regla de Ocha, including "presentations," in which the iyawó (new initiate) is presented before Añá (the deity of the batá), and anniversaries of santeros' initiations (cumpleaños de santo) (Schweitzer 2013). In these contexts, the voice of Añá, mobilized by the execution of the batá by male ritual drummers, functions as a medium of communication enticing the oricha to "come down" (bajar) and offer advice, dancing, and healing to those gathered (Schweitzer 2013; Vaughan and Aldama 2012; Vélez 2000). The Cuban batá, then, are not traditional to the specific ritual ceremonies of Ifá,

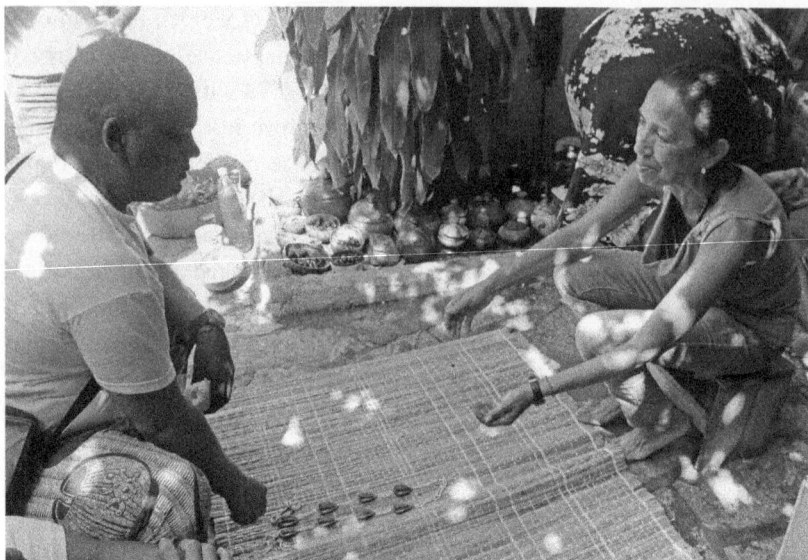

FIGURE 3.4. Babaláwo Enrique Orozco Rubio and Nagybe Madariaga Pouymiró, Letra del Año yearly divination reading, Ẹgbé Irán Átele Ilogbon Odugbemi. June 2015. Photo by the author.

which forms an interrelated but increasingly divergent branch of oricha worship from that of Regla de Ocha (Holbraad 2012, 109; D. Brown 2003; Larduet Luaces 2014).[22]

Second, Pouymiró's didactic project of teaching batá to women and men for future ritual use circumvents all-male lineages of initiation and apprenticeship in Añá (Jassey 2019; Schweitzer 2013; Vaughan and Aldama 2012; Vélez 2000). In so doing, her didactic approach radically reconfigures the bases of ritual and epistemic access to the batá for both men and women. In Regla de Ocha, the *lavado de manos* (hand-washing initiation) and *juramento* (full Añá initiation) are reserved exclusively for heterosexual men (Vincent 2006, 117–18). In assuming didactic leadership over the passage of knowledge to students with the purpose of using tambores de Añá to officiate future rituals, Pouymiró circumvents the all-male master-student relationship of Añá lineages that have been maintained for generations.[23] Furthermore, Pouymiró explicitly feminizes access to the Añá deity that resides within the batá, upending the theological strictures that justify the prohibition of female contact with consecrated batá and with the oricha Añá.[24]

Third, Pouymiró's female-centered vision of crafting novel toques inspired by an explicitly feminist interpretation of Ifá-Òrìṣà radically breaks with conceptions of the rich, complex corpus of batá toques as a relatively fixed set of "archetypes" tied to specific orichas and sequences. Despite histories of regional variation, fluidity in execution, and the value placed on personal style, these archetypes are approached with a certain degree of fidelity in Regla de Ocha (Schweitzer 2013; Vaughan and Aldama 2012). As Umi Vaughan notes, toques aren't merely static; rather, "improvisation on gestural and rhythmic 'archetypes' enhances the divine potential of the performance" (Vaughan and Aldama 2012, 24). Even so, Pouymiró's generative approach to creating new toques that aim to break the "plainly patriarchal and masculine interpretation" she views as pervasive in Regla de Ocha moves beyond the fluidity of personal style. Rather, this project proposes a generative form of creating a novel batá liturgy engendered by female interpretation and craft, demonstrating Pouymiró's vision for explicitly feminist forms of intervention into consecrated batá playing and Regla de Ocha more broadly.

The First *Ensayo de fundamento de mujeres*

When I first met Nagybe Madariaga Pouymiró in 2015, she was in the process of rehearsing with female initiates in the ẹgbẹ́ in preparation for that year's Festival de Fuego, hosted by cultural research institute Casa del Caribe. Occurring annually at the beginning of July in the weeks immediately preceding Santiago de Cuba's Carnival celebrations, the festival's academic conferences and workshops have long served as a stage for Pouymiró in voicing her arguments—theological, socialist-egalitarian, and otherwise—in favor of female access to the consecrated batá. The festival also serves as a meeting ground for international academics, female percussionists, and *santeras* interested in the same goal of achieving female access to the batá or even the creation of female-headed lineages of tambores de Añá. In 2013, for example, Pouymiró assisted in organizing the First Encounter of Women Batá Percussionists and Female Percussion as part of the thirty-third annual festival, a meeting that included panels and performances by female percussionists and *bataleras* (female batá players) from Obiní Batá (Havana), Obiní Irawó (Santiago de Cuba), Obiní Aché (Cienfuegos), and Ojalá (the United States), along with the participation of German percussionist Dorothy Marx (Pouymiró 2015b; Radio Encyclopedia 2013). Reflecting the global-local nexus of the politics of delimitation of Afro-Cuban religion, as well as the self-constituting dynamics in which academic scholarship and religious praxis craft one another within "autopoietic pattern[s] of relationality" (Palmié 2013, 29), Pouymiró intended to use the nationally and internationally focused academic and musical Festival de Fuego as the perfect stage for presenting the first *tambor de fundamento de mujeres* (consecrated batá set playing by women) to the world and thereby publicly breaking the prohibition against women playing the batá or channeling Añá.[25] However, despite having consulted Ifá and received confirmation from Orozco Rubio that playing the consecrated batá was pre-destined for her (ìyánífá Caridad Rubio Fonseca of the ẹgbẹ́ and Pouymiró, pers. comm., June 20, 2015), Pouymiró had not yet received authorization for this specific goal from Orozco Rubio.

On an otherwise ordinary Monday afternoon in late June 2015, some two weeks before the inauguration of the Festival de Caribe, Orozco Rubio issued the authorization that Pouymiró had awaited several decades to receive: she, ìyánífá Caridad Rubio Fonseca (Orozco Rubio's mother, b. 1949), and ìyánífá Anais López Rubio (Orozco Rubio's sister, 1979–2017) would be the first three women authorized to play a set of tambores de Añá in Cuba, and they would do so that afternoon in the Ẹgbé Irán Átele Ilogbon Odugbemi using Orozco Rubio's consecrated set. Undoubtedly, this authorization came on that par-ticular day because I was planning to be at the ẹgbẹ́ interviewing Pouymiró and Fonseca with audio equipment and cameras. It was made clear during informal conversations surrounding the event and during the recording of the event itself that as a North American academic, my presence served as documentation and validation of the event, and it was expected that I would bear witness to the event and photograph, videotape, and write about the events for dissemination abroad.[26] Notably, the first documented instance of three women playing the consecrated batá set would not be a *tambor*, or ritual event, at all; rather, it would constitute an initial instance of access to the consecrated drums outside of the context of ritual by Pouymiró, Fonseca, and López Rubio with the intent of enabling the women to officiate ceremonies using the batá at a later date.[27] Notably, as well, Orozco Rubio called to give the official blessing, saying that he would be unable to make it that afternoon but that the women were fully authorized and encouraged to approach the batá on their own, thus authorizing the event yet refraining from overseeing it directly.

The ẹgbẹ́, located in the back of Fonseca and López Rubio's home, en-compasses an open-air ritual space divided into discrete spatial realms: a central, open-air patio, the Ìgbò Odù (room with a sacred altar) on the far left of the patio, the *cuarto de Eggún* (room for the ancestors, in which the batá are kept) to the right of the entranceway, and an altar to the òrìṣà Èṣù, purposefully kept in the farthest corner of the patio away from the home. After Orozco Rubio's call, Fonseca went to the cuarto de Éggun to retrieve the consecrated drums and, noting that it was too hot to rehearse in the late June sun, carried the consecrated batá from the outdoor ẹgbẹ́ patio into the liv-ing room for the first official "rehearsal" (*ensayo*). Nagybe—euphoric, tearful, and anxious all at once—clasped her hands together and smiled tearfully at the drums as Fonseca carefully removed them from their black cases. Fonseca wrapped Nagybe in a blue ceremonial cloth, and we set up a practice stage for the first ensayo, arranged so that I would film with my audio equipment and camera from the back of the room while the three women faced me, seated in a semicircle of three chairs, in the front.

Self-consciously proclaiming the moments to come as a "historic event," Pouymiró sat down to record a statement before initially approaching the drums. In it, she emphasizes that she, Fonseca, and López Rubio execute the tambores de Añá within the tenets of YTR and that, as ìyánífá and female initiates, they possess the theological foundations and spiritual formation to do so: "We are not going to violate—nor will we be violating—any natural law, or anything that is not normal. I don't believe that if men come from the wombs of women, there can be any impediment against us executing the tambores de Añá. . . . Today, June 22, 2015, for the first time in Cuba and in the world, we women will play the *fundamentos*. I believe that this is something important that can revolutionize music [and] that will revolutionize the religion. All things are subject to change."[28]

Fonseca added to Pouymiró's statement, saying that in addition to "breaking all of the molds" and "taboos" that had been created "against women" in Regla de Ocha (as stated by Pouymiró), they would also leave "a legacy for others, so that other religious women can play their drums without issue."[29]

In honor of the ẹgbẹ́'s titular òrìṣà, Ògún, Pouymiró, Fonseca, and López Rubio began the ensayo with a liturgical sequence dedicated first to the Òrìṣà Ògún and second to Ọ̀rúnmìlà, with Pouymiró as lead drummer on the *iyá* (largest) drum, Fonseca on the midsized *itótele*, and López Rubio on the smallest *okónkolo*. Pouymiró and Fonseca alternated as akpwón lead singers, with all three women participating in the choruses. After a pause, the women set the three drums on a stand so that Pouymiró could play all three drums simultaneously, a technique popular in secular presentations of the batá but not in ritual ones, and initiated another sequence to Ògún and Ọ̀rúnmìlà. After a short break, in which a few neighbors and relatives began to pass through, they continued with a sequence of toques and *cantos* (songs) dedicated to Yemọja—Orozco Rubio's titular deity—with Pouymiró again taking the lead as akpwón (see fig. 3.5).

In the songs to Ògún, Ọ̀rúnmìlà, and Yemọja, the three women played rhythms taken directly from the Regla de Ocha batá corpus and combined them with vocals that mixed traditional Ocha songs and phrasings with new, Yorùbá-style wordings and pronunciation. In the sequence to Ifá, however,

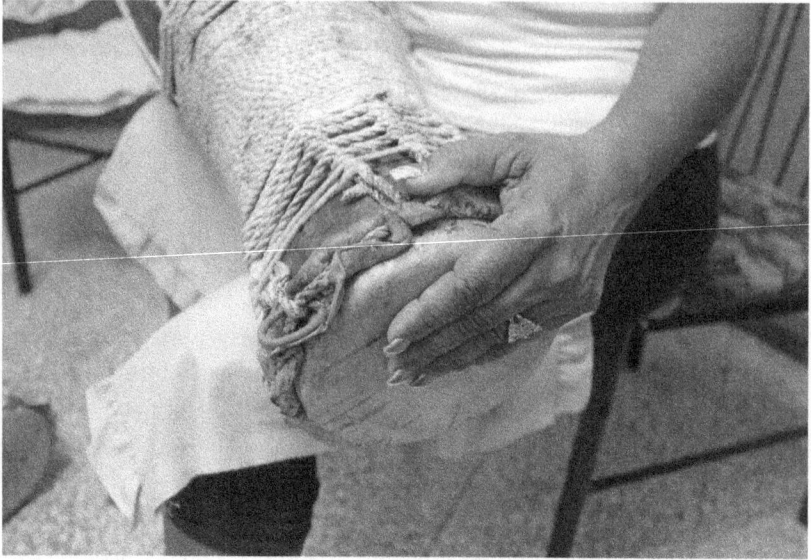

FIGURE 3.5. Ìyánífá Caridad Rubio Fonseca plays the consecrated *itótele*. June 22, 2015. Photo by the author.

the women discarded Cuban texts altogether in favor of a praise song taken directly from contemporary Yorùbáland:

Ó dọwó èyin baba wa,	Your hands reach us, our father.
ìṣèṣe dọwó èyin baba wa	The tradition is guided by your hands, our father.
Ẹ má jé ó bàjé èsìn ìṣèṣe	It doesn't allow [us] to lose the spirituality of our tradition.
ìṣèṣe dọwó èyin baba wa	The tradition is guided by your hands, our father.[30]

Notably, the three women learned this praise song to Ifá from the well-known Nigerian ìyánífá Asabioje Afenapa's album *Ìṣèṣe Làgbà* (released in 2007).[31] Afenapa's album presents a series of songs and praises to various òrìṣà recorded over the bàtá and dùndún drums, with rhythms that differ markedly from the Cuban toques of Regla de Ocha.[32] Throughout the song, Fonseca, López Rubio, and Pouymiró recontextualized the canto (lyrical text and melody) by juxtaposing the song over the Cuban toque *obanlá*, played on all three consecrated bàtá by Pouymiró (ex. 1).

As noted, Pouymiró's execution of obanlá on all three bàtá simultaneously presents a highly idiosyncratic approach to playing the consecrated instruments. This decision inevitably influences the interpretation of the toque. In playing all three instruments herself, Pouymiró highlights notes that outline the skeletal rhythmic structure of obanlá while eliminating others that would be played in three-person ritual contexts. As a comparative example, percussionist and olubatá Michael Spiro's transcription of a Havana-style approach to obanlá (also called the fourth "road," or *camino*, to Osain) outlines the toque as shown in example 2 (Spiro and Hill 2017, 34).[33]

In comparing these two performances (exs. 2 and 3), it's clear that Pouymiró's execution of the toque sounds the structure of obanlá as produced by Jiménez, Naní, and Suárez in the mid-1990s while also offering variations. Both interpretations emphasize the two open unison tones on the downbeat

EXAMPLE 1. Nagybe Madariaga Pouymiró plays the toque obanlá on all three consecrated batá drums, while ìyánífá Fonseca and ìyánífá López Rubio join her in singing the chorus of a praise song to Ifá. As performed on June 22, 2015. Transcription by the author.

EXAMPLE 2. Sketch of Michael Spiro and Justin Hill's transcription of the Havana-style approach to the fourth road of Osain as played by Regino Jiménez, Fermin Naní, and José Pilar Suárez in the mid-1990s. Transcription adapted by the author from Spiro and Hill (2017, 34).

EXAMPLE 3. Excerpt from Nagybe Madariaga Pouymiró's interpretation of the fourth road of Osain (mm. 1, 4, and 8 from ex. 1). Transcription by the author.

of the iyá; however, Pouymiró diverges by switching her hands to the two smaller instruments for the remainder of the sequence to produce the hocketed itótele and okónkolo tones that give structure to obanlá, notably playing a comparatively reduced lead iyá part. As a player with only two hands at her disposal (as opposed to six), Pouymiró necessarily plays fewer notes, outlining key aspects of the toque while also offering stylistic distinctions. On the itótele, Pouymiró produces the same notes on the *enú* (low-pitched, larger instrument head) as her Havana-style counterparts, simultaneously eliminating or offering a slight eighth-note variation on the *chachá* (high-pitched, smaller instrument head). On the okónkolo, Pouymiró offers a rhythmic variation on both the enú and chachá heads in the first half of the measure, proceeding to reproduce the second half of the measure verbatim.

This combination of variation and consistency between two spatially and temporally separated interpretations of obanlá—one capturing a Havana-style performance in the mid-1990s and the other a Santiago de Cuba performance in the mid-2010s—speaks to the batá corpus as a living, breathing tradition, one in which regional and individual stylistic variations produce both contrast and aural recognizability among diverse players. At the same time, Pouymiró's technique of adapting the three-instrument batá set for solo performance on a stand marks a profoundly gendered rupture in consecrated batá performance. While Pouymiró's use of a stand builds on the established practice of adapting the aberinkulá set for solo performance in Cuban popular music, the practice is unheard of in ritual contexts (Jassey 2019, 164).[34] In this case, Pouymiró's use of the stand underscores the long histories of prohibition from three-person ritual performance contexts for bataleras, including Pouymiró, who learned to play the three aberinkulá batá together for solo performance in secular and folkloric settings. Additionally, Pouymiró's idiosyncratic choice builds on longer gendered histories of innovation in the use of stands in Cuba. The all-female batá troupe Obiní Batá, for example, innovated the use of individual stands for each player for secular and folkloric group performance (a practice taken up by two other all-female groups, Afro America and Batá Show) (Jassey 2019, 163).[35]

In this instance, Pouymiró explained that she decided to use the Cuban toque obanlá, specifically, for this newly acquired Yorùbá-language song because it is a "shared" toque (*ritmo suelto*) in the Cuban batá tradition, or a toque that is used as an underlying rhythm for many different orichas. As Vaughan notes, shared toques such as *iyakotá, ñongo,* and *chachalokuafun* are used as underlying rhythms to sing for "many" deities in the Regla de Ocha tradition, unlike other batá rhythms linked exclusively to specific oricha (Vaughan and Aldama 2012, 122, 128).[36] Pouymiró felt that obanlá, as a shared toque, was appropriate for use in a song praising Ifá and also fit the rhythm and cadence of the newly introduced Yorùbá melody.

In looking at examples 1 and 3, it is worth also noting the selective Yorùbá-centrism that Pouymiró and the other women involved exhibit in their approach to Nigerian-style ritual music in eastern Cuba. In this case, fidelity to the Cuban-style batá rhythmic archetypes and technique in contrast with a preference for contemporary Nigerian praise songs indicates a selective Yorùbá-centrism within the realm of Nigerian-style ritual sound. On the one hand, claims of fidelity to the pronunciation, tonal characteristics, and semantics of the contemporary Yorùbá language as a more potent and pure channel of communication with the òrìṣà than Afro-Cuban Lucumí, or the vestigial, nonsyntactic ritual lexicon used in Regla de Ocha-Ifá, indicate what Ana María Ochoa Gautier (2006) terms "epistemologies of purification" in the realm of the linguistic that look to the Yorùbá language of contemporary Nigeria as a model for fate-changing efficacy in Ifá and òrìṣà ritual. On the other hand, this linguistic claim is not matched by parallel ideologies of aurality in the realm of the instrumental (Ochoa Gautier 2014), where the Cuban batá are maintained as a faithful vessel for Añá/Àyàn despite divergences in the rhythmic archetypes and techniques of their Nigerian counterparts.[37]

The Aftermath

After finally achieving the decades-long goal to which she had dedicated much of her personal and professional life, Pouymiró's euphoric tears, excitement, laughing, and crying—shared by all three women and myself, but especially notable in Pouymiró—gradually gave way to the darker emotions of fear, anxiety, and dread. "I know the Yoruba Cultural Association [of Cuba] will show up," Pouymiró growled apprehensively (Pouymiró, interview, June 22, 2015). "There will have to be police surrounding the whole building at the

FIGURE 3.6. Anais López Rubio, Nagybe Madariaga Pouymiró, and Caridad Rubio Fonseca (*left to right*) play the consecrated tambores de Añá of babaláwo, omo Añá, and olúbatá Enrique Orozco Rubio. June 22, 2015. Photo by the author.

Festival de Caribe," she worried. "I imagine that with the world's Ocha religious community, there won't be a safe place in the world for us!" Moments of pride and bravery emerged and faded in tandem with feelings of anxiety and apprehension, and in a moment of determined strength and conviction, Pouymiró turned to the camera and clarified: "We take on the challenge of what comes from now onward. We know that there will be many skeptics, but, well, living is a risk. In the end . . . we know where we're headed, we know what we want, and we know why we're doing it. We have been the first to do it so that in the future, new generations of women percussionists of *tambores de fundamento* will arise, and in equal conditions [to men]" (see fig. 3.6).

The tendencies of fear to swell and unfurl in the face of the obscurity of the unknown underscores here the emotional toll of enacting what can be framed as an act of political "dissensus" as put forward by Jacques Rancière ([2004] 2009). The first *grupo de fundamento de mujeres* (group of women to play the tambores de Añá) marks a reconfiguration of the boundaries of collectively held sense and perception that self-evidently delimit that which is held in common—in this case, the gendered, ecclesiastical, and acoustic boundaries of proper femininity in Regla de Ocha and the ontological bases of the oricha Añá—and that which is not. Furthermore, the ominous fear associated with a state-linked apparatus (the ACYC) underscores the degree to which the perceived towering of the state within the Cuban imagination awakens monolithic notions of hidden powers and reach, including in the case of "Afro-Cuban religions" (Routon 2010).

The historic "breaking of the mold" had occurred, however, and Pouymiró planned to demonstrate to the local and global Ocha community present at the upcoming Festival de Caribe that women had in fact broken the barriers of prohibition and were playing the consecrated batá in Cuba. In preparation for her academic paper at the festival, tentatively entitled " 'Menstruation: Blessing or Curse' by Enrique Orozco Rubio," Pouymiró prepared a statement and a video using images, sound, and interviews taken from the day that she, Fonseca, and López Rubio played the tambores de Añá. These images would show that women could—and already had—played the consecrated batá and that, additionally, they had the foundations to do so. The video would also incorporate the paper's central thesis, which aimed to theologically discredit the prohibition against women playing batá based on their menstruation.

On Monday, July 6, Pouymiró presented at the Festival de Caribe's academic conference, held at the grand Teatro Heredia theater in Santiago de Cuba. Pouymiró prefaced the presentation by saying that she would offer a statement and then, at the end of the presentation, illustrate with a video. The twenty-minute paper announced that women had already played the consecrated batá within the theological foundations of African traditionalism:

> Today, this work aims to demonstrate that it is possible for those women motivated by and interested in practicing as percussionists of the tambores de fundamento [to do so]. It is completely possible. This serves, then, to help overthrow a myth [based on menstruation] lacking in solid argument. Therefore, I exhibit the reasons by which a group of women, thanks to the liberties that the traditionalist African religion offers us, has already been able to access and practice with the sacred tambores de fundamento consecrated to the deity Añá, without endangering the integrity of those traditional omo Añá already in existence. (Pouymiró 2015a)

Following this statement, Pouymiró outlined her theological justifications, emphasizing her *fundamento* (foundation) in both Santería and Ifá. When it came time to show the videos and photographs of Pouymiró, Fonseca, and López Rubio performing on the tambores de Añá, however, Orozco Rubio announced to the technician running the event from his seat in the audience, "No salen las imagenes" (The images don't come up), shaking his head. An ambiguous wording, the comment could mean either "the images are not working" or "the images will not be shown." The statement surprised Pouymiró, who had not been warned and who had used her presentation as a segue into the demonstration, aural and visual, of her participation in the first known case of women playing the consecrated batá in Cuba or internationally.

In the Q&A section following Pouymiró's presentation, a prominent male santero and academic, the first to respond, initially praised Pouymiró's presentation as interesting and important within the contexts of female access to unconsecrated batá; however, he then flatly dismissed the principal thesis of the paper, proclaiming that, as an academic setting, this was not the space for a discussion of access to consecrated batá. "This is a religious problem," he emphasized, and the question of female access to consecrated batá truly falls to (male) "religious leaders," "babalaos," and "great priests." The flat repudiation of feminine theological argumentation within the spaces of the academic festival stood the following day in stark contrast to the same male academic's subsequent flowered praise for other male presenters, such as Orozco Rubio and babaláwo Enrique Machín Hernández, whose presentations, which also explicitly incorporated theological argumentation based on interpretations of the odù of Ifá, he deemed well-researched and "scientific."

The multiple ways in which Pouymiró's presentation of the first grupo de fundamento de mujeres, which constituted, for her, a lifelong goal and achievement, were maneuvered, delimited, and received at the Festival de Caribe underscore the ways in which the boundaries of proper femininity in Regla de Ocha and Ifá are regulated and enforced in both academic and non-academic contexts. The maneuvering of ownership and control over the details of the event by Orozco Rubio in this case demonstrates the ways in which male control over events rooted in lifelong female struggles for religious egalitarianism renaturalize the hierarchies of male-controlled knowledge and access, even within an ostensibly more open and "emancipatory" Nigerian-style Ifá. Additionally, this case reveals tensions between the discrete, if at times overlapping, intentions of the female and male participants in the first grupo de fundamento de mujeres, including Pouymiró, Orozco Rubio, and Fonseca and López Rubio. Orozco Rubio, who openly authorized the event as part of an emancipatory African traditionalist philosophy, later tempered publicizing the details of the event in the face of the nascent potential of future repercussion or lost legitimacy. Pouymiró, on the other hand, felt that this story was her own and that it constituted the culmination of a lifelong struggle to break the taboos surrounding female prohibition in Regla de Ocha. However, Pouymiró's one crucial sentence announcing the fact that she and the other initiated women had, in fact, already accessed the tambores de Añá through the tenets of traditional African-style Ifá did reach members of the audience.

Following the male academic's comments, several Cuban and international santeros/as stood to praise and congratulate her efforts, as well as the efforts of her authorizing priest, Enrique Orozco Rubio.

Conclusion

The case of the first grupo de fundamento de mujeres underscores the novel theological and gendered revolutions wrought in Cuban oricha worship by the polemical and burgeoning African traditionalist movement. Through reconnections with the Yorùbá traditional religion anchored in the contemporary Nigerian homeland, Cuban women and men have carved out novel spaces for generative acts of reconfiguration in Regla de Ocha-Ifá. In consecrated batá performance, Nigerian-style Ifá-Òrìṣà provides alternative models of participation that enact possibilities—and transatlantic justifications for these possibilities—that conflict with gendered prohibitions at home. Nagybe Madariaga Pouymiró's history of intervention into consecrated batá performance since the 1980s, including publications, academic conference presentations, performances, and her eventual involvement with the African traditionalist movement, demonstrates the ways in which these reconnections with Yorùbáland have converged with decades-long efforts on the part of Cuban women to alter gendered prohibitions in Regla de Ocha. Furthermore, Pouymiró's story speaks to the ways in which the perceived efficacy of Nigerian-style Ifá opens up novel, futurist spaces of potentiality for female ritual musicians. Harnessing the efficacy of efficacy itself (or "the uses of use," as Ahmed [2019] states), Pouymiró and other ìyánífá mobilize African traditionalism as an avenue to achieve deep-rooted personal desires for gendered egalitarianism and heightened ritual participation, specifically in the realm of sacred drumming. In this way, women in Cuba harness the transformative potentiality of gendered norms in contemporary Yorùbáland to enact desired changes on the island itself. Larger questions remain, however: Will the first ensayo de fundamento de mujeres engender further cases of women accessing the sacred batá within the tenets of African traditionalism or even within Regla de Ocha? Or will this case remain a singularity, ignored by the community in Cuba and elsewhere?[38] The case of women and consecrated batá underscores the ongoing ways in which engagement with the contemporary African continent continues to shape gender and ritual music in present-day Cuba. Additionally, these women's interventions point to the convergence of desires for religious equality with transatlantic forms of reimagining within the landscape of gender and ritual music globally.

4

Ìyánífá: Gendered Polarity and "Speaking Ifá"

In the eastern Havana neighborhood of Alamar, *iyánífá* Yamilka Gámez Oliva stands barefoot on the outdoor patio of the Aworeni Temple of Havana, facing the upright, iron *osùn babaláwo*, or "diviner's staff" of Ifá.[1] One of a babaláwo's "most important possessions" in Yorùbáland, the osùn babaláwo is stuck into the ground, standing straight up, during important Ifá gatherings and ceremonies (H. Drewal 2016, 333).[2] Facing the diviner's staff, Gámez Oliva rattles the wooden *ìróké* continuously in her right hand, alternating Yorùbá language chants of the verses of Ifá with praise songs to Osùn, animating the iron staff's *àṣẹ*, or manifesting authority.[3] As Henry J. Drewal (2016, 333) notes, Yorùbá language chants and songs invoke the manifesting force of the osùn babaláwo, which, "when used with incantations," replenishes the àṣẹ of the owner and "acts as a weapon against death and other destructive forces." Behind her, a semicircle of babaláwo, ìyánífá, and other members of the Temple of Havana help her summon this power, punctuating her verses with calls of affirmation and repeating her intoned choruses in call-and-response. Her short-cropped hair, still growing out from the ritual head-shaving of her recent initiation, and the blue, beaded necklace with the intricately sewn word "IYANIFA" highlighted in white beads around her neck, announces her newfound authority as priestess of Ifá. As she pauses to pour a series of substances over the small, iron bird perched on top of the staff, representing the "lone bird" (*eyẹkàn*) or àṣẹ of Ọ̀rúnmìlà (Abiodun 2014),[4] her husband, also a babaláwo in the temple, calls out a corresponding series of odù verses and songs. The members of the temple interject the verses with the call, "Àṣẹ!" as Gámez Oliva proceeds to communicate with the deity Osùn via the coconut (*obi*) oracle. Posing a series of questions to Osùn in Yorùbá before dropping a series of small pieces of coconut to the earth, Gámez Oliva and other members of the temple gauge the deity's response by reading the distribution of the shells—either face-up or face-down—on the ground.[5]

In Cuba, an ever-increasing number of ìyánífá are breaking the taboo against female participation in Ifá by "speaking Ifá" (*hablar Ifá*) in a variety of ritual and informal settings.[6] This common colloquialism in Cuba tradition-ally refers to the "more-or-less informal manners of conversation" between Cuban-style *babalaos*, in which these men "strive, often competitively . . . [to demonstrate] their command of the mythical knowledge of Ifá signos," as Martin Holbraad (2012, 102) notes. To speak Ifá, then, is to command knowl-edge over Ifá's corpus and to be able to wield that knowledge in ritual settings and in everyday life. Beyond the informal associations of the phrase, the fre-quent assertion that ìyánífá now speak Ifá in Cuba underscores the centrality and potency of the word—and the voice—in the Yorùbá traditional religion (YTR) of Nigeria. The Yorùbá language, when invoked with correct pronun-ciation and intentionality, is perceived as "reactivating" the conditions of the sacred odù verses, creating the conditions of possibility for transformations of fate.[7] As ìyánífá Fatunmise (2013, 11) explains, "The power of the word is the power to enter the astral plane . . . from this plane the power of 'ofe se' is used to change the condition of life on earth." That ìyánífá in Cuba now "speak Ifá" underscores their newfound command and authority of the mani-festing power of Ifá divinatory practice as well as their novel entrance into the previously restricted all-male priesthood.

Notably, controversies surrounding ìyánífá mark the most antagonizing, vitriolic point of difference between Cuban-style and Nigerian-style Ifá prac-titioners in Cuba. The polemic surrounding ìyánífá directly fuels repeated calls for the blacklisting of African traditionalist babaláwo and ìyánífá and their exclusion from the state-linked Yoruba Cultural Association of Cuba (ACYC, chapter 2). Here, I trace the ìyánífá debate in Cuba, exploring the pointed controversies surrounding the newfound capacity of women to wield the manifesting power of the voice and the word in Ifá ritual. Through an analysis of an annual Letra del Año (Letter of the Year) divination ceremony in Santiago de Cuba, I interrogate the ways in which African traditionalists assert ìyánífá as central to Yorùbá-rooted philosophies of community health and gendered polarity. I explore how, in African traditionalist ẹgbẹ́, ìyánífá are centered in ceremonies as a means to heighten ritual success through in-toned and sung presence. Additionally, I explore gender in Nigerian-style Ifá-Òrìṣà in relation to debates on sexuality in African traditionalism, pointing to the ways in which mandates of heterosexuality in Nigerian-style Ifá priest-hoods versus homosexual inclusivity in òrìṣà lineages reinscribe the sexual boundaries of Cuban-style Regla de Ocha-Ifá as it historically developed on the island. In so doing, this chapter takes an intersectional approach toward the racial, gendered, and sexual complexities of Ifá priestess- and priesthoods in Cuba, with an eye toward the global controversies erupting in and through them.

"Ìyánífá" Arrive in the Americas and Cuba: 1978–2016

In 1978, the Nigerian playwright and Àràbà of Òṣogbo Ifáyẹmí Ẹlẹ́buìbọn spoke to the public in Miami in a conference organized by his Cuban American godchild, the babalao José Miguel Gómez Barberas (Palmié 2013, 278). Facing the Cuban American community of babalaos in Miami, Ẹlẹ́buìbọn caused an uproar by explaining that, in Nigeria, women are initiated into the Ifá priesthood alongside men. This upsetting revelation threatened the gendered boundaries of Cuban-style Ifá in Cuba and its "secondary" diasporas in the United States (Frigerio 2004), where initiation into Ifá and access to Ifá's sacred corpus of *odù* is reserved exclusively for heterosexual men (Beliso-De Jesús 2015a). Ẹlẹ́buìbọn's announcement caused such an outcry among the Cuban American community in Miami that the event was covered in the *Miami Herald* in December of that year (Palmié 2013, 278). Seven years later, in 1985, Ẹlẹ́buìbọn continued his pivotal role in the Yorubizing turn in the diaspora by overseeing the initiation of Dr. Patri D'Haifa, a Jewish psychiatrist based out of New York, as the first documented ìyánífá in the Americas (Padilla Pérez 2006). Ẹlẹ́buìbọn's gendered revelation and active role in ìyánífá initiations in the United States instigated a "contentious process" that would ultimately divide Cuba's babalaos into two factions: those aligned with Cuban-style Regla de Ocha-Ifá and those aligned with Nigerian-style Ifá-Òrìṣà (Palmié 2013, 278–79).

From the first historical moments marking the Yorubizing turn in the Americas, in other words, controversies surrounding gender played a central role. Across distinct ritual communities, these gendered controversies were furthermore informed by intersectional issues of race and sexuality. In the United States, the outcry surrounding the initiation of ìyánífá in the 1980s and 1990s was deeply imbricated with race, especially among Black American Yorùbá revivalists associated with the Ọ̀yọ́túnjí Village in South Carolina. Clarke notes that the initiation of the White US American woman "Olúfadékẹ́ the Ìyánífá" in 1990 caused an uproar among the members of the Ọ̀yọ́túnjí Village, who, unlike many of their Cuban American peers, espoused Yorùbá revivalism as a form of Black nationalist separatism in the United States in the 1970s and 1980s (Clarke 2004, 18, 147). As Clarke notes, "Because she was not only a woman but was also seen as racially Other, the politics of race and gender brought to the fore critical questions about what constitutes Yorùbá practice" and "who should be included" (18). In this sense, Ẹlẹ́buìbọn and other Nigerian babaláwo's initiations of White and non-Black women as ìyánífá across the Americas underscored the divergent racial logics at play between the universalizing approach of YTR (and, historically, Cuban-rooted ritual lineages) and those of other revivalist communities throughout the Americas, including the United States.[8]

In Cuba, meanwhile, the initiation of the first ìyánífá is believed to have occurred in the year 2000, when African traditionalist pioneer and babaláwo Victor Betancourt Omolófaoló Estrada claims to have initiated two Cuban women (María Cuesta and Nidia Águila de León) as ìyánífá in his Ifá Ìranlówo temple in Havana (Machado Tineo 2013).[9] Done "quietly," this first instance of female initiation remained unsurfaced until the "Iyanifa debate" erupted in Cuba in 2004 (Beliso-De Jesús 2015a, 820). This debate followed a global controversy surrounding the US American ìyánífá Chief Yeye Araba-Agbaye (Dr. Patri D'Haifa, the same ìyánífá initiated by Ẹlẹ́buìbọn), who circulated claims of seeing the òrìṣà Odù, the reproductive mechanism of Ifá that is forbidden for women to see or receive in both Cuban-style Ifá and the globalizing lineages of YTR based in Nigeria (Abímbọ́lá 1997, 87; Beliso-De Jesús 2015a, 818).[10] Additionally, D'Haifa claimed to have directly initiated a male priest into Ifá, an impossibility without the forbidden reproductive mechanism of the òrìṣà Odù restricted to male babaláwo (Beliso-De Jesús 2015b; Landry 2015). The International Council for Ifá Religions, based in Ilé-Ifẹ̀, promptly "disputed D'Haifa's claims and circulated an online press release revoking her [chieftancy] title" (Beliso-De Jesús 2015b, 200).[11] This global controversy underscored the policed gendered boundaries of òrìṣà worship in the diaspora and reached the ACYC and Cuba's babalaos, who perceived the initiation of women such as D'Haifa as the work of "profaners" who threatened to "tarnish" the religion (Yoruba Cultural Association of Cuba [2004] 2013). In 2004, the controversy became "a national Cuban issue" when it was revealed that a Venezuelan practitioner of Regla de Ocha, Alba Marina Portales, was traveling to the island to be initiated as ìyánífá in the house of Ernesto Acosta Cediez in Matanzas and under the guidance of Betancourt's Ifá Ìranlówo lineage (Beliso-De Jesús 2015a, 820; Rossbach de Olmos 2014, 72–73).[12] In response, the ACYC released a "worldwide proclamation to oricha practitioners condemning the practices of Iyanifa" and blacklisting the associated babaláwo and ìyánífá (Beliso-De Jesús 2015a, 820; Rossbach de Olmos 2014, 72–73). As Aisha Beliso-De Jesús (2015b, 202) notes, the Cuban state "unofficially aligned itself against iyanifá ceremonies by hassling and policing" African traditionalists in 2004 and 2005, "threatening some members of

Ifá Iranlówo with fines for housing foreigners in their home without permission" and condoning "the call to blacklist African-style priests."

Despite opposition from the ACYC, the initiation of ìyánífá in Cuba gained momentum in the late 2000s, and initiations spread among other African traditionalist lineages and ẹgbẹ́. In 2006, the first ìyánífá initiation in eastern Cuba occurred in Holguín when the Venezuelan babaláwo José Hidalgo Edibere Gamés initiated Cuban babaláwo Félix Arsenio Fuentes Cáceres's wife, Kirenia del Carmen Mejías, as ìyánífá (Martínez Betancourt and Orozco Rubio 2016).[13] That same year, Victor Betancourt and the African traditionalist babaláwo Enrique de la Torre initiated Anais López Rubio, who would become one of the first women authorized to play the consecrated batá set in Cuba (chapter 3), as the first ìyánífá in Santiago de Cuba. In 2009, Victor Betancourt Estrada's son, Víctor Yasmani Betancourt Águila,[14] initiated *santera* Dulce María Rodríguez Sánchez (b. 1960) as ìyánífá along with four other women in the city of Holguín (Martínez Betancourt and Orozco Rubio 2016).[15] In 2012, María Rodríguez Sánchez founded the Egbè Fermina Gómez ati Echu-Dina (*sic*) in Holguín, becoming, to this day, the only female founder and "rector" (leader) of any African traditionalist ẹgbẹ́ in Cuba.[16] Unlike the other African traditionalist ẹgbẹ́ across Cuba's provinces, María Rodríguez Sánchez's Egbè Fermina Gómez ati Echu-Dina is headed by five ìyánífá (including her daughter Yadira Flamand Rodríguez) rather than a community (or titled council) of male babaláwo.

Gendered and Sexual Philosophies of Polarity

Although significantly smaller in number than the initiation of African traditionalist babaláwo, the initiation of ìyánífá in Cuba has expanded significantly over the last decade. By 2016, for example, the African traditionalist babaláwo Enrique Orozco Rubio had initiated fifty-four women as Ìyánífá, or slightly less than one-third the total number of babaláwo he has initiated into Nigerian-style Ifá (Martínez Betancourt and Orozco Rubio 2016). In Cuba, the initiation of ìyánífá has expanded along with African traditionalism itself, with ìyánífá practicing in the Cuban provinces of Havana, Matanzas, Ciego de Ávila, Holguín, and Santiago de Cuba (Machado Tineo 2013).

In Nigerian-style Ifá-Òrìṣà, babaláwo and ìyánífá alike frame the initiation of women into the Ifá priesthood as "the emancipation of women" and as a corrective to the "lacunas" evident in Regla de Ocha-Ifá, particularly as these relate to philosophies toward female participation in Ifá (Orozco Rubio 2015a). One such lacuna, according to practitioners of Nigerian-style Ifá-Òrìṣà, is the interpretation accorded to references to the "wife or wives of

Orunmila" (in Cuba, also known as "Orula") in the Ifá corpus (Beliso-De Jesús 2015a, 821; D. Brown 2003, 145–46; Machado Tineo 2013). In Cuban-style Ifá, babalaos interpret the references to the wife/wives of Orunmila as—in practical terms—"wives of the Babalawo or priest of Ifá" (Machado Tineo 2013, my translation). Called the *apetebí ayanfá* in Cuba, this "highest" ritual ranking for women designates that a woman is "forever bound to the Babalao" while ascribing her "the position of server" within rituals and ceremonies (Beliso-De Jesús 2015a, 820–21). As a ritual "server," the apetebí ayanfá in Cuban-style Ifá "is in charge of organizing all domestic ritual activities such as serving food for the feast tables as well as cleaning, cooking, and plucking the hens for the sacrifice" (821). As Beliso-De Jesús notes, the ACYC defends this circumscribed role of women as apetebí ayanfá—in other words, as domestic "servers"—as a "privileged" and "celebrated" position. In the ACYC's public declaration against ìyánífá in 2004, for example, the ACYC stated: "Orula granted woman with the role of server of Ifá, and when we say server, we mean it in the best sense of the word, because we give women the utmost consideration and respect, not only within the religion but also as a worker, wife, mother, and principal educator of our children" (820–21). In Cuban-style Ifá, in other words, the highest consecration that a woman receives is apetebí ayanfá, or domestic server. As such, women are denied epistemic access to the study of the odù Ifá and the actionable capacity to wield Ifá's instruments of divination.

In Nigerian-style Ifá-Òrìṣà, references to the "wife or wives of Orunmila" in the Ifá corpus are interpreted instead as ìyánífá, "mother who has Ifá" or "mother in the work of Ifá" (Oládémọ 2022, 23) (also termed "Iyá Onífá," the "mother of Ifá," or *iyalawo*, "mother of secrets," in other Yorùbá revivalist movements throughout the Americas) (Clarke 2004; Machado Tineo 2013; Murrell 2010, 120, 122).[17] Following the gender norms surrounding female initiation into Ifá in Yorùbáland, ìyánífá in Cuba are initiated into Ifá and permitted to use Ifá's sacred instruments of divination. These include the *ọpẹlẹ* (called *ókuele* in Cuba) (Holbraad 2012, 149), a divining chain of "eight half seed shells" (Bascom 1969a, 3; Beliso-De Jesús 2015b, 203). In certain—though not all—ẹgbẹ́, ìyánífá are additionally permitted to utilize the sacred *ikin Ifá*, or palm nuts, the principal implements of Ifá divination.[18] Additionally, ìyánífá study the sacred odù of the Ifá corpus and are allowed to "sacrifice four-legged animals," both of which form "strict prohibitions" in Regla de Ocha-Ifá (Beliso-De Jesús 2015b, 203).[19] As Machado Tineo (2013) notes, these discrepancies in the interpretation of references to the "wife" of Ọrúnmìlà/Orula in the Ifá corpus constitute the "cornerstone" of the contentious ìyánífá debate between Cuban-style Regla de Ocha-Ifá and Nigerian-style Ifá-Òrìṣà.

These discrepancies translate, in relative terms, into a "minimum power (as apetebí) or maximum (as Iyanifá)" regarding the usage of the divining implements of Ifá ritual and the oversight of divination ceremonies (Machado Tineo 2013, my translation).

Despite the significant ritual, conceptual, and actionable differences in divination between the designations of apetebí ayanfá and ìyánífá, African traditionalist men continually emphasize that the category of ìyánífá is not equivalent to that of a babaláwo. "Ìyánífá is not a woman babaláwo," African traditionalist babaláwo often state (Orozco Rubio, interview, June 23, 2015). Significantly, ìyánífá lack access to the òrìṣà Odù, the reproductive mechanism that allows babaláwo to initiate other babaláwo and to build descent-based ritual lineages, a transnational point of contention that erupted with the scandal surrounding ìyánífá Dr. Patri D'Haifa in the early 2000s (Abímbọlá 1997, 87; Beliso-De Jesús 2015a, 818). If an ìyánífá, such as the female rector Dulce María Rodríguez Sánchez in Holguín, wishes to initiate a babaláwo into her temple and build her own ritual lineage, she must call on another African traditionalist babaláwo to oversee the consecration and preside over the crucial òrìṣà Odù (which women are prohibited from seeing) (Rodríguez Portuondo 2016).

In justifying the exclusion of female access to the reproductive òrìṣà Odù, African traditionalist babaláwo point to a Yorùbá traditional philosophy of polarity that undergirds a gendered and sexual construction of equilibrium of opposites—male and female—as central to spiritual and community well-being. As Orozco Rubio outlines, in the initiation of a babaláwo or an ìyánífá, the initiate reencounters their respective gender-opposite "sensibility" through a spiritual marriage to the female òrìṣà Odù (in the case of the male babaláwo) or to the male òrìṣà Ọ̀rúnmìlà/Ifá (in the case of the female ìyánífá). The consecration of a babaláwo or ìyánífá thus reestablishes "spiritual equilibrium" through the heterosexual, spiritual marriage with the equivalent gender-opposite òrìṣà: Odù or Ifá/Ọ̀rúnmìlà.[20] Since women are already born with the "capacity" to sexually reproduce and bear children, they are excluded from access to—or even seeing—the reproductive òrìṣà Odù. Male babaláwo, however, are given access to the òrìṣà Odù as a means to reproduce through the "birth" of ritual children, providing them with the power to initiate others and build their own ritual lineages.[21] Needless to say, the hetero- and cisnormative gendered pairing of babaláwo-òrìṣà Odù and ìyánífá-Ifá/ Ọ̀rúnmìlà presumes ontological, binary gender stability, wrought cosmologically as an unbreachable, (cis)gendered "stasis" (Spencer 2015, xix) whose latent male-female spiritual disequilibrium is ritualistically canceled through the act of initiation. This cisgendered and heterosexual marriage between babaláwo-òrìṣà Odù and ìyánífá-Ifá/Ọ̀rúnmìlà through the act of initiation is also mobilized to justify the exclusion of homosexual men and women from the high spiritual ranks of ìyánífá and babaláwo.[22] Many African traditionalists frame "gays" and "lesbians" as representing a "philosophical contradiction" with respect to this heterosexual spiritual marriage, negating the possibility for their participation in the foundational rites of initiation (Orozco Rubio, interview, July 25, 2015).

The debate concerning homosexual initiation into Ifá—for women and men—is however, a point of contention among African traditionalists. During the ìyánífá debate of 2004, African traditionalist members of Ifá Ìranlówo responded to the ACYC's outcry concerning female initiation into Ifá by "accus[ing] the Cuban-style priests of an 'even worse' crime than initiating women: initiating 'undercover effeminate foreigners,' or homosexual male tourists, for money" (Beliso-De Jesús 2015a, 823). During many of my conversations in Cuba, African traditionalist women and men reiterated this purported sexual point of difference from Cuban-style Ifá, pointing to what they frame as the hypocrisy of Cuban-style babalaos who decry the initiation of women yet are more than willing to initiate foreign "effeminate" men for payment. Such beliefs concerning sexuality and Ifá among African traditionalists point to homosexuality as a foundational taboo in Cuban Ifá priesthoods. That said, individual views concerning the ban on homosexual initiates among African traditionalists diverge, reflecting the heterogeneity of the individual beliefs (and sexualities) of practitioners themselves. Other babaláwo and ìyánífá, for example, pointed out to me in our conversations that it is impossible to know a client's sexuality prior to initiation—what one does in bed, so to speak—and therefore equally impossible to claim a ban on non-heterosexual babalaos/babaláwo in Ifá. Furthermore, several noted the open (if, for many, uncomfortable) secret in Cuba that a number of Cuban-style babalaos are known to have had homosexual relationships with other men, at times openly, without being stripped of their ritual authority or legitimacy. Cuban-style *santero* and academic Tomás Fernández Robaina, for example, wrote of this phenomenon in the 1990s: "Of course there cannot be a rule without an exception. Despite the fact that Regla de Ifá [the Ifá priesthood] is so insistent upon prohibiting homosexuals from becoming *babalaos* . . . some *babalaos* are known to be homosexual. How can this be? Quite simply they were initiated when they were too young to have acquired a sexual orientation, so that as they grew up and became homosexual they were able to retain their role of *babalao*, regardless of criticism and rejection by conservatives" (Fernández Robaina 1996, 206, in Conner and Sparks 2004). Orozco Rubio adds another explanation to the acceptance of babalaos known to engage in male-to-male sex despite the purported homosexual ban in Cuba. In one of our conversations, Orozco Rubio tellingly stated that he knows of Cuban babalaos who are openly known to be gay or have sexual relationships with men yet who "are the most *guapos*, the most babalaos, the most gangster-ish [*mafiosos*], if you know what I mean" (Orozco Rubio, interview, July 25, 2015). Here, Orozco Rubio correlates being the "most babalao" in Cuba not with being heterosexual, per se, but rather with embodying tropes of masculinity tied to *guapería*, a Cuban archetype of masculinity that embodies the tough, aggressive, or brave, in other words, being a man who is bold, even vulgar, and ever-ready for a fight (Fernández 2010; Lundgren 2013, 17).[23] Saying that he personally knows of homosexual babalaos who are "the most guapos," Orozco Rubio uses the Cuban Spanish adjective *guapo* to reference an archetype of masculinity tied to "cocky, gutsy, rough behavior" (Lundgren 2013, 17),[24] also correlating guapería with the ideal, and archetypal, Cuban babalao. As Orozco Rubio points out, homosexual babalaos who exhibit the characteristics of hypermasculinity associated with guapería are known to practice openly in Cuba without lost legitimacy. As such, the issue governing whether a babalao who engages in known homosexual acts can practice Ifá openly is rooted less in his sexuality per se but rather in what Orozco Rubio frames as the individual's "conduct," in other words, their public-facing gender expression. Mobilizing the archetype of the hypereffeminate, gay *loca*, or "screaming queen" (Morad 2014, xv) as guapería's antithesis and as an example of a sexually inflected gender presentation prohibited among Cuban babalaos, Orozco Rubio states: "What denotes a gay [individual] who is babalao and a gay [individual] who is not babalao is conduct. There may be gays [*sic*] who are very histrionic, and you note [their sexuality] by their gestures . . . but, I imagine, there are a ton of [homosexual men] who are babalaos. And what happens is that [given] the conduct they must have in front of society, and what is expected of them socially, they comport themselves a different way. But they are as gay as the others" (Orozco Rubio, interview, July 25, 2015).[25] Here, Orozco Rubio notes that one's ability to openly practice Ifá as a babalao in Cuba is tied not to one's heterosexuality, strictly speaking, but rather to whether a man presents as guapo, denoting a specific Cuban ideal of "tough" masculinity. The discursive controversy surrounding homosexual initiations in Ifá, in other words, is grounded more deeply in public displays of effeminacy than in private—or even openly known—sexual acts with other men.

In Cuba, this dynamic in Ifá reflects a broader historical tendency toward heightened societal acceptance of what are construed as "masculine" versus "effeminate" men who have sex with men, a dynamic itself intimately tied to colonially inflected, patriarchal ascriptions of the differential role and power of women and men in postcolonial American societies. As Moshe Morad (2014, 17) notes in his study of sexuality during Cuba's Special Period in the 1990s, "masculine" and, by extension, "'active'/'top' homosexuals" have historically been placed in opposition to their sexual counterparts in the public imaginary: namely, effeminate (and, by assumption, "bottom" or sexually penetrated) men. Morad states, "[perceived] masculine 'active'/'top' homosexuals (penetrators) are not stigmatized in the way [perceived] sexually passive (penetrated) homosexual men are, who, in the Latino understanding, take the role of women both in their social behavior and in bed" (17). Reflecting the relative nonstigmatization of masculine-presenting and presumably "active/top" homosexual men in Cuba, Morad also states that "occasional male-to-male sex was not necessarily seen as a threat to normal heterosexual relations and family life, whereas leading a public life as gay was seen as a threat" (Morad 2014, 18, citing C. Hamilton 2012, 153). Public "gay" identities—specifically, in this case, gendered presentations of homosexual effeminacy—have historically been stigmatized in comparison with those of "masculine" and "active/top" men who have sex with men, who are also able to lead (and enjoy) the societal benefits of heteronormative public life.

These Cuban attitudes toward male sexuality inflect and inform debates surrounding the initiation of "homosexual" (read: effeminate) men in Ifá, who are rebuked differentially from their masculine-presenting peers who nonetheless also engage in sex with men. Additionally, Orozco Rubio underscores that Ifá has chosen, through divinatory revelation and on innumerable occasions, to allow these "homosexual" men to "pass" or "go through," in other words, to become initiated in Ifá: "You can see the face of a person in an initiation but not their preferences or their feelings. So you [the client] can feel homosexually [sic], yet when you arrive in front of Ifá, Ifá permits you to pass. He knows why he permits you. We human beings can't see this" (Orozco Rubio, interview, July 25, 2015). Here, Orozco Rubio underscores both the inability of babaláwo or ìyánífá to definitively discern a given person's sexuality prior to initiation and, secondly, the indisputable historical acceptance by the òrìṣà Ifá of homosexual male initiates into the Ifá priesthood through revelatory divination. This acceptance by the òrìṣà Ifá, whose knowledge goes beyond the human ability to "see," has led to the entrance and open acceptance of known babalaos who have sex with men in Cuba despite the purported foundational taboo against homosexuality.

Despite this acknowledgment, Orozco Rubio and other African traditionalists nonetheless insist that initiating known homosexual men as babaláwo or homosexual women as ìyánífá presents a "philosophical contradiction" regarding the underlying rites of initiation, and Orozco Rubio personally refuses to do so. Likewise, I didn't meet a single African traditionalist babaláwo or ìyánífá who admitted to knowingly initiating or participating in the initiation of a known homosexual woman or man into the Ifá priestess- and priesthoods, despite claims that they know of Cuban-style babalaos who have done so. Perspectives on the initiation of homosexual practitioners in Ifá among ìyánífá and babaláwo, however, vary. A prominent ìyánífá, for example, insisted to me that the discrimination against homosexual individuals in Cuban Ifá mirrors the discrimination against the initiation of women as ìyánífá in Cuban-style Ifá. For her, this discrimination reflects broader trends toward male-instigated misogyny and patriarchy in Regla de Ocha-Ifá. "We aren't condemned in heaven, we are condemned by men," she stated in refer- ence, first, to ìyánífá, before continuing: "[People say], 'homosexuals can't be initiated into Ifá.' Who said this? In what odù is it? Why reprimand a man who the heavens sent through his sign to be consecrated into the cult of Ifá? And because of their sexual orientation, we're going to suppress this?"[26] This same ìyánífá also stated that she would gladly participate in the initiation of a homosexual woman or man into Ifá if Ọ̀rúnmìlà dictated this was destined for them in their odù, which, of course, would require the presence of a baba- láwo to access the reproductive òrìṣà Odù.

In Yorùbáland, meanwhile, prominent Nigerian babaláwo also reference the odù Ifá as the ultimate authority on any given individual's right to Ifá priesthood/priesthesshood initiations, although the interpretation of whether or not homosexual men or women should be initiated into the Ifá priesthoods varies considerably. The esteemed babaláwo and scholar Wándé Abímbọ́lá, for example, the designated "messenger and ambassador of the Yoruba re- ligion for the world" (Àwíṣẹ Awo Ní Àgbáyé) (Konen 2013), notably draws on the odù to promote homosexual tolerance and inclusivity in regard to Ifá initiations. As Tony Van Der Meer (2017, 155) outlines, Abímbọ́lá responded to a conference paper addressing gay rights in Ifá at the World Òrìṣà Con- gress at the University of Ilẹ̀ Ifẹ́ in 2013 by emphasizing the "principles of good character" as key to one's merit as a potential initiate into Ifá. Following the statement, Abímbọ́lá began chanting the well-known song "Eni a rere," drawn from the odù Ifá (see chapter 2):

Eni a rere la n wa o	We are looking for a few good people
Eni a rere la n pe	We are only looking for a few good people
Eji Ogbe gba wa se	Eji Ogbe bless this person
Gba wa se o	
Eni a rere la n wa o	We are looking for a few good people
	(Van Der Meer 2017, 155–56)

After singing, Abímbọ́lá then "expressed that if gay people have good character, or ìwà pẹ̀lẹ́, then perhaps there may be something others could learn from them," drawing applause from the audience (Van Der Meer 2017, 156). Dating to at least the 1990s, Abímbọ́lá has "insisted that sexuality is a personal issue that is irrelevant to Ifá initiation, and one should not pry into the personal life or sexuality of an initiate" (Villepastour 2015a, 144, referencing Abímbọ́lá 1997, 28). Speaking to Ivor Miller on the Cuban taboo against the initiation of homosexual men in Ifá, for example, Abímbọ́lá (1997, 28) also stated, "A babaláwo must not impose his way of life on anyone. Who are we to probe the personal life of another person?"

The esteemed Nigerian babaláwo's views on homosexuality, though significant given his official position as the global spokesperson for YTR, diverge significantly from other prominent Nigerian babaláwo who have influenced the development of African traditionalism in Cuba. The babaláwo Ṣọlágbadé Pópóọlá, for example, espouses "that the practice of a gay lifestyle is not acceptable to mankind" and "views non-heterosexual sex as a perversion," a category to which he also includes "oral sex, cybersex, and phone sex" (Van Der Meer 2017, 155–56).

Amid these discrepant logics informing homosexual initiation into Ifá among prominent Nigerian babaláwo and globally minded YTR messengers, African traditionalists in Cuba have notably mobilized the sexual logics of priesthood and priesshood initiations as they developed historically in Regla de Ocha-Ifá. Specifically, African traditionalists maintain a division between òrìṣà priesthoods as inclusive of openly homosexual priests and priestesses and Ifá as purportedly exclusive of them. In Cuba, this division in Regla de Ocha-Ifá relates to the historical divergence of Ifá and oricha ritual as increasingly separate, yet intertwined, ritual fields (D. Brown 2003). In adapting YTR to the island, African traditionalists have mobilized this sexual division between Ifá- and oricha-centric ritual fields, introducing novel, Yorùbá-inspired òrìṣà priesthoods inclusive of openly homosexual women and men and Ifá priesthoods that deny them initiation, ultimately mirroring the logics of Cuban-style Regla de Ocha-Ifá.

This maintenance of the sexual boundaries of Regla de Ocha-Ifá in Ifá and òrìṣà initiations continues despite African traditionalists' awareness of other YTR ritual communities, particularly in the United States, who openly initiate gay babalaos.[27] Additionally, the sexual prohibition against homosexual Ifá initiates remains despite other significant ruptures in Nigerian-style Ifá-Òrìṣà, particularly in terms of gender. As Orozco Rubio states in reference to homosexual Ifá initiations: "We've broken all the other taboos: the taboo of women in Ifá, the taboo of women in *el tambor* [consecrated batá performance].... We're the 'taboo-breakers'" (Orozco Rubio, interview, July 25, 2015). For Orozco Rubio, this particular taboo remains "because of the finality of the [initiation] rite," which presents, for him, "a contradiction." In terms of òrìṣà initiations, however, Orozco Rubio and other babaláwo and ìyánífá openly acknowledge, and even celebrate, the presence of homosexual òrìṣà initiates in their ẹgbẹ́. Orozco Rubio states, "I have ahijados that are homosexuals... of very good human quality and very good people," who are also "very good religious [practitioners]," a sentiment I heard from others as well. These openly homosexual òrìṣà priestesses and priests can receive "*mano de Orula* [an initial, nonpriesthood Ifá initiation] and participate in all of the Ifá rituals, except those that have to do with initiation," Orozco Rubio clarifies, "the secret part of Ifá." At the annual Letter of the Year ceremony discussed later in this chapter, openly gay òrìṣà priests (including priests of the newly introduced, Yorùbá-inspired Egúngún òrìṣà priesthood [see chapter 5]), participated in the collective Ifá divination ritual, which did not involve initiations.

The exclusion of openly homosexual women and men from the Ifá priesthood purportedly persists in Nigerian-style Ifá because of a central logic of heterosexual, cisnormative gendered polarity between ìyánífá and babaláwo, as previously discussed. This polarity operates as central logic key to Ifá initiation rites, ritual success, and, more broadly, Yorùbá-inspired philosophies of community health and gendered equilibrium, also operating as an exclusionary mechanism for homosexual women and men. For African traditionalists, the symbolic marriage between babaláwo-òrìṣà Odù and ìyánífá-Ifá/Ọ̀rúnmìlà in initiation rites is additionally said to represent but one facet of the "law of polarity" informing Yorùbá traditional philosophy (Orozco Rubio, interview, July 25, 2015).[28] In Ifá, the universe is conceived as encompassing a constant, dynamic "equilibrium between two opposing poles": for example, "the negative and the positive," "day and night," "cold and heat," "the world of the living and the world of the ancestors" (Orozco Rubio, interview, July 25, 2015). Orozco Rubio frames this law of polarity as a "dynamic equilibrium" represented, for example, by the opposition between Olódùmarè and the òrìṣà Èṣù. As he outlines, Olódùmarè, or the "Supreme Being" and "apex of the Yorùbá pantheon" (Abimbola 2005, 51), represents the force of creation, while Èṣù, the neutral, policing "trickster God" (51), represents the "principle of opposition" that "stands against" the force of creation (Orozco Rubio, interview, July 25, 2015). As Abímbọ́lá and Orozco Rubio note, Èṣù is a "neutral entity" (Abimbola 2005, 58) that constitutes "the principle not of destruction or malignancy, but of opposition" (Orozco Rubio, interview, July 25, 2015). As Deji Ayegboyin and George Jegede (2009) elaborate, the dynamic equilibrium between Olódùmarè and Èṣù that informs the law of polarity finds its correlate in the neutral Yorùbá conception of the dynamic interplay between *ire* (good) and *ibi* (evil), or "the two major forces that control the universe." In Yorùbá traditional philosophy, ire and ibi are conceived as informing and constituting one another, as demonstrated in the phrase "ibi nini ire, ire ninu ibi" (evil is in what is good and good is an evil) (Ayegboyin and Jegede 2009). The centrality of Èṣù to òrìṣà worship and Ifá in Yorùbáland and its diaspora likely owes its prominence (Falola 2013), in part, to the òrìṣà's capacity to "open doors" and "spiritual pathways" by constituting "the energy that travels constantly between these two values": "the negative and the positive" (Orozco Rubio, interview, July 25, 2015). In Cuban Regla de Ocha-Ifá the "law of polarity" finds its correlate in the conception of *iré* (positive energy) and *osogbo* (negative energy), which Santera Marta Moreno Vega (2000) likens to the dual nature of the orichas and the "elements of nature they represent" as both "life-giving" and "destructive."

In Nigerian-style Ifá-Òrìṣà, the "law of polarity of the universe" as engendered through gendered equilibrium between male and female—and, by extension, masculine and feminine energy—constitutes a cornerstone of Ifá philosophy and ritual practice.[29] For Orozco Rubio and other African traditionalists, the restoration of the role of ìyánífá in accordance with the gender norms of contemporary Yorùbáland marks the rebalancing of gendered equilibrium in Nigerian-style Ifá-Òrìṣà, an equilibrium ostensibly lost during the transformation of the Yorùbá religion in colonial- and early republican-era Cuba. For African traditionalists, the reinstatement of the traditional female gender roles of ìyánífá as well as the study and worship of central òrìṣà of the Yorùbá pantheon ostensibly lost in Cuba (such as the òrìṣà and cult of Ìyámi Òṣòròngà)[30] serves as a corrective to (dis)equilibrium in the gendered formulations of Regla de Ocha-Ifá. As Castro Figueroa (2012) notes, Cuban Regla de Ocha-Ifá indeed favored the development of rituals and rites related to "protection and divination" during and after the transatlantic slave trade, deemphasizing those related to rites of fertility and maternity. And Orozco Rubio elaborates: in Yorùbáland "women are the center of equilibrium of the society," and "unlike our society . . . the adoration of the principle of motherhood is vital" (Orozco Rubio, interview, June 23, 2015). In a broad sense, the initiation of (cisgendered, heterosexual) women into the Ifá priesthood is framed as restoring community health and well-being by enhancing the dynamic interplay of male-female polarity and thus enriching gendered spiritual equilibrium. On an individual level, meanwhile, the introduction of ìyánífá into the landscape of Cuban Ifá is framed as restoring women's "right to know and rectify their destiny" through Ifá practice and divination.[31]

Beliso-De Jesús (2015b, 208) notes in her ethnography in Matanzas in the 2000s, however, that discourses of female emancipation in Nigerian-style Ifá-Òrìṣà depict Nigerian-style Ifá as "seemingly more gender egalitarian" than Cuban-style Ifá but "not necessarily feminist." In the "Iyanifa debate" of 2004, for example, members of the Ifá Ìranlówo lineage framed "feminist impulses" such as those represented by the US American ìyánífá Patri D'Haifa, who claimed to have "initiated the first openly gay Babaláwo" (Ifá Foundation International 2014), as "imperialist feminisms" (Beliso-De Jesús 2015b, 204). Beliso-De Jesús (2015b, 204, 209) writes: "Perceived extensions of Western (read white American) imperialisms, feminist impulses have been diagnosed within African diaspora assemblages as co-opting and distorting diasporic traditionality. . . . This invoking of a rhetoric against American exceptionalism orders (neo)liberal, modern, and democratic feminists and gays to the realm of the global imperialist Other—the United States." While African traditionalists outside of the Ifá Ìranlówo lineage with whom Beliso-De Jesús conducted her fieldwork do frame their gendered interventions in Nigerian-style Ifá-Òrìṣà as explicitly feminist (e.g., Nagybe Madariaga Pouymiró, see chapter 3), the rhetoric surrounding ìyánífá in Cuba overwhelmingly values these priestesses in a purportedly African "traditional" sense, for example, emphasizing their capacity to bear children and to be good wives and mothers. Orozco Rubio, for example, likens the role of the babaláwo and the ìyánífá within an ẹgbẹ́ to that of a "mother and father," each with a specific and noninterchangeable role. He states, "It is necessary that both [the babaláwo and ìyánífá] are together in order to procreate, and it is necessary that they are together in order to consti-tute a family."[32] This metaphor of a heteronormative, cisgendered coupling of male and female as the basis for the biological family extends here to the baba-láwo and ìyánífá as the basis for the creation of ritual family and community well-being. In so doing, Orozco Rubio's formulation depicts homosexual indi-viduals as "philosophical contradiction[s]" located outside of the purview of the highest priesthood rankings of Ifá. Additionally, such formulations frame "imperialist feminisms" such as those represented by the American D'Haifa's claim of female access to the reproductive òrìṣà Odù in the United States or to the initiation of an openly gay babalao as disruptive of Yorùbá traditionality (Beliso-De Jesús 2015b, 204) and, specifically, disruptive of the male-female polarity necessary for gendered equilibrium and community health.

The rhetoric of female "emancipation" in Nigerian-style Ifá-Òrìṣà addi-tionally fuels larger discourses surrounding Ifá's "universal" character (Orozco Rubio, interview, June 24, 2015; Gómez Rodríguez, interview; Otto William Sabina de León, interview by the author, Morón, May 18, 2016). Tropes of universalism in Nigerian-style Ifá-Òrìṣà, for example, serve to promote racial inclusivity among ẹgbẹ́ members and normalize non-Black leadership while simultaneously eliding the sexual exclusion of homosexual, queer, trans, and gender-nonconforming individuals from the Ifá priest- and priestesshoods. Overwhelmingly, African traditionalist ẹgbẹ́ in Cuba promote ideologies of racial universalism that effectively disarticulate "true" Africanity (and African traditionality) from Blackness and ancestral African heritage. Such ideologies of racial universalism in Nigerian-style Ifá are also deeply imbricated with claims of gendered inclusivity, an assertion that belies the circumscribed gender and sexual roles accorded to the exclusively heterosexual, cisgender men and women initiated into the babaláwo and ìyánífá priesthoods. Discourses of gendered egalitarianism in Nigerian-style Ifá likewise frame African traditionalism as the emancipatory antidote to Cuban Regla de Ocha-Ifá, which is framed as "*machista* and ignorant" (García Basulto 2016). As the Olúwo of the Aworeni Temple of Havana, Erick Gómez Rodríguez succinctly states: "Ifá is for everyone" (Gómez Rodríguez, interview). Despite the ostensible universality of Ifá, however, Nigerian-style Ifá-Òrìṣà exhibits highly circumscribed gender and sexual roles predicated, in part, upon purported Yorùbá philosophical edicts of heterosexual, cisgender male-female polarity. More centrally, these edicts in Nigerian-style Ifá-Òrìṣà build on the preexisting sexual and gendered boundaries of Regla de Ocha-Ifá in Cuba as it historically developed on the island.

Here, I turn to an annual Letra del Año divination ceremony at the Ẹgbẹ́ Irán Átele Ilogbon Odugbemi in Santiago de Cuba as a means to examine the relationship between ìyánífá and ontological constructions of female personhood, potency, and power in Ifá. I point to how the role played by ìyánífá in Nigerian-style Ifá ritual ceremonies underscores the centrality of philosophies of male-female polarity and dynamic gendered and sexual equilibrium in Nigerian-style Ifá. Through an analysis of the efficacy of sound in a Letra del Año ceremony, I explore how discourses and practices surrounding sound and listening posit specific aspects of the sonic as imbuing the Letra del Año ceremony with àṣẹ, or the necessary capacity to effect change, enhance community well-being, and "rectify destiny" (Gómez Rodríguez, interview). Specifically, I interrogate the importance accorded to the female voice—and to the incantation of the Yorùbá language by ìyánífá—as exemplary of the Yorùbá-inspired philosophical and ritual tenets of gendered polarity and equilibrium.

Ìyánífá and the Voice

On Saturday, June 27, 2015, the Ẹgbẹ́ Irán Átele Ilogbon Odugbemi held its annual Letter of the Year divination ceremony in Santiago de Cuba, led by

the temple's founder and leader, babaláwo Enrique Orozco Rubio. In line with
the Yorùbá religious calendar, which holds the annual Yorùbá Letra del Año
ceremony in the summer in Nigeria, members of Orozco Rubio's ẹgbẹ́ celebrated the ceremony in June rather than in January (as is the custom in Regla
de Ocha-Ifá) to mark the beginning of the Yorùbá calendar and new year.
The annual Letter of the Year ceremony forms a foundational yearly ritual
that culminates in the prognostication—via the revelation of an odù—of the
potential blessings and perils to be faced by the community and its individual
members over the course of the coming year. The daylong ceremony begins
before 6:00 a.m. and lasts until slightly after 4:00 p.m. in the afternoon, encompassing a sequence of preparations, divination rituals (using the various
implements of Ifá, including the ọpẹlẹ, divining chain, and the ikin palm tree
nuts), plant and animal sacrifices, and *obras* (works). The ceremony provides
a set of forecasts and guidelines that "allow us to minimize the impact of
[the] negative," such as potential dangers and obstacles, and "maximize the
positive" over the course of the coming year.[33] On this hot summer Saturday, approximately forty of Orozco Rubio's *ahijados* from Santiago de Cuba
as well as other surrounding eastern provinces, including the city of Baracoa
in the province of Guantánamo, gathered at the temple for the yearly ritual.
The temple is located at the home of ìyánífá Caridad Fonseca Rubio, Orozco
Rubio's mother, also one of the first women authorized to play a set of consecrated batá in Cuba (chapter 3). Attendees included ìyánífá, babaláwo, and
lower-ranked initiates dressed in Afrocentric, Yorùbá-inspired ritual dress,
all of whom brought their individual sets of sacred ikin to be ritually washed
as part of the yearly Ifá ritual and festival.

The washing of the ikin Ifá in a ritual herbal bath known as *omi ẹrọ*
(*omiero* in Lucumí) forms one of the central acts of the annual Letter of the
Year ceremony.[34] The omi ẹrọ, or "water of softening," consists of a bath
of *ewé*, or herbs and plants, used within rituals and consecrations to placate
"the malign influences that afflict" (Matory 2005, 130) and to release "secret
ingredients" that serve specific ends (Orozco Rubio, interview, July 23, 2015).
As J. Lorand Matory notes, the term *omi ẹrọ* makes evident a Yorùbá "logic
of pacification" that, rather than viewing malignant forces as presences to be
eliminated, aims for the neutralization of forces that will continue to "coexist"
with an individual. As Wándé Abímbọ́lá explained to Matory in 1999: "No,
you don't drive things off. They would just come back. You soften or placate them so you can coexist" (Matory 2005, 130). This logic reflects the Yorùbá philosophy of dynamic equilibrium between opposites—polarities—as
the basis for "the processes of health and life in all of the universe" (Orozco
Rubio, interview, June 24, 2015). In the case of the omi ẹrọ, a carefully

selected assortment of herbs and plants, each of which holds "a determined spiritual power" (Orozco Rubio, interview, July 23, 2015), is carefully prepared throughout the ceremony. The preparation of the omi èrò culminates when the bath is joined with animal sacrificial blood, which charges it with its potency as "cool, or cooling water" (Brandon 1983, 295).

The preparation of the omi èrò begins before the ceremony, when the sixteen herbs and plants to be used in the ritual bath are laid on a mat in the patio of the temple.[35] Each *ewé Ifá*, or "herb of Ifá," is carefully selected and carries a ritual potency of specific utilization for the bath of the sacred ikin. The *rinrin* plant, for example (*renren* in Nigeria, *Peperomia pellucida*), is a plant with "great mystic powers" used to "assuage the fire of the negative things we have in our destiny" (Orozco Rubio, interview, July 23, 2015; Wiart 2006, 43).[36] The Pèrègún plant (*Dracaena fragrans*, or cornstalk dracaena), on the other hand, confers the "spiritual powers to fight" and to face "difficult" situations in life (Orozco Rubio, interview, July 23, 2015).

The ceremony formally opens with the *mojuba*, or an introductory prayer of "homage" and "greeting" to the òrìṣà and ancestors (Smith 2016, 82; Oló-gundúdú 2009).[37] A babaláwo begins the ceremony by kneeling before the sixteen herbs and plants displayed on the mat (figs. 4.1 and 4.2). To his left and right, babaláwo shake the *àdá òrìṣà*, or a multifunctional, metal bell knife. On one side, the àdá òrìṣà resonates when shaken, while on the other, it curves into a functional, cutting edge. This sonorous knife is at once an instrument and an implement, used in ritual to "achieve the energy" necessary through sonorous resonance and as a functional tool used as a knife during ritual sacri-fice.[38] As the babaláwo shake the àdá òrìṣà, animating and energizing the baba-láwo's prayers, the kneeling babaláwo intones the opening mojuba prayer, using melodic cadences familiar to mojuba recitation in Regla de Ocha-Ifá (Audio Example 5: Excerpt of opening incantation).[39] The mode of incantation of the verses at the boundary point of spoken word and ritual song underscores what Bode Omojola frames as the Yorùbá language's frequent utility "as a recitative," in other words, as a "mode of discourse [that] operates in the interstice between speech and song," a dynamic also audible in Cuban Lucumí (Omojola 2011, 85). Speaking to the power of praise recitatives in invoking the manifesting power of the òrìṣà in Yorùbáland, Omojola notes that "the attributes of [the òrìṣà] . . . are most vividly and powerfully expressed" through oríkì, or praise poetry recita-tives (85). Omojola elaborates, "Oriki is more than just a performance. It is also an action-laden rendition that spurs spirits and deities into action" (86).[40] In YTR ritual, *oríkì* (praise poetry) and *orin* (song) form a continuum of nature-imbued, linguistic manifesting force, one in which Yorùbá language vocaliza-tions are perceived as imbued with the capacious power to inspire action.

FIGURES 4.1 and 4.2. Babaláwos prepare herbs and plants for the *omi ẹ̀rọ̀*. Annual Letra del Año ceremony, Ẹgbé Irán Átele Ilogbon Odugbemi, Santiago de Cuba, June 2015. Photo by the author.

After the recitative mojuba, the ceremony begins with the babaláwo ritually preparing the plants and herbs, consecrating them with rum and vital substances before placing them in a large, clay bowl filled with water. As the babaláwo place the sixteen plants in the bowl, they rip them open, releasing and "spilling" the secret ingredients of the ewé into the water while singing a contemporary Yorùbá praise song:

Bí mo dúró, bí mo wúre	If I am standing while I pray
Ire tèmi kà ẏ̀àì gba	It allows my prayers to be accepted (by Olódùmarè)
Bí mo jòkó, bí mo wúre	If I am seated while I pray
Ire tèmi kà ẏ̀àì gba [sic]	It allows my prayers to be accepted (by Olódùmarè)[41]

As Orozco Rubio explains, this verse of the odù culminates in an invocation: "Even when I am lying down, and I no longer have strength, may what I ask and invoke have the capacity to manifest" (Orozco Rubio, interview, July 23, 2015).

Orozco Rubio and his ahijados learned this contemporary Yorùbá song from a pirated, digitally circulated copy of a book published by the US-based, Nigerian ìyánífá Chief FAMA (FAMA Àìná Adéwálé-Somadhi, b. 1953), a highly influential and hemispherically minded YTR missionary-entrepreneur. Born in 1953 in the village of Emùré Ilé (Ondó state, Nigeria), Chief FAMA Àìná Adéwálé-Somadhi has carved out a space as an authority on Ifá divination and òrìṣà worship as practiced in her birthplace of Yorùbáland, transforming since the 1990s into a successful, globally oriented YTR entrepreneur and prolific author. After studying Ifá for several years in the 1980s, Chief FAMA initiated as ìyánífá in Nigeria in 1988 (Adéwálé-Somadhi 2006a). Two years later, Chief FAMA immigrated to the United States, where she established herself as "one of the best-known leaders of the [Ifá-Òrìṣà] religion in Southern California," as journalist David Olson (2008), of the *Monterey Herald*, describes. In San Bernardino, California, Chief FAMA founded an import business for West African ritual materials, Ilé Ọ̀rúnmìlà Afrikan Imports, in conjunction with her husband, babaláwo Ifábọ̀wálé Sohma Somadhi.[42] While running the imports business, Chief FAMA also pursued a career publishing internationally distributed, multilingual books and newsletters dedicated to YTR through a sister company, Ilé Ọ̀rúnmìlà Communications.[43]

Chief FAMA's English-, Yorùbá-, and Spanish-language publications bridge the heterogeneous linguistic terrain of Ifá divination and òrìṣà worship between Nigeria, the United States, and the Hispanophone Américas. With over two dozen books to her name, Chief FAMA's publications include *Fundamentals of the Yorùbá Religion: Adoring Òrìṣà* (2006); *Reflections on the Wisdom of Ifá* (2009); two Yorùbá-English dictionaries focused on òrìṣà language (*FAMA's Èdè Awo: Òrìṣà Yorùbá Dictionary*, 2001, and *Ogbho Dictionary*, 2015), and three Spanish-language translations of her English-language texts (*Manual para el Profesional que Práctica Ifá*, 2006; *Dieciséis Historias Mitológicas de Ifá*, 2008; *Reflexiones Sobre la Sabiduria de Ifa*, 2010). Through the promotion of West African materiality, Yorùbá language praise poetry and songs, and step-by-step instructions for ritual, Chief FAMA joins a growing number of globally minded Ifá-Òrìṣà entrepreneurs who find—and cultivate—an emerging market for Yorùbá-English and Yorùbá-Spanish ritual publications and West African materials for Hispanophone and Anglophone practitioners.

Notably, Chief FAMA's Spanish-language ritual text, *Manual para el Profesional que Práctica Ifá* (Adéwálé-Somadhi 2006b), or *Practical Manual for Ifa Professionals* (its original, English-language title, Adéwálé-Somadhi 2020), includes a chapter specifically dedicated to the preparation of the omi ẹ̀rọ̀ for "wash[ing] the Ikin Ifá during the Ifá anniversary" (2020, 281). With line-by-line instructions for the ewé Ifá to be placed in the bath, a specific sequence of ritual steps and explanations of their significance, and translated, Yorùbá language songs for Ifá and the òrìṣà (including Òsányin, Ọ̀ṣun, Èṣù, and Olódùmarè), the book provides an invaluable resource for African traditionalists in Cuba and across the Spanish-speaking Americas for preparing the omi ẹ̀rọ̀ for the "Ifá anniversary." Instructed by informal audio recordings from Chief FAMA (also passed hand-to-hand through flash drives), African traditionalists in Cuba "work" the actionable, circulating ritual knowledge of contemporary YTR provided by the Nigerian ìyánífá and chief.

Orozco Rubio's pirated, digital text copy of Chief FAMA's *Manual* also notably diverges in significant ways from the ìyánífá's original Yorùbá-Spanish book (see Adéwálé-Somadhi 2006b), pointing to the complexities of translative acts that empower practitioners to harness contemporary YTR approaches to ritual in Cuba. The digital text document that Orozo Rubio shared with me, for example, is renamed "preparacion del omiero [*sic*]" (or "preparation of the *omiero*," in Spanish and Lucumí) and exhibits prominent—and unmarked—additions and discrepancies. These include alterations of Yorùbá-Spanish translations; the addition of Spanish-language phrases and supplemental information (including the scientific names of Yorùbá language plant names, or phytonyms, to aid with plant identification); significant formatting, font, and orthographic discrepancies; and, idiosyncratically, the excision of a final prayer to ikin Ifá meant exclusively for a "trained Babaláwo" rather than "a novice" or "a student of Ifá," as Chief FAMA instructs (see Adéwálé-Somadhi 2020, 388). Across the digital document, the text also displays spelling and diacritics highly inconsistent with Chief FAMA's original book and, in many cases, with Standard Yorùbá itself (e.g., the use of ß and ÿ as replacements for the Yorùbá consonant ṣ or ê as a replacement for

the vowel ẹ). The multiplicity of fonts and font sizes (YorubaOK for Yorùbá and Lucumí; Arial for Spanish) for the languages represented likewise
reveal a palimpsest-like nature to the text, suggesting the likelihood of extensive copy-and-paste (and additive) procedures.[44] Together, these divergences
point to the complex and often anonymous translative acts attendant to the
circulations of such digital text documents across the YTR ritual diaspora.[45]
Additionally, these divergences point to the fractured—and yet generative—
processes through which African traditionalists gain access to and employ
contemporary Yorùbá praise poetry and songs in Nigerian-style ceremonies.

In the Letter of the Year ceremony, Orozco Rubio and other babaláwo
and ìyánífá mobilize Chief FAMA's publication—via the pirated book chapter—as a crucial YTR resource for heightening the manifesting power of the
ritual during the preparation of the omi èrọ̀ and the washing of the ikin Ifá.
Throughout, they highlight the essential link between the voice, the Yorùbá
language, and potent, magic-infused plant materiality in the preparation of
the omi èrọ̀, underscoring the centrality of the efficacy of sound to the
manifesting force of the ceremony. As Orozco Rubio notes, the recitation of
the sacred verses of the odù and the contractions of the verses that constitute
Ifá's repertoire of songs are so crucial to Ifá that "without the word and invocation, there can be no ritual" (Orozco Rubio, interview, June 23, 2015). He
states, "[Even with] the most refined tureens [soperas] in the world, the best
stones, the best snails [caracoles] . . . the biggest and most beautiful animals,"
if participants were to "cover their mouths" the fate-transforming capacity
of the ritual would be negated. The voice in Ifá ritual animates the natural
elements used in ceremonies (e.g., water, plants, and other ingredients) with
àṣẹ, the generative potency and power of transformation. This link between
voice, materiality, and actionability predicates the fate-changing efficacy of
natural elements and material objects on incantation, which communicates
to the rituals' listeners—the òrìṣà—the actions and aims of participants. As
babaláwo "spill out" the ingredients of the ewé for the omi èrọ̀ bath during
the Letter of the Year, babaláwo and ìyánífá animate their actions with Yorùbá
language song, "extolling the power of the leaves" and "projecting, through the
incantations, the spiritual power of the leaves in order to use them in [their]
favor" (Orozco Rubio, interview, July 23, 2015). This simultaneity of word and
action imbues the material with manifesting capacity and communicates intentionality to òrìṣà listeners.[46]

While crouched around the clay bowl of the omi èrọ̀, the babaláwo
crush and wring the plants and herbs in the water as Orozco Rubio leads
the ẹgbẹ́ in a call-and-response of the odù's contracted Yorùbá language
song. Following the instructions and song texts outlined by Chief FAMA

(Adéwálé-Somadhi 2006b, 205–7), Orozco Rubio unites action, incantation, and intentionality:

Leader:	Êrún, êrún	Squeeze, squeeze
Chorus:	O o, êrún	Yes, squeeze
Leader:	Érún j'ogbó	Wringing will bring us good health
Chorus:	O o, êrún	Yes, squeeze
Leader:	Êrún j'atö	Wringing will bring us a long life
Chorus:	O o, êrún …	Yes, squeeze …
Leader:	Êrún ÿ'àÿeyôrí	Wringing will bring us a world of success
Chorus:	O o, êrún …	Yes, squeeze …
Leader:	Êrún n'iré gbogbo [sic]	Wringing will bring us all of the ire[47]

Orozco Rubio and other African traditionalists discursively frame the incantation of the verses and songs of Ifá in the contemporary Yorùbá language as the most "pure" means of communication with the òrìṣà (González Ramírez, interview). This notion of the purity of the Yorùbá language draws from a YTR philosophical conception of the relation between the tonal qualities of the Yorùbá language and the sonority of nature. As Orozco Rubio elaborates, "The Yorùbá language emerges, according to these models of belief, from the onomatopoeic sounds produced by the different elements of nature" (Orozco Rubio, interview, June 23, 2015). As such, "it is said that this sacred language, already perfected as a language, is the mother tongue [la lengua matriz] that allows man to communicate directly with nature through sounds and intentionality" (Orozco Rubio, interview, June 23, 2015). This emphasis on "pure" communication with the elements of nature resonates with writings on the relationship between the òrìṣà and nature in Yorùbá traditional and philosophical thought (Karade 1994; Vega 2000). Described by McKenzie as a "nature religion" (McKenzie 1997, 556), YTR and its correlates in the diaspora frame the òrìṣà/oricha alternatively as "aspect[s] of nature's energy" or as representations of "the infinite elements in nature: water, earth, wind, fire, trees, flowers and animals" (Vega 2000, 14). The ontological slippage between òrìṣà as a manifestation of nature itself (e.g., the ocean, thunder, or a tsunami), as "an aspect of nature's energy" (Vega 2000, 14), or as a "natural law" governing the manifestation of nature conveys, in multitudinous ways, the centrality of "the study of nature" to Yorùbá traditional philosophy and thought.[48] Elaborating on the connection between the Yorùbá language, nature, and the òrìṣà, Orozco Rubio continues: "Speaking Yorùbá, with adequate pronunciation, with correct timbre, with correct tones … is the only form you have to guarantee a spiritual connection of force directly with the òrìṣà" (Orozco Rubio, interview, June 23, 2015).[49]

Following "Êrun," the babaláwo continue to wring and squeeze the herbs and plants in the clay pot with their hands as Orozco Rubio leads the ẹgbẹ́ in a series of songs dedicated to Òsányin, the òrìṣà of "herbal medicines" (Whalman 2001, 148). The Yorùbá songs reference Òsányin's dominion over "the healing properties of leaves and herbs," which, within YTR, hold the capacity to offer practitioners "relief from physical suffering" (Bay 2008, 30). Significantly, a number of songs to Òsányin at this point in the ceremony mirror Lucumí correlates common in Regla de Ocha-Ifá, reflecting an effort by certain babaláwo such as Victor Betancourt Estrada to "restore," "decipher," and "correct" the verses and songs of the Cuban Regla de Ocha-Ifá tradition, in certain cases through their translation into contemporary Yorùbá.[50] These songs unite action and word as the babaláwo animate the wringing of the plants and herbs with descriptions for listening humans and òrìṣà: "Mo yùn ewé mo saa rawó / Ewé lò ya omí [sic]," "I cut the leaves and rub them with both hands / I tear the leaves up in the water."[51] As members of the ẹgbẹ́ follow Orozco Rubio's call-and-response, Orozco Rubio speeds up his singing, transitioning quickly between over a dozen distinct verses and choruses dedicated to Òsányin. In so doing, Orozco Rubio tests the ẹgbẹ́ members' dominion and agility in transitioning between songs. "Ewé, ewé òrìṣà, ewé o dára, Òsányin ewé [sic]," he calls out. "The leaves, the leaves of the òrìṣà, the leaves are good, the leaves of Òsányin." Bridging the entrance into the next song with an accelerating pickup note at the ending of the previous chorus, Orozco Rubio speeds into the next verse: "Òsányin a wá ni ilé o, Òsányin a wá ni ilé o / Gbogbo ewé iré nbò wá [sic]," "Òsányin, come to my house / all of the blessings of the herbs are also coming."

Once Orozco Rubio and members of the ẹgbẹ́ cycle through the *cantos* to Òsányin, the ìyánífá of the temple, including Caridad Rubio Fonseca and Noerlinda Burgal Hechevarría, replace the babaláwo at the clay pot, rubbing and crushing the herbs and plants together in the water with their hands. At this point in the ceremony, the venerated batá player Buenaventura Bell Morales and other percussionists that Orozco Rubio has hired for the ceremony accompany the singing with *tumbadoras* and *chékere*,[52] using rhythms inspired by the ritual *toques* of the Cuban *güiro* ensemble.[53] As the ìyánífá take over the wringing of the herbs and plants, Orozco Rubio intones a two-bar, asymmetric *clave* common in ritual toques to the oricha in Cuban Regla de Ocha-Ifá on the *güataca* (metal hoe blade), guiding the other percussionists and singers as he begins a call-and-response. In it, he references the presence of the ìyánífá in this moment of preparation of the omi èrò: "Tobinrin lèrò / Ba wa gbo / Tobinrin lèrò / ki o ba wa gbo [sic]." Orozco Rubio offers the meaning of this chorus as follows: "There can be many men in this place, but

FIGURE 4.3. Ìyánífá prepare to wring and crush the herbs and plants of the omi èrò. Annual Letra del Año ceremony, Ẹgbé Irán Átele Ilogbon Odugbemi, Santiago de Cuba, June 2015. Photo by the author.

if there isn't a single woman, èrò won't manifest" (Orozco Rubio, interview, July 23, 2015).[54] Èrò (of omi èrò), which Orozco Rubio translates as "the spirit of maternal consolation," "water that gives life," or, alternatively, "water that encloses the mysteries of maternity," holds the power to convert mundane objects into sacred ones through their "impregnation" with "vitality and life." This revitalization and conversion of the mundane into the sacred through its "impregnation" with the vitality of the feminine, "maternal" power of the *omi èrò* forms the first crucial step in preparing an object (in this case, the ikin Ifá) for the moment of animal sacrifice. "Women are the ones who have the power of èrò in an innate, natural way," Orozco Rubio explains, underscoring the necessity of their presence in the preparation of the omi èrò (Audio Example 6: Ìyánífá wring the herbs and plants) (see fig. 4.3).

With the omi èrò sufficiently prepared—and in balance—through the wringing and crushing of the herbs and plants by both male babaláwo and female ìyánífá, the washing of the ikin Ifá of each individual ẹgbé member begins. Orozco Rubio calls out variations on songs for Ọ̀rúnmìlà, returning to the instructions and ritual texts contained within his digital copy of Chief FAMA's *Manual* (Adéwálé-Somadhi 2006b, 2020). The chorus responds, "Ṣùṣù o, Aládé mà mí wẹ, ṣùṣù o" (*Ṣùṣù o*, the King is taking his bath, *Ṣùṣù o*).[55] After one run-through, Orozco Rubio again intones the clave on the güataca as the chékere and tumbadora players fall into rhythm. The gathered ìyánífá and babaláwo audibly shake their ìróké and àdá òrìṣà as the ẹgbé follows his calls with the response, "*Ṣùṣù o*, the King is taking his bath,

Ṣùṣù o." Two ìyánífá sit before two divided pots containing the omi ẹ̀rọ̀ as two babaláwo slowly pass each of them a small gourd bowl (*jícara*), filled with the ikin of an individual member. Giving the ikin their "bath," the ìyánífá dip the jícaras in the omi ẹ̀rọ̀ one by one, bathing them with their hands in the sacred, herb-filled water before returning each gourd bowl to the attending babaláwo. Orozco Rubio cycles through the verses and choruses, individu-ally naming the sixteen *méjì*, or principal odù (Ojú Odù Mërìndínlógún), of the Ifá corpus: "Bàbá Èjì Ogbè, King among the Odù Ifá," "Bàbá Oyeku Meji, King among the Odù Ifá," "Bàbá Iwori Meji, King among the Odù Ifá."[56] The babaláwo and ìyánífá respond, "Ṣùṣù o, the King is taking his bath, Ṣùṣù o." Through the dual forces of action and incantation, the ìyánífá animate the omi ẹ̀rọ̀ and revitalize the sacred ikin throughout the course of their ritual bath (Audio Example 7: Ìyánífá give the ikin Ifá their bath).

For members of the ẹgbẹ́, the washing of the ikin by the ìyánífá in the annual Letra del Año ceremony reflects their status as the "wives of Orun-mila" and, therefore, as the best-suited to give the ikin, also termed "Ifá," their baths. Reflecting the hetero- and cisnormative gendered and sexual logics underpinning Nigerian-style Ifá-Òrìṣà, ìyánífá are habitually framed as the best-suited to "touch" the male òrìṣà Ifá. As ìyánífá Yamilka Gámez Oliva explains: "Our elders say that the person who can best attend to a man is a woman. A man doesn't like to be touched a lot. So, it's better that a woman attends to Ifá. 'My Ifá is attended to by my wife.' The Ifá of any babaláwo is going to be attended to by his wife [*mujer*, literally 'woman'], including [in] sacrifice. . . . Ifá is a man; [he] is the voice of Ọ̀rúnmìlà. So the most appropriate person to attend to Ọ̀rúnmìlà is an ìyánífá. Because, also, this woman is consecrated [to Ọ̀rúnmìlà]."[57] Here, Ifá, as a man, "doesn't like to be touched"—specifically, by other men—making a babaláwo's wife, or, even better, an ìyánífá, the most appropriate person to touch, bathe, and handle the ikin Ifá. This gendered and (hetero)sexual logic is reinforced by a latent homophobia—a fear of and disinclination toward men touching and bathing the male òrìṣà—that is ritualistically enforced in the ceremony by the empha-sis on ìyánífá both as innately possessing ẹ̀rọ̀, or the life-giving "mysteries of maternity" crucial to the preparation of the omi ẹ̀rọ̀ itself, and, addition-ally, as the most appropriate to wash the male ikin in the omi ẹ̀rọ̀'s sacred bath. This heterosexual ritualistic pairing of ìyánífá-babaláwo and ìyánífá-Ọ̀rúnmìlà extends to the justification of ìyánífá's exclusion from the female òrìṣà Odù during their, and other babaláwo's, initiations. As Gámez Oliva continues, "This is why [ìyánífá] cannot initiate anyone, because she can't sleep with a woman [i.e., òrìṣà Odù], because [their union does not enable] procreation" (Gámez Oliva, interview).

Conclusion

A year after I attended the Letra del Año ceremony at the Ẹgbẹ́ Irán Átele
Ilogbon Odugbemi in 2015, I returned to Santiago de Cuba to conduct follow-
up research and interviews with members of the ẹgbẹ́ and with the percussionists who had played at this, and other, African traditionalist ceremonies.
One such percussionist was an *olubatá*, son of Changó, and *oriaté*, or "leading
head," of Regla de Ocha in Santiago de Cuba (D. Brown 2003, 152). Although
not a practitioner of Nigerian-style Ifá-Òrìṣà himself, the percussionist participated on occasion as a hired *akpwón* to sing cantos to *eggún*, or the dead,
at African traditionalist egúngún ceremonies for Orozco Rubio's ẹgbẹ́ (see
chapter 5). After reviewing several videos of egúngún ceremonies with him,
I pulled up videos of the Letra del Año ceremony in order to clarify a few
questions I had concerning percussion, including one of the ìyánífá washing
the sacred ikin in the omi ẹ̀rọ̀. Abruptly, he asked his wife, whom he had
invited to sit in on the interview with us, to leave the room. Once she left,
he turned to me and politely explained that, although his wife is initiated in
Regla de Ocha as *hija de Yemayá*, or a child of the oricha Yemayá, he did not
want her to witness the images of ìyánífá participating in the Letra del Año
ceremony or handling the sacred ikin—both of which are strictly prohibited
in Regla de Ocha-Ifá. Even though he had directly participated as a hired
percussionist and akpwón in Nigerian-style ceremonies involving ìyánífá
himself, including this one, and knew that I was showing him videos of the
ceremony in that moment, the oriaté nonetheless wished to prevent his wife
from witnessing the images. The immediacy and force of the oriaté's censor-
ing of his wife's access to audiovisual evidence and information surrounding
the role of ìyánífá in Nigerian-style Ifá-Òrìṣà underscores the contentious,
and at times ambiguous and contradictory, divide separating the two domains of òrìṣà/oricha and Ifá worship in Cuba. Additionally, it underscores
the centrality of gender to this divide.

In Nigerian-style Ifá-Òrìṣà, the initiation of women into Ifá as ìyánífá
and their participation in African traditionalist ritual is often framed as the
"emancipation" of Cuban women from the machismo of the Regla de Ocha-
Ifá tradition. Despite such discourses of liberation, however, the role of
ìyánífá within Nigerian-style ritual reflects highly binary gendered philosophies of male-female polarity and balanced gendered and sexual equilibrium
that discursively locate "imperialist feminisms"—including radical, absolute
gendered equality (or, even, gendered binary dissolution) (Spencer 2015) and
homosexuality—as ostensibly falling outside of Nigerian-style Ifá (Beliso-De
Jesús 2015a, 2015b). Nonetheless, ìyánífá now "speak Ifá," wielding command

over Ifá's corpus and dominion over its implements of divination. As evidenced in the annual Letra del Año ceremony, the voice—when intoned in the Yorùbá language, with intentionality, by ìyánífá—serves as central means to animate ritual with the efficacious force of àṣẹ and the capacity to manifest desires and transform fates for individual members and the community at large. As such, Nigerian-style Ifá-Òrìṣà offers ìyánífá, at once, vastly increased access to and dominion over the fate-transformative knowledge and actionable implements of Ifá in relation to Cuban-style Ifá while simultaneously circumscribing these womens' roles within highly hetero- and cisnormative philosophies of gendered polarity and community equilibrium. As such, ìyánífá are valued as mothers and wives, as beings holding the "mysteries of maternity" and the innate "capacity" for (human) reproduction, and as essential gendered counterparts to male babaláwo.

The Efficacy of Pleasure and the Utility of the Close: Regionalism and All-Male *Egúngún* Masquerade

On May 27, 2016, I huddled against the concrete wall of a small, packed foyer in the eastern Cuban city of Baracoa. Shoulder to shoulder with members of the Ẹ̀gbẹ̈ Íran Àtelé Ilôgbôn Baracoa and the ẹgbẹ́'s visiting parent temple from Santiago de Cuba, we waited in eager anticipation for the appearance of the city's first *egúngún* masquerade.[1] The room vibrated with an air of expectancy and suspense as Enrique Orozco Rubio, the parent temple's *Olúwo*, entered the room from an adjoining hallway and warned the crowd that the two masqueraders who would momentarily manifest in the temple were not to be touched. Several charged minutes followed, the relative silence of the thirty-five standing participants punctuated by sporadic hushed voices and low murmurs. Suddenly, Orozco Rubio reentered the foyer and broke into song. He called out a contemporary Yorùbá traditional religion (YTR) praise song: "Fe lé egùn Ojá re, fe lé egùn [*sic*]" (We want the spirits to appear, to cover themselves with Ojá, and to be friendly).[2] As the awaiting crowd echoed the call, Orozco Rubio played a *clave* pattern characteristic of Cuban *bembé* drumming on the *güataca* (metal hoe). Behind him, two *tumbadora* players seated in the far corner of the room began elaborating a *toque* also drawn from the drumming traditions of eastern Cuban bembé, or religious parties for the oricha, with a third percussionist punctuating the polyrhythms with the high-pitched, distinctive sounds of the chékere.[3] Orozco Rubio and the other participants alternated the verse in a call-and-response, building momentum in anticipation of the emergence of the egúngún masqueraders.

As the call and the drumming strengthened in volume and energy, two masked figures, covered head-to-toe in brightly colored, full body masks (*agò egúngún*), emerged from the hallway, dancing in stylized gestures and whirling the vibrant yellows, reds, greens, purples, and golds of their hand-

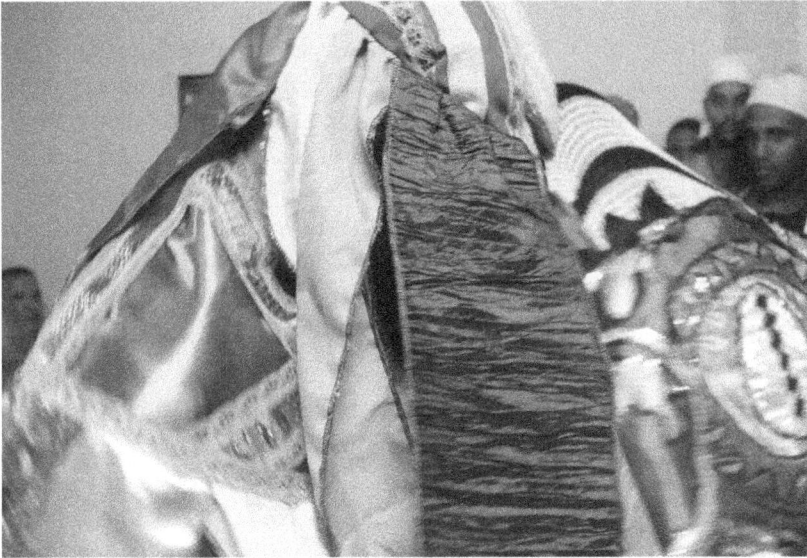

FIGURE 5.1. Cuban-made egúngún masks. Êgbë Íran Àtelé Ilôgbôn Baracoa, Baracoa, 2016. Photo by the author.

tailored, satin-and-sequined suits across the space of the foyer. The faces of the masqueraders were obscured as to be rendered unidentifiable, in one case with a white-and-black mesh netting and, in the other, with a series of dark-red, gold-inlaid cloths. In addition to their faces, all other potentially iden-tifying human features were covered, including the skin of the arms, legs, and feet. As the two egúngún danced in the center of the room, at first with measured gestures and then with increasingly wild and frenetic movements, several babaláwo separated the masqueraders from the crowd by wield-ing brightly colored, wound pàsán egúngún, or egúngún "whipping-canes" (Boscolo 2009, 204). These pàsán egúngún prevented onlookers from acci-dentally touching the egúngún. As the drumming intensified and the sing-ing grew louder, the egúngún began emitting low, guttural noises as they flailed in stylized movements throughout the room, holding palm fronds that swished through the air in sweeping motions. The peculiar, guttural sounds emitting from the mouths of the egúngún transferred an otherworldly, non-human quality to the dancing figures, an aural strangeness that augmented the nonhuman quality of the egúngún's "amorphous" masks and suits (M. Drewal 2003, 124) (see fig. 5.1).

The dancing of the egúngún masqueraders in the Êgbë Íran Àtelé Ilôg-bôn Baracoa marked the first appearance of egúngún, or a "secret society" dedicated to ancestor worship in Yorùbáland (Clark 2007, 85), in the eastern city of Baracoa in Guantánamo province. In Yorùbáland, egúngún constitute "the collective spirits of the ancestors" who watch over the lives of the living and are invoked through masquerade to "protect the community against evil spirits, epidemics, famine, witchcraft, and evildoers" (Babayemi 1980, 1). Egúngún masked figures manifest the reemergence of an individual ancestor "among the living" in a nonfigurative (i.e., nonrepresentative) way (Asante 2009, 231; M. Drewal 2003, 124). As Migene González-Wippler (1994, 83) notes, egúngún masqueraders are "believed to be the materialized spirit, not just a person possessed by the dead." Additionally, an egúngún figure may manifest "the entire spirit of the Egungun," or the collective spirit of the ancestors, in the realm of the living (Asante 2009, 231; Babayemi 1980, 1). In Yorùbáland, the line between individual and collective ancestral manifestation is blurred, and the "Yoruba teach that, in the traditional African religion, we are not individuals, but parts of a coherent, collective legacy that ties all the spirits together in one massive community" (Asante 2009, 233). The egúngún masquerader, as "an autonomous, yet collective, entity" (Boscolo 2009, 194), exemplifies this bridging of the individual and the collective, demonstrating the Yorùbá philosophical conception that life "contains within it manifestations of the ancestral, the living and the unborn," all of which "are vitally within the intimations and affectiveness of life" (Soyinka 1976, 144, in Boscolo 2009, 194).

In Yorùbáland, the egúngún masquerade in public spaces with intricately constructed costumes that inspire fascination, awe, and fear in the community, making explicit the intimate connection between the living and the dead. As Cristina Boscolo (2009, 196) notes, the "varied, richly imaginative" egúngún masks "convey . . . [the] presence and power [of the ancestors] in the life of the living." She further details that "in Yoruba thought, death is not the end of life; when somebody dies, it is only the body, the 'temporal mask', that perishes. The departed become *ará òrun* (denizens of the other world) and possess 'limitless potentialities which . . . [they] can exploit for the benefit or detriment of those who still live on earth.' Making use of these potentialities, the *ará òrun* at times materialize as masquerade: they are *egúngún*, the sacred mask of the ancestors. They invest the performer—wearing the mask—with their particular powers" (192).[4] The egúngún masqueraders manifest the connection between the living and the dead in Yorùbá traditional philosophy, their appearance underscoring the ways in which "*òrun* (the other world) . . . comes to bear tangibly on *ayé* (this world)" (196). Through ará òrun, masqueraders harness and exploit the "limitless potentialities" of the Egúngún, exploiting the potentialities offered by the materialization of the ancestors in this world.

The particularities of the ways in which the first egúngún masquerade manifested in the small, eastern Cuban city of Baracoa underscores the dynamic interplay of heterogeneity, regionalism, and an aesthetics of pleasure on the spread of African traditionalism in Cuba. The intimate ties between the novel, Yorùbá-inspired egúngún society and local ritual music traditions dedicated to worshipping the ancestors in Guantánamo province, including bembé and Espiritismo, points to the ways practitioners adapt contemporary, Yorùbá ancestral traditions according to regional logics of ancestral worship, ritual pleasure, and ritual success. Here, I explore how the adaptation of egúngún masquerade to novel and idiosyncratic Cuban environments underscores, in this case, the imbrication of ritual sound with an efficacy of the close in African traditionalist ritual.

Finally, this chapter highlights the novel transformations wrought in ancestral and òrìṣà worship through Ifá revisionism. African traditionalists notably conceive of egúngún as "an òrìṣà" (òrìṣà Egúngún).[5] This conception resonates with many—though not all—formulations of egúngún in Yorùbáland, where the precise nature of egúngún in relation the òrìṣà and the ancestors varies (see H. Drewal 1978, 18).[6] Nonetheless, egúngún masquerade and its secret society have emerged specifically through—and in tandem with—Nigerian-style Ifá in Cuba. This diverges significantly from the case of Yorùbáland, where egúngún masquerade falls under the historical domain of the Òjè society and not under the domain of Ifá temples or lineages.[7] As I argue here, the emergence of the òrìṣà Egúngún through Nigerian-style Ifá underscores the centrality of the Ifá-centric ritual domain (and male babaláwo) to African traditionalism. Furthermore, the specificities of the emergence of egúngún masquerade in Cuba points to the unique conceptual conjunction of "Ifá-Òrìṣà" ritual practice on the island, a conjunction that enlivens—and yet tellingly inverts—the phrase "Regla de Ocha-Ifá" in Cuba itself. Ultimately, these idiosyncrasies point to the unique adaptation of YTR—including its ancestral and òrìṣà practices—to a profoundly Ifá-centric, revisionist ritual complex on the island.

Aural Empowerment and Strangeness: Egúngún Masquerade

In Yorùbáland, the egúngún secret society dates back centuries to the heart of the Òyó empire, where ancestral masquerade consolidated as a ritual cult with strong political ties from the sixteenth to the eighteenth century (Babayemi 1980; Thabiti Willis 2017).[8] Members of the egúngún society (now commonly termed Òjè) served an integral role in the social, political, and ritual fabric of Òyó, performing crucial—and fearsome—politico-religious functions (Babayemi 1980, 41).[9] The Òjè society and its masquerading egúngún acted as a "political agent" of the Aláàfin (king) of Ọ̀yọ́, for example, "spear heading his wars" during the imperialist expansion of the empire (Babayemi 1980, 29). During the subsequent upheavals of the eighteenth and nineteenth centuries, the egúngún society and ancestral masquerade disseminated across Yorùbáland alongside fleeing residents of Ọ̀yọ́ (30). Across Yorùbáland, the Ọ̀jẹ̀ continued to serve politico-religious functions in the midst of the sociopolitical and religious reconfigurations of Yorùbá society. The local ọba (king) of various Yorùbá towns and communities, for example, would gain the "support of the society in warding off evil spirits" through recourse to the egúngún and the Alágbàá, or "the ritual head of the egúngún cult" (41–42). Through the support of the society of ancestors, the ọba could "claim supernatural power and invincibility" (41–42). As a relatively autonomous political counterforce, however, the Ọ̀jẹ̀ also held the power to "condemn a wicked Ọba of any town" (28), underscoring the imbrication of the ritual power of the ancestors (egúngún), harnessed by the Ọ̀jẹ̀, with Yorùbá political institutions.

Today, egúngún masquerade continues to fall under the domain of egúngún societies and the Ọ̀jẹ̀ (Omosule 2007), even as their explicitly political and military functions have "dwindled" significantly (Babayemi 1980, 45). In the annual egúngún festivals held in various Yorùbá towns, for example, egúngún masquerade continues to underscore the Yorùbá philosophical belief that death is not merely the end of life but rather a "journey" to another realm: "the world of the ancestors" (Asante 2009, 231). In this world, the ancestors continue to intervene in and "take an active interest" in the lives of the living (Eades 1980, 123). As Molefi Kete Asante (2009, 231) notes, the "ancestral spirits . . . can assist the community in carrying out its daily activities" and offer guidance to community members "in their ordinary lives." In this way, when a person dies, the deceased becomes "an òrìṣà to his own family" (Abímbọ́lá 1973, 75; Eades 1980, 123), reflecting the Yorùbá proverb "A kú tán làá dère," or "to die is to become deified" (Afolayan and Pemberton 1996, 25, in Boscolo 2009, 191).[10] The ancestors actively communicate with the living through dreams, spirit possession, divination, or masquerading egúngún (Clark 2007, 84; Thabiti Willis 2017). The ancestors also depend on the living and must be "ritually remembered" in order to continue to "watch over the society" (Asante 2009, 231). As Richards (1994, 7) notes, this "remembrance of the ancestors is vital to the success of human endeavors" and "to ignore them will result in witchcraft, plagues and social dissolution." The egúngún masquerade offers a central form of ritual remembrance through what Boscolo describes as "a fireworks display of colours, dance, music, and poetry" that "materializes" the past and connects "ọ̀run and ayé" (Boscolo 2009, 203). As Margaret Drewal (2003, 121) astutely notes, the Yorùbá words for "visual representation" (àwòrán), spectator (awòran), and spectacle (iran) derive etymologically from the "verb radical ran," itself linked to memory and repetition.[11] The egúngún masquerade, as visual spectacle, both conjures the memory of individual and collective ancestors through performative ritual remembrance and manifests the presence of the ancestors in the lives of the living.

Beyond its potent visuality, the egúngún masquerade depends on sound as a central aspect of both the Egúngún's journey between ọ̀run and ayé and in maintaining the ontology of egúngún as the manifestation—and not figurative representation—of the ancestors. As Boscolo (2009, 208) notes, "The ancestor's journey is an arduous one; the distance between the two worlds is great. Egúngún needs to be empowered and encouraged . . . it is the devotee's attention and care that play the crucial role in empowering the òrìṣà." Karin Barber (1991) echoes Boscolo's assertion, stating, "The power of egungun depends on human action to maintain and restore it. After being kept in store . . . the egungun has become limp and feeble; its powers have to be deliberately restored by human action" (77, in Boscolo 2009, 208–9). Drumming and incantation are crucial human actions in empowering and drawing out the egúngún in their "arduous" journey between ọ̀run and ayé (Boscolo 2009, 208). In Yorùbáland, bàtá and dùndún drummers are an "indispensable requisite of egúngún display" (218) and crucial to the revitalization of the Egúngún. During the ọdun egúngún, or egúngún festivals, in Yorùbáland, for example, bàtá drumming "announces the imminent arrival" of the egúngún as they emerge from the interior of homes and into public space, the masqueraders manifesting only once the bàtá drumming reaches a sufficiently powerful level of volume, momentum, and "crescendo" (208).[12] In Cuba, Orozco Rubio echoes this assertion by noting that the tambores (drums) are used to "attract" the Egúngún, who, once they have emerged, danced, and "enjoyed themselves" to the accompaniment of the tambores, walk around and converse with members of the community as the tambores stop playing. "When they are at peace, everything stops," he says, "that's key."[13]

In addition to the centrality of bàtá and dùndún drumming in revitalizing the egúngún in their journey between ọ̀run and ayé, the invocation of oríkì through both vocalization and drummed speech surrogacy forms a crucial aspect of the empowerment and manifestation of the egúngún in Yorùbáland. As Boscolo (2009, 209) states, "Whether interpreted by women's voices or by bàtá drummers, the performance of oríkì is an essential part of the process of empowerment." Barber elaborates:

It is not the *oríkì* by themselves but the process of attributing them, the action of uttering them and directing them at the subject that is effectual. The longer you will go on, the more effectual it will be. . . . *Oríkì* performance . . . is not just a matter of piling up prestigious and reputation-enhancing encomia. It actually affects changes of state. . . . The spiritual world is translated into the human world, brought in and localized . . . [enacting] an intensification of the powers of the spiritual beings. It is by being invoked, called upon that the *òrìṣà* or *egúngún* attains its most concentrated beings. (Barber 1991, 78, in Boscolo 2009, 209)

Notably, in Yorùbáland women are centrally responsible for the empowerment of the egúngún as they emerge into the world of the living and for the manifestation of an egúngún's "most concentrated beings." Women chant oríkì that praise the ancestors and recount "salient moments in the history of the family" as the egúngún emerge from the interior spaces of homes (Boscolo 2009, 208). The central role of women in empowering the egúngún through invocation of the oríkì counterposes—and, in a sense, defies—the purported male exclusivity of the egúngún secret society (208), which "like [the] *Oro* [cult], emphasises the separation between men and women" and prohibits women from wearing or even touching the egúngún masks (Eades 1980, 123).[14] In addition to female invocation of the oríkì through vocalization, male drummers empower the egúngún by "speaking" the oríkì through drummed speech surrogacy on the bàtá and dùndún. In so doing, male drummers in Yorùbáland echo the Yorùbá proverb "onílú ẹni abọwọgbede bí ofe," or "it is one's drummer whose hand can render the most fluent praise about one" (Boscolo 2009, 208).

In addition to its prominence as a site of empowerment for the egúngún, ritual sound serves as a central domain for enacting a sense of aural strangeness that maintains the ontology of the egúngún as the physical, nonfigurative manifestation of the ancestors. This sense of the strange maintains the underlying "secret" of the human wearer of the egúngún mask during the masquerade (Boscolo 2009, 196). The "nonhuman qualities" of the egúngún are communicated through the visuality of the masks, the bodily gestures of the Egúngún's dance, and the fear associated with touching the manifested ancestors, among other factors (M. Drewal 2003). The egúngún "wear amorphous cloth forms conceived and sewn in ways to obscure or to alter human features, carry dangerous medicines on their person that prohibit outsiders and the uninitiated from touching them out of fear of sickness or death, and perform highly stylized dances" that communicate a separation of the status of the masked ancestor from that of the living (M. Drewal 2003). In addition to the otherworldly visuality of the egúngún mask, the egúngún masquerader emits a "low," "grumbling," "hoarse," or guttural voice that obscures the identity of the human wearer (Asante 2009, 231; Clark 2007, 84; Thabiti Willis 2017, 12). The guttural, "unrecognizable" utterances give the egúngún a "strange and unknown" quality that underscores the fact that the Egúngún, "as an ancestral relative does not have the voice of someone living in the village" (Asante 2009, 231; Thabiti Willis 2017, 12). "When an Egungun speaks," Mary Ann Clark (2007, 84–85) notes, "it is believed to be the voice of the dead ancestor that listeners hear." Through aural estrangement, the egúngún masquerader grounds its ontology as a nonfigurative ancestor manifested in the world of the living, one with fate-transformative potentiality and the ability to intervene in the life of the community.

Egúngún Masquerade in Eastern Cuba

As the egúngún masquerade in Guantánamo province intensified, the two masked figures whirled throughout the room with increasing speed, swishing the palm fronds they held in their covered, gloved hands throughout the air as a surrounding circle of babaláwo enclosed them with brightly colored, cloth-wrapped pàsán egúngún, attempting to shield the crowd from the masqueraders. Provoking and animating the egúngún dancers with intensifying volume and speed, the two *tumbadora* percussionists elaborated a single and ongoing bembé rhythm drawn from local "religious parties" in 12/8 time.[15] Together, the drummers constructed the repeated rhythmic figure by weaving a polyrhythmic texture on the deeper-pitched *tumbador* and the midregister *seis por ocho*, building momentum and energy in tune with the dancers' movements by alternately punctuating the ostinato with extended and consecutive sixteenth-note runs. As the momentum and volume of the rhythm built in line with the increasingly frenetic movements of the whirling figures, Orozco Rubio alternated the called choruses of the songs in rapid succession, offering vocalized praise to the manifested ancestors. Discursively linking the palm fronds (*màrìwò*) to the Egúngún's capacity to "carry away" those "troublesome" elements that may "disturb the peace of the community" (Asante 2009, 231; Babayemi 1980),[16] Orozco Rubio invoked the power of the agò egúngún (the egúngún dress or mask)[17] and the màrìwò to "bring good things and ward off the bad." He calls out, "Màrìwò re rè eee [sic]," "the palm fronds thrash about to bring good things and ward off the bad." The chorus responds, "agò n re rè [sic]," or "the agò thrashes about to attract good things and ward off the bad."[18] The invocation links voice, word, and actionability, manifesting the power of the whirling, thrashing movements of the agò egúngún and the màrìwò to bring good and ward off bad fortune as the

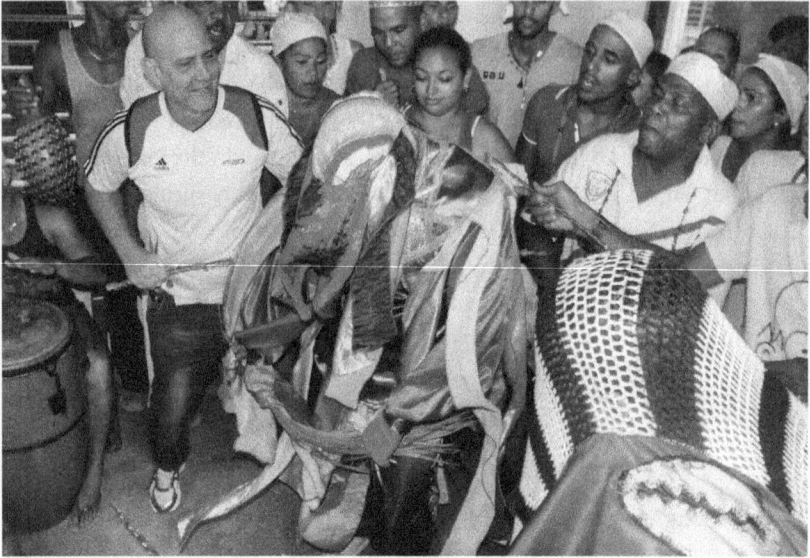

FIGURE 5.2. Babaláwos separate the crowd from the masquerading egúngún with pàsán egúngún ("whipping canes"). Êgbë Íran Àtelé Ilôgbôn Baracoa, Baracoa, 2016. Photo by the author.

egúngún masqueraders dance and toss around with increasingly rapid movements in the center of the foyer. Meanwhile, the call-and-response continues: "Màrìwò tu yà ri yà ri yà [sic]," "the palm fronds come undone and open the path." Orozco Rubio alternates the call with "Agò n tu yà ri yà ri yà [sic]," "the cloths of the egúngún dress come undone and open the path" (Audio Example 8: Egúngún masquerade in Baracoa) (see fig. 5.2).

After several minutes, the egúngún figures gradually recede toward the back of the room, making their way to the adjoining hallway before disappearing from view. As they leave, the drumming and singing continue at a fever pitch. At this point in the ceremony, the ritual crosses more explicitly from egúngún masquerade into local, eastern Cuban traditions of *Espiritismo cruzado*, or mediumship. Suddenly, a young doctor in his midtwenties who is known as a spirit medium of Espiritismo in Baracoa falls into trance. His eyes close and his lips puff outward as he draws his arms in front of his face, crossing them as he stumbles backward and forward in jerked, erratic motions. Shortly after, another young man, also well-known as a local Espiritismo medium, falls into trance behind him, exhibiting what Wirtz (2014, 57) describes as the "puffed out cheeks," "pursed lips," and other "unusual and exaggerated facial expressions [that] are distinctive markers of possession trance" in Cuba. The fitful motions and exaggerated expressions of the two Espiritismo mediums echo a similar sense of estrangement from the status of the living that the egúngún earlier exhibited, though with gestures, movements, and vocalizations characteristic of specifically Cuban ritual modalities of spirit possession (e.g., in Regla de Ocha or Espiritismo cruzado).[19] With their faces and arms exposed, the Espiritismo mediums manifest a sense of the nonhuman through gestures and motions that draw attention to the ways "in which the spirits of the dead . . . must operate human bodies they are alien to" (57). After several minutes, the two mediums are carefully led outside of the space of the foyer and into the back rooms of the home, directed on by the gentle guidance of several members of the crowd. As the drumming and singing stop, the participants burst into cheers and applause, lauding the resounding success of the first egúngún masquerade.

In witnessing the first egúngún masquerade in Cuba's easternmost city of Baracoa, I am struck by the ways in which members of the Êgbë Íran Àtelé Ilôgbôn Baracoa and the surrounding community incorporate key sonic, visual, and sartorial elements of Yorùbá egúngún masquerade while adapting the manifestation of the egúngún ancestors to specifically eastern Cuban modalities of ancestor worship, including those of bembé, *muerterismo,* and Espiritismo cruzado (see Bodenheimer 2015; Dodson 2008; Millet 1999; Warden 2006). Hailed as the *tierra de muertéras* (the land of the dead ones) (Dodson 2008, 128), eastern Cuba, or Oriente, holds a rich history of ritual traditions rooted in cultivating the active relationship between the living and the dead. As Santiago de Cuba researcher José Millet emphasizes, "muerterismo," or "sacred rituals honoring dead ancestors," encompassed the most widely practiced ritual practices in eastern Cuba before the arrival of Santería and Palo from western Cuba in the early twentieth century (Millet 2000, 110–11, in Bodenheimer 2015). In colonial Oriente, large celebratory events known as bembés were held that "invoked ancestral and other spirits to visit the world of the gathered descendants" (Dodson 2008, 86).

In the nineteenth century, the Espiritismo ritual movement also gained wide traction in Oriente (Bodenheimer 2015; Bolívar, González, and del Río [2007] 2013; Dodson 2008). As Diana Espírito Santo (2015, 14) describes in her rich ethnography of Espiritismo in Cuba, Espiritismo emerged "at the crossroads of a number of cosmologies of the person, including nineteenth-century European, Asian, Christian, and West African." Practiced across Cuba and the broader Hispanophone Caribbean, Espiritismo utilizes mediumship to communicate with the dead (*muertos*) and other spirits. In Cuba, specifically, Espiritismo first emerged in Oriente before traveling westward to Havana and other parts of western Cuba (Bodenheimer 2015). Now, multiple variants of Espiritismo, including Espiritismo cruzado, *Espiritismo de cordón, Espiritismo de mesa,* and *Espiritismo de Caridad* are practiced throughout Cuba, though with notable regional variations (Dodson 2008, 126–27). Espiritismo cruzado, or "crossed" or "mixed" Espiritismo, forms one of the most popular variants in Cuba and combines elements from Palo, Regla de Ocha, and "Cuban folk Catholicism" (Dodson 2008, 127; Santo 2015). *Cajón al muerto* ceremonies in Havana and Matanzas, for example, incorporate rhythms and songs from African-inspired Palo ritual and form one of the most popular expressions of Espiritismo cruzado in western Cuba. Drawing on the influences of Christianity and African-inspired ritual, these ceremonies proceed from Spanish-language "Catholic plegarias" to songs "sung in *bozal*, an Africanized form of Spanish associated with slaves and mixed with Bantu words" (Dodson 2008, 127).

In Baracoa, specifically, Espiritismo cruzado and Espiritismo de cordón form two of the most prominent ritual practices of the small eastern city, reflecting but one facet of the rich historical importance of ancestor worship in Guantánamo province and the larger eastern region.

As Baracoan art historian and Alágbàá Egúngún (egúngún "priest") Rosendo Romero Suárez notes,[20] the widespread popularity of Espiritismo cruzado and Espiritismo de cordón in Baracoa has only recently been challenged by the spread of Protestant Christianity, which is gaining notable traction in the small city (Romero Suárez, interview). The recent arrival of egúngún masquerade in Baracoa, then, marks only the most recent manifestation of ancestor worship within a rich and variegated history of spiritual practices aimed at cultivating the relationship with the dead.

Notably, the egúngún masquerade was held in the home of Francisco "Pancho" Reyes Sollet, the rector of the newly formed Êgbë Íran Àtelé Ilôgbôn Baracoa and the son of one of Baracoa's most prominent *espiritistas*, or mediums. The egúngún masquerade culminated a three-day ceremony marking the foundation of the first African traditionalist ẹgbẹ́ in Baracoa, Êgbë Íran Àtelé Ilôgbôn Baracoa, and the initiation of five babaláwo, including Reyes Sollet. As the culminating event in the foundation of the African traditionalist temple, the masquerade inaugurated the official arrival of Nigerian-style Ifá-Òrìṣà and its specific forms of ancestor worship in the small eastern city.

Baracoa, which means the "existence of the sea" in Arawak, is Cuba's easternmost city and its first colonial establishment (Scarpaci 2006, 84). Columbus is believed to have landed in Baracoa when he first traveled to Cuba, and the island's first governor, Velázquez de Cuéllar, made the "large Indian town" the island's first capital in 1511 (Corzo 2003, 35; Humboldt 2011). Between 1511 and 1521, eastern Cuba became the "springboard" for the conquest of Mexico and also a center for the indigenous slave trade, "first [with slaves] from the

Lucayas (the Bahamas) and parts of Florida" (Zeuske 2007, 122). Between 1518 and 1530, the African slave trade began in Cuba, with the first slaves imported "directly from the Cape Verde islands, São Tomé, or from the Kongo region to Santiago de Cuba [and] Baracoa" along with other sites in central and western Cuba (122). In subsequent years, Baracoa declined steeply in prominence, remaining relatively isolated from the rest of the island. It wasn't until 1964 that a paved highway (La Farola) was built linking the small city to Santiago de Cuba and the rest of the country (Scarpaci 2006, 84). For centuries, maritime (and, subsequently, air) travel were the principal means of arriving at the relatively isolated "corner of the island" (84). Now a "tourist pole," the city of some 100,000 residents "serves as a springboard to pristine forests and beaches . . . [and its] mountain slopes form part of the UNESCO biosphere that house unique flora and fauna" (84).

For members of the Ẹ̀gbẹ́ Ìran Àtẹ́lẹ́ Ilôgbôn Baracoa and its egúngún society, Baracoa's unique history—including its strong precolonial indigenous populations, its status as the first site of European conquest, and its early history of indigenous and African slaving—makes the city a particularly rich site for ancestral worship. "Baracoa has great spiritual potency," the ẹgbẹ́'s rector, Reyes Sollet, repeatedly told me.[21] "When you come to Baracoa," Alágbàá Egúngún Romero Suárez echoed, "you feel an energy that vibrates and that is distinct; you don't feel it in any other place in Cuba" (Romero Suárez, interview). The Alágbàá Egúngún Ricardo "Buzzy" Pérez, elaborated, stating, "Baracoa is very rich in the tradition of the ancestors. Baracoa was one of the first settlements of our Taíno ancestors, the original natives of this area. It was the first settlement discovered by Columbus; it was the first founded villa, the first Spanish settlement on the island. It was the capital for almost three years."[22] When people die, he notes, "this ancestral legacy gets rooted . . . [and] washed down into the earth." Within the widespread practice of Espiritismo in Baracoa, Romero Suárez adds that "it is rare to find anyone in Baracoa who doesn't have an indigenous person [of Baracoan origin] in his *cordón espiritual* ['spiritual cord' or 'spiritual lineage']" (Romero Suárez, interview). Pérez adds that, with the establishment of the African traditionalist temple and the egúngún society in Baracoa, "our African ancestors come to take part [here], in Baracoa" (Pérez, interview).

The use of tumbadoras and rhythmic toques drawn from local Espiritismo cruzado and bembé traditions marks the adaptation of the first egúngún masquerade to specifically Baracoan modalities of ancestor worship. Following the ceremony, Baracoan practitioners described the single, repetitive rhythmic toque played on the tumbadoras during the duration of the egúngún

Clave bembé

EXAMPLE 4. *Clave bembé*. Transcription by the author.

masquerade as that used in bembés and Espiritismo cruzado ceremonies in eastern Cuba, referencing an array of rituals dedicated to the orichas and/or honoring the dead.

Terminologically, the use of the term *bembé* by Alágbàá Egúngún to refer to ceremonies for the oricha and Espiritismo cruzado in Baracoa points to the broad usage of the term to reference varied, and often "crossed," African-inspired ritual traditions in eastern Cuba. Whereas in western Cuba the term is often used synonymously with *toque de santo* or *tambor* in Regla de Ocha, in other words, with "any ritual drumming ceremony for the orisha" (Schweitzer 2013, 209), Alágbàá Egúngún consistently used the term *bembé* in Baracoa to reference a wide array of ceremonies honoring the ancestors, including and beyond those tied specifically to Regla de Ocha.[23]

During the egúngún masquerade in Baracoa, the clave pattern played by Orozco Rubio was the same as that played in western Cuban bembés for the oricha (see Warden 2006, fig. 4, 57). This *clave bembé*, also known as the seis por ocho clave (or six eight clave) in Havana and western Cuba, constitutes a "standard" bell pattern or timeline found widely across West Africa, including in Ewe music in Ghana (Agawu 2003, 157) and in the *wóòròò* (*konkolo*) rhythm of Yorùbá traditional music (Dada 2015, 33).[24] As Kofi Agawu (2003, 157) relates, this standard bell pattern "has a latent off-beat feel and an extensive anacrusis [unaccented pickup note] that confers on it a strong, forward-pointing dynamic" (see ex. 4).

Employing this forward-propulsive pattern, the tumbadora percussionists, each local players from Baracoa, inflected their own rhythmic sensibilities into the performance, drawing powerfully on local traditions of Espiritismo cruzado. The interlocking rhythm on the tumbadoras and the repetitiveness of a single toque over the entirety of the egúngún masquerade further elicited the "highly repetitive nature" of Palo drumming, which, as Bodenheimer (2015, 105) notes, is also characteristic of the cajón al muerto ceremonies associated with Espiritismo cruzado in western Havana. Ultimately, the use of the term *bembé* to index various African-inspired ritual traditions in eastern Cuba, many of them "crossed" (*cruzado*), mirrored the "crossing" of contemporary Yorùbá and Cuban ritual practices in the first Baracoan egúngún masquerade itself. The closing of the masquerade—in which two well-known Baracoan practitioners of Espiritismo cruzado fell into spirit possession following the departure of the masked figures—manifested this "crossing."

The Alágbàá Egúngún present at the ceremony emphatically underscored this crossing of egúngún with Espiritismo cruzado as a "logical" and "aligned" integration of Nigerian forms of ancestral worship, via the Yorùbá-inspired òrìṣà Egúngún, within the rich landscape of practices dedicated to cultivating the relationship with the dead in Baracoa. "One of the greatest virtues of the religion that we practice is precisely that it is favorable to *mestizaje* [mixing], but, to logical mestizaje, not to illogical mestizaje," notes Romero Suárez (Romero Suárez, interview). Framing the arrival of egúngún and its crossing with local ritual as aligned and preordained, Romero Suárez continues, "I am sure that this [crossing of egúngún and Espiritismo cruzado] comes from the alignment that exists between the heavens and the earthly space in which we live. It occurs because it is by divine mandate; it doesn't happen by chance." Here, Romero Suárez frames African-inspired religions in Cuba, including Ifá-Òrìṣà and Espiritismo cruzado, as incorporative, absorptive, and flexible, a position that exists in tension with discourses of "inventions" and "illogical" adaptations that often inflect African traditionalist discourse surrounding Regla de Ocha-Ifá and its transformations in the African diaspora. In Baracoa, however, Romero Suárez frames the arrival of egúngún and of African traditionalism itself as preordained and aligned with the rich histories of ancestral worship in eastern Cuba. Connecting this perspective to my own ethnographic research and the lens with which he'd like my future academic writings to take, Romero Suárez continues: "The expression of this religiosity, here, is unique. . . . Baracoa is unique. Baracoa is extremely spiritual, and the egbẹ́ has been born under this spirituality. There is a common thread. There is a logical, logical, absolutely logical and harmonious relationship between the parts and the whole. And I think it is beautiful and intelligent, in the study that you are doing, that you see it from this perspective, the relation that exists, the logical relation that exists between the parts and the whole" (Romero Suárez, interview). Romero Suárez's statement echoes the ethnographic insights of anthropologist Brendan Jamal Thornton in his studies of religious "difference" in the space of the Hispanophone Caribbean. In a provocative study of Pentecostalism and masculinity in the Dominican Republic, Thornton (2016, 79) challenges notions of "religious difference locally" by arguing for the ontological congruence of seemingly disparate traditions—for example, Dominican *vodú*, Catholicism, and Pentecostalism—in working-class neighborhoods. Rather than framing these religious practices as oppositional and divided along axes of individual and collective systems of "belief," Thornton argues that African-inspired ritual and the practices of Christianity (Catholicism, Pentecostalism) coexist for Dominican practitioners as parts within a cohesive ontological whole, in other words, within a consensus of shared ascriptions and logics. Here, Romero Suárez frames the introduction of Nigerian-inspired egúngún lineages into the rich ritual landscape of Baracoa as a logical, aligned "part" within a larger, cohesive ontological "whole" of ancestral worship traditions. While "there's a total resistance from criollo babalaos to convert to *el tradicionalismo*," Romero Suárez notes, pointing to the contentious divisions between Cuban-style and Nigerian-style Ifá-Òrìṣà in Cuba, "what we're really doing is taking advantage of the millenary potentialities that have arrived to us from Nigeria, from Ilé-Ifẹ̀ and other [sites] . . . that we readjust here, to Cuba" (Romero Suárez, interview). Framing the ritual crossings and readjustments in Baracoa as aligned and brimming with "potentialities," Romero Suárez states affectionately, following the ceremony: "The fiesta for egúngún was totally mestizo, totally crossed [*cruzado*], because Baracoa is that way, and no other."

This valuation of the local as a valid form of ancestral worship in Baracoa in relation to the arrival of contemporary Nigerian forms of ancestral ritual in African traditionalism points to the ways in which local forms of ritual practice continue to be valued as efficacious in their capacities to communicate with, animate, provoke, and/or produce pleasure for òrìṣà and the ancestors. This occurs despite heterogeneous, and often more contentious, forms of relation between African traditionalist ẹgbẹ́ and local forms of oricha practice across Cuba's regional provinces. In the realm of ritual music, especially, Alágbàá Egúngún of the Odùgbemi lineage argue that local forms of ritual drumming used to honor the ancestors, including bembé and güiro (chapter 4), offer an efficacious means of drawing out, animating, and producing pleasure for the egúngún, the ancestors, and those gathered. Orozco Rubio states: "I'll tell you something. For me, it's more meritorious to do it with these [local ritual drums], that are the drums of our ancestors, than to do it with Nigerian drums" (Orozco Rubio, interview, May 12, 2016). In contradistinction with the Aworeni lineage in Havana, which has made a concerted effort to integrate Nigerian ritual drums into African traditionalists practice (chapter 2), Orozco Rubio and other African traditionalists in eastern Cuba frame local drum ensembles dedicated to the oricha and the ancestors as a more useful form of pleasure and provocation for the egúngún than Nigerian bàtá or dùndún. For them, these local, regional instruments are the ritual instruments of "our ancestors."[25]

Regional Aesthetics of Pleasure and Provocation

In eastern Cuba, the use of *tumbadoras* by the Odùgbemi lineage for the egúngún masquerade rather than the Cuban *bàtá* drums marks a notable difference from egúngún performance in western Cuba and, more broadly, Yorùbáland. In Yorùbáland, the bàtá drums are directly associated with egúngún in addition to their well-known association with the òrìṣà Ṣàngó (A. Euba 1990). The talking bàtá set serves a crucial function in drawing out the egúngún in their travels between the world of the ancestors and the world of the living, as noted previously (Boscolo 2009). Additionally, the bàtá "talking drums" serve the role of prompting, provoking, and reprimanding the masquerading egúngún during performances (Boscolo 2009). Likewise, the dùndún, a pan-Yorùbá ensemble increasingly prominent within contexts of òrìṣà worship (see chapter 2), is associated with egúngún masquerade in Yorùbáland and also used to provoke and draw out the "personality" of the egúngún (A. Euba 1994, 166).[26] Akin Euba states:

> Every *egúngún* has his own individual personality, be it aggressive, comical, fearsome, or whatever. It is the drummer who helps him realize that personality. Although considered the *egúngún* helper, the drummer is not above taunting and provoking the *egúngún*. On occasion when an *egúngún* meets an opponent, the *ìyáàlú* drummer's musical patterns can either help to avert a confrontation or actually provoke one. The drummer's discretion on such occasions is crucial. Assuming that, after provocation, a fight does develop between two opposing *egúngún*, there follows a display of magical powers by them to show who is superior. Each of the *egúngún* must then rely on his drummer to inspire him to a great performance. (A. Euba 1994, 166, in Boscolo 2009, 218)

The crucial role of the bàtá and the dùndún within egúngún masquerade in Yorùbáland points to the efficacy of specific forms of ritual instrumentation in drawing out and inspiring a successful, often competitive egúngún performance. The instruments animate the Egúngún, drawing out their rawest, greatest potentialities and powers through the divergent and forceful affective modalities of bothering, reprimand, and provocation.[27]

In the Ilé Tuntún African traditionalist temple in Havana, practitioners use the batá drums in òrìṣà ceremonies and to draw out and animate egúngún masquerade. The African traditionalist babaláwo Frank Cabrera Suárez, who is considered the first Cuban babaláwo to receive a *fundamento* (or consecrated emblem) of egúngún from Nigeria in the late 1990s (Martínez Betancourt 2016),[28] masquerades the five Nigerian-consecrated agọ̀ egúngún in his possession to the sounding of the Cuban batá. Cabrera and Ilé Tuntún's use of the batá for egúngún masquerade mirrors the link between the bàtá and egúngún in Yorùbáland while also pointing to the prominence of the Cuban batá as the premier ritual instrument of the oricha in western Cuba. The five egúngún masks that Cabrera owns were elaborated in Nigeria and sent to Cuba by means of Cabrera's connections with Wándé Abímbólá during the years that I conducted fieldwork in Cuba (Cabrera, interview, April 4, 2016).

Cabrera's trajectory of connection with Nigerian egúngún lineages, specifically through Táíwò Abímbólá and his father Wándé Abímbólá, in comparison with Orozco Rubio's discrete connections with egúngún masquerade through the Odùgbemi lineage points to the heterogeneity of contact points with Yorùbáland among distinct African traditionalist ẹgbẹ́. These discrete connections, in turn, inform heterogeneous ritual practices and procedures among different lineages. While Cabrera's five agọ̀ egúngún were constructed and consecrated in Nigeria before being brought to Cuba, for example, Orozco Rubio received his agọ̀ egúngún as part of his initiation into the priesthood of egúngún in accordance with the ritual edicts of the Odùgbemi lineage established by the exiled Cuban founder Ifáshade Odùgbemi (Orozco Rubio, interview, May 12, 2016). Accordingly, the egúngún masks of the Odùgbemi lineage in eastern Cuba are elaborated and consecrated in Cuba rather than imported from Nigeria. Notably, as well, the Odùgbemi lineage is the only African traditionalist lineage in Cuba that masquerades agọ̀ egúngún as part of a formal egúngún society, in other words, by what its members frame as "Alágbàá Egúngún" (egúngún "priests") initiated into an egúngún "lineage." While Cabrera owns five agọ̀ egúngún and masquerades them in conjunction with Ilé Tuntún ritual ceremonies, he is not himself initiated into a Nigerian-rooted egúngún ritual society.[29] When I asked about the relationship of the masks to initiated egúngún societies, Cabrera pointed to Wándé Abímbólá's knowledge and prestige on the matter, emphasizing that Abímbólá personally insisted Cabrera receive the Nigerian egúngún masks and suggesting that being initiated as babaláwo is enough to "work" the Egúngún. This dominion over the egúngún masks by babaláwo in western Cuba, which also mirrors the introduction of egúngún priesthood societies in eastern Cuba through babaláwo in the Odùgbemi International Association for Traditional Yoruba Religion (OIATYR), demonstrates a marked difference from Yorùbáland, where egúngún masquerade historically fell under the purview of the Ọ̀jẹ̀ and not under Ifá lineages and babaláwo (Babayemi 1980).

In 2012, Cabrera received the first three masks through Abímbólá, each embodying an important babalao in Cuba's history and in Cabrera's own *rama* of Ifá. These included "Remigio Herrera Adechina (1811–1905), Eulogio Rodríguez Tata Gaitán (1861–1945) and Martín Cabrera Escudero (1919–1966)" (Martínez Betancourt 2016).[30] In 2014, Cabrera received an additional two masks embodying "Miguel Febles Padrón (1910–1986) and Pablo Sevilla

(1930–2002)" (Martínez Betancourt 2016). Notably, Cabrera emphasizes that the masks are less for honoring the ancestors than for "working with them." "They are òrìṣàs," Cabrera states, and as such they are brought out "to be worked, so that they help you." Here, Cabrera emphasizes the functional efficacy of the egúngún as nonrepresentational ancestors "worked" to resolve particular issues (Cabrera, interview, April 4, 2016). In order to work with these five ancestors and the collectivity of ancestors that the egúngún represent, Cabrera holds regular egúngún masquerades in Ilé Tuntún, including masquerades for *itàdógún* ceremonies and toques for specific ancestors. In conjunction with other African traditionalist ẹgbẹ́ in and around Havana, Cabrera also masquerades the Nigerian-consecrated agò egúngún as part of the annual Ifá festival held annually in conjunction with the Yorùbá calendar.

Egúngún Masquerade at the Ifá Festival: Western Cuba

The first time that I witnessed an egúngún masquerade in Cuba was during the annual Ifá festival hosted by Ilé Tuntún in June 2015. Held in conjunction with other neighboring African traditionalists ẹgbẹ́ in and around Havana, the seventeenth annual Yoruba Calendar Festival, as it was called, lasted from June 4 to 10 with events and ceremonies held daily in various African traditionalist temples and homes throughout the city and surrounding area. On this particular day, the Ẹgbẹ́ Ifá Olodu, headed by babaláwo Yunieski González Ramírez (b. Havana, 1977), hosted the masquerade of Cabrera's five agò egúngún at the Finca Tirabeque, a rural property in Santiago de las Vegas. I arrived at the event a few hours early with babaláwo and ethnobotanist Julio Martínez Betancourt, who resides in Santiago de las Vegas. Through his extensive knowledge of ritual plants and their uses in African-inspired ritual in Cuba, Martínez Betancourt has helped González Ramírez convert part of the Finca Tirabeque property into a "sacred forest," or an ecological site cultivated with ritual plants and used in Ifá-Òrìṣà initiations and rituals.[31] Together, Martínez Betancourt, González Ramírez and I conversed with members of Ẹgbẹ́ Ifá Olodu and other African traditionalists gathered at the rural property as we waited for Cabrera and other members of Ilé Tuntún to arrive from Havana.

As soon as the truck arrived at the property carrying the five masked Egúngún, the members of Ilé Tuntún, and the batá players, the egúngún immediately inspired a sense of fascination and awe among those gathered, including myself. The Nigerian-crafted agò featured impressive headdresses with multicolored, loosely hanging lappets descending over the varied, multi-patterned cloths of the underlying suits, and the faces of the masks, with their

FIGURE 5.3. Frank Cabrera Suárez's Nigerian-made egúngún masks, masking as the Cuban babalaos Pablo Sevilla (*front*) (1930–2002) and Martin Cabrera (*back*) (1919–1966). Santiago de las Vegas, 2015. Photo by the author.

covered white-and-black mesh netting, offered an intimidating obstruction of the faces of the wearers. The masks were, quite simply, unlike any attire I had witnessed in Cuban ritual ceremonies. Unlike the agọ̀ egúngún that I would later witness in Baracoa, with their bright colors and satin cloths designed in accordance with the visual aesthetics of Regla de Ocha ritual dress in Cuba, these masks were darker and of Nigerian construction, using cloths and materials typical of Yorùbáland (see figs. 5.3 and 5.4).

Once the truck parked, three batá players set up on the back patio of the property's house, initiating the festival event by playing the Cuban toque *iya-kotá*. As they played, a standing *akpwón* called out a contemporary, Yorùbá language song, the melody and lyrics of which were passed to Cabrera by Táíwò Abímbọ́lá.[32] The song celebrates the arrival of the Egúngún Festival (*ọdun egúngún*) in Yorùbáland (see fig. 5.5):

FIGURE 5.4. Frank Cabrera Suárez's five Nigerian-made egúngún masks. José Reinaldo Ilin Montano, lead *iyá* batá player, seated left. Santiago de las Vegas, 2015. Photo by the author.

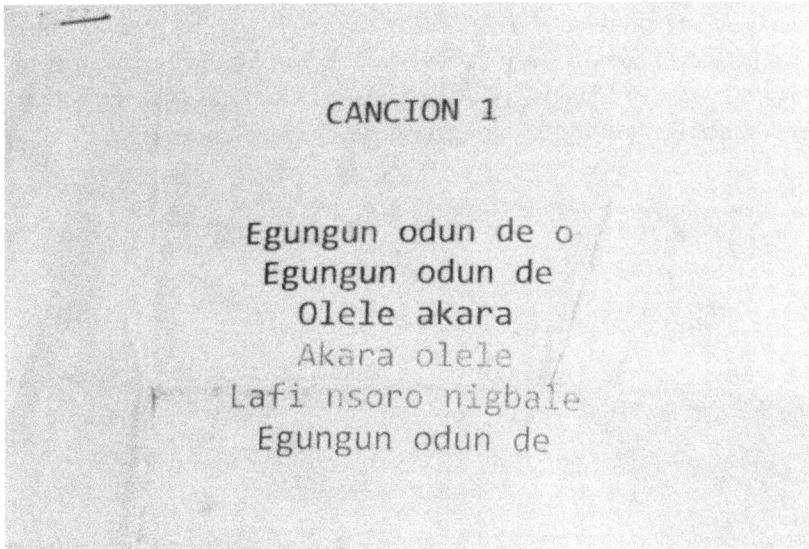

CANCION 1

Egungun odun de o
Egungun odun de
Olele akara
Akara olele
Lafi nsoro nigbale
Egungun odun de

FIGURE 5.5. Copy of egúngún song passed to Frank Cabrera Suárez by Táíwò Abímbólá. Photo by the author.

> The Egúngún Festival has arrived
> The Egúngún Festival has arrived
> We celebrate it with *olele* and *akara*[33]
> We celebrate it with *akara* and *olele*
> We celebrate it in the grove with *olele* and *akara*
> The Egúngún Festival has arrived[34]

The percussionists and the akpwón overlayed the Cuban toque with the Yorùbá lyrics in call-and-response as the five egúngún began to shuffle, dance, and spin on the space of the back patio (Audio Example 9: Egúngún masquerade in Havana). As the momentum of the song built, the masked egúngún whirled the multicolored lappets of their elaborate cloth suits in increasingly fast motions, echoing the words of the egúngún verse I would later hear in Baracoa: "Agọ̀ n tu yà ri yà ri yà [*sic*]," "the cloths of the egúngún dress come undone and open the path." The dancing gained momentum as the drummers switched to the toque *Olokun*, transitioning to a second song in praise of egúngún passed from Abímbọ́lá to Cabrera (see fig. 5.6):

> Egúngún exists
> Òrìṣà exists
> We adore them as they were adored in that era
> You don't adore them as they were adored in that era[35]

Mirroring their counterparts in eastern Cuba, the instrumentalists and singers adapt the recently introduced, Yorùbá language songs to the rhythms and logics of performance of regional, western Cuban òrìṣà and ancestor traditions. Indeed, almost a year later, I heard the same egúngún song (fig. 5.5) played in eastern Cuba by a different lineage (OIATYR), with very different connections to Nigeria, during the first egúngún masquerade in Baracoa.

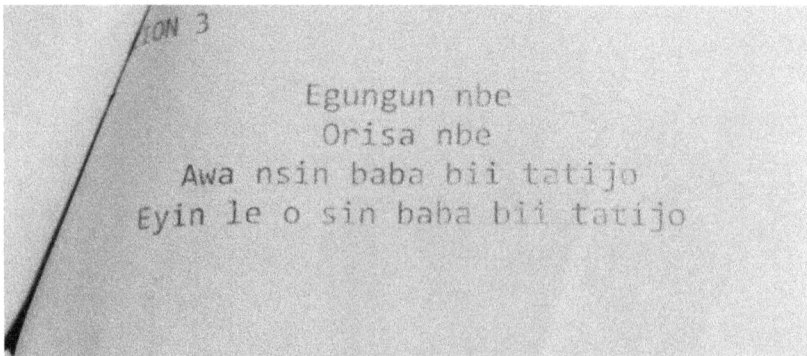

> Egungun nbe
> Orisa nbe
> Awa nsin baba bii tatijo
> Eyin le o sin baba bii tatijo

FIGURE 5.6. Copy of additional egúngún song passed to Frank Cabrera Suárez by Táíwò Abímbọ́lá. Photo by the author.

Immediately, I noted the differences in the Baracoan adaptation of the Yorùbá language song to the rhythmic sensibilities of eastern Cuban bembé, from the intricacies and inflections of the melody to the underlying percussion and clave bembé. Like their eastern Cuban counterparts, Cabrera also points to the contemporary, Yorùbá language ritual songs as "better" than local Regla de Ocha ritual songs dedicated to the *eggún*, or ancestors, specifically "because these have the translation" (Cabrera, interview, April 4, 2016). In so doing, Cabrera echoes a common assertion made by African traditionalists throughout Cuba concerning the efficacy of contemporary Yorùbá language verses, placing emphasis on their semantic intelligibility as the "living language" of the Yorùbá and the òrìṣà ancestors (see fig. 5.6).

While the Yorùbá language is heralded by African traditionalists as "better" as a ritual tongue than Cuban Lucumí, Cabrera and others nonetheless emphasize that regional ritual instruments offer a highly efficacious means of animating the Egúngún. The lead *iyá* player of the batá ensemble, José Reinaldo Ilin Montano, related to me that in adapting the Yorùbá language praise songs to the Cuban batá corpus, he chose the iyakotá Cuban batá rhythm to accompany the egúngún songs because iyakotá is a "shared" toque, meaning that it can be used as an underlying rhythm to sing for different deities in the Regla de Ocha tradition (Vaughan 2012, 122, 128).[36] Likewise, the toque Olokun can be used while singing for multiple orichas, including Elegguá and Yemayá, as well as for eggún.[37] Ilin Montano related to me that he chose these specific rhythms to accompany the egúngún songs in the absence of contemporary Nigerian bàtá rhythms precisely because of this flexibility, mirroring the choices made by batalera Pouymiró in eastern Cuba (chapter 3). Additionally, he chose the toque Olokun because of the preestablished relationship between the toque and eggún in the Cuban batá corpus of Regla de Ocha.

Ritual Pleasure and Success

In western and eastern Cuba alike, egúngún and Ifá practitioners of the Ilé Tuntún and the Odùgbemi lineages mobilize specific local and regional forms of ritual percussion as efficacious forms of animating the òrìṣà. Notably, these practitioners frame these regional percussion ensembles as efficacious specifically in their capacity to produce ritual pleasure—a crucial modality of òrìṣà animation and engagement. For African traditionalists, pleasure constitutes a structure of feeling at the core of both òrìṣà manifestation and ritual success.[38] González Ramírez, for example, who hosted the egúngún masquerade at his Finca Tibareque, frames the batá as effective in animating the òrìṣà through an aesthetics of pleasure and festivity (*festejo*). He states:

Although in Africa they don't have the same form of consecrating Añá or of making *omo Añá*[,] . . . I do think that the Cuban batá are very good. They have good spirituality. Therefore, I believe in them a lot. . . . In Africa, whenever possible, every ritual ends or begins with Añá. It's the form of communication . . . with the ancestors. In communication with the òrìṣà, it's the dance form of the òrìṣà. . . . Whenever a ritual ends in Africa, it's customary to play *el tambor* because it's like a fiesta. Now, when we have a fiesta here, we put on reggaeton or we put on, for example, salsa. In reality, what they put on there is a tambor which is of the òrìṣà. Listen! The òrìṣà listens, and the òrìṣà likes it. (González Ramírez, interview)

Here, González Ramírez highlights the importance of party-imbued celebration to the success of Ifá-Òrìṣà ritual, emphasizing that many òrìṣà were once living beings now animated, just like humans, through festivity and song. Likening a tambor for the òrìṣà to the popular musical forms of reggaeton and salsa, González Ramírez additionally frames the tambor as the preferred party music of the òrìṣà, a description that resonates with the common characterization of African-inspired drumming ritual for the òrìṣà as a "religious party" (Romero Suárez, interview). Additionally, González Ramírez notes that the verses of the odù Ifá contain a section called *orin*, or the "song" section of the verse, that is explicitly tied to a ritual mandate of festive celebration (festejo): "After [the *itán*, or the story section of the odù Ifá,] is the song, which is called orin. The orin is a festejo [celebration], like praising that things turned out well. There is a part that is used to sing with joy. It is said that at the end of a ritual, you should sing and you should finish with joy. And joy is orin" (González Ramírez, interview). González Ramírez highlights the festive ritual pleasure of the òrìṣà and the celebration of that pleasure by gathered humans as central to the success of òrìṣà ritual. Underscoring his belief that Cuban batá are efficacious in animating the òrìṣà—that they have "good effect"—González Ramírez further emphasizes that holding "a tambor is very important." Orozco Rubio echoes González Ramírez's statement from the opposite side of the island: "Remember that traditions aren't carved in stone," he states, referencing the incorporation of the tumbadoras into African traditionalist egúngún ritual in Baracoa. "They adjust to the moment. What can't happen is losing the tradition through an absence of tambor [drummed ritual performance]" (Orozco Rubio, interview, May 12, 2016).

While the festive ritual pleasure of the òrìṣà through the tambor is vital to ritual success, African traditionalists additionally emphasize the centrality of festive ritual pleasure to humans as well. Babaláwo Damián Francisco Paula Valdés, of the Aworeni lineage, elaborates: "We practice a culture of Ifá-Òrìṣà, but with the understanding that it's a fiesta, that the rituals are festivities. You have to call good energy, positive vibes, and [you do] this simply by making a ritual a fiesta, warming hearts, so that people feel content."[39] Connecting this sense of ritual festivity to public-facing initiations and ritual events that might been seen by the broader community or even attract noninitiates, Valdés states:

> If the ceremony is open, it's a fiesta, and that's how we do it. We enjoy. Every initiation of Ifá-Òrìṣà that's done in this temple, we begin in the street and we finish here inside the temple, everyone singing, everyone praying, everyone— like Cubans say—*gozando* [experiencing pleasure/enjoying]. Now, when the moment of the secret arrives, it's secret. Those who aren't in the [forbidden] area put themselves in the area that they can be, and the secret is secret. Now, the fiesta is *fiesta* because you have to call positive energy. You have to call good spirits, and this is done singing, dancing, eating. That's how it's done. It can't be any other way. (Valdés, interview)

Here, Valdés frames the imperative of human enjoyment—gozando—through ritual song and dance as crucial to the capacity to draw positive energy and "good spirits" to rituals. For Valdés, the "open," nonsecret parts of ceremonies are in fact fiestas (parties). Through singing, dance, and food, Ifá-Òrìṣà fiestas animate human initiates—and even broader, noninitiated community members—to draw out positive energy and "good spirits" to ritual ceremonies and initiations.

Valdés's, González Ramírez's, and Orozco Rubio's statements surrounding ritual pleasure point to the centrality of pleasure and party-inflected festivity to Ifá-Òrìṣà practice in Cuba. More broadly, their statements point to the importance of recognizing pleasure and festivity as integral affective modalities in studies of ritual music in Cuba and beyond (see, e.g., Catlin-Jairazbhoy 2012; Tallotte 2018). In music studies, pleasure has increasingly been recognized as an affective force that entangles the personal, the collective, and the political, particularly in the realm of popular and secular music studies (Danielsen 2006; Frith 1988; Guilbault 2010, 2019; Neill 2002; Rowe 1995; Shain 2018, xxii). Music scholar and anthropologist Nomi Dave (2019, 2), for example, succinctly states in relation to Guinean popular music that "pleasure matters. Pleasure works beyond the individual and individual experience to create shared meaning and feeling within and across groups. Shared experiences and ideas of pleasure shape the way in which people interpret and invest in social life, generating alliances and allegiances, influencing collective memories, and crafting collective aspirations."[40] Likewise, US American queer of color writer adrienne maree brown's (2019) generative work on "pleasure activism" robustly theorizes pleasure as a site of imaginative social reconfiguration. In her work, brown points to the relation of "aliveness" and the "pleasure politic" to "personal, relational, and communal power" (6). Through "efforts to promote, impede, or direct social, political, economic, or environmental reform" via feelings of "enjoyment" or "happy satisfaction" (13), individuals harness the power of "pleasure activism," potentiating the possibility of "shifting the ground beneath us, inside us, and transforming what is possible" (11).

In scholarship on Cuban and Cuban American popular music, queer studies has especially contributed to our understanding of the ways that collective experiences of musical pleasure serve as powerful catalysts for engendering novel forms of identity, belonging, social reconfiguration, and resiliency (Amico 2006; Morad 2014; Muñoz 2009, 2012; Soares 2020). Queer scholarship on Cuban and Cuban diaspora music attends to the ways that queer acts of musical consumption and appropriation engender novel sites of belonging and queer ("gay") identity (Morad 2014); the ways that Cuban American and Latinx queer performances "reterritorialize" stigmatized class identities (e.g., *chusmería*) and other majoritarian forms of "injurious speech" (Muñoz 1999, 185); and how performances of joy and hope constitute acts of survival and resilience in the queer Cuban and Hispanophone Caribbean diaspora (Soares 2020).

Beyond queer studies, Kjetil Klette Bøhler's recent work on *timba* in Havana also compellingly argues for "groove" as a crucial modality of the political potentialities of pleasure in African-inspired Cuban popular music. Bøhler demonstrates that the interactive, polyrhythmic musical structures of timba—a working-class, Afro-Cuban style characterized by its high-energy fusion of rumba and *son* with hip-hop, funk, jazz, and salsa—craft "particular forms of 'presence and pleasure'" that make audible (and visceral) the political potentialities of *coros* (lyrical choruses) (Danielsen 2006, in Bøhler 2021, 198).[41] Bøhler also historizes scholarship on the social and affective possibilities of Cuban musical pleasure in the mid-twentieth-century writings of Fernando Ortiz: "[Ortiz] argued that Afro-Cuban music has for centuries mobilized its sonic pleasures to create new ways of being together on the island" (Bøhler 2021, 196). In *La africanía de la música folklórica cubana* ([1950] 2001), for example, Ortiz writes: "Afro-Cuban music is fire, tastiness and smoke, syrup, sensual flavour [sandunga], comforts/relief [alivio]; it is like a sonic rum that you drink through your ears, that brings the people together, making them equal and bringing forth life through the senses" (Ortiz [1950] 2001, 13, in Bøhler 2021, 196, Bøhler's translation). Here, musical pleasure through *sandunga* (sensual flavor) brings "forth life through the senses" and potentiates novel forms of "equal" social relationality,[42] acting as a "sonic rum" grounded in the interactive, polyrhythmic possibilities of Afro-Cuban music and dance (Ortiz [1950] 2001, 13, in Bøhler 2021, 196).

In eastern and western Cuba, González Ramírez, Valdés, and Orozco Rubio's framing of festive pleasure likewise highlights the importance of pleasure and party-infused festivity—via the polyrhythmic groove of el tambor—to the success of African traditionalist ritual. Beyond popular and secular music studies, their comments also underscore pleasure as a crucial affective modality of African-inspired ritual music and dance in Cuba. Additionally, their framing implicates the festive ritual enjoyment of both the human and the nonhuman (the òrìṣà and ancestors) as central to the efficacy of ritual. Through the tambor, African traditionalists enact a regionally grounded aesthetics of ritual pleasure for human and nonhuman listeners and dancers crucial to the efficacy and success of Ifá-Òrìṣà ceremony. For them, festivity (festejo) and party-inflected pleasure (*el gozo*) capacitate practitioners to successfully "work with" the Egúngún, the ancestors, and the òrìṣà. Additionally, festive ritual pleasure allows African traditionalists to call "positive energy," "good spirits," and "good people" (chapter 2), highlighting the importance of musical pleasure to efforts aimed at social and ritual reconfiguration in a contentious ritual movement.

Conclusion

In March 2016, a year after first witnessing Cabrera's five agò egúngún at the annual Ifá festival in Santiago de las Vegas, I attended another egúngún masquerade at Ilé Tuntún, in this case as a culmination of a tambor in homage to the late Cuban babalao Filiberto O'Farrill. The three batá percussionists initiated the homage by playing a Cuban *toque a eggún*, or a tambor for the ancestors, using rhythmic sequences characteristic of Regla de Ocha. Toward the end of the tambor, José Reinaldo Ilin Montano switched to the Olokun toque, calling out the lyrics to "Egungun nbe." From the back of the house, the egúngún emerged, traveling through the small foyer in which the batá players and other members of Ilé Tuntún gathered and moving outside and into the streets. Without dropping the toque, the batá players took turns strapping the instruments to their bodies while seated so that they could stand and follow the masquerading egúngún by foot. Two other percussionists joined the procession, playing interlocking rhythms on two imported, Nigerian agogo Ifá bells as the drummers, the Egúngún, and other members of Ilé Tuntún followed. In this procession, the outdoor egúngún masquerade in this relatively isolated Havana neighborhood more closely mirrored the public dynamics of egúngún masquerade in Yorùbáland, where egúngún masquerades often take place in the streets with family members following the egúngún as the bàtá or dùndún animate the òrìṣà and participants (Babayemi 1980; Boscolo 2009; A. Euba 1990). In parading Havana's streets, the participants in Cuba violated state law regarding freedom of public assembly (see chapter 2), though in a neighborhood relatively removed from the center of the capital city. This outdoor procession contrasted with the indoor masquerade I would witness a few months later in Baracoa where, although members of the Êgbë Íran Àtelé Ilôgbôn Baracoa openly debated the risks of holding the masquerade outdoors, they ultimately decided against the potential legal repercussions due to the proximity of the ẹgbẹ́ to Baracoa's city's center, only blocks away. Despite this difference, both ẹgbẹ́ engaged an efficacy of the close to animate African traditionalist ritual, mobilizing the capacious power of local ritual instrumental ensembles in line with regional logics of ritual pleasure to animate human and nonhuman listeners.

Throughout Cuba, egúngún masquerade (and, in the case of the Odùg-bemi lineage, priesthood societies), are gaining traction as a Yorùbá-inspired means of worshipping and "working with" the dead in Nigerian-style Ifá-Òrìṣà. In eastern Cuba, the adaptation of Yorùbá egúngún masquerade to local contexts and practices of ancestor worship, including bembé and Espiritismo cruzado, reflects the grounding of novel Yorùbá traditions within localized logics and practices of working with the dead. The incorporation of sonorous practices of aural estrangement that maintain the ontology of the egúngún as nonhuman, manifested ancestors and the use of Yorùbá language praise songs to invoke and empower the egúngún points to the centrality of Yorùbá-inspired logics of sonorous efficacy to the transplantation of egúngún in Cuba. At the same time, the use of instruments, rhythms, and ritual modalities of festivity (festejo) and pleasure (el gozo) drawn from eastern Cuban practices of ancestor worship, including bembé and Espiritismo cruzado, give a decidedly eastern bent to the sounding and force of egúngún masquerade. Through an efficacy of the close, practitioners ceremonially "cross" the egúngún with the rich, deep-rooted historical traditions of the tierra de muertéras in Oriente (Dodson 2008, 128).

In egúngún masquerades in western Cuba, where the egúngún masquerade first (re)gained prominence, African traditionalist ẹgbẹ́ hold egúngún masquerades as part of celebrations and homages that mark both novel, Yorùbá-inspired ceremonies of recent import (e.g., the Yorùbá Ifá Festival and ìtàdógún) as well as toques to eggún characteristic of Regla de Ocha. In line with regional logics surrounding the efficacy of sound, the egúngún masquerades I witnessed in Ilé Tuntún utilized the batá to draw out and animate the Egúngún, mirroring the historical and contemporary link between the bàtá and egúngún in Yorùbáland. In western Cuba, like eastern Cuba, Yorùbá songs are likewise adapted to localized and regionally prominent rhythms associated with ritual pleasure and festivity in ancestor and òrìṣà worship. The rich and contextually rooted adoption of egúngún masquerade in Havana (western Cuba) and Baracoa (Oriente) underscores the dynamic interplay of heterogeneity and regionalism in Nigerian-style Ifá-Òrìṣà in Cuba.

The "Leopards" of Nigerian-Style Ifá-Òrìṣà: Visions from Cuba to Yorùbáland

In the small city of Morón, in the central province of Ciego de Ávila, the African traditionalist *babaláwo* Otto William Sabina de León sat in a wooden chair on his back patio explaining how Nigerian-style Ifá-Òrìṣà arrived to him in this relatively secluded area of Cuba. Far from the central hubs of Regla de Ocha-Ifá in the urban poles of western and eastern Cuba, the city of Morón didn't have *babalaos* when Sabina de León was a teenager. Around that time, his aunt worked in the tourist beach resorts of the nearby Cayo Coco islands off the northern coast and there befriended a babalao from Havana who invited Sabina de León to the capital to be initiated in 2000. Shortly after, one of Sabina de León's *ahijados* began to bring him books on the Yorùbá traditional religion from Spain, including American anthropologist and Yorùbá scholar William Bascom's seminal *Ifá Divination: Communication between Gods and Men in West Africa* (1969). For Sabina de León, this book offered his first glimpse at the Yorùbá traditional religion of contemporary Nigeria. After reading about the use of "tan" and "green" beads for the left-wrist *ide* bracelet in Yorùbáland rather than the yellow and green beads used in Cuban Ifá (Bascom 1969, 84), Sabina de León replaced his yellow-and-green ide, which he considered "something Afro-Cuban," with a brown-and-green one. This marked his "first step" toward Nigerian-style Ifá-Òrìṣà. Shortly after, when the Yoruba Cultural Association of Cuba (ACYC) issued its vitriolic, nationwide proclamation blacklisting Victor Betancourt's Ifá Ìranlówo and all African traditionalists involved with ìyánífá initiations in 2004, the proclamation had the opposite-of-intended effect on him. Fascinated, he traveled to Havana to seek out African traditionalism's most prominent babaláwo, including Frank Cabrera and Victor Betancourt. Hitting it off particularly well with Victor Betancourt, Sabina de León spent days and then weeks every month traveling to Havana and learning about Nigerian-style Ifá in Betan-court's home. Ultimately, Sabina de León became a self-anointed "disciple" of Betancourt's, carrying the Ifá Ìranlówo lineage to Morón and establishing a subsidiary ẹgbẹ́ there.[1]

Sabina de León's trajectory toward African traditionalism reveals the mul-titudinous means by which women and men arrive at Nigerian-style Ifá-Òrìṣà throughout Cuba's regional provinces. Predicated on several key historical antecedents, including the opening of Cuba's economy to tourism and foreign travel as well as heightened access to Cuba's ritual diasporas abroad, Sabina de León's journey additionally hinges on the national vigilance of Afro-Cuban religion by Cuba's state-linked ACYC. In his case, the association's national (and international) diatribes against Nigerian-style Ifá-Òrìṣà and attempts to delegitimize and ostracize its practitioners created an opposite-of-intended desire, ultimately heightening his—and his wife's—awareness of and curiosity about the gendered and theological upheavals occurring through Nigerian-style Ifá.[2]

During our conversation, Sabina de León criticized the underlying mis-sion of the ACYC to organizationally unite and police the boundaries of oricha worship in Cuba by evoking a provocative symbol of authority and self-sufficiency in Ifá: the leopard. According to Sabina de León, African tra-ditionalism has flourished throughout Cuba's provinces, despite the oppo-sition of the ACYC, precisely because babaláwo and ìyánífá are ultimately "leopards," not "sheep." Solitary and territorial, leopards live in relative isola-tion from one another, he states, associating in small packs, primarily with their offspring.[3] This evocative metaphor of independence, self-sufficiency, and autonomous ritual family among the relatively small and marginalized African traditionalist ritual lineages and ẹgbẹ́ in Cuba also draws on the cen-trality of the leopard in West and Central African indigenous societies as symbols of "royals," "political power," "social power," and "power elites" (Blier 2015, 326; Miller 2009, 54). In Yorùbáland, the Ọ̀ọ̀ni of Ilé-Ifẹ̀ is "held as the 'leopard' " (Blier 2015, 326, citing T. Euba 1985, 13). As related to me by Cuban babaláwo, when a woman or man initiates as ìyánífá or babaláwo, they are also believed to "convert into a leopard."[4]

As Sabina de León's metaphor implies, the symbol of the leopard evokes the heterogeneous and relatively independent nature of the emergence of Af-rican traditionalism—and African traditionalist ẹgbẹ́—throughout Cuba's provinces. In 2015, there was a notable attempt by African traditionalists and foreign babaláwo affiliated with Yorùbá traditional religion (YTR) abroad to unite the various ẹgbẹ́ in Cuba through a formal meeting, the "First His-panophone Encounter of the Ifá-Òrìṣà Tradition" (the Primer Encuentro

Hispanoparlante de la Tradición Ifá-Òrìṣà) organized by Victor Betancourt and Mexican babaláwo Eli Torres Gongora. As numerous attendees noted after the event, the unification of the heterogeneous ẹgbẹ́ into a unified umbrella African traditionalist organization, mirroring to a degree the state-linked ACYC, ultimately failed. Participants pointed to the autonomous nature of individual ritual communities and their heterogeneous, transatlantic hierarchies of ritual authority with discrete Nigerian-rooted lineages as a reason for the idea's disintegration. Others pointed to the ways the meeting unearthed broad disagreements concerning who would constitute the "leader" of such an ostensibly national organization rooted in profoundly divergent, transnational ritual hierarches. The Aworeni lineage and its various ẹgbẹ́ in western Cuba, for example, uphold Dr. William Vera as the eminent, Ilé-Ifẹ̀-appointed "Àràbà of Cuba," or Ifá-Òrìṣà ritual head for all practitioners on the island (chapter 2). Other African traditionalists reject the Aworeni lineage's claims to such far-reaching ritual and institutional authority. Members of Ifá Ìranlówo pointed to early pioneer and lineage head Victor Betancourt Estrada as the reigning authority on Nigerian-style Ifá and the ideal choice to head such a Cuban organization. Others still denied the very notion of the ritual and organizational immanence of a single individual outright, holding instead to the heterogeneous, transnational hierarchies of authority among individual, Nigerian-root ẹgbẹ́.

Indeed, apart from this effort, the development and proliferation of Cuba's discrete African traditionalist lineages has overwhelmingly been marked by dynamics of autonomy, heterogeneity, and idiosyncrasy. The variegated means by which information about YTR arrives in the hands of practitioners throughout Cuba's provinces and the marginalization of these ritual communities on the fringes of the boundaries of Regla de Ocha-Ifá as dictated by the ACYC has restricted the public face of African traditionalism while, simultaneously, providing advantages. The ability to operate as a leopard—with a tremendous amount of autonomy in individual and community approaches to Ifá-Òrìṣà—provides ample, generative possibilities.

Africanists and the ACYC: Potential Futures

The marginalization of African traditionalists from the ACYC has arguably facilitated the autonomy necessary for the multitudinous manifestations and interventions of Nigerian-style Ifá-Òrìṣà practitioners in Cuba, contributing to the expansive growth of a ritual movement that has more than doubled in size in only five years (Martínez Betancourt, pers. comm., 2020). Given this, the ACYC appears to be reevaluating its position in light of the thriving, expanding influence of Nigerian-style Ifá-Òrìṣà on the island. In 2016, the new president of the ACYC, Babalao José Manuel "Manolo" Pérez Andino,[5] made a series of symbolic yet contradictory gestures toward the "inclusion" of African traditionalists in the association. In January, Pérez Andino facilitated the unification of the two opposing Letter of the Year (Letra del Año) commissions in Havana, incorporating the members of the ACYC's competing Organizing Commission of the Letter of the Year (Comisión Organizadora de la Letra del Año Miguel Febles Padrón) into the official Letter of the Year held by the ACYC's Counsel of High Priests of Ifá (Consejo de Sacerdotes Mayores de Ifá).[6] This unification was significant because of the protagonizing role played by African traditionalist pioneer Victor Betancourt Estrada in the previously unaffiliated Organizing Commission of the Letter of the Year (see D. Brown 2003, 342; Hearn 2008, 49–51). Several months later, Pérez Andino additionally made Betancourt an official member of the ACYC, giving him a formal position as the advisor of the association's Supervising Council of Eastern Provinces.[7] The inclusion of Betancourt as the first African traditionalist babaláwo granted official membership to the ACYC since the ìyánífá debate of 2004, however, was predicated on Betancourt's agreement that he would desist from initiating further women as ìyánífá—a condition to which, surprisingly, he agreed. When I sat down with Pérez Andino that summer, he stated,

> My policy as a babalao is to unify, to bring all of the religions that have to do with Africa [together] as one. There were wars between the Africanists and the others, and after entering [as president of the ACYC], I was able to unify the two Letras del Año that existed. . . . Today, I am giving Africanists access [to the ACYC] . . . under the concept that they cannot initiate women into Ifá. . . . [Women] can't "make Ifá" because they are women.[8] There is no woman pope. That is the destiny of the religion, of life. . . . It has been signaled that way over the course of centuries. (Pérez Andino, interview)

Pérez Andino's rhetoric of unification frames the unity of African traditionalists and Regla de Ocha-Ifá practitioners as largely (or, even, already) achieved, with himself in the protagonist's role. Pérez Andino refers, first, to the successful unification of the two Letras del Año and, second, to the entrance of Betancourt into the association under his tenure. Furthermore, the new "welcoming" of "Africanists" into the ACYC is conditioned on the termination of the initiation of women by babaláwo and, additionally, by the caveat that ìyánífá who have already been initiated in Cuba relinquish their newly achieved status and "defer and dedicate themselves to being Apetebí de Orúla [i.e., domestic servers]" (Pérez Andino, interview). Pérez Andino's statement further naturalizes the exclusion of women from the Ifá priesthood by comparing the status of babalao to that of the pope, drawing on the historical precedent of centuries of patriarchal exclusion of women in the Catholic Church and other worldwide religious organizations. With this rhetoric of "unification," it seems that Pérez Andino's friendship and professional ties with one prominent African traditionalist pioneer, Betancourt, stands in for the purported "unity" of all African traditionalists and Regla de Ocha-Ifá practitioners under the state institutional umbrella of the ACYC.

Clearly, this discourse belies the ongoing exclusion of African traditionalists—and the patent exclusion of ìyánífá—from the ACYC. Shortly after Betancourt was appointed as the advisor to the eastern provinces by Pérez Andino, the female rector of the Egbẹ́ Fermina Gómez ati Echu-Dina, ìyánífá Dulce María Rodríguez Sánchez, stated from her *casa-templo* in Holguín, "We will never negate the consecration of ìyánífá. To the contrary, we are going to stick around, studying [Ifá]. And we will combat all that wants to eliminate us."[9] Despite the protests of Rodríguez Sánchez and other ìyánífá and babaláwo across the island, Pérez Andino's rhetoric of unification points to the expanding strength of African traditionalism in Cuba and to the increasingly unavoidable implications of its influence on the association. The leopards of Nigerian-style Ifá-Òrìṣà, with their competing logics of ritual efficacy and their gendered and institutional interventions, are clearly leaving a broader mark on the boundaries of Ifá and oricha worship in Cuba. The ACYC president's changes in rhetoric, if not in policy, indicate the potential for future reevaluations of the state-linked organization's official stance toward African traditionalism (and ìyánífá, in particular). In the meantime, as the African traditionalist movement continues to expand in strength, practitioners of Nigerian-style Ifá-Òrìṣà will undoubtedly continue to reshape and reformulate Ifá-Òrìṣà worship on the island, acting, in idiosyncratic and heterogeneous ways, as the resourceful, fate-transformative "leopards" of translocal Ifá-Òrìṣà worship.

Global Ifá-Òrìṣà Ritual Efficacy: A View from Yorùbáland

Two years after leaving Cuba for the United States in 2016, I traveled to Táíwò Abímbọ́lá's ritual compound in the city of Ọ̀yọ́ during my first trip to Nigeria. After researching Nigerian-style Ifá-Òrìṣà in Cuba for years, I was grateful and eager to have the opportunity to meet with one of the pioneering progenitors of YTR on the island and travel to the Yorùbá "homeland," a site of promise for so many.[10] Immediately, I was struck by the remarkable similarities between Ifá divination in African traditionalist ritual houses in Cuba and Nigeria. From the cadences of the recited verses of Ifá to the plucking, preparing, and eating of sacrificial guinea fowl, pigeons, and chickens before and after rituals, the visuality and sonority of Ifá ritual powerfully evoked the specificity of African traditionalist ritual in Cuba, from Sabina de León's casa-templo in Morón to Enrique Orozco Rubio's ẹgbẹ́ in eastern Santiago de Cuba. The ọpọ́n Ifá divination tray, the osùn babaláwo diviner's staff and its decorative, etched artistic relief on the walls of Abímbọ́lá's compound, and the giant West African snails that Cuban babaláwo now import as a form of efficacious, West African materiality—all of these evoked the uncanny specificity of Nigerian-style Ifá on the island itself. During divination readings, the revelation of the need for a material sacrifice (ebó), the counting of bills, and the sending of a babaláwo or apprentice to neighborhood stores to gather supplies recalled the familiarity of the everyday ritual hustle and monetary sacrifice of Ifá in the ritual diaspora. The pouring of beer over ritual sacrifices instead of rum—one of the products most closely associated with Cuba's particular postcolonial history in the Caribbean (see Gjelten 2008, 3)—nonetheless offered one idiosyncrasy.

Within a day of staying with Abímbọ́lá, I gradually became aware of the spatialization of the ritual compound and, specifically, the ways the layout and design speak to Abímbọ́lá's cultivated engagement with practitioners from abroad. Abímbọ́lá has converted the space into an impressive guest house, Ifá-Òrìṣà learning center, ritual space, small neighborhood store, and personal family home that takes up the space of a large city block, surrounded on all sides by immense walls and a guarded entrance. In the back of the compound, a recently constructed guest residence with two suites on the bottom and three renovated suites on top—each with a separate bathroom and a large, common living room area with couches and a flat-screen TV—is built to host dozens of ritual tourists and guests from the Americas and Europe on any given visit. Abímbọ́lá's fluency in Spanish, gained during his years studying tropical medicine in Havana (see chapter 1), allows the Nigerian babaláwo to engage ritual visitors from the Hispanophone Americas, including Cuba, Argentina, and other sites across Latin America where YTR-oriented revisionist movements are gaining strength. Through a Spanish-language ritual orientation, Abímbọ́lá now joins other prominent Nigerian priestesses and priests who also orient their global ritual authority toward the Hispanophone Américas through Spanish-language ritual publications, West African material export businesses geared toward Latinx and Latin American clients, and the cultivation of transnational ritual tourism and travel. To the right of Abímbọ́lá's principal home, an open-air patio with dozens of stacked chairs and a series of classroom-style chalkboards etched with diagrams and writings on Ifá anticipates the arrival of guests, who travel internationally to study with the renowned Nigerian babaláwo and receive readings and consecrations. In the back of the compound, an open-air ritual area houses three egúngún masks (agọ̀ egúngún), displayed standing upright in human-like form. The impressive visuality of Abímbọ́lá and his family's three masks instantaneously conjures the rich designs of the five masks owned by Abím-bọ́lá's close Cuban friend and collaborator Frank Cabrera Suárez in Havana that were sent to the Cuban babaláwo by Abímbọ́lá's father, Wándé Abímbọ́lá (chapter 5).

Abímbọ́lá's orientation toward foreign ritual visitors and godchildren in Nigeria mirrors, to a significant degree, the translocal efficacy of international ritual tourism and the cultivation of globally oriented ritual lineages among African traditionalists in Cuba itself. Amid the global dynamics of economic precarity that afflict postcolonial nations in West Africa and the Caribbean, Ifá and òrìṣà priests and priestesses in Nigeria, Cuba, and other sites across the Americas mobilize foreign ritual tourism and the building of transnational ritual lineages as a vital source of translocal engagement and economic empowerment and opportunity. In Cuba, where the effects of the US embargo compound the economic vagaries of the revolutionary state, African traditionalist ìyánífá and babaláwo confront the everyday hustle to survive and *resolver* through the efficacious promise of YTR, including the potential it holds for building transnational lineages. Cabrera's Nigerian-rooted Ilé Tuntún in Havana, which was founded in collaboration with Abímbọ́lá in 1997, now boasts godchildren in Spain, Mexico, Venezuela, Italy, and France, many of whom travel to the ẹgbẹ́ in Cuba to receive initiations and consecrations.[11] African traditionalist ẹgbẹ́ across Cuba, including the Aworeni and Odùgbemi lineages, also actively craft transnational lineage institutions with subsidiary temples (and proliferative *ahijados*) in Panama, Ecuador, Mexico, Spain, and other sites across the Americas and Europe. In Nigeria, likewise, babaláwo and ìyánífá mobilize their own efficacious engagements with Yorùbá-inspired ritual diasporas abroad, crafting novel global constituencies of Ifá-Òrìṣà ritual followers and revitalizing an "endangered" ritual tradition in Yorùbáland itself. In the face of the steep ebb of YTR traditions and affiliation in Nigeria (chapter 2), Abímbọ́lá and other Yorùbá Ifá and òrìṣà priests and priestesses mobilize the heightened interest in YTR across the Global South to maintain the vitality of Ifá and òrìṣà traditions and cultivate ritual tourism to the Yorùbá homeland.

From Havana to Ọ̀yọ́

Within a few hours of my arrival at Abímbọ́lá's compound, the Nigerian babaláwo called his close friend Frank Cabrera Suárez in Cuba on his cell phone and put me on the line. The two babaláwo—one in Ọ̀yọ́ and the other in Havana—have talked on the phone, often daily, since Abímbọ́lá left Cuba in the late 1990s. Despite the prohibitive costs of paying for international phone calls between the island and Nigeria (over $1USD per minute during my research years, an astronomical price in Cuba), the frequent calls between the two became an everyday part of my fieldwork with Ilé Tuntún in 2015 and 2016. Now, I found myself on the opposite end of the line as I heard Cabrera's voice enthusiastically connecting with me from Havana. "Táíwò is the one who advises me in all religious aspects," Cabrera emphasized to me two years earlier, shortly before I left Cuba in 2016 (Cabrera, interview, April 9, 2016). "He's the one who attends to us personally. . . . If you don't know something, you have to ask." This ability to ask, now, from ritual authorities in contemporary Yorùbáland rather than from fellow babalaos on the island itself, forms a cornerstone of African traditionalist ritual rupture in Cuba. No longer separated from contemporary YTR ritual knowledge by over a century of geotemporal isolation, "Africanists" in Cuba use their connections with contemporary Yorùbá practitioners to forge novel hierarchies of knowledge and ritual authority. Centrally, African traditionalists such as Cabrera use their connections with Yorùbá ritual authorities to heighten the efficacy of ritual "works," a driving logic that ties them to other Yorùbá-inspired revisionists across the Global South.

When speaking of his own visit to Nigeria in 2013, for example, Cabrera framed his trip with Abímbọ́lá less as a tour of Yorùbáland and more as a form of *trabajo* (work). "We traveled, doing the work [of Ifá]," he emphasized, describing one of the only times the babaláwo have seen each other in person since the 1990s.[12] "You have to study," Cabrera continued, seemingly drawing the conversation back to the present moment and the need for continued work, hustle, and sacrifice in Cuba itself. "Right now, I have chants I have to learn," Cabrera stated. Underscoring the African traditionalist imperative to learn the contemporary Yorùbá language *orin* (songs) and *oríkì* (chants and praise poetry) passed to him by Abímbọ́lá and to vocalize them with correct intelligibility and intonation, Cabrera concluded, succinctly, "and the chants have to be learned by heart."

Efficacy, Use, Potentiality

The case studies in this book delineate just a few ways that women and men harness efficacy as a potentiality-filled promise in Cuba. Throughout, I explore efficacy—and, centrally, the efficacy of sound—as a powerful force animating contemporary engagement with the African continent and with YTR ritual movements across the Global South. Through translocal, Nigerian-style Ifá, African traditionalists reshape sound, listening, and language to heighten efficacy and success in Cuban ritual. Additionally, Ifá-Òrìṣà priests (babaláwo), priestesses (ìyánífá), and female batá players (*bataleras*) harness the efficacy of efficacy (or "the uses of use," Ahmed 2019) in the service of divergent projects and desires. African traditionalists mobilize logics of heightened ritual efficacy to challenge gendered prohibitions in Cuban ritual music, disrupt the monopoly of state-linked religious institutions and restrictions on Cuba's burgeoning civil society, and heighten their own personal efficacy in the realization of goals and desires. Nigerian-style practitioners' positioning between two broad and often competing domains of Ifá and òrìṣà worship—Cuban-style Regla de Ocha-Ifá and Nigerian-style Ifá-Òrìṣà—also allows them to generatively harness in-betweenness in the service of idiosyncratic desires and needs. The interstitial potentiality of Nigerian-style Ifá offers a powerful resource for ìyánífá, babaláwo, and bataleras, allowing them to harness, at will, the efficacy of the close or the usefulness of the far to transform their fates and lives.

In this book, I've used efficacy to examine how notions of use and utility offer a powerful lens through which to explore the promise and potentiality of translocal forms of engagement. I've shown how individuals draw on the utility of the close and the far to create alternate futures and craft novel possibilities. Throughout, I underscore how translocal logics of efficacy can drive powerful ruptures in local hierarchies of knowledge, action, and authority. Through the promise of reinvention of ritual and self, Nigerian-style Ifá-Òrìṣà in Cuba capacitates individuals to personally manifest as *eficaz* (efficacious), allowing them to resculpt the conditions of their lives within the contingencies of a precarious present.

Acknowledgments

This book began over a decade ago, and countless individuals in Cuba, the United States, Nigeria, and elsewhere helped shape its contents. First and foremost, I'd like to thank ethnobotanist Julio Martínez Betancourt, who first introduced me to Nigerian-style Ifá during a fortuitous encounter in Santiago de las Vegas, Havana, in 2012. Looking back, the insights contained within these pages came to fruition only through Martínez Betancourt's insatiable academic curiosity, openness, and friendship. To Martínez Betancourt, who opened the path for this research and generously shared his own publications, intellectual interests, and contacts over the course of a decade, I am extremely grateful.

Innumerable others in Havana, Santiago de Cuba, and other locales across Cuba contributed insights, conversations, and meals and opened their homes and house-temples (*casa-templos*) to me. Ruddy Fernández García, Nagybe Madariaga Pouymiró, Enrique Orozco Rubio, and Frank Cabrera Suárez were especially generous in offering time, friendship, contacts, patience, conversation, and insights. This project would not have been possible without them. In eastern Baracoa, Rosendo Romero Suárez and Ricardo "Buzzy" Pérez were also especially generous. I'd also like to acknowledge and thank three incredible women who passed during the course of my research in Cuba and who each greatly impacted me: Katherine Hagedorn, Anais López Rubio, and Ania.

This project was born out of my time at the University of Pennsylvania (2009–17) and, subsequently, my appointment as resident director of Penn Global's study abroad program at the University of Havana and the New Latin American Cinema Foundation (Fundación del Nuevo Cine Latinoamericano) (fall semesters 2012–16). Thank you to Danielle Scugoza for providing me with such an incredible and massively enjoyable opportunity. Thank you also to my Penn Abroad students, who offered rich perspectives on their experiences in Cuba and were a joy to get to know and spend time with. At the University of Pennsylvania, Timothy Rommen offered an endless source of enthusiasm, fun, encouragement, wisdom, and support, and continues to do so into my professional career. Thank you, Tim! At the University of Pennsylvania, I also benefited from a number of excellent colleagues, and I would especially like to thank Jairo Moreno, Carol Muller, Guthrie P. Ramsey Jr., and John L. Jackson. Stephan Palmié and Jairo Moreno gave generative critiques and comments on earlier drafts of this manuscript. Likewise, Amanda Villepastour offered extensive commentary and editing, greatly improving the manuscript. I am immensely grateful for her time and expertise. Villepastour also helped organize my first trip to Nigeria in 2018, a unique and beneficial opportunity for which I am extremely grateful. At the University of Pennsylvania, thanks go to Carolyn Fornoff, Evelyn Owens Malone, Lee Veeraraghavan, Laura Donnelly, Darien Lamen, Jessamyn Doan Ewing, Helena de Llanos, Daniel Villegas Vélez, Lina Martinez Hernandez, and Christine Dang for encouragement, friendship, and a vital intellectual community during our graduate years. Two School of Arts and Sciences Research Grants at the University of Pennsylvania funded the initial fieldwork for this research, and a Dean's Grant for Research and New Media provided funds for the audiovisual and recording equipment I used for photographs and audio and video recordings in Cuba.

In Havana, the Cuban Ministry of Culture's Juan Marinello Cultural Research Institute (El Instituto Cubano de Investigaciones Culturales Juan Marinello) supported my research and provided the visa/carnet necessary for three full years of research as a foreign ethnomusicologist and temporary resident affiliated with the institute (January 2014–August 2016). I'd especially like to thank Henry Heredia and Martha Esquenazi Pérez for their support and encouragement at the institute during these years. Thank you also to fellow US American ethnographers Hope Bastian Martínez and Maya J. Berry for facilitating initial contacts with the institute and for delightful friendships that greatly enriched these years. Other friendships and relationships shaped these years in beautiful ways: a special thank you to Nora Kratz, Suzanne Gardinier, Kepa Izaguirre, Marilyn G. Miller, and Dachelys Valdés Moreno.

My position as assistant professor of ethnomusicology at the University of Nevada–Reno (UNR) allowed this project to come fully to fruition. Thank you so very much to my wonderful musicology colleagues, Louis Niebur and Julianne Lindberg, who provide an absolutely joyful, creative, and collaborative environment to work in. I feel so lucky for you both! Thank you also to my excellent colleagues in the Department of Music and to our incredible administrative staff (Cynthia Prescott, Vicki Bell, and Neva Sheehan). A special thanks go to Olga Perez Flora and James Flora, who offered a home away from home at UNR and beautiful opportunities to continue performing Cuban music in Reno. Thank you also to Chance Utter for the opportunity to play batá here. I'm grateful for your upbeat, energizing spirit. So many other colleagues supported this work directly or indirectly. A special thanks to Caitlin Early for a generative book writing retreat and innumerable writing sessions. Thanks also to Brettón Rodríguez, Gaby Ortiz Flores, Ignacio Montoya, Jenna Hanchey, Vivian Zavataro, Anushka Peres, Isabelle Favre, Pardis Dabashi, Nasia Anam, and Daniel Enrique Pérez for providing such a beautiful intellectual community here. Our former dean of the College of Liberal Arts at UNR Debra Moddelmog facilitated vital start-up research packages for junior faculty, and the College of Liberal Arts provided funding for follow-up research trips to Cuba (2020) and my first trip to Nigeria (2018).

Colleagues at other institutions also greatly supported this work. Immense thanks to Marysol Quevedo and Cesar Favila for an exceptionally supportive writing group over the course of years. It's been a true pleasure to collaborate with you two. Thanks also to Jessica Swanston Baker, who changed the course of writing entirely with a necessary, and delightful, writing retreat and transformative comments on the book proposal. Thank you also to M. Myrta Leslie Santana and Marceline Saibou for support on early presentations of this material and for ongoing encouragement over the years.

Lots of love and gratitude go to my family. Thank you to Lynn Shapiro, Gina Meadows, Glenn Meadows, and Elizabeth Meadows for your support and love during the book writing years. To Lynn Shapiro, thank you for introducing me to your immense love for music (always audible in our childhood home) and encouraging my passion for playing music as a kid. My grandparents on my father's side, Wanda Meadows and Junior Meadows, constantly filled their own home with harmonica, accordion, and bass, proving to me from the youngest age that women can play electric bass, too. My nana on my mother's side, Marian Blanck Shapiro, greatly encouraged and supported me during her lifetime, including during my graduate years, and continues to inspire me through her life story. Gina, thank you immensely for being in my life the way that you have since I was a teenager. I'm so grateful for you. A special thanks to Leah Meadows for a fantastic brainstorming session in DC and for endless joyful times together. Thank you also to Ryan, Blake and Grace, Ted, Stephen, Kathleen, and Joel for all the fun and love.

Finally, I'm grateful to my partner, Lydia Huerta. Thank you, Lydia, for being such an immense source of adventure, encouragement, joy, and love during years of writing and revision. ¡Gracias por todo, mi amor! ¡Te amo!

Material for chapter 3 was adapted from an article entitled "El tradicionalismo africano: Women, Consecrated Batá, and the Polemics of 'Re-Yorubization,' in Cuban Ritual Music," published in *Ethnomusicology* 65, no. 1 (Winter 2021): 86–111.

Glossary

agọ̀ egúngún *egúngún* masks
agogo Ifá metal bell
ahijados ritual godchildren
àṣẹ in Yorùbá philosophy, the manifesting force of transformation (*aché* in Lucumí)
babalao priest of Ifá (Cuban Lucumí spelling)
babaláwo priest of Ifá (Yorùbá spelling)
batalera female batá drummer
bembé religious party for the oricha/òrìṣà
dafá Ifá divination reading
ẹgbẹ́ African traditionalist ritual communities, conceived as ritual brother and sisterhoods
eggún ancestors (Lucumí)
ikin (also ikin Ifá) palm nuts used for Ifá divination
iróké a tapper and bell used in Ifá divination
iṣẹṣe a Yorùbá language term used to reference the Yorùbá traditional religion (YTR) of Nigeria
iyánífá priestess of Ifá
Lucumí ritual lexicon of Cuban Regla de Ocha-Ifá
odù "signs" of Ifá divination (256 total). Also *odù Ifá*.
omi ẹ̀rọ̀ ritual herbal bath
ọpọ́n Ifá divination tray
oricha deity (*òrìṣà* in Yorùbá, *orixá* in Brazilian *candomblé*)
oríkì praise poetry
orin ritual songs
òrìṣà deity of the Yorùbá traditional religion (*oricha/orisha* in Cuban Regla de Ocha, *orixá* in Brazilian *candomblé*)
Ọ̀rúnmìlà òrìṣà of divination (Orunmila/Orula in Cuban Lucumí)
osùn babaláwo diviner's staff
Regla de Ocha Cuban-style oricha worship, also termed Santería
Regla de Ocha-Ifá Cuban ritual complex of oricha worship (Regla de Ocha) and Ifá divination
toque rhythm or rhythmic archetype

Notes

Preface

1. Also *ikin Ifá*. In Cuban Lucumí, the ritual lexicon of Regla de Ocha (Santería) and Ifá, the palm nuts are termed *ikines*.

2. Ifá Ìranlówo, founded by Cuban *babalao* Victor Betancourt Estrada in Havana in 1991 (Martínez Betancourt 2014), is widely considered to be the first African traditionalist *casa-templo* (house-temple) established in Cuba (Larduet Luaces 2014). The clip of Yadira Flamand Rodríguez in the documentary *Ìyánífá: La necesaria evolución* was filmed in the casa-templo of ìyánífá Dulce María Rodríguez Sánchez in Holguín (Egbè Fermina Gómez ati Echu-Dina). Rodríguez Sánchez's temple forms a subsidiary temple of Betancourt's Ifá Ìranlówo lineage located outside of Havana.

3. *Àṣẹ* (rendered *aché* in the Cuban Lucumí ritual lexicon) also constitutes a central concept in the practices of Regla de Ocha and Ifá in Cuba.

4. *Oricha* (in the Cuban Lucumí ritual lexicon) is rendered *òrìṣà* in the Yorùbá language and in the Yorùbá traditional religion of Nigeria.

5. Anthropologist Aisha M. Beliso-De Jesús (2015a, 817) notes that the term *styles* (*estilos*) is often used to distinguish between "different regional lineages of Santería" in Cuba (e.g., Matanzas versus Havana) and, more broadly, between the "African-style" practices of "Nigerian Ifá" throughout the Americas and Cuban-style practices on the island. In this book, I also using the terms *Nigerian-style* and *Cuban-style* to make this distinction, building on African traditionalists' own use of the terms *Nigerian-style*, *Yorùbá-style*, and *Cuban-style* during my research.

6. In Nigerian-style ritual communities in Cuba, revisionists often spell *oricha* "òrìṣà," in accordance with Standard Yorùbá orthography in Nigeria (see "On Terminology and Orthographic Choice" in the preface).

7. Yorùbáland extends beyond Nigeria's borders into the southeastern region of Benin and the north-central region of Togo, where Ifá and òrìṣà practices flourish. "Nigerian-style" practitioners in Cuba have thus far engaged exclusively with Nigerian *babaláwo* and ìyánífá, however, informing this nationally specific linguistic designation for the practices of the Yorùbá traditional religion of West Africa.

8. This phenomenon reflects broader tendencies toward ideologically informed spelling choice across the African ritual diaspora (Johnson 2002; Schieffelin and Doucet 1994; Wirtz 2007a). Linguistic anthropologist Kristina Wirtz (2007a, 273) notes of her fieldwork in eastern

Cuba: "The choice of orthographic representation is never neutral." Rather, orthographic choice in African-inspired ritual in Cuba, Brazil, and other locales indicates a specific ideological relationship to African "sources" and "African diasporic history" (Wirtz 2007a, 242; Johnson 2002).

9. For a detailed argument for Lucumí's status as a ritual "lexicon" rather than a "language" or "dialect," see Villepastour 2020.

10. Standard Yorùbá orthography conforms to the guidelines set by the Nigerian Joint Consultative Committee on Education in 1974 (see Joint Consultative Committee on Education 1974; Olúmúyìwá 2013). For a timeline of historical efforts to standardize Yorùbá orthography in Nigeria since 1875, including heightened efforts at standardization in the postcolonial period of the late 1960s and early 1970s, see Olúmúyìwá 2013.

11. Olúmúyìwá (2013, 40) notes that "there remains a great deal of contention over writing conventions-spelling, grammar, the use of tone marks" in Yorùbá orthography, even despite repeated historical efforts at standardization. The numerous dialects of the language further complicate these efforts.

Introduction

1. These economic policy changes were announced between September 2010 and November 2011 (see P. Peters 2012, 8, 11).

2. At the time of writing, President Biden delayed years in fulfilling (and only partially fulfilling) a campaign promise to reverse the Trump administration's aggressive sanctions against Cuba and its reversal of Obama's policies, moving to increase international flights and expand allowances on remittances in May 2022 (see Sanger 2022).

3. Although both embassies remained closed, during Jimmy Carter's US presidency in 1977, Cuba and the United States signed an accord to open a US Interests Section (USINT) in Havana and a Cuban Interests Section in Washington, DC, both of which "operated under the protection of the Embassy of Switzerland." See US Embassy 2020. In 2017, the Trump administration again drastically reduced personnel and operations at the US embassy, including processing visas for Cubans, as part of a hardening of diplomatic relations (and presumably in response to the so-called Havana Syndrome attacks; see Aljazeera 2022).

4. Tighter US sanctions against Cuba imposed by the Trump administration in 2017 (restricted flights and sanctions against individuals and companies that visit or do business with Cuba) alongside the COVID-19 pandemic crisis have since "devastated" the tourism industry in Cuba (Nicoll 2022). The war in Ukraine beginning in 2022 further impacted Russian travel to Cuba, a significant source of tourism to the island (Kahn 2022). In 2022, the severe economic crisis instigated the migration of "nearly 250,000 Cubans, more than 2 percent of the island's 11 million population," to the United States, often via precarious, homemade boats (Augustin and Robles 2022). A number exceeding both "the [number of migrants of the] 1980 Mariel boatlift and the 1994 Cuban rafter crisis combined," the migration crisis "has no end in sight and threatens the stability of a country that already has one of the hemisphere's oldest populations" (Augustin and Robles 2022).

5. Before being incorporated into the municipality of Havana in 1976, Santiago de las Vegas was a separate city with its own government (Kelly 2022).

6. Villepastour (2015b, 282–83) defines egbé as "society, fraternity, or age mates," differentiating it from the òrìsà Egbé, the "Òrìsà of heavenly accomplices."

7. As of 2020 (Martínez Betancourt, pers. comm., 2020).

8. Also termed *odù Ifá*.

9. In the Yorùbá language, words are not pluralized with an *s* as in Spanish and Lucumí. Thus, *babaláwo* indicates both the singular and the plural in Yorùbáland and in YTR ritual parlance. In this book, I follow Nigerian-style academic and ritual practitioners in Cuba, including Julio Martínez Betancourt, who also use *babaláwo* to indicate both the singular and the plural (without the addition of an *s*) (see Martínez Betancourt 2014; Martínez Betancourt and Barrero 2017, 56). Cuban-style Regla de Ocha-Ifá practitioners, meanwhile, pluralize *babalao* as *babalaos* in accordance with the rules of the Spanish language (and Lucumí).

10. Notable exceptions include Ned Sublette's *Cuba and Its Music: From the First Drums to the Mambo* (2004), which ends in 1959 (at the entrance of the Cuban Revolution) and linguistic anthropologist Kristina Wirtz's *Performing Afro-Cuba: Image, Voice, Spectacle in the Making of Race and History* (2014). Wirtz's monograph offers an ethnography of African-inspired folkloric and musical performance in eastern Cuba, where Santería has historically been overshadowed by other African-inspired ritual practices (for a recent treatment of Santería and the history of the batá in eastern Cuba, see Larduet Luaces 2014). In a promising turn, recent scholarship on music and Santería has also increasingly focused on questions of homosexuality (Morad 2014) and intersectional issues of sexual subjectivity, trans subjectivity, gender performance, and race (Leslie Santana 2019).

11. For US American–authored studies that focus on the batá ritual instruments of Regla de Ocha, specifically, see Schweitzer 2013 and Vaughan and Aldama 2012.

12. Lino Neira Betancourt's book *La percusión en la música cubana* ([2004] 2014), for example, dedicates an entire chapter to "Yoruba Antecedents" in Cuban percussion, outlining the *chequeré*, *tambores de bembé*, *tambores iyesá*, and *batá* without making any reference to Ifá (including the prominence of the *irofá* percussion instrument in Cuban Ifá ritual). Book-length studies that do focus specifically on Ifá divination in Cuba and Nigeria, meanwhile, overwhelmingly approach divination from the perspective of anthropology (see Bascom 1952, 1969a; Holbraad 2012; McClelland 1982; Olupona and Abiodun 2016) or, alternatively, from the perspective of babaláwo's own ritual and theological writings (see Abímbọ́lá 1997; Adegbindin 2014). Notable exceptions include Ifáyẹmí Ẹlẹ́buìbọn's *Ìyèrè Ifá: Tonal Poetry, the Voice of Ifá: An Exposition of Yorùbá Divinational Chants* (1999) and Wándé Abímbọ́lá's chapter "Continuity and Change in the Verbal, Artistic, Ritual, and Performance Traditions of Ifá Divination" (2016), both of which focus on Ifá in Nigeria.

13. For examples of those that have, see Beliso-De Jesús 2015a and 2015b and Palmié 2013. In the context of Brazil, see Díaz 2016, 2020, and 2021 and Matory 1999 and 2005.

14. Here, I also follow scholars who point to language as a domain conceptualized not as outside of sound or the sensorial but rather as foundationally constitutive of each (see, e.g., Feld 2017; Ochoa Gautier 2014; Porcello et al. 2010; Wirtz 2014).

15. See, for example, scholarship on language as an "acoustic signature" of an individual (Truax 2001, in Porcello et al. 2010) and as an indicator and expression of class (Fox 2004), gender identity (Davies et al. 2015; Zimman 2018), and emotional states (Friedhoff, Alpert, and Kurtzberg 1962). See also the voice and language as a "sonic geography" indicative of place and race and crucial in the construction of local identities (Boland 2010) and localized, in-community forms of musical expression (Rose 1994).

16. Yunieski González Ramírez, interview by the author, Santiago de las Vegas, April 18, 2016; Otto William Sabina de León, interview by the author, Morón, May 18, 2016; Nagybe Madariaga Pouymiró, interview by the author, Santiago de Cuba, May 14, 2016; Humberto Torres Hurtado,

interview by the author, Santiago de Cuba, April 23, 2016. All interviews in Cuba conducted in Spanish and translated by the author.

17. Enrique Orozco Rubio, interview by the author, Santiago de Cuba, June 23, 2015.

18. In a provocative look at "transgender 'transformistas'" (transgender gender performers) in Cuba, M. Myrta Leslie Santana (2020, 2022) generatively highlights the abundance and resonance of discourses of dignity (*dignidad*) within Cuban contexts of "social and material precarity."

19. The word *culto* is commonly used to describe African-inspired ritual practices by practitioners in Cuba and does not in and of itself carry the negative connotations associated with the word *cult* in English. Larduet Luaces also cofounded the eastern Cuban carnival festival, Festival del Caribe / Fiesta de Fuego, in Santiago de Cuba in the 1980s (see chapter 3). The terms *palero/a* and *santero/a* index a practitioner (-o, male/ -a, female) of Palo and Santería (Regla de Ocha), respectively.

20. In the case of happiness, Ahmed (2010a) complicates the notion of the object of sociocultural desire as guaranteeing a positive outcome, critiquing societal investments in upholding such failed (and, for many, unattainable) promises.

21. The phrase *horizons of potentiality* draws on queer of color and performance scholar José Esteban Muñoz's (2009, 1) influential and poetic formulation of queerness as an "ideality" that can be felt as "the warm illumination of a horizon imbued with potentiality." I find this description apt for the forms of potentiality, intimacy, and futurity demonstrated in Orozco Rubio's statement here. For more on the complexity of views on homosexuality in Nigerian-style Ifá-Òrìṣà, see chapter 4.

22. Orozco Rubio has, however, engaged with Nigerian babaláwo who visit Cuba directly. See chapter 3.

23. Here, I draw on Ochoa Gautier's (2014, 26) formulation of aurality, which points to how contested understandings of sound often "entangle the ontological and epistemological." See chapter 1.

24. On "Expanding the Idea of América" and the possibilities of "Américan rhetoric," see Olson and De los Santos 2015, 194.

Chapter One

1. McDonnell 1990b. US officials at the time claimed the "exposed" agents were merely "legitimate American diplomats" harassed by Cuban propaganda campaigns (see D. Williams 1987).

2. The drug-trafficking scandal ended with the execution of decorated war hero General Arnaldo T. Ochoa Sánchez and constituted one of the biggest scandals of Fidel Castro's decades-long presidency (see Pear 1989).

3. After decades, the "wet foot, dry foot" policy was eliminated by the Obama administration following the temporary normalization of relations with Cuba in 2017 (see Labott, Liptak, and O 2017).

4. De La Fuente's (2001) and Clealand's (2017) studies on race in Cuba underscore the discrepancies between racial designations in Cuba, the United States, and other locales across the Americas. Additionally, their studies historicize the specificity of Cuban notions of Whiteness, Blackness, and mixed-race categories (e.g., mestizo and mulato) from the colonial to revolutionary eras. In reference to individuals in revolutionary Cuba, Clealand generatively makes explicit that she uses terms such *Black* to describe persons who would be considered as such in Cuba itself (14). Clealand states, "I use the term 'black' to describe persons who would be considered

black or in some cases *mulato* by Cuban standards," while noting that "there is not a definitive line separating dark *mulatos* and blacks of lighter brown skin," nor one separating these from categories such as *moro* (used to "describe dark-skinned *mulatos*") (14). Here, I follow Clealand in using terms such as *White*, *Black*, and *mestizo* to describe such designations as they would be interpreted in Cuba itself and based, especially, on individuals' self-identifications in conversations and interviews. This keeps present the observation that, in Latin American countries outside of Cuba, "research . . . has found that often racial self-identification does not match with interviewer identification primarily due to nonwhites identifying as lighter than they may be identified by others," and, presumably, by foreign or lighter-skinned ethnographers (Clealand citing Telles 2004, 14). While researchers in Cuba, including Clealand (2017) and Mark Sawyer (2006), have generally found "that there was significant agreement with both interviewer and self-identification not only among blacks, but all races" in Cuba itself (Clealand 2017, 14), as a US American White ethnographer, I nonetheless use racial self-identifications spoken explicitly in conversations and interviews when possible.

5. Mwakikagile refers specifically here to the era before the fall of Apartheid in South Africa.

6. For differing estimations of the exact number of extant ethnic and linguistic groups in Nigeria, see Adegbija 1997 and Gandonu 2011.

7. For more on the interactions of Christianity and Islam in Nigeria, see Dowd 2015; Hunwick 1992; and Peel 2016.

8. Also referred to as the "postcolonial" Africa diaspora(s). See Adepoju 2010; Konadu-Agyemang, Takyi, and Arthur 2006; Koser 2003; and Okpewho and Nzegwu 2009.

9. Notably, such framings are often accompanied in the popular press with overtly racist overtones, such as in the article "Black China: Africa's First Superpower Is Coming Sooner Than You Think" (Hill 2020). Such characterizations speak to ongoing narratives of African underdevelopment that plague interpretations of the continent's growing economic and technological strength. See Maliki 2018.

10. As Brown notes, "Ifá's 256 compound *odù* signs are permutations of a set of sixteen ranked principal or parent signs, called *melli* (Yoruba *méji*), i.e., $16 \times 16 = 256$" (D. Brown 2003, 339). For more on the odù of the Ifá corpus, see Bascom 1952, 1969a and Holbraad 2012.

11. See Lydia Cabrera's ([1954] 1993) seminal mid-century ethnographic text, *El Monte*, on the links between the ecological materiality of ritual practice in African-inspired Cuban ritual and alternative ontologies of place and perception among practitioners of Regla de Ocha, Palo, and other African-inspired ritual practices in Cuba. Martínez Betancourt's rich ethnography of *yerberos*, or commercial plant vendors, in Havana likewise points to the imbrication of plant materiality, preservationist ecology, generational ritual knowledge, and instrumental actionability in African-inspired ritual in the urban capital (Martínez Betancourt 2013; see introduction).

12. For more on competing global assemblages of "Nigerian-style" and "Cuban-style" Ifá and oricha/òrìṣà worship, see Beliso-De Jesús 2015a.

13. I have not found evidence to dispute this claim by Rodríguez, although it may belie other, previous lineages founded by foreigners in Yorùbáland.

14. "Nuestro Fundador," *Linaje-Odugbemi*, accessed September 4, 2019, https://www.linaje-odugbemi.com/nuestro-fundador/.

15. On the economic disadvantages faced by Black and African-descendant Cubans since the Special Period, see Roland 2011.

16. Victor Betancourt Estrada, interview by the author, Havana, June 11, 2016; Frank Cabrera Suárez, interview by the author, Havana, April 9, 2016.

184 NOTES TO PAGES 25-30

17. Manuel de Jesús Rabaza Torres, interview by the author, Havana, April 27, 2016.

18. For Regla de Ocha-Ifá's travel from western Cuba to eastern Santiago de Cuba, see Larduet Luaces 2014.

19. See Ochoa 2010.

20. See Miller 2005, 2009; Torres Zayas 2010.

21. See Andreu Alonso 1995, in Holbraad 2012, 12; D. Brown 2003.

22. See Brandon 1993; Omojola 2014; Peel 2000.

23. For more on the cabildos de nación, or the Spanish colonial institutions crucial to the preservation of African traditions in Cuba, see I. Moreno 1999 and Ortiz 1921.

24. For a generative examination of coeval temporality, see Fabian 1983.

25. The extent of just how absolute the isolation was between Cuban practitioners of Regla de Ocha-Ifá and their counterparts in Yorùbáland throughout the twentieth century is a matter of some debate. Anthropologist Alain Konen, for example, who conducted ethnographic research with the African traditionalist *babaláwo* Frank Cabrera and the Nigerian-rooted Ilé Tuntún in Havana beginning in 2002, relates an oral narrative from his Cuban interlocutors that claims that the Cuban babalao Tata Gaitán received the Yorùbá religious title of Àràbà of Cuba from three visiting African Àràbà in the "second-quarter of the twentieth century" (Konen 2013, my translation). Though Konen acknowledges that "no written historical data confirms this narrative," he finds the twentieth-century travel of Yorùbá religious leaders to Cuba as "plausible," citing Pierre Verger's accounts of the travel of Dahomean dignitaries to Cuba and Brazil for years at a time in the nineteenth century (Verger 1952, 157, in Konen 2013, my translation). If this visit of Yorùbá practitioners did occur in Cuba during the first half of the twentieth century, Konen notes that "no comparable event seems to have been repeated for decades," at least until the 1987 exchange between Cuban babalao Filiberto O'Farrill and the visiting Ọọni of Ilé-Ifẹ̀, explored in this chapter (Verger 1952, 157, in Konen 2013, my translation).

26. See Langley 1983; Perez 1986.

27. See Bonsal 1971; Freyre 2006.

28. See Ayorinde 2004; Baloyra and Morris 1993; Castro Figueroa 2012; Menéndez 2002; Olorunnisola and Akinbami 1992.

29. As Romeu and others note, the Fourth Congress of the Cuban Communist Party announced that "its members and government officials . . . [could] join religious and fraternal organizations and vice versa," effectively legalizing open religious practice for the first time in decades (Romeu 2013, 263).

30. As Edward George (2005) notes, in a country with a population of only eleven million people, the Cuban revolutionary government sent as many as half a million Cuban citizens to serve in the military conflict in Angola between the mid-1960s and 1991, a conflict that "would shape the lives of a generation of Cubans."

31. In the case of Nigeria, this did include Nigerian writer and Nobel Prize winner Wole Soyinka (Yorùbá: Akínwándé Olúwọlé Babátúndé Ṣóyíinká), who took numerous trips to Cuba (Castro Figueroa 2012).

32. La Isla de la Juventud is an island separated from the mainland off Cuba's southwestern coast. As Fiddian-Qasmiyeh notes: "Formerly known as La Isla de Pinos, this small island's name was formally changed to La Isla de la Juventud (the Island of Youth) in 1978. . . . The transformation of this previously under-populated Cuban island into an International Centre for Studies revolutionised both the islands demography and its economic capacity" (Fiddian-Qasmiyeh 2015, 139; see also Alsonso Valdés 1984).

33. During my years in Cuba, this continued South-South solidarity and medical internationalism was evident in Cuba's response to the outbreak of the Ebola virus in Africa in 2014–15,
when Cuba sent 256 Cuban doctors and medical professionals to provide perilous "direct care"
in Sierra Leone, Liberia, and Equatorial Guinea (see Beldarraín Chaple and Mercer 2017, 134),
and in the medical response to the 2015 earthquake in Nepal, to which Cuba sent 49 health care
professionals (see Granma 2015).

34. C. Peters (2012) translates *una fuente viva* to "well spring."

35. Castro Figueroa (2012) and Moore (2006) both offer summaries of Cuban revolutionary policies toward religion—including Catholicism and Afro-Cuban religions—from the early
years of the revolution to the Fourth Congress of the Cuban Communist Party in 1991. Citing
Clark (1992), Kirk (1989), and Vázquez Montalbán (1998), for example, Moore outlines how the
Cuban revolutionary government's earliest conflicts with religion were primarily with the Catholic Church, which—though exhibiting less power and influence than in other Latin American
nations—became "a refuge for oppositional movements" against Castro's new regime following
the 1959 revolution (Kirk 1989, in Moore 2006, 202). As early as 1961, Cuba's vast and vibrant
popular religious festivals—with their ideological links to Catholicism and saints' festivals—
were effectively eliminated through a lack of allocation of state resources (Moore 2006, 202).
Additionally, "images of Santa Claus and the use of Christmas trees" were banned (202) and
important Christian holidays were renamed and reframed as secular, revolutionary traditions.
The week preceding Easter, for example, was coined "Playa Girón week" (referencing the failed
US Bay of Pigs invasion of 1961) and dedicated to "mass voluntary labor" (Moore 2006, 202;
Millet and Brea 1989, 93–94). By the late 1960s, the Cuban government had effectively banned
religion by no longer allowing "anyone professing a faith to be a member of the Communist
Party" or trade unions, affiliations that were "extremely beneficial to one's educational opportunities and career" (Fernández Robaina 1994, 36, in Moore 2006, 208). During the first decades of
the revolution, Afro-Cuban ritual traditions were alternately framed as "primitive," "misguided,
confused, backward, [and] uncultured" (Moore 2006, 210) or, in more extreme examples in
government and social scientist publications, as "pathological" (McGarrity 1992, 199, in Moore
2006, 211) or evidence of "mental disorder" (Moore 2006, 211).

36. Castro Figueroa sums up the equivalency between nonpersecution and tolerance on the
part of the revolutionary state between the mid-1970s and mid-1980s when he states—referring
to the 1986 reestablishment of the Letra del Año: "And of course, if this happened, it was because
the government permitted it" (Castro Figueroa 2012, 91). See also Argyriadis and Capone 2004;
Hearn 2008.

37. As Abímbọ́lá notes, the lack of Spanish speakers in Yorùbáland and English- or Yorùbá-
speakers in Cuba has made exchange and communication between Cuba and Yorùbáland particularly difficult. During his first visit to Cuba in the 1980s, Abímbọ́lá hoped to establish a
Spanish-Yorùbá exchange program between the University of Ife (now Obafemi Awolowo University) and Cuba modeled on the successful Portuguese program that he previously designed
as dean of Faculty of Arts between the University of Ife and Brazil. The Cuban embassy sent the
University of Ife Spanish instructors following Abímbọ́lá's visit and his establishment of a certificate course in Spanish but failed to set up Yorùbá language instruction in Cuba as Abímbọ́lá
originally envisioned (Abímbọ́lá 1997, 112).

38. Other Cuban *babalaos*, however, were skeptical of the Ọ̀ọ̀ni's visit. Palmié (2013) relates
how Cuban babalaos recalling the event years later framed it as "an attempt on the part of the
Cuban government to strike an oil deal with Nigeria" rather than as the return of "their true

sovereign," pointing to the Ọ̀ọ̀ni's status as a born-again Christian and a wealthy businessman (see Palmié 2013, 108).

39. According to the Ọ̀ọ̀ni's vision, the Yorùbá Congress would likely be modeled after the "International Congress of Òrìṣà Tradition and Culture" that a group of globally minded oricha/òrìṣà/orixa visionaries—including Wándé Abímbọ́lá, the Puerto Rican santera Marta Vega, and Brazilian "candomblé-priest cum ethnographer" Deoscoredes Maximiliano dos Santos—organized in 1981 under the Ọ̀ọ̀ni's own "patronship" (Palmié 2013, 61, 72).

40. Claudia Rauhut (2014) notes how unusual it was for Cuban babalaos to have significant contact with foreigners in the late 1980s. According to her interviews with Betancourt in 2007, his earliest contacts with written sources on the Nigerian Yorùbá religion came from contacts with practitioners in Mexico and the United States in the late 1980s (Rauhut 2014, 187). In my own interviews with Betancourt in 2016, Betancourt stated that his first direct contacts with Nigerian babaláwo—which took the form of letters and mailed correspondence—were facilitated by an Italian *ahijado*. Larduet Luaces's account of Betancourt claims Ṣọlágbadé Pópóọlá as Betancourt's first Nigerian contact (though Betancourt didn't meet Pópóọlá until 2004–5, significantly later) (Betancourt, pers. comm., 2016) and also points to an "Italian friend" as Betancourt's initial point of contact with babaláwo of contemporary Yorùbáland (Larduet Luaces 2014, 163). In my interview, Betancourt didn't name the specific Nigerian babaláwo with which he first had correspondence during this early period.

41. Martínez Betancourt 2014; Rauhut 2014, 187.

42. Brown (2003) notes that a turn-of-the-century innovation by "Efuche Ña Rosalía, Obadimelli Octavio Samar, and the Society of Santa Bárbara (1900)" in the development of Regla de Ocha included an effort to "restructure the 'African' 'head-and-foot' initiation in favor of the 'modern' 'pantheonized Lucumí initiatory system" (117). This points to the (re-)adoption of *pie y cabeza* initiations as a return to practices from an earlier, nineteenth-century Cuban era. Brown adds that "as late as 1924," practitioners would "perform the head-and-foot initiation" if in a financial bind "and receive the other orichas later when they were needed, or affordable" (137).

43. In relation to the history of ìyánífá in the Americas, Beliso-De Jesús (2015a, 820) relates: "According to Maybell Padilla Pérez (2006, 3), the first ìyánífá in the Americas was initiated in 1985 in the United States. In 2000, two Cuban women were initiated to Ifá in Havana. In 2003, a Cuban woman living in Spain, Ìyáonifá Ifáunke Maria Antonia Regojo Soto, was initiated in Ile Ife." It's important to note, however, that Betancourt's claims to this first date of initiation (2000) are contested by some in Cuba (see chapter 4).

44. According to Frank Cabrera and others, Táíwò Abímbọ́lá only stayed in Cuba for three to four years, establishing the Nigerian-rooted institution Ilé Tuntún in Havana but never completing his medical degree (Cabrera, pers. comm., 2016).

45. Frank Cabrera Suárez, interview by the author, Havana, April 4, 2016.

46. In his writings and placards, Cabrera alternately spells Ilé Tuntún as Ilé Tüntun, Ilè Tuntun, and Ile Tun Tun.

47. According to the registry of the Corporate Affairs Commission of the Nigerian Federal Ministry of Commerce and Tourism, the "Ile Tuntun Organisation" was officially incorporated in Nigeria in 2004, with both Táíwò and Wándé Abímbọ́lá as sponsors (Corporate Affairs Commission 2016).

48. Also rendered as *Ogbe She* (Castro Figueroa 2012) and *Obeché* (Konen 2013).

49. While Cabrera frames Nigerian-rooted, Yorùbá evangelism as prophecy, others are

much more skeptical. Numerous interlocutors during my fieldwork framed Nigerian babalá-wo's increased travels to Cuba in the 1990s and 2000s as commercially, rather than spiritually, motivated.

50. For more on the uses and resonance of "Africa" in the Afrofuturist artistic visions of contemporary US Black American musicians, from Kool Keith and Labelle to Janelle Monáe, see Murchison 2018 and Rollefson 2008.

51. For a powerful look at how "tropes of Africanness" are mobilized by African descendant musicians in Brazil, see Díaz 2021, 4.

52. Notably, however, remnants of òrìṣà such as Ẹgbẹ́ and Orí survive through selected practices, such as in loosely related eggún rituals and feeding the head in Regla de Ocha-Ifá (Villepastour, pers. comm., 2017). Additionally, praise songs dedicated to the òrìṣà Ẹgbẹ́ in YTR persist in Cuban Lucumí correlates, even as the texts and translations of the songs have significantly transformed over time (Villepastour 2020, 23).

53. My translation.

54. The Cuban Lucumí ritual lexicon is widely considered to be historically rooted in the Yorùbá language of colonial-era West Africa, both by practitioners and scholars alike (Palmié 2013; Wirtz 2007a). This framing dates to the pioneering and oft-cited comparative works of Cuban scholar Fernando Ortiz (beginning with Ortiz [1906] 1973; see Palmié 2013), who influenced the writings of subsequent twentieth-century Cuban and foreign practitioners and academics, including Nicolás Angarica (2010 [circa 1940s]), Lydia Cabrera (1957), and William Bascom (1950, 1969a, 1969b) (Palmié 2013; Villepastour 2020, 2021). Although Cuban Lucumí undoubt-edly holds a "vestigial" relationship with the linguistic precursor(s) to contemporary Yorùbá (Wirtz 2007b, 111, in Villepastour 2021, 154), recent critiques of these twentieth-century works and their potential oversimplification of the complex histories of the emergence of the Lucumí lexicon in Cuba have emerged (Palmié 2013; Villepastour 2020, 2021). These studies point to the complexity of Lucumí's at times coeval relationship with the historical development of Yorùbá dialects and of Standard Yorùbá itself in the nineteenth and twentieth centuries; they also point to the early dependence of the scholarly study of Lucumí-as-Yorùbá in Cuba on the study of Yorùbá antecedents in Brazil (Palmié 2013; Villepastour 2020, 2021).

55. For further historiographical analyses of the transnationally informed emergence of a Yorùbá ethnicity, language, and tradition in nineteenth and twentieth century Yorùbáland, see Peel 1989, 2000.

56. Here, I draw on Palmié's (2008) formulation of "predications of Africanity" on and off the African continent.

57. In certain cases, Nigerian ìyánífá, such as Chief FAMA, have published Spanish-language translations of their own Yorùbá-English ritual books for Hispanophone audiences, which also circulate in Cuba via amateur, copy-and-paste digital Word documents (see Adéwálé-Somadhi 2006b, chapter 4).

Chapter Two

1. Ìyáàlù, literally "mother-drum" in Yorùbá (Omojola 2014, 24), is a generic designation used for the lead drum of various Yorùbá ritual ensembles. These include the lead drum and "primary talker" of the bàtá ensemble (Villepastour 2010, 23) and a specific instrument that is commonly (though not always) the lead drum of the dùndún ensemble (A. Euba 1990, 19). Kayode Samuel (2008/2009, 52; 2021, 4) notes that the curved, wooden stick, termed kọ̀ngọ̀ or

ọpá in Yorùbá, has a flattened tip at the end that is often covered with rubber or animal skin to protect the surface of the instrument.

2. As discussed below, the Yorùbá language utilizes three tone levels (high tone, mid tone, and low tone) (see Eme and Uba 2016; Laniran and Clements 2003) and tonal contours (shifts in pitch over a single syllable or word) (Akinlabi and Liberman 2000). While the high tone and low tone are marked by diacritics, the mid tone "is indicated by no accent mark over a vowel" (Oládémọ 2022, vii).

3. Cuban percussion is overwhelmingly characterized by fixed-pitched construction and techniques. There are some exceptions, however, such as the highly secretive Abakuá society's incorporation of sliding-pitch techniques on the *Ékue* sacred friction drum during rituals and initiations (see Miller 2000, 2009). As Ivor Miller notes (Sexteto Habanero [1928] 1995, in Miller 2000, 171), Abakuá members who played in foundational popular *son* groups of the 1920s, such as Agustin Gutiérrez of Sexteto Habanero, imitated the sliding-pitch "roar" of the Ékue drum on *bongó* percussion (a technique audible in popular recordings such as "Dónde estás corazón" from 1928).

4. Translations given by the Àràbà of Cuba, Chief Ángel William Viera. See also Adéwálé-Somadhi 2006a.

5. There is, however, an unconfirmed oral narrative of the potential crowning of an Àràbà in Cuba by visiting Nigerian babaláwo in the first half of the twentieth century. Anthropologist Alain Konen, who conducted ethnographic research with the African traditionalist babaláwo Frank Cabrera Suárez and the Nigerian-rooted Ilé Tuntún in Havana beginning in 2002, relates an oral narrative from his Cuban interlocutors that claims that the Cuban *babalao* Tata Gaitán received the Yorùbá religious title of "Àràbà of Cuba" from three visiting African Àràbà in the "second-quarter of the twentieth century" (Konen 2013, my translation). Notably, the Àràbà of the United States, the Nigerian Àràbà Adedayo Ologundudu, was crowned the year after Dr. Viera, on June 28, 2014, and was born in Ilé-Ifẹ̀ (ChiefDayo 2014). As such, he is a Nigerian babaláwo residing permanently in the United States. These two coronations of Àràbà for region's outside of Yorùbáland—Cuba and the United States—mark the only two such coronations made by the former Àràbà Àgbáyé Chief Adisa Makoranwale Aworeni before his death in 2018, pointing to the importance of Cuba and the United States in the global Yorùbá ritual diaspora. For more on the former Àràbà Àgbáyé Chief Adisa Makoranwale, see Adelaja 2018.

6. José Manuel "Manolo" Pérez Andino, interview by the author, Havana, June 20, 2016.

7. All biographical information received through interviews with Viera, 2016.

8. Also called "itẹfa," See M. Drewal 1992, 64.

9. Palmié uses the term *transatlantic messenger* in reference to the mid-twentieth-century French "photographer, inveterate traveler, ethnographer, and historian" Pierre Verger, who "had been criss-crossing the Atlantic" from Benin and Nigeria to Brazil and Cuba "ever since the late 1940s" (Palmié 2013, 69).

10. Numerous Cuban practitioners of Regla de Ocha-Ifá notably make similar counterarguments on the damaging effects of colonialism and postcolonialism on Yorùbá traditionality in Nigeria itself, citing, for example, the decline of YTR in the face of Islam and Christianity (see Clarke 2004; Villepastour 2010).

11. Brown (2003, 286) refers to these "vessels" interchangeably as "receptacles" for the *oricha*, also drawing on Matory's formulation of these material objects as "containers" (Matory 1986, 84–91, in D. Brown 2003, 286) "of *fundamentos* . . . in which the orichas, and by extension, their priests, are nourished."

12. Ángel William Viera Bravo, interview by the author, Havana, June 17, 2016.

13. At the time, Owólabí served as a member of Òkè Ìtasè's council of high priests. After the former Àràbà Àgbáyé, Chief Adisa Makoranwale Aworeni, died in 2018, his son, Owólabí, was chosen as the next Àràbà Àgbáyé, assuming the position on August 19, 2018, after his appointment by a council (National Insight News 2018). For more on Àràbà Àgbáyé Owólabí Awódòtun Awóreni Mákòránwálé II, see his interview with Roots and Rooted (2010).

14. Called Olofin, Olofi, or Odun in Cuba and, often, Odù in Nigeria (see Villepastour 2015a, 288; D. Brown 2003, 87; Marcuzzi 2006).

15. The former president of the Association of Black Psychologists in the United States, Grills's academic research explores the intersections of African and Black psychology (Grills 2018).

16. Quotations of Ẹlẹbuìbọn taken from video footage of Viera's consecration ceremony as "Àràbà of Havana" in Òṣogbo, Nigeria. Courtesy of Ángel William Viera Bravo.

17. As De Ferrari (2014) notes, the lifting of the exit visas did not, however, enable all Cubans to travel freely. As he states, "The decree defends the right to deny exit to some people 'in order to preserve the human capital created by the Revolution.'" Additionally, Girish Gupta (2013) notes that the lifting of the exit visas does little to lift the extreme monetary restrictions that most Cubans have to traveling abroad: "For many the benefits will likely be more psychological than practical."

18. Frank Cabrera Suárez, the founder of Ilé Tuntún, also traveled to Nigeria for the first time in 2013, staying with his Nigerian ritual advisor, Táiwò Abímbọ́lá. By 2013, other Cuban practitioners of Nigerian-style Ifá-Òrìṣà living outside of the island had traveled directly to Nigeria (indeed, dating back to Barberas's travels decades before). However, few Cuban practitioners permanently residing in Cuba have traveled to Nigeria itself.

19. Ẹlẹbuìbọn referred to Viera as an official "representative" of the Yorùbá traditional religion in Viera's consecration ceremony as "Àràbà of Havana" in Òṣogbo, Nigeria. Video footage courtesy of Ángel William Viera Bravo.

20. The (re)introduction of the dùndún in Cuba by Viera was first explored in research by Cuban ethnographer Julio Martínez Betancourt (see Martínez Betancourt 2015 and Martínez Betancourt and Barrero 2017). As Martínez Betancourt and Carmen Barrero (2017, 53, my translation) note, instruments demonstrating "morphological characteristics, uses and symbologies analogous to the [dùndún instruments] recently introduced from Nigeria" by Viera were notably documented by Cuban ethnographers on the island in the mid-twentieth century. Fernando Ortiz, for example, documented the existence of a drum similar to the ìyáàlù (what Martínez Betancourt and Barrero refer to as ilú iyá in the article) called bajú in a store in Havana in the 1950s. This instrument was constructed based on African "prototypes," as Ortiz (1994, 175–76, in Martínez Betancourt and Barrero 2017, 53) described, and was commissioned by a US company building instruments for a US orchestra. Likewise, Martínez and Barrero note that drums termed gangá (framed as similar to the ìyáàlù) and requeté (framed as similar to the gúdúgúdú) were documented as part of bembé instruments in Cienfuegos by mid-twentieth-century ethnographers (Sáenz Coopat 1997, in Martínez Betancourt and Barrero 2017, 53). Marcuzzi (2011, 224) ventures that the hourglass-shaped tension drum ganga found in Cuba and analyzed by Sáenz Cooper was more likely "analogous to the Yoruba gángan" while the gangá "is likely a descendant of the Hausa gangá."

21. Ángel William Viera Bravo, interview by the author, Havana, April 22, 2016.

22. On the common grouping of Yorùbá traditional musical instruments into families and familial relational structures, see Samuel (2008/2009, 50). The gúdúgúdú drum, for example, is considered the "father" and "progenitor of all drums that make up dùndún" (50).

23. The gúdúgúdú, as a nontension drum, notably differs from the other subfamilies in construction and, subsequently, the ability to glide between pitches in imitation of the contours of Yorùbá speech (A. Euba 1990; Samuel 2008/2009).

24. Durojaye et al. (2021, 4, citing Akpabot 1986 and Durojaye 2019) note that "although there are different dialects spoken among the Yorùbá, the dùndún only imitates the Ọ̀yọ́ dialect," which is "believed to be the standard Yorùbá" (A. Euba 1990, in Durojaye et al. 2021, 4). Villepastour (2020) notes that although Standard Yorùbá is "commonly said to be Ọ̀yọ́ dialect," the development of the "Yorùbá koiné (a standard language arising from mutually intelligible regional dialects)" was also influenced by the Ègbá dialect as well as by Hausa, Arabic, and English lexical content and syntactic structures in the nineteenth century (6, citing Fagborun 1994).

25. In relation to the reproduction of syllables on the gángan, as described here, Samuel (2021, 5) notes that the drum membrane is struck obligatorily for consonant-vowel and word-initial vowel syllables and optionally, rather than obligatorily, for "word-medial" vowel syllables.

26. Even the fixed-pitch gúdúgúdú, which produces two principal pitches (a low pitch created by hitting the "surface of the ida," or a black paste affixed to the drum head, and a higher pitch produced by hitting the surface membrane) is also said to emulate a specific series of linguistic texts, according to Samuel's (2008/2009, 59–60) fieldwork with informants in Nigeria.

27. Amanda Villepastour notes that the Yorùbá language is also "best suited" to speech surrogacy because "it has three tone bands. Languages with two tone bands increases ambiguity, while band languages with four or more become too complex" (Villepastour, pers. comm., 2017).

28. On the continued linguistic capacities (and limitations) of the batá set in Cuba in relation to the Nigerian bàtá and their capacity for drummed speech surrogacy, see Villepastour 2010.

29. As Villepastour outlines, the dùndún were introduced from the Hausa in the north (Vincent 2006). Notably, the bàtá were also introduced from the Hausa (Vincent 2006), though scholars and players often view the bàtá as older, "Yoruba" instruments in relation to the dùndún (see Omojola 2014).

30. Much scholarship on the bàtá also frames the drumming ensemble as historically restricted to egúngún masquerades and ritual contexts related to the worship of the òrìṣà Ṣàngó (see, e.g., A. Euba 1990). This restriction is often contrasted with the use of the batá for most of the oricha in Cuba (see, e.g., Sublette 2004, 216; Vaughan and Aldama 2012, 258). Villepastour, however, suggests that the extensive bàtá repertoire extant in Yorùbáland throughout the twentieth century (including repertoire dedicated to "dozens" of òrìṣà) along with "transatlantic cognate rhythms" between the Nigerian bàtá and Cuban batá repertoires without evidence of recent exchange provides evidence that the bàtá were already used for òrìṣà beyond Ṣàngó and Egúngún by the time the instruments arrived in Cuba in the nineteenth century (Villepastour, pers. comm., 2017).

31. Even on the ìyáàlù, however, the "restricted capacity for glissando" has led drummers to code the glides between tones with flams (Villepastour 2010; Villepastour, pers. comm., 2017).

32. The ṣẹ̀kẹ̀rẹ̀ are termed chékere in Lucumí.

33. Cantos and toques (batá rhythms) dedicated to Orúnmila/Orúnla/Orúla (the oricha of divination) and Ifá do, however, exist in Cuban-style Regla de Ocha ritual ceremonies for the oricha.

34. A cappella singing accompanied by the iróké, however, is also common in Yorùbáland.

35. Àyàn in Yorùbáland (see Villepastour 2015b).

36. When I questioned Àràbà Viera about the term dùndún, for example, he was unfamiliar with the name. Given that the Aworeni drummers use the Yorùbá language correlates of the individual instruments of the ensemble, this may point to the lack of the usage of the collective

term dùndún in Yorùbáland (as argued by A. Euba 1990, 19). Writing in 1990, Akin Euba claimed that dùndún drummers refer to the ensemble not as "dùndún" but rather by the names of a given ensemble's leading instruments, that is, as "ìyáàlù, gángan, àdàmọ̀, kànàngó" or "kósó" (19). As he stated, "indeed, the musicians do not appear to have a ready conception of the overall definition of dùndún" (19). On the other hand, Villepastour, who has conducted fieldwork in Nigeria since 1999 and spoke with Viera in 2016, argues that the term dùndún is now "generic" in Yorùbáland, suggesting that, perhaps, Viera's unfamiliarity with the term may be due to his self-confessed lack of knowledge of the Yorùbá language and reliance on interpreters during two trips to Nigeria in 2013 and 2015.

37. Ivor Miller, in his far-reaching interview with Wándé Abímbọ́lá, notes that the Havana-based batá player and drum maker Jesús Pérez was bestowed with the title Obá-Ilú in Cuba in the 1960s and 1970s, which was translated for him as both " 'king of the drum' (rey del tambor) and as 'king of the people' (rey del pueblo)." In response, Abímbọ́lá notes that while "Ọba ìlù" means "king of the drum" in Yorùbá, the similarly spelled but tonally distinct Yorùbá word ìlú means, instead, "people" or "a town." The collapse of the similar, yet tonally and semantically distinct Yorùbá words in Cuban Lucumí led to the use of ilú to indicate both "drum" and "people" in Cuba (Abímbọ́lá 1997, 133).

38. The Nigerian-born babaláwo Adedayo Ologundudu was crowned as the Àràbà of the United States on June 28, 2014, following Viera's coronation as Àràbà of Havana in 2013 (Chief-Dayo 2014). Notably, I encountered these recordings by Ologundudu and Afenapa in various African traditionalist ẹgbẹ́ during my fieldwork in both eastern and western Cuba (see chapter 3).

39. Martínez Betancourt and Barrero (2017) note that members of the Aworeni lineage incorporated the dùndún into specific moments of ritual ceremonies, including during the preparation of the ritual "purifying" bath (omi ẹ̀rọ̀/omiero, see chapter 4) used in initations and during ritual songs dedicated to the òrìṣà Òsányin (55). Further ceremonial and processional uses of the dùndún in Cuba are discussed below.

40. As Vélez (2000, 90) notes, the Office of Religious Affairs was established in 1984 as a part of the Central Committee of the Communist Party, marking a "radical change" in state policy toward religion in the 1980s.

41. All Águila de Ifá (2015) quotes my translation.

42. Casas particulares are rooms in private homes that Cubans can rent to foreigners for overnight stays with the appropriate license. The legalization of casa particulares in Cuba came in 1993, during the Cuban government's turn toward tourism as a means to revive the economy following the collapse of the Soviet Union and the onset of the "Special Period" (see Becker 2016).

43. Daily Rondon Ocaña, interview by the author, Havana, June 18, 2016.

44. As of this writing—and due to the relative infancy of the Aworeni temples in Cuba—the national and subsidiary Aworeni temples in Cuba do not yet hold a full council of sixteen coronated chiefs (though the number of coronated chiefs grows incrementally each year).

45. As Bascom (1969a, 92) explains, the Akọda is the senior babaláwo "who calls the others at the annual Festival and thus precedes them."

46. For more on the relationship between familial lineages, extended familial compounds, and occupational and ritual practices in Yorùbáland, see Olajubu 2003 and Barber 1991 (in Olajubu 2003). For a discussion of the Àyàn bàtá drumming lineages and compounds, see Villepastour 2015a.

47. Oyěwùmí (2006, 20) has controversially intervened against the common gendering of the translation of babaláwo as "father of the secret" or "father has secrets," arguing that the accurate translation of the term "refer[s] to both male and female diviners." Oyěwùmí's assertion,

however, has been heatedly contested, particularly by J. Lorand Matory (see Strongman 2019, 22–24, on the "Oyěwùmí/Matory debate").

48. Oyeronke Olajubu (2004, 53) notes that in YTR, practitioners broadly distinguish between *awo* and *ogberi*, or "initiates into the sacred knowledge of a deity or a religious society" (awo) versus "novices and uninitiated people" (ogberi) within a particular ritual society.

49. Palmié draws on Peel's (1989) notion of "Yoruba ethnogenesis" in nineteenth-century Yorùbáland to speak to the novel reformulation of ritual kinship (Yoruba ecclesiogenesis) in nineteenth-century Cuba. Here, I use this phrase to describe the reformulation of transatlantic, Yorùbá-inspired ritual and institutional hierarchies in Cuba in the 2010s.

50. As noted in the preface, *àṣẹ* (*aché* in Cuban Lucumí) also constitutes a foundational concept in Cuban-style Regla de Ocha-Ifá.

51. As Abosede Omowumi Babátúndé (2017, 364) notes, "*Orí* is regarded as one's spiritual destiny and is therefore often personified as *òrìṣà* (deity)."

52. At the Àràbà Aworeni Ilè Ìfè Ifá Temple of Cuba, I met African traditionalist babaláwo who aspired to a chieftaincy title but were unable to afford it, including percussionists who played the dùndún.

53. Scholars of religion have likewise pointed to the imbrication of religious participation and conversion with possibilities for heightened personal power and prestige within environments of material and economic precarity globally (Richman 2008; Thornton 2016; Virani 2022). K. E. Richman (2008, 4), for example, highlights religious conversion to evangelical Protestantism as a means of "mastering a model of individual, social, and economic success" for Haitian immigrants in the United States. Brendan Jamal Thornton (2016, 190) likewise points to the social benefits awarded to individuals who outwardly perform their newfound status as converted "saints" in Pentecostal communities in working-class neighborhoods in the Dominican Republic, including the ways such performances confer the heightened "social currency" of "respect" in the urban barrio. Vivek Virani's (2022, 107) work also compellingly points to the imbrication of spiritually grounded "aspirational subjectivities" and "new pathways for mobility" for Malvi *nirguṇ bhajans* musicians in India, particularly within the contexts of India's liberalized capitalist and globally oriented consumer economy since the 1990s.

54. Timothy Rommen's (2007, 65–66) formulation of "the negotiation of proximity" in the Full Gospel community in Trinidad likewise points to the ways that practitioners negotiate the distant and the near through ritual music as a means to navigate aspirational ideals of gnostic spirituality in their translocal ritual communities. Rommen's formulation of "the negotiation of proximity" informs my formulation of "the efficacy of the far" and "the efficacy of the close" here, particularly in illustrating how ritual music styles from abroad (e.g., the United States), "thanks to their distanced point of origin . . . [can be] less bounded, more useful" (66) than local, Trinidadian styles (see also chapter 5).

55. The bestowal of the title "Chief Yeye Araba-Agbaye" to the US American ìyánífá Dr. Patri D'Haifa in 1995 marks one of the most notable examples (Kumari 2014, 365; Edemodu 2002). For more on the controversies surrounding Dr. Haifa, see chapter 4.

56. An Ifá ceremony, of recent arrival in Cuba, that is "observed once every 17 days" (Avorgbedor 2003, 57).

57. Osniel González, interview by the author, Havana, June 20, 2016.

58. Many prominent Nigerian-style babaláwo in Cuba, furthermore, were previously initiated into Cuban-style Ifá before turning to Nigerian-style Ifá, a ritual domain notorious for its female exclusion (and homophobia) (see chapters 3 and 4).

59. This gendered concern among Owólabí, González, and others in the Aworeni lineage did not, noticeably, extend to a concern regarding the lack of women who participated in dùndún drumming, which is also all-male in Cuba. As Samuel (2014, 15) notes in his study of female dùndún drummers in Yorùbáland, female dùndún drumming has increasingly "[emerged] as an established musical art form" among the Yorùbá, at least within the secular domain. Women, however, do perform in the outdoor spaces of festivals linked to the òrìṣà (i.e., female dùndún drummer Ayannike Fasola's performance at the annual Ọṣun-Òṣogbo Festival, one of the largest and most highly visible òrìṣà festivals and pilgrimage sites in Nigeria), and female dùndún drummers such as Ayanbanke Lawani have even become "household names" in Ọ̀yọ́ state (32). Ongoing beliefs among male "hardliners" used to exclude women from ritual drumming persist, however (32). These include a belief in the decline of sexual satisfaction among men who have sex with female drummers (32), the "notion that women are usually more susceptible to spiritual attacks during public performance" (33), and women's ritual exclusion from specific ritual sites (e.g., shrines and groves) and the "knowledge of esoteric matters" necessary to adequately perform ritual drumming in ceremonies (34). Furthermore, all of Samuel's female informants— even those who performed at outdoor festivals linked to the òrìṣà—"testified that they neither belonged to any cult nor ever participated in any private forms [e.g., indoor rituals] of festivals," with their performances "limited to the social [and outdoor] aspect of festivals" (36). This ongoing exclusion of women from dùndún ritual drumming in Yorùbáland likely inflects Owólabí, González, Viera, and other babaláwo's lack of concern regarding the lack of female dùndún drummers in Cuba, even when concerns regarding the lack of women more broadly arise. Likewise, the very recent arrival of the dùndún ensemble in Nigerian-style Ifá; the general lack of familiarity with the instruments; and the relative lack of women in the Aworeni lineage (including drummers) have likely all contributed to making this a nonissue (thus far). This lack of interest in female dùndún drumming, however, diverges significantly from a passionate interest in the right of women to play the consecrated bátá ritual drums in Regla de Ocha (and, more recently, Nigerian-style Ifá-Òrìṣà), particularly among women and ìyánífá in eastern Cuba (chapter 3).

60. With the globalization of revisionist Ifá and òrìṣà worship, Ifá and other òrìṣà festivals modeled on YTR practice in Nigeria are celebrated in innumerable locales in the United States and Latin America, including in the Ọ̀yọ́túnjí Village in South Carolina (Clarke 2004; Pinn 1998), the Ile Ise Ejiogbe Ifá Temple in Washington, DC (Adogame 2009), the Orisa Lifestyle Academy in Oakland, California (Origunwa n.d.), and the Ẹgbẹ́ Mimo Awo Bàbá Eégúngún Digbolègún Elekuro Olúwo Ifátéjú Aworeni in Argentina (DarkRaven66675 2013), among others. In the case of the "Odunfa" Ifá Festival in Oakland, California, in 2016, the festival was presided over by none other than Ifáyẹmí Ẹlẹ́buìbọn (Origunwa n.d.).

61. The *agogo Ifá* was the first imported instrument that Àràbà Viera received directly from Nigeria after his turn from Regla de Ocha-Ifá to Nigerian-style Ifá-Òrìṣà in 2008–9, and he received it circa 2011 (Viera, interview, April 22, 2016).

62. On the use of glass beads among Yorùbá royalty, Bascom (1969b, 102) notes that excavations of glass beads at Ilé-Ifẹ̀ indicate "that it was a center of the glass making industry in precontact times." In the 1930s, when Bascom conducted fieldwork in Nigeria, he noted that the Yorùbá kings wore beaded crowns as "the symbols of their authority" and that the beads themselves were often imported from Europe, though "coral, red stone beads, and a highly prized tubular blue bead (sẹgi) were probably of African origin" (30, 102).

63. Àràbà Viera provided this approximate translation from the original Yorùbá (Viera, interview, June 17, 2016).

64. Viera notes that the Oyugbona is also in charge of sacrificial offerings to the òrìṣà (Viera, interview, June 17, 2016).

65. The *clave* audible in the procession is notably reduced from the ritual claves sounded in *bembé* ceremonies in Regla de Ocha (and in Nigerian-style Ifá-Òrìṣà ceremonies in eastern Cuba), such as the *clave bembé* (see chapters 4 and 5).

66. Although often referred to in the singular as "the clave" (*la clave*), numerous claves (e.g., specific timelines/patterns) exist depending on the style or songs being played in a given repertoire. The term *timeline* was coined by A. M. Jones in 1956 and subsequently adopted by African musicologists such as Ghanaian scholar J. H. Kwame Nketia throughout the twentieth century.

67. For debates concerning what the clave is and how it relates to meter, *topoi*, timeline, and other concepts, see Agawu 1987, 2003; Díaz 2021; Paulding 2017; and Peñalosa 2009. On the clave's "return" to West Africa, see Carwile 2017 and Shain 2018.

68. See, for example, the recordings of Dundun Ensemble of Adjarra, Benin (1996).

69. This performance also demonstrates other notable innovations. Delgado Iglesias, for example, holds the ìyáàlù diagonally across his chest with the strap over his right shoulder (figs. 2.1 and 2.9). This marks a subtle but notable difference from Yorùbá drummers who place the strap of the larger dùndún instruments (e.g., ìyáàlù, *isáájú*, and *kẹríkẹrì*) over the left shoulder while resting the instruments directly against their hip bone (Samuel 2014). This placement allows them to use the hip as a "counterforce" when tightening or loosening the cluster of tension cords gripped with the left hand in imitation of Yorùbá speech (Carter-Ényì 2018, 281). Additionally, the Aworeni lineage employs the ìyáàlù and the gángan simultaneously—both "talking" drums that serve as lead instruments in Yorùbáland (Samuel 2008/2009, 2014). A. Euba (1990, 157–58) notes that "it is unusual to include the gángan" in "*ìyáàlù* type" ensembles in Yorùbáland, although one informant, who was "one of the musicians of the Aláàfin [king] of Ọ̀yọ́," noted that ensembles "performing dancing music for the Ọba [king] would consist of *ìyáàlù*, *gúdúgúdú*, *isáájú*, *ìkẹhìn*, *kẹríkẹrì*, and *gángan*."

70. While Frank Cabrera's Ilé Tuntún also braves the Cuban law by holding ritual processions in an outlying neighborhood off the Calzada de Bejucal road in Havana (see chapter 5), African traditionalist ẹgbẹ́ in Cuba's regional provinces expressed concern for the law, which is "punishable by up to three months in prison and a fine" (Boyle and Sheen [1997] 2003, 125). In eastern Cuban cities, practitioners of Nigerian-style Ifá-Òrìṣà opt out of processions that constitute otherwise indispensable features of the recently introduced Yorùbá worship lineages of egúngún (see chapter 5).

71. Ìyánífá Asabioje Afenapa's (2007) album *Ìṣẹ̀ṣe Làgbà* translates *ìṣẹ̀ṣe* as "tradition and culture," while Fatoba (2005) translates it as "foundation/beginning." In Cuba, the term is used interchangeably with the Yorùbá traditional religion and Nigerian-style Ifá-Òrìṣà.

72. As Samuel (2008/2009, 50) notes, it is common to see the ṣẹ̀kẹ̀rẹ̀ played with dùndún in Yorùbáland.

73. My translation of the anonymous Yorùbá-Spanish digital document provided by babaláwo and Chief Akọda Santiago Ariosa Hercey.

74. Erick Gómez Rodríguez, interview by the author, Havana, 2016.

75. For more on pitch contrast and melodic contour in Yorùbá language song in relation to the tonal characteristics of Yorùbá speech, see Omojola 2011, 95.

76. Here, Villepastour is speaking specifically to the case of the bàtá drums of Nigeria, not the dùndún. Nonetheless, this dynamic of isolation between Cuban percussionists and Nigerian percussionists applies to dùndún drummers as well. See Villepastour 2015b.

Chapter Three

1. "Community of descendants of the great mystic house of Ifá of the Odugbemi lineage" in Yorùbá (*Comunidad de descendientes de la gran casa mística de Ifá*), my translation.

2. Orozco Rubio's ẹgbẹ́, founded in 2007, did not receive official authentication as part of the Nigerian-rooted Odùgbemi lineage until Orozco Rubio's (re-)initiation as an African traditionalist babaláwo in 2014 (Orozco Rubio, pers. comm.).

3. On the relationship of actionable knowledge to power, prestige, and secrecy in Afro-Cuban religions, Todd Ramón Ochoa (2010, 71) states, "it is a truism that madrinas and padrinos, godmothers and godfathers, the people who initiate 'godchildren' into Palo and Ocha/Santo practice, are possessive of their initiates." This possessiveness can translate into purposeful withholding of guarded knowledge to keep initiates perpetually economically and ritually bound to the *padrino/madrina* or *casa-templo* (see Ochoa 2010).

4. As Ned Sublette (2004) notes, Regla de Ocha-Ifá has served as one of the most dynamic facets of the informal economy in revolutionary Cuba since the 1950s. For priests and ritual leaders of Ocha-Ifá and Palo in Cuba and internationally, Palo and Regla de Ocha-Ifá can, at times, be highly lucrative.

5. On the associations of "Afro-Cuban religions" to Blackness, witchcraft, and criminality, see Beliso-De Jesús 2015a, De la Fuente 2001, Sublette 2004, and Ortiz (1906) 1973.

6. All quotations of Enrique Orozco Rubio are taken from interviews with him in Santiago de Cuba, June–July 2015.

7. Called *mano de Orula* (hand of Orula) for men and *icofá* for women, this entry-level initiation into Ifá offers "spiritual protection" and the promise of a "beneficial effect on health" to the initiate, also indicating for men whether becoming a babalao is destined for them (see Ayorinde 2004, 214; Jassey 2019, xxi).

8. This, and all other biographical information on and quotations from Orozco Rubio, come from interviews conducted with him in 2015.

9. *Falta de respeto.* In Cuba, it's a common colloquial phrase denoting mild to serious offense and often directly spoken to the offender.

10. Internet access has been notoriously and restrictively limited by the Cuban state, and Cubans were only granted official, public access to (very limited and slow) Wi-Fi hotspots in July 2015. Nonetheless, some Cubans have been able to receive dial-up access in their homes through the accounts of foreigners (among the only people in Cuba granted access to internet in their homes).

11. Before this, women from Santiago de Cuba had been initiated as ìyánífá through travel to Victor Betancourt's ẹgbẹ́ in Havana, but none had yet been initiated directly by a priest in eastern Cuba.

12. Enrique Orozco Rubio, interview by the author, Santiago de Cuba, June 23, 2015.

13. For more on the distinct lineages of Ifá in Yorùbáland, see Adegbindin 2014; Bascom 1969a; Olupona and Rey 2008; Peel 2000.

14. Nagybe Madariaga Pouymiró, interview by the author, Santiago de Cuba, June 20, 2015.

15. Also spelled *aberikulá*.

16. Jassey (2019) notes that the ritual distinction between aberinkulá drums and tambores de Añá has transformed over time. Rituals using aberinkulá drums, "although once quite common in Cuba," for example, "are now extremely rare," as stated by her informants (179). Jassey also observes that "the associated prestige and religiosity of *fundamento* [consecrated] *batá* means that although much more expensive to hire, they are by far the preferred ritual instrument" (179).

This occurs despite the fact that "like *fundamento*, *aberikulá* can bring down the orichas to possess the bodies of devotees" in ritual (179). Likewise, percussion ensembles such as *bembé* and *güiro* are widely used in oricha ritual across Cuba's provinces, also inspiring oricha possession in the bodies of practitioners (63; see also Schweitzer 2013, 23).

17. For extensive histories of women aberinkulá players in Havana, see Hagedorn 2001 and Jassey 2019. Victoria Jassey notes that the earliest account of a woman playing the aberinkulá drums in Cuba is of Aleida Socarras, daughter of Fermín Nani, an instructor at the Conjunto Folklórico Nacional de Cuba (CFNC, the premier state folkloric ensemble in Havana). According to interviews, Socarras began playing with her father around 1978 at the age of eleven (Jassey 2019, 147). In 1979, aberinkulá batá and folkloric drumming were included in the curriculum of the Instituto Superior de Arte (ISA), or the University of Arts of Cuba, where "possibly for the first time, White people, women and foreigners were taught how to play batá drums" (20). This led to an uproar among ritual practitioners and a subsequent decision within the CFNC "that it would be safest to teach only foreign women" (21), as they were considered "far less likely to trespass into the religion with their newfound *batá* skills and likely would confine themselves to playing in secular *batá* groups," as related to Katherine Hagedorn by ritual drummer Alberto Virreal (Hagedorn 2001, 89–90, in Jassey 2019, 21). This resulted in yet another "contentious debate" among ritual practitioners and excluded Cuban women until certain male batá drummers "agreed to teach Cuban women" to play the aberinkulá drums in the late 1980s (22). Villepastour (2013) also highlights the protagonism of the "esteemed, yet controversial," Havana-based *santera* and *akpwón* (ritual singer) Amelia Pedroso, who "was almost certainly the first Cuban women to cross a traditional gender line and perform publicly with her own all-women group on the drums, the batá, which accompanied her vocal performances" (54). By 1993, Pedroso was touring the United States with esteemed akpwón Lázaro Ros and "began to make an impression on U.S. American women, occasionally playing the batá at parties with her male colleagues" (56). Pedroso, however, "died in 2000 before she could fulfill her deeper, far more radical mission: to own and play her own consecrated batá drums" (54–55).

18. Jassey (2019, 23) notes that the ACYC's views on women playing unconsecrated, aberinkulá batá (though not, notably, *tambores de Añá*) have since shifted considerably. The highly successful, all-female batá group Obiní Batá, for example, who play aberinkulá drums, receive state institutional support and now hold a weekly residency at the ACYC.

19. Famously, Fermina "Lucumí" and Carlota purportedly used Yoruba "talking drums" to announce the initiation of the rebellion (Godfried 2006).

20. Elizabeth Sayre (2000), drawing on her interview with Michael Marcuzzi, outlines a few of the varied (and often contradictory) menstruation arguments as follows: "Women cleanse themselves through menstruation and therefore do not need to play batá, because playing is itself a cleansing"; "because women menstruate, it is dangerous for them to approach the consecrated drums, because their menstrual blood may be mistaken as an offering to Añá"; and "because the menstrual cycle is associated with the Aje, or 'witches'—anti-social, feminine spiritual forces—female contact with Añá will void the consecration of the drums."

21. Pouymiró has started composing these novel toques based on this feminist and African traditionalist interpretation (using Western notation); however, because the toques are unedited drafts and have not yet been completed or performed in nonritual or ritual contexts, I have chosen not to reproduce them here.

22. Cuban *babalaos* are however, integrated in specific ways into Cuban consecrated batá and Añá worship. As Schweitzer (2013, 223) notes, Cuban babalaos "play an important role in

preparing new sets of batá de fundamento, including overseeing the making of the medicines that are sealed within the body of the drums." Likewise, Cuban batá ritual drummers often "have a padrino in Ifá, who as a babalao is responsible for giving them the Hand of Ifá, a ritual initiation that connects one with one's destiny," in addition to their padrino in Añá (217). In Regla de Ocha-Ifá, Nigerian-style Ifá-Òrìṣà, and YTR, likewise, Ifá divination can reveal the need to hold a *tambor* (or hire a bàtá ensemble, in the case of Nigeria) for the oricha/òrìṣà (Schweitzer 2013; Vincent 2006, 83).

23. The first set of consecrated batá drums is claimed to have been created by Lucumí slaves in Cuba in 1830 (Ortiz 1954).

24. As Sayre (2000) outlines, these include varying—and often contradictory—views, including that "Añá (the orisha of the drums) is a feminine force, therefore a woman playing the drum creates an improper imbalance of gendered energies" and "the batá drums belong to the orisha Changó, the epitome of virility, and a woman player cannot enact the masculinity appropriate to this situation."

25. The Festival del Caribe has included African-inspired ritual ceremonies (including of Santería, Palo, Vodú, and Espiritismo) as part of its official festival programming for decades (Herrero Beatón 2003).

26. This dynamic has been a staple of charged attempts to publicize, authenticate, and bear witness to changes in Afro-Cuban religion for decades. See, for example, Palmié 2013 and Wirtz 2014.

27. Jassey (2019) found that while the prohibition against women playing consecrated batá stands throughout Cuba (and internationally), female batá drummers in Cuba occasionally play the aberinkulá for ritual ceremonies, despite the fact that for many men such an "act is considered profane" (188). Likewise, female batá drummers in the UK (including Jassey herself, both in Cuba and the UK) have played aberinkulá during ritual ceremonies (186). Although uncommon and controversial, women in Cuba have also played other ritual drums and percussion for *güiro* ceremonies dedicated to the oricha (64). This includes four sisters of the Pelladito family in the municipality of Guanabacoa in eastern Havana, "who perform *güiro* ritually several times a week" (64). Jassey notes, however, that the Pelladito sisters "were the only female group" that she encountered during her research "who work professionally as ritual musicians in Cuba" (64).

28. Nagybe Madariaga Pouymiró, interview by the author, Santiago de Cuba, June 22, 2015.

29. Caridad Rubio Fonseca, interview by the author, Santiago de Cuba, June 22, 2015.

30. My translation of the anonymously authored Yorùbá-Spanish translation provided by Orozco Rubio.

31. Orozco Rubio received a pirated version of Afenapa's album through his interactions with African traditionalist babaláwo visiting Cuba (Enrique Orozco Rubio, interview by the author, Santiago de Cuba, May 30, 2016).

32. For an extensive analysis of the differences between Cuban and Nigerian batá/bàtá playing techniques, morphology, and relation to speech surrogacy, see Villepastour 2010.

33. My gratitude goes to percussionist David Gervais for pointing out the similarity of Pouymiró's execution of obanlá to Michael Spiro's transcription.

34. Umi Vaughan credits the popular dance and jazz fusion group Irakere, formed by Chucho Valdés in 1973, with popularizing the use of the batá drums in nonritual, popular music settings (Vaughan and Aldama 2012). As he notes, however, Irakere wasn't the first group to play the batá outside of ritual settings, as the instruments had occasionally been shown in academic, art music, and cabaret settings throughout the twentieth century (Vaughan and Aldama 2012;

see also Moore 1997, 220). Jassey (2019, 164) adds that the technique of placing three batá on a stand to play solo was popularized by Cuban percussionist Octavio Rodríguez of the group Mezcla before being incorporated into other Cuban popular music groups. This technique is now widely used in secular, nonritual settings.

35. Such moves resonate with other gender-inflected adaptations for women playing African-inspired percussion in Cuba. Obiní Batá, for example, uses a highly idiosyncratic legs-crossed, side-saddle position to play the *tumbadoras*, a move that "prevent[s] them playing with their legs open," as men do (Jassey 2019). Ultimately, such innovations point to the historical imperative to prevent breaching expectations of musical femininity during the public performance of male-coded, Afro-Cuban drums, even for female Cuban musicians playing within overtly secular and folkloric contexts.

36. Schweitzer (2013) describes such toques as "generic" rather than "shared." In his taxonomy, Schweitzer conceptually organizes the batá toques along a "continuum," characterized on one extreme by what he terms "dedicated" toques, or toques that "identify with individual, specific orishas" and, on the opposite extreme, "generic" toques, or toques that "have no particular associations and accompany the songs for many, if not all, of the orishas" (74). Generic toques, within Schweitzer's taxonomy, encompass a wide range of toques ranging from those "associated with as few as three orishas or extended across the entire pantheon" (90).

37. This sentiment, in which the Cuban batá are maintained as efficacious vessels for Añá/Àyàn among certain African traditionalists despite divergences with the Nigerian bàtá, was echoed by some, though not all, Nigerian-style practitioners in Cuba. Babaláwo Yunieski González Ramírez, for example, underscored in our interviews that "the Cuban Añá, yes, has good effect" in Nigerian-style rituals, despite divergences between the Cuban batá and their Nigerian counterparts (Yunieski González Ramírez, interview by the author, Santiago de las Vegas, April 18, 2016). Members of the Aworeni lineage in western Havana, however, specifically argue that the batá are inappropriate for the ritual contexts of Nigerian-style Ifá, instead pointing to the *ilú Ifá* (dùndún) as the only instruments adequate for Ifá worship based on their perceived contemporary use in Yorùbáland (for a discussion of the ways that the dùndún have been reontologized as ilú Ifá, or drums of Ifá, in the Aworeni lineage in Havana, see chapter 2). Ultimately, these debates underscore the divergent conceptualizations of the efficacy of particular approaches to ritual sound among discrete, and widely heterogeneous, African-style ẹgbẹ́ across the island (see chapter 5).

38. For further discussions of the aftermath and potential future repercussions of this event, including the question of whether or not this "fracture in the status quo" might "[develop] into a gaping crack" for future consecrated *bataleras*, see Jassey 2019, 141.

Chapter Four

1. Also called *opa osun Orunmila* (H. Drewal 2016, 333). It is placed in front of a *babaláwo*'s house, marking the "residence of a diviner," and is also always carried in the front of any public procession (333). Wándé Abímbọ́lá defines Olúwo as "chief priest" (Abímbọ́lá 2016, 32).

2. During rituals, the *osùn babaláwo* is fed as an altar to Ọ̀rúnmìlà, the *òrìṣà* of divination (H. Drewal 2016). On this day, this particular diviner's staff belongs to the chief priest (*Olúwo*) of the Aworeni Temple of Havana, Erick Gómez Rodríguez, whose residence served as the temple and as the meeting place for this gathering.

3. During my fieldwork, the *osùn babaláwo* was referred to as *Osùn* and ritually fed along with other deities, such as Èṣù and Ifá.

4. Abiodun states that the "lone bird" symbolically alludes "to Orunmila's à̩șé̩" (Abiodun 2014). Bird (2009, 69) translates osùn babaláwo as the "Bird of Ifá staff."

5. The "*obi-coco* oracle," or "the four shards of coconuts," served as a replacement in Cuba for the Yorùbá "kola nut system" given the absence of kola nuts on the island (D. Brown 2004, 813; see also Abímbó̩lá 2016, 38). Many African traditionalist *egbé̩* now use kola nuts, which have been reintroduced on the island, if available, while others continue to use the Cuban *obi* oracle (or both).

6. Also "talking Ifá."

7. Enrique Orozco Rubio, interview by the author, Santiago de Cuba, June 23, 2015.

8. E̩lé̩buìbo̩n came to prominence as an authority and "religious entrepreneur" of Ifá and òrìșà worship in Ò̩șogbo in the 1960s shortly after the White, Austrian artist Suzanne Wenger turned toward the project of revitalizing the Ò̩șun Grove (now a UNESCO World Heritage Site and home to the Ò̩șun-Ò̩șogbo Festival) in 1958 (Probst 2004, 57–76, 352). Wenger's influence in the revitalization of Ò̩șun Grove from the 1950s to the 1980s and her initiation as a priestess of Ò̩șun ultimately affectionately known as "Adunni Olorisa" in Ò̩șogbo (Osundare 2008) may have influenced local, and then globally minded, Yorùbá ritual practitioners' views on initiating foreign, and particularly White, women into YTR (Villepastour, pers. comm., 2022).

9. Many in Cuba, however, contest Betancourt's claim.

10. Villepastour, however, informed me of an interlocutor who claims knowledge of marginal lineages in Nigeria where women are permitted to "see" Odù (in the Ijebu area, specifically, dating back at least two generations), suggesting that the prohibition against women accessing Odù within the principle, globalizing lineages of Yorùbáland may not be absolute in Nigeria (Villepastour, pers. comm., 2017).

11. See Eledá.org 2003. Then Chief Yeye Araba-Agbaye D'Haifa claimed that her intention to initiate a babaláwo in Nigeria was first affirmed through Ifá oracular divination in Miami, Florida, and subsequently approved and overseen by the Àràbà Àgbáyé himself, Chief Adisa Makoranwale Aworeni, in Ilé-Ifè̩, Nigeria, following written correspondence between D'Haifa, the Àràbà Àgbáyé, and the sixteen-member council of elders at the Òkè Ìtasè̩ temple (Edemodu 2002; see also Landry 2015). The worldwide rebuttal of D'Haifa's claim by the ICFIR following the global controversy, however, takes special care to note that the Àràbà Àgbáyé served as the chairman of the board of trustees of ICFIR at the time of the proclamation, implying his tacit approval of the organization's decision to revoke her title (Eledá.org 2003). Landry (2015) astutely notes that this global proclamation also marked a move toward publicity, self-validation, and international authority for ICFIR in the early 2000s. Landry states: "While the International Council for Ifa Religion was clearly trying to use D'Haifa's case as a way of setting an international standard, at least where the initiation of women is concerned, they were also trying to bring attention to their organization by arguing in the same press release that 'all temples and associations of Ifa worship in all parts of the world are hereby advised to register with the Council unfailingly'" (88).

12. In 2005, Portales helped to finance the initiation of three Cuban women as ìyánífá in Matanzas (Beliso-De Jesús 2015a, 820).

13. Later that year, the Egbé Òrìsà-Oko (*sic*) temple in Holguín changed its name to Egbé-Ifá-Barapetun-Alabalese (*sic*) (Indigenous African Faith Ifá E̩gbé̩) (Martínez Betancourt and Orozco Rubio 2016).

14. Víctor Yasmani Betancourt Águila was initiated into Nigerian-style Ifá directly by the Nigerian babaláwo S̩o̩lágbadé Pópó̩o̩lá in Havana in 2006 (Martínez Betancourt and Orozco Rubio 2016).

15. Yadira Flamand Rodríguez, Lídice María Peña, Raquel Ávila de la Peña, and Ilya María Trasovares Infante (Martínez Betancourt and Orozco Rubio 2016). At the time of her initiation into Ifá, ìyánífá Dulce María Rodríguez Sánchez was a respected *santera* in Holguín, having practiced Regla de Ocha (as a child of the oricha Yemayá) for thirty-five years, and she held a leadership position in the provincial branch of the ACYC as president of the Council of Elders (Consejo de Mayores) for the province of Holguín. Upon her initiation as ìyánífá, María Rodríguez Sánchez was expelled from the ACYC and from her leadership position, also losing many of her *ahijados*, or godchildren, in Holguín (Dulce María Rodríguez Sánchez, interview by the author, Holguín, May 16, 2016).

16. During my fieldwork years, all of the other twenty-one ẹgbẹ́ were headed by male babaláwo (Martínez Betancourt, pers. comm., 2016).

17. These translations mirror contemporary Yorùbá terminological divisions between babaláwo and ìyánífá according to the gender of the diviner, although the historical root of the emergence of such divisions between male and female diviners is a matter of debate. In a provocative (and controversial) study of contemporary Yorùbá conceptualizations of gender, for example, Nigerian scholar Oyèrónkẹ́ Oyěwùmí problematizes the gendered translations of *babaláwo* and *ìyánífá* as "father of the secret" and "mother of secrets," respectively, arguing that ìyánífá "is an elision of *Ìyá nínú Ifá* meaning master of expert of Ifá, which is identical to the [nongendered] meaning of *babaláwo*" (Oyěwùmí 2006, 24). Furthermore, Oyěwùmí argues that the term *ìyánífá* is of relatively recent coinage in Yorùbáland, emerging "[as] a necessary development in reaction to the increasing gendering of *babaláwo* as male." She continues, "The trend to create gendered vocabulary in Yorùbá is an interesting one, and may be a practical solution to female marginalization as Yorùbá social categories are increasingly interpreted according to the-male-as-norm standards of the dominant colonial language—English" (24). Furthermore, Oyěwùmí argues that "the term *ìyán'fá* is gaining currency in certain circles as the accepted mode for referring to female Ifá diviners but knowledge of the word is hardly widespread" (24). Oyěwùmí's critical historicization of the term *ìyánífá* points both to a potential recent trend toward gendering Yorùbá language in Ifá in Yorùbáland and holds provocative consequences for the notions of gendered polarity in Nigerian-style Ifá in Cuba, as discussed in this chapter. Notably, however, Oyěwùmí's analyses have been passionately rebuked by other scholars, including J. Lorand Matory. For more on the "Oyěwùmí/Matory debate," see Strongman 2019, 22-24.

18. As I discovered during fieldwork, approaches to ìyánífá's access to and use of Ifá's implements of divination, particularly the ọpẹlẹ and ikin, vary among Cuba's African traditionalist ẹgbẹ́. In Dulce María Rodríguez Sánchez's Egbè Fermina Gómez ati Echu-Dina in Holguín and Erick Gómez Rodríguez's Ilé Ijuba Olafemi Orímolade Aworeni Temple in Havana, for example, ìyánífá utilize both the ọpẹlẹ and ikin for Ifá rituals and divinations. In others, however, ìyánífá's access to the ọpẹlẹ and ikin is more restricted.

19. Despite this prohibition, historical accounts point to the presence of women permitted to sacrifice "plumed animals and four-legged animals" throughout the history of Regla de Ocha-Ifá. Rubiera Castillo (2020), for example, notes that the renowned *oriaté* (a Regla de Ocha post historically held by women that has become male dominated, considered the "king" or "head of the mat" for initiation and divination rituals; see D. Brown 2003, 150) Maria Towa, "considered queen of the Lucumíes," is said to have "introduced the knife (Pinodo) and the possibility of killing (sacrificing four legged animals) to all Santeros and babalawos who followed" (Castillo 2020, 94). Likewise, the historical figure Mercedes la Balogún, also known as Ogún Toyo, was

permitted to sacrifice four-legged animals, "thus decreasing the criteria that limited women from sacrificing because of lack of physical strength" (94).

20. Enrique Orozco Rubio, interview by the author, Santiago de Cuba, July 25, 2015. Chief Fagbemileke Fatunmise (2013) elaborates on the interplay between feminine and masculine energy in the initiation of babaláwo. As she outlines, during initiation, the babaláwo is presented with "female energy" via the "Odù Pot," in which the "Divine Feminine Energy" and "items representing the four cardinal points of the Universe" are housed (43). This reencounter allows the initiate to receive the àṣẹ necessary to "enhance his masculine energy to be elevated to a Babaláwo" (43). The àṣẹ is "passed down through the 'Woman,'" as "it is impossible for men to pass this energy unless he is already a full-fledged Babaláwo" (43). Here, the enhanced masculinity necessary for ritual reproduction is predicated on encounter with the female energy of the òrìṣà Odù, as found in the sacred "Odu Pot."

21. For more on the language of "birth" in Regla de Ocha-Ifá and the Yorùbá traditional religion, see Villepastour 2015a.

22. During my years in Cuba (2012–16), the babaláwo and ìyánífá I spoke with referred specifically to individuals who were "gay," "homosexual," and "lesbian," occasionally also using derogatory terms such as *tortillera* (resonant with "dyke") or *maricón* (a derogatory term for effeminate gay men; see Lumsden 1996). No one made reference in our conversations to the experiences of *travesti* or *transgénero* individuals or categories of transgender subjectivity in Cuba that have often been collapsed with queerness and/or *transformismo* (drag performance) by Cubans and foreign scholars alike (Leslie Santana 2022). Rather, practitioners referred to "homosexuality" in the form of the aforementioned terms. I attribute this lack of reference to trans subjectivities, in part, to what I assume to be the relative lack of everyday conversations and visibility surrounding the specificity of trans subjectivity (including the "distinction and overlap between queerness and transness," as Leslie Santana [2022, 48] astutely notes) in these specific ritual contexts in Cuba during the years I conducted research. Notably, however, other ethnographers, including M. Myrta Leslie Santana, have since documented trans subjectivity in Cuba in relation to transformismo and sexuality with much more nuance than I (see Leslie Santana 2019, 2020, 2022).

23. Nadine Fernandez also explicitly connects *guapería* in Cuba to lower-class status (Fernandez 2010, in Lundgren 2013, 17).

24. In Cuban Spanish, specifically, *guapo* does not reference someone who is "handsome" in this case (the traditional translation of *guapo* in Spanish). See Fernández 2010 and Lundgren 2013.

25. I've chosen to reproduce these words here verbatim, despite the potential offense taken by using such wording to describe homosexual men. I do this in order to illustrate the ways in which such terms and conceptions of homosexuality are mobilized among African traditionalists in Cuba.

26. Interview with a Cuban ìyánífá. I've chosen not to reproduce the speaker's name here for her own protection.

27. See, for example, the Ifá Foundation based in Crescent City, Florida, who claim to have initiated the first openly gay babalao in the United States: https://www.ifafoundation.org/.

28. For more on the concept of polarity in Yorùbá ritual philosophy, see Edwards and Mason 1998, 4, and Oladipo 2002, 158.

29. For more on the idea of male and female polarity in Ifá, see Fatunmbi 1992–93.

30. On the òrìṣà Ìyámi Òṣòròngà as "the dynamic force of Divine Feminine Energy" in Yorùbáland, see Fatunmise 2013, 22.

31. Erick Gómez Rodríguez, interview by the author, Havana, 2016.

32. Enrique Orozco Rubio, interview by the author, Santiago de Cuba, June 24, 2015.

33. Enrique Orozco Rubio, interview by the author, Santiago de Cuba, July 23, 2015.

34. Preparation of the *omiero* (as it is termed in Lucumí) also constitutes a central aspect of ceremonies in Regla de Ocha-Ifá, where the powerful "purifying liquid" of the ritual bath is used to wash ritual implements and bathe the initiate in preparation "for contact with the santos" (Brandon 1991, 61; Martínez Betancourt 2013, 120).

35. The number, and type, of herbs and plants used for the *omi ẹ̀rọ̀* varies widely and depends on the òrìṣà, consecrations, or bath in question. Orozco Rubio uses sixteen specific herbs and plants for the omi ẹ̀rọ̀ for Ifá (Orozco Rubio, interview, July 23, 2015).

36. *Peperomia pellucida*, or "shiny bush" plant, known as the *corazón del hombre*, or the "heart of man" in Cuba (Wiart 2006, 43).

37. A widely diasporic invocation prominent in YTR, Regla de Ocha-Ifá and *candomblé* ceremonies in Brazil, the *mojuba* sonorously forges a "palimpsestic collapsing of time and space" through recourse to "the act of naming as creative commemoration" (Otero 2010, 20, citing Peel 1989; C. Smith 2016, 83, citing Alexander 2006).

38. Yunieski González Ramírez, interview by the author, Santiago de las Vegas, April 18, 2016.

39. See Domingo Hernández's vocalization of "Mojuba Olodumare," recorded by Lydia Cabrera and Josefina Tarafa in Cuba in 1957, for an example of a Cuban rendition of the mojuba (Santa Cruz et al. [1957] 2003).

40. Here, Omojola (2011, 86) draws on A. Euba (2003, 64) to point to the action-inflected, manifesting force of the *oríkì* in Yorùbáland.

41. I've reproduced the idiosyncratic spelling and diacritics of Orozco Rubio's anonymously authored, digital Yorùbá-to-Spanish language translation of the text here. The provenance of the song (and digital word document) from the book by Chief FAMA (Adéwálé-Somadhi 2006b, 2020) is discussed in this chapter. In Adéwálé-Somadhi's original publication (Spanish edition [2006b], English edition [2020]), the Yorùbá song and its Spanish-language translation are written as follows: "Bí mo dúró, bí mo wúre / Si estoy de pie mientras rezo [If I'm standing while I pray] / Ire tèmi kà ṣàì gba / Permita que mis oraciones se manifiesten [por Olódùmarè] [My prayer will be accepted (by Olódùmarè)]" (Adéwálé-Somadhi 2006b, 205, my translation of Spanish text). Chief FAMA's English language publication provides the Yorùbá-English translation as follows: "If I pray while I'm standing / My prayer will be accepted (by Olódùmarè)" (Adéwálé-Somadhi 2020, 310).

42. Numerous African traditionalists in Cuba request and receive West African ritual materials from Ilé Ọ̀rúnmìlà Afrikan Imports through the visits of US-based babaláwo to the island (e.g., red *osùn* powder made from the camwood trees, *Pterocarpus osun*, of central-west Africa and used in Ifá initiations, or *iyere*, West African black pepper seeds, *Piper guinense*, used for working with Èṣù). See Ifeka 2009.

43. In 2000, Chief FAMA also received a bachelor's degree in English from California State University–San Bernardino after initiating her university studies as a nontraditional student in her forties (Adéwálé-Somadhi 2006a).

44. Many of the idiosyncratic diacritics present in this and other digital documents have also notably entered Nigerian-style Ifá as well (as in the spelling of Êgbë Íran Àtelé Ilôgbôn Baracoa, see chapter 5), seemingly contributing to a novel orthography for Nigerian-style Ifá rooted in the copy-and-paste procedures attendant to the circulation of digital documents across the YTR ritual diaspora.

45. The discrepancies between the Spanish translations evident in the digital document and Chief FAMA's own Yorùbá-Spanish book translation of the original English text also point to the possibility that the anonymous author (or authors) unofficially translated this version of the chapter from the original English publication, also idiosyncratically removing specific sections and displaying idiosyncratic formatting, font, orthographic, and translation discrepancies (see Adéwálé-Somadhi 2020).

46. Chief FAMA makes this imperative explicit in the text, noting that "the process should be explained" to Òsányin, who should also be asked to "bless" the *ewé* (herbs) (Adéwálé-Somadhi 2020, 290).

47. I've reproduced the idiosyncratic spelling, diacritics, and translations in Orozco Rubio's anonymously authored Yorùbá-to-Spanish language text here. In Adéwálé-Somadhi (2006b, 205–7), Chief FAMA spells this section as follows: "Líder [Leader]: Ẹ̀rún, ẹ́rún / Exprime, exprime / Coro [Chorus]: O o, ẹ́rún, Si, exprime" (*sic*, my English language translation).

48. Enrique Orozco Rubio, interview by the author, Santiago de Cuba, May 12, 2016. Karin Barber frames the "gaps, inconsistencies, and contradictions" that characterize heterogeneous formulations of the òrìṣà as constituting, rather than "[a] regrettable untidiness," an "essential trait of the Yorùbá cosmology," one that "[points] to its inherent flexibility" (Barber 1990, in Boscolo 2009, 217).

49. For a detailed discussion of how African traditionalists claim the Yorùbá language as a source of heightened ritual efficacy despite steep barriers to linguistic fluency in the tonal phonology of Yorùbá in Cuba, see chapter 2. Notably, this claim to heightened ritual efficacy through recourse to the contemporary Yorùbá language has been passionately decried by Cuban practitioners since the 1990s (see Menéndez 1995, chap. 1) and even, more recently, by notable, foreign academics (see Villepastour 2020). Amanda Villepastour (2020), for example, states: "Demonstrating that Lucumí has only a loose relationship to Yorùbá should not be harnessed to argue that sacred song performance in Cuba is less efficacious than in Nigeria" (25). Villepastour adds: "The emotional intensity invoked by uttered Lucumí contributes to its spiritually efficacy, as evidenced by routine trance induction in Cuba, and remarkably, its intercultural efficacy" (referencing an instance in which visiting Nigerian òrìṣà priestess, Doyin Faniyi, fell into trance in a Cuban *batá* ritual) (25). Despite such practitioner and academic protestations, however, logics of heightened linguistic efficacy continue to serve as a core discourse justifying the turn to contemporary YTR among Nigerian-style practitioners in Cuba (chaps. 2, 3, and 4). Villepastour (2021, 157) acknowledges the centrality of language to these debates, stating: "Yoruba language knowledge resides at the heart of this revisionist drive."

50. Humberto Torres Hurtado, interview by the author, Havana, April 23, 2016; Victor Betancourt Estrada, interview by the author, June 11, 2016. Victor Betancourt Omolófaoló Estrada is widely credited as spearheading the effort to "restore," "decipher," and "correct" the *ese Ifá*, or sacred verses of the odù, as well as the songs of the Regla de Ocha-Ifá tradition in Cuba through their translation into contemporary Yorùbá (Dulce María Rodríguez Sánchez, interview by the author, Holguín, May 16, 2016; Orozco Rubio, interview, July 25, 2015; Torres Hurtado, interview; Otto William Sabina de León, interview by the author, Morón, May 18, 2016; Betancourt, interview). Betancourt relates that he began a concerted effort to learn Yorùbá and to translate the odù verses and songs of Regla de Ocha-Ifá tradition as a communicative imperative in Ifá-Òrìṣà practice when it came to his attention that Cuban *babalaos*, including himself, didn't "know what they were singing" or "know what they were saying" in rituals (Betancourt, interview). This linguistic premise for the turn to Nigerian-style Ifá-Òrìṣà was echoed by numerous

babaláwo throughout Cuba's provinces. Betancourt worked in collaboration with a French professor of Yorùbá who traveled to Cuba and, additionally, with books, texts, dictionaries and other materials in order to "fill the empty spaces" of the Regla de Ocha-Ifá tradition (Betancourt, interview). For a critique of linguistic efforts to "back-translate Lucumí into Yorùbá," see Villepastour 2020, 15, 25.

51. This and all other translations of songs to Òsányin are my translation of Orozco Rubio's anonymously authored, digital Spanish-language text. Notably, variations of this song have been published in books on Cuban-style Regla de Ocha (see Madan 2021, 206).

52. The *tumbadoras,* or "conga drum[s]" (Sublette 2004, 266) used in Cuban *rumba* (as well as in varied ritual contexts, e.g., Regla de Ocha-Ifá, bembé, and Palo) include three drums of "different diameters, echoing the mula, caja, and cachimbo of the Congo baile yuka" (Schweitzer 2013; Sublette 2004, 266). These include the deepest-pitched *tumbador* (also called *conga, hembra,* or *salidor*), the midregister *segundo* (also called *macho, seis por ocho,* or *tres dos*), and the highest-pitched *quinto* (Daniel 1995, 80).

53. The Santiago de Cuba percussionist and batá player Félix Escobar Griñan pointed out the connection between the rhythms played on the tumbadoras and *chékere* at the Letra del Año ceremony and the güiro ensemble (Félix Escobar Griñan, interview by the author, Santiago de Cuba, 2016). As Kenneth Schweitzer notes, "Lucumí" rituals dedicated to the òrìsà "can be supported by one of a variety of percussion ensembles" in Cuba, including—beyond the "most prestigious" batá *tambores de Añá* ensemble—"aberikulá, bembé, guiro, cajón, and iyesá" (Schweitzer 2013, 23). As he describes, the güiro ensemble "consists of two or three beaded gourds (known as either güiros or *chekerés*), a single conga drum, and a güataca" (24).

54. In an alternate translation that Orozco Rubio provided via a digital, anonymous, Spanish-language text, the translation is rendered as follows: "If there are one thousand men in this place but no women, this place isn't complete. In the moment that women join this place, this place will change because women will bring èrò."

55. In the original, pirated (and notably altered) digital text document held by Orozco Rubio, the chorus is idiosyncratically written as "ßùÿù o, Aládé mà mí wê, ÿùÿù o." This contains letters and diacritics (ß, ÿ, and ê) not consistent with Standard Yorùbá, as noted in this chapter. For clarity, and following the ẹgbẹ́'s Spanish-inflected pronunciation of the chorus, I've written "sùsù" here as published in Chief FAMA's original book ("Sùsù o, Aládé mà mí wẹ̀, sùsù o," Adéwálé-Somadhi 2006b, 210). Notably, the Spanish language digital document held by Orozco Rubio includes specific phonetic instructions for the word *Sùsù* (ßùÿù), with the pronunciation clarified as "shu." This reflects the Yorùbá pronunciation of the consonant s as /ʃ/ (approximating the English language "sh" spelling sound). Chief FAMA's original Yorùbá-Spanish translation also includes this phonetic indication, written as "Shu, Shu" and clarified as the onomatopoeic "splashing sound that the water makes, when the herbs are washed" (Adéwálé-Somadhi 2006b, 210, my translation). In Audio Example 7: Ìyánífá give the ikin Ifá their bath, members of the ẹgbẹ́ pronounce the Yorùbá consonant s in "Sùsù o"/ "ßùÿù o" using the Spanish phoneme /s/, approximating the English language s spelling sound. This move reflects the common replacement of the non-Spanish phoneme /ʃ/ with /s/ among Spanish language second-language learners when approaching languages where the /ʃ/ phoneme is common (e.g., Yorùbá and English) (see Raynolds and Uhry 2010, 499, citing Bear et al. 2003 and Yavas 2006).

56. The sixteen *méjì,* or principal *odù,* of the Ifá corpus are, in sequential order, Èjì Ogbè, Oyeku Méjì, Iwori Méjì, Odi Méjì, Irosun Méjì, Oworin Méjì, Obara Méjì, Okanran Méjì, Ogunda

Méjì, Osa Méjì, Ika Méjì, Oturupon Méjì, Otura Méjì, Irete Méjì, Oshe Ofun Méjì, and Ofun Ofun Méjì (Karade 1994, 12).

57. Yamilka Gámez Oliva, interview by the author, Havana, 2016.

Chapter Five

1. The Ẹ̀gbë Íran Àtelé Ilôgbôn Odugbemi. See chapter 4 for a discussion of the idiosyncratic diacritics and orthography used in this and other African traditionalist ẹgbẹ́ titles.

2. My translation of Orozco Rubio's anonymously authored digital text document, titled "Cantos de Ègúngún" (Songs of ègúngún), containing the Yorùbá-Spanish translation.

3. The term *bembé*, in this context, refers to a "religious party" in which participants pay homage to the orichas through drumming and dance (Rosendo Romero Suárez, interview by the author, Baracoa, 2016). Ambiguity in the usage of the term within specifically eastern Cuban ritual contexts, and its potential link to *Espiritismo cruzado* in addition to *toques de santo*, is elaborated in this chapter.

4. Here, Boscolo quotes Idowu (1962, 192).

5. Enrique Orozco Rubio and Ricardo Pérez, interview by the author, Santiago de Cuba, May 12, 2016; Frank Cabrera Suárez, interview by the author, Havana, April 4, 2016.

6. Henry Drewal (1978, 18) notes that egúngún are believed to be òrìṣà among some, though not all, egúngún worshippers in Yorùbáland, a conceptualization that varies from site to site. Babayemi (1980, 1), for his part, distinguishes between egúngún and the òrìṣà, stating that "the Yorùbá keep in constant communion with their ancestors whose spirits are believed to be closer to them than the orisa."

7. Egúngún secret societies are, however, closely linked with Ifá divination in Yorùbáland (Babayemi 1980; Beier 1958). H. U. Beier (1958, 3) states that "it is always the priest of the Ifá oracle, who will decide what spirit [deceased person] must thus receive special worship" through the creation and masquerade of an egúngún mask. Babayemi (1980, 6–7) likewise notes that origin myths of the egúngún abound in the odù Ifá, which mythically "[illustrate] the origin of egúngún."

8. See Thabiti Willis (2017) and Babayemi (1980, 17–29) for extensive discussions of divergent scholarly accounts of the emergence of the egúngún, including egúngún's relation to the bordering Nupe and Bariba peoples and the imbrication of the egúngún society with political struggles across the history of the Ọ̀yọ́ empire.

9. Ọlajubu and Ojo (1977, 262) also defines "Ọ̀jẹ̀" as "professional maskers."

10. The full proverb states "A kú tán làá dère, ènìyàn ò suwòn láàyè," "to die is to become deified; no one venerates a living person" (Afolayan and Pemberton 1996, 25, in Boscolo 2009, 191).

11. As she notes, the "Yoruba use this root [*ran*] for the verb 'to remember' (*ranti [ran eti]*) and 'to recite Ifá verses' (*ranfá [ran Ifá]*) as well as 'to send a message by way of a messenger' (*ranse [ran ise]*). In the latter case, the message delivered is the messenger's interpretation of the original. Each repetition is a revision of the initial material" (M. Drewal 2003, 121).

12. *Ọdun egúngún*, or egúngún festivals, often take place between May and July for a period of seventeen days (Boscolo 2009, 203). In certain areas, egúngún festivals take place between December and March (Babayemi 1980, 30).

13. Enrique Orozco Rubio, interview by the author, Santiago de Cuba, May 12, 2016.

14. Women, however, hold key titles within the egúngún lineage in Yorùbáland, "even if they mainly operate behind the scene" (Familusi 2012, 308). Babayemi (1980, 4) notes that the

"most senior women titles" in the egúngún cult include Iyámọde and Yèyéṣọrun, though titles vary from site to site. "Such women are not to divulge the secrets of the cult," Babayemi warns, stating that they adhere to the saying, "If a woman knows cult secrets, she must never tell" (4). In Cuba, I'm not aware of any titles for women introduced as part of the novel egúngún lineages or societies, which were all-male during my fieldwork years.

15. *Fiestas religiosas* (Romero Suárez, interview).

16. Asante (2009, 231) defines such elements as "troublesome" or "disgruntled people."

17. Also referred to as a "costume"; see Lindfors 1977, 154–55.

18. My translation of Orozco Rubio's provided digital document with the Spanish transla-tion. I've translated the verb *sacudirse* as "thrash about," although it could alternately be trans-lated as "to shake off," "to throw off," "to jerk," or "to toss about."

19. Wirtz (2014, 58) notes that these gestures are more typical of "muertos, or spirits of the dead" than they are of oricha spirit possession in Regla de Ocha-Ifá, though they "can some-times be seen in possessions by the orichas of Santería as well." In various *cajón al muerto* cere-monies that I witnessed in Havana between 2013 and 2014 (which are associated with *Espiritismo cruzado*, see Warden 2006), individuals possessed by the dead exhibited similar gestures to those exhibited in this chapter.

20. In the OIATYR lineage in eastern Cuba helmed by Orozco Rubio at the time of this fieldwork, members of both the Ẹgbé Irán Átele Ilogbemi Odugbemi (Santiago de Cuba) and the Ẹ̀gbë Íran Àtelé Ilôgbôn (Baracoa) used the term "Alágbàá Egúngún" to refer to initiated priests of egúngún in the newly instituted egúngún society in eastern Cuba. The use of the term Alágbàá Egúngún to indicate a *sacerdote* ("priest" in Spanish) of egúngún notably diverges from Babayemi's description of the title of Alágbàá in Yorùbáland as, more specifically, "the ritual head of the egúngún cult" (Babayemi 1980, 41). H. U. Beier (1958, 3) likewise states: "Egungun is a secret society of maskeraders headed by a hereditary chief called the Alagba." In eastern Cuba, however, members of Orozco Rubio's lineage notably used the term *Alágbàá Egúngún* to refer, in the plural, to "priest[s] of Egúngún," which, at the time of this fieldwork, included the initiation of twelve Alágbàá Egúngún in the ẹgbẹ́ in Santiago de Cuba, one Alágbàá Egúngún in Holguín, and one Alágbàá Egúngún in Baracoa (Romero Suárez) (Romero Suárez, interview; Orozco Rubio, interview, May 12, 2016).

21. Reyes Sollet, interview by the author, Baracoa, May 29, 2016.

22. Ricardo "Buzzy" Pérez, interview by the author, Santiago de Cuba, 2016.

23. Ethnographer Jualynne Dodson (2008, 128), in her study of ritual traditions in Oriente, notes that her research informants also linked the term *bembé* to the ritual traditions of "muer-téra" and "bembé de Sao" in eastern Cuba. In reviewing the research of investigators at the Casa del Caribe in Santiago de Cuba, Dodson further notes that the term *bembé* is used more broadly to refer to celebrations and parties during the colonial era in eastern Cuba aimed at invoking the ancestors "to visit" the world of the living (86).

24. For a study of the standard timeline and its uses in Brazil based on circular rotations of the "regulative time point" (Anku 2000), in other words, using alternate downbeats rooted in the shifting perception (and uses) of the downbeat in cyclical, timeline-based music, see Díaz (2021, 97–105).

25. See also discussions on the continued use of the Cuban batá as an efficacious means of channeling Añá/Àyàn in Nigerian-style Ifá-Òrìṣà ritual (chap. 3).

26. In Yorùbáland, the individual egúngún demonstrate a wide variety of names, types, and functions that vary from town to town and city to city (Boscolo 2009, 194). Types of egúngún

may include egúngún aláré (egúngún entertainers) (194), Olóùgun (herbalists), Láyèwú / Ọdẹ (hunters) (195), or Jénjù ("the *egúngún* believed to execute witches to the power of Àgan" in Ọ̀yọ́, called Gbajẹẹro in Ede) (194), among others.

27. In Yorùbáland, the direct association between *bàtá*, *dùndún*, and the manifestation of egúngún further underscores the historical significance of Ọ̀yọ́ in the development of the lineage-based egúngún society and its diffusion, in tandem with the "expansion of Ọ̀yọ́'s sphere of influence," throughout the region in the eighteenth and nineteenth centuries (Boscolo 2009, 201). This historical expansion and the resultant "hegemony" of Ọ̀yọ́ precipitated the prominence of the batá drums in western Cuba as well. As Miguel Ramos (2000, viii) notes, the prominence of the Cuban batá as the premier instruments of the oricha "illustrate[s] the vitality of Ọ̀yọ́ cultural hegemony" in contemporary Regla de Ocha practice.

28. Martínez Betancourt has traced a genealogy of the revival of egúngún in Cuba, via African traditionalism, between 1998 and 2016 (Martínez Betancourt 2016). As he notes, Frank Cabrera Suárez received the *fundamento* (emblem) of egúngún in 1998. In 2003, Victor Betancourt Estrada held a public display of egúngún masks in conjunction with the Casa de la Amistad Cuba–Angola in Havana. In 2009, the Cuban expat Frank Alberto Hernández Reyes was initiated into the priesthood society by Juan Manuel Rodríguez Camejo (Ifáshade Odùgbemi), and he subsequently initiated the first three egúngún priests in Cuba in November 2011, officially instating the egúngún society on the island (Martínez Betancourt 2016).

29. The separation of owners (or holders) of egúngún masks, or "lineage egúngún," from the Ọ̀jẹ̀ secret society, or "professional maskers" themselves, however, is also typical of Yorùbáland (Babayemi 1980, 30; Ọlajubu and Ojo 1977, 262). In Yorùbáland, Babayemi notes that "each lineage would have to arrange with the Ọ̀jẹ̀ when their lineage egúngún could come out" (Babayemi 1980, 30), pointing to the dominion of egúngún masquerade as provenance of the Ọ̀jẹ̀.

30. Martín Cabrera Escudero (1919–66) was Cabrera's father.

31. Yunieski González Ramírez, interview by the author, Santiago de las Vegas, April 18, 2016.

32. Cabrera also received audio from Táíwò Abímbọ́lá in which the Nigerian babaláwo sings the song, demonstrating its melody (Cabrera, pers. comm., 2016).

33. *Ọ̀lẹ̀lẹ̀* and *àkàrà* are Yorùbá foods associated with the òrìṣà. Akinyemi (2015) describes *ọ̀lẹ̀lẹ̀* as a "cooked pudding made from black-eyed pea paste wrapped in leaves" and *àkàrà* as "fried bean cake."

34. My translation of the Yorùbá-Spanish translation of this song provided to Cabrera by Táíwò Abímbọ́lá.

35. My translation.

36. Also referred to as "generic" toques (see Schweitzer 2013).

37. José Reinaldo Ilin Montano, interview by the author, Havana, 2016.

38. Raymond Williams influentially coined the phrase "structures of feeling" in the 1970s (R. Williams 1977, 27; see also Sharma and Tygstrup 2015).

39. Damián Francisco Paula Valdés, interview by the author, Havana, April 30, 2016.

40. Despite progressive analyses of music's affective force, musical pleasure has also been linked to divisive and regressive stances and forms of action, including authoritarianism and violence (Dave 2019, 3).

41. For more on *timba*, see Perna 2005.

42. For a provocative look at *kwaito* music as "above all else a declaration of sensory and intellectual equality" for Black musicians and listeners within conditions of pervasive material inequity in post-apartheid South Africa, see Steingo 2016, 14.

Epilogue

1. Otto William Sabina de León, interview by the author, Morón, May 18, 2016.

2. Sabina de León's wife initiated as an ìyánífá in 2006, only two years after Sabina de León met Victor Betancourt Estrada in Havana following the ACYC's 2004 proclamation (Sabina de León, interview).

3. Leopards, the "most solitary and secretive of Africa's big cats" (McIntyre 2015, 509), live in relative isolation from one another, associating primarily during mating season, the weaning of offspring, and, occasionally, in the adult lives of offspring (Estes 1991; Kingdon et al. 2013; Nowak 1999).

4. Humberto Torres Hurtado, interview by the author, Havana, April 23, 2016. During initiations, for example, women and men are ritually painted with spots using red *osùn*, "blood-colored camwood" in Yorùbá, and *efun*, "white chalk" (Matory [1994] 2005, 192). Although interpretations of these designs vary considerably in Cuba (D. Brown 2003, 201), many African traditionalist babaláwo claimed in our interviews that the spots invoke the bravery, fearlessness, and vitality of the leopard (Enrique Orozco Rubio, interview by the author, Santiago de Cuba, June 23, 2015; Torres Hurtado, interview; Yunieski González Ramírez, interview by the author, Santiago de las Vegas, April 18, 2016). On the relationship of *Abakuá* in Cuba to the "leopard societies" of the Cross River basin in southeastern Nigeria, including the "Àbàkpà (Ejagham), Efut, and Èfik peoples," see Miller 2000, 164. As Ivor Miller notes (2000, 167), the term for the sacred Ékue drum of Abakuá "derives from the Èfik [word] *ékpè* (leopard)."

5. Elected in 2014 following the death of the ACYC's previous president, Antonio Castañeda Márquez (1946-2014).

6. For more on the history of the competing Letra del Año ceremonies in Havana, see D. Brown 2003, 342; Castro Figueroa 2012; and Hearn 2008, 49-51.

7. Victor Betancourt Estrada, interview by the author, Havana, June 11, 2016; José Manuel "Manolo" Pérez Andino, interview by the author, Havana, June 20, 2016.

8. *Hacer Ifá*, that is, become Ifá initiates.

9. Dulce María Rodríguez Sánchez, interview by the author, Holguín, May 16, 2016.

10. My visit to Ọ̀yọ́ and other sites in Yorùbáland in 2018 was kindly and graciously facilitated by scholar and musician Amanda Villepastour, who mapped our itinerary between Lagos, Ọ̀yọ́, and Òṣogbo.

11. Frank Cabrera Suárez, interview by the author, Havana, April 9, 2016.

12. Frank Cabrera Suárez, interview by the author, Havana, April 4, 2016.

References

Abimbola, Kola. 2005. *Yorùbá Culture: A Philosophical Account*. Birmingham, UK: Ìrókò Academic Publishers.

Abímbọ́lá, Wándé. 1979. "Continuity and Change in the Verbal, Artistic, Ritual, and Performance Traditions of Ifá Divination." In *Ifá Divination: Knowledge, Power, and Performance*, edited by Jacob K. Olupona and Rowland O. Abiodun, 32–42. Bloomington: Indiana University Press, 2016.

———. 1996. "Wapele: The Concept of Good Character in Ifá Literary Corpus." In *African Intellectual Heritage: A Book of Sources*, edited by Molefi Kete Asante and Abu S. Abarry, 98–106. Philadelphia, PA: Temple University Press.

———. 1997. *Ifá Will Mend Our Broken World: Thoughts on Yoruba Religion and Culture in Africa and the Diaspora*. Interviews and introduction by Ivor Miller. Roxbury, MA: AIM Books.

———. 1976. "Yoruba Religion in Brazil: Problems and Prospects." In *Actes du 42e Congrès International des Américanistes*, 619–39. Paris: Société des Américanistes.

Abiodun, Rowland. 2014. *Yoruba Art and Language: Seeking the African in African Art*. Cambridge: Cambridge University Press.

Adebajo, Adekeye. 2002. *Liberia's Civil War: Nigeria, ECOMOG, and Regional Security in West Africa*. London: Lynne Reinner Publishers.

Adedeji, W. 2016. "The Nigerian Music Industry: Challenges, Prospects and Possibilities." *International Journal of Recent Research in Social Sciences and Humanities* 3 (1): 261–71.

Adegbija, Efurosibina. 1997. "The Identity, Survival, and Promotion of Minority Languages in Nigeria." *International Journal of the Sociology of Language* 125: 5–27.

Adegbindin, Omotade. 2014. *Ifá in Yorùbá Thought System*. Durham, NC: Carolina Academic Press.

Adegoke, Yemisi. 2017. "UN: Half of World's Population Growth Is Likely to Occur in Africa." CNN, June 26. https://www.cnn.com/2017/06/25/africa/africa-population-growth-un/index.html.

Adelaja, Tayo. 2018. "Araba Agbaye, Custodian of Orunmila dies at 86." Infotrust, August 1. https://infotrustng.com/araba-agbaye-custodian-of-orunmila-dies-at-86/.

Adepoju, Aderanti, ed. 2010. *International Migration within, to, and from Africa in a Globalized World*. Legon, Ghana: Sub-Saharan Publishers.

Adesoji, Abimbola. 2010. "The Boko Haram Uprising and Islamic Revivalism in Nigeria." *Africa Spectrum* 45 (2): 95–108.

Adéwálé-Somadhi, FAMA Àìná. 2006a. *Fundamentos de la religión Yorùbá: Adorando òrìṣà*. San Bernardino, CA: Ilé Ọ̀rúnmìlà Communications.

———. 2006b. *Manual para el profesional que practica ifa*. San Bernardino, CA: Ile Orunmila Communications.

———. 2020. *Practical Manual for Ifa Professionals*. Self-published.

Adogame, Afe. 2009. "Practitioners of Indigenous Religions in Africa and the African Diaspora." In *Religions in Focus: New Approaches to Tradition and Contemporary Practices*, edited by Graham Harvey, 75–100. New York: Routledge.

Afenapa, Asabioje. 2007. *"Isese L'agba" (Tradition and Culture Is the Best)*. Okanran-onile Productions 634479649189, compact disc.

Afolabi, Niyi. 2005. "Axé: Invocation of Candomblé and Afro-Brazilian Gods Brazilian Cultural Production." In *Fragments of Bone: Neo-African Religions in a New World*, edited by Patrick Bellegarde-Smith, 108–23. Urbana: University of Illinois Press.

Afolayan, F. S., and John Pemberton III. 1996. *Yorùbá Sacred Kinship*. Washington, DC: Smithsonian Institution.

Agawu, V. Kofi. 1987. "The Rhythmic Structure of West African Music." *Journal of Musicology* 5 (3): 400–18.

———. 2003. *Representing African Music: Postcolonial Notes, Queries, Positions*. New York: Routledge.

Águila de Ifá. 2015. "Apetebí: La iniciación en Ifá de la mujer de la tradición afrocubana; Una respuesta a los capos y sus sicarios religiosos de la tradición nigeriana." In *Yorùbá Cultural Association of Cuba* (Havana, Cuba), Boletín no. 4, February.

Aguilar Amaya, Rodolfo Javier, Mey-King Romero Hung, Ángel William Viera Bravo, Cheryl Tawede Grills, Cristina V. Hernández Roca, and Ana Sarracent Sarracent. 2014. "Relación de los efectos nocivos laborales y comunitarios en adictos al alcohol y cocaína." *Revista de Hospital Psiquiátrico de la Habana* 11 (1). https://www.medigraphic.com/cgi-bin/new/resumen.cgi?IDARTICULO=50113.

Augustin, Ed, and Frances Robles. "'Cuba Is Depopulating': Largest Exodus Yet Threatens Country's Future." *New York Times*, December 10, 2022. https://www.nytimes.com/2022/12/10/world/americas/cuba-us-migration.html.

Ahmed, Sara. 2010a. "Happy Objects." In *The Affect Theory Reader*, edited by Melissa Gregg and Gregory J. Seigworth, 29–51. Durham, NC: Duke University Press.

———. 2010b. "Orientations Matter." In *New Materialisms: Ontology, Agency, and Politics*, edited by Jane Bennett, Pheng Cheah, Melissa A. Orlie, and Elizabeth Grosz, 234–57. Durham, NC: Duke University Press.

———. 2006. *Queer Phenomenology: Orientations, Objects, Others*. Durham, NC: Duke University Press.

———. 2019. *What's the Use? On the Uses of Use*. Durham, NC: Duke University Press.

Akinlabi, Akinbiyi, and Mark Liberman. 2000. "The Tonal Phonology of Yoruba Clitics." In *Clitics in Phonology, Morphology and Syntax*, edited by Birgit Gerlach and Janet Grijzenhout, 31–62. Amsterdam: John Benjamins Publishing Company.

Akinyemi, Akitunde. 2015. *Orature and Yorùbá Riddles*. New York: Palgrave Macmillan.

Akpabot, S. 1986. *Foundations of Nigerian Traditional Music*. Ibadan, Nigeria: Spectrum Books.

Alarcón, Jessica M. 2008. "Babalawo." In *Encyclopedia of the African Diaspora: Origins, Experiences, and Culture*, vol. 1, A–C, edited by Carole Boyce Davies, 138–39. Santa Barbara, CA: ABC-CLIO.

Alexander, M. Jacqui. 2006. *Pedagogies of Crossing: Meditations on Feminism, Sexual Politics, Memory, and the Sacred*. Durham, NC: Duke University Press.

Aljazeera. 2022. "US Issues Visas in Cuba for First Time in More Than Four Years." May 3. https://www.aljazeera.com/news/2022/5/3/us-issues-visas-in-cuba-for-the-first-time-in-more-than-4-years.

Alsonso Valdés, C. 1984. *Población, migración internacional y desarrollo regional: Una experiencia cubana*. Isla de la Juventud, Cuba: Ponencia de contribución, Seminario internacional de población y Nuevo Orden Económico Internacional.

Amico, Stephen. 2006. *"Su casa es mi casa*: Latin House, Sexuality, Place." In *Queering the Popular Pitch*, edited by Sheila Whiteley and Jennifer Rycenga, 131–51. New York: Routledge.

Andreu Alonso, Guillermo. 1995. *Los Ararás en Cuba: Florentina, la princesa dahomeyana*. Havana: Editorial de Ciencias Sociales.

Anku, Willie. 2000. "Circles and Time: A Theory of Structural Organization of Rhythm in African Music." *Music Theory Online* 6 (1): 1–8.

Angarica, Nicolas Valantin. 2010. *El lucumí al alcance de todos*. Edited by Angel Rodríguez Alvarez. Self-published.

Anguelovski, Isabelle. 2014. *Neighborhood as Refuge: Community Reconstruction, Place Remaking, and Environmental Justice in the City*. Cambridge, MA: MIT Press.

Argyriadis, Kali, and Stefania Capone. 2004. "Cubanía et santería: Les enjeux politiques de la transnationalisation religieuse (La Havane–Miami)." *Civilisations* 51: 81–137. http://civilisations.revues.org/668.

Asante, Molefi Kete. 2009. "Egungun." In *Encyclopedia of African Religion*, vol. 2, edited by Molefi Kete Asante and Ama Mazama, 231–33. Thousand Oaks, CA: SAGE Publications.

Ayegboyin, Deji, and Charles Jegede. 2009. "Evil." In *Encyclopedia of African Religion*, vol. 1, edited by Molefi Kete Asante and Ama Mazama, 249–50. Thousand Oaks, CA: SAGE Publications.

Avorgbedor, Daniel Kodzo. 2003. *The Interrelatedness of Music, Religion, and Ritual in African Performance Practice*. New York: E. Mellen Press.

Ayorinde, Christine. 2004. "Santería in Cuba: Transition and Transformation." In *The Yoruba Diaspora in the Atlantic World*, edited by Matt D. Childs and Toyin Falola, 209–30. Bloomington: Indiana University Press.

Azorena, Marcelino. 1961. "Los cabildos de nación ante el registro de la propiedad." *Actas de Folklore* 1 (3): 13–22.

Babátúndé, Abosede Omowumi. 2017. *"Orí* and *Ẹlédàà* in Poverty Conceptualization in Traditional Yorùbá Religion: Challenging Developmental and Aid Organizations' Understandings of Poverty." *Journal of African Cultural Studies* 29 (3): 362–76.

Babayemi, Solomon Oyewole. 1980. *Egúngún among the Ọ̀yọ́ Yorùbá*. Ibadan, Nigeria: Board Publications.

Baker, Jessica Swanston. 2020. "Small Islands, Large Radio: Archipelagic Listening in the Caribbean." In *Contemporary Archipelagic Thinking: Towards New Comparative Methodologies and Disciplinary Formations*, edited by Yolanda Martínez-San Miguel and Michelle Stephens, 383–401. Lanham, MD: Rowman & Littlefield.

Baloyra, Enrique A., and James A. Morris, eds. 1993. *Conflict and Change in Cuba*. Albuquerque: University of New Mexico Press.

Barber, Karin. 1990. "*Oriki*, Women, and the Proliferation and Merging of *Orisa*." *Africa* 60 (3): 313–37.

———. 1991. *I Could Speak until Tomorrow: Oriki, Women, and the Past in a Yorùbá Town*. Edinburgh: Edinburgh University Press.

Barnet, Miguel. 1997. "La Regla de Ocha: The Religious System of Santería." In *Sacred Possessions: Vodou, Santería, Obeah, and the Caribbean*, edited by Margarite Fernández Olmos and Lizabeth Paravisini-Gebert, 79–100. New Brunswick, NJ: Rutgers University Press.

Bascom, William. 1950. "The Focus of Cuban Santeria." *Southwestern Journal of Anthropology* 6 (1): 64–68.

———. 1952. "Two Forms of Afro-Cuban Divination." In *Acculturation in the Americas*, vol. 2 of *Proceedings and Selected Papers of the Twenty-Ninth International Congress of Americanists*, 3 vols., edited by Sol Tax, 169–79. Chicago: University of Chicago Press.

———. 1969a. *Ifá Divination: Communication between Gods and Men in West Africa*. Bloomington: Indiana University Press.

———. 1969b. *The Yoruba of Southwestern Nigeria*. New York: Holt, Rinehart, and Winston.

———. (1980) 1993. *Sixteen Cowries: Yoruba Divination from Africa to the New World*. Bloomington: Indiana University Press.

Bastian Martínez, Hope. 2018. *Everyday Adjustments in Havana: Economic Reforms, Mobility, and Emerging Inequalities*. Lanham, MD: Lexington Books.

Bay, Edna G. 2008. *Asen, Ancestors, and Vodun: Tracing Change in African Art*. Urbana: University of Illinois Press.

Bear, D., S. Templeton, Lori A. Helman, and T. Baren. 2003. "Orthographic Development and Learning to Read in Different Languages." In *English Learners: Reaching the Highest Level of English Literacy*, edited by G. Garcia, 71–95. Newark, DE: International Reading Association.

Becker, Hilary. 2016. "Tourism in Cuba: Barriers to Economic Growth and Development." In *Handbook of Contemporary Cuba: Economy, Politics, Civil Society, and Globalization*, edited by Mauricio A. Font and Carlos Riobó. New York: Routledge.

Beier, H. U. 1958. "The Egungun Cult among the Yorubas." *Présence Africaine*, no. 18/19: 33–36.

Beldarraín Chaple, Enrique and Mary Anne Mercer. 2017. "The Cuban Response to the Ebola Epidemic in West Africa: Lessons in Solidarity." *International Journal of Health Services*, 47 (1) (January): 134–49.

Beliso-De Jesús, Aisha M. 2015a. "Contentious Diasporas: Gender, Sexuality, and Heteronationalisms in the Cuban Iyanifa Debate." *Signs: Journal of Women in Culture and Society* 40 (4): 817–40.

———. 2015b. *Electric Santería: Racial and Sexual Assemblages of Transnational Religion*. New York: Columbia University Press.

Berry, Maya J. 2010. "From Ritual to Repertory: Dancing to the Time of the Nation." *Afro-Hispanic Review* 29 (1): 55–76.

Betancourt, Lino Neira. (2004) 2014. *La percusión en la música cubana*. Havana: Fondo Editorial Casa de las Américas.

Bird, Stephanie Rose. 2009. *A Healing Grove: African Tree Remedies and Rituals for Body and Spirit*. Chicago: Lawrence Hill Books.

Blier, Susan Preston. 2015. *Art and Risk in Ancient Yoruba: Ife History, Power, and Identity, c.1300*. Cambridge: Cambridge University Press.

Bodenheimer, Rebecca M. 2015. *Geographies of Cubanidad: Place, Race, and Musical Performance in Contemporary Cuba*. Jackson: University Press of Mississippi.

Bøhler, Kjetil Klette. 2021. "The Political Force of Musical Actants: Grooves, Pleasures, and Politics in Havana D'Primera's 'Pasaporte' Live in Havana." *Twentieth-Century Music* 18 (2): 185–222.

Boland, Philip. 2010. "Sonic Geography, Place and Race in the Formation of Local Identity: Liverpool and Scousers." *Geografiska Annaler*, Series B, Human Geography 92 (1): 1–22.

Bolívar Aróstegui, Natalia. 1990. *Los Orishas en Cuba*. Havana: Ediciones Unión.

Bolívar, Natalia, Carmen González, and Natalia del Río. (2007) 2013. *Corrientes espirituales en Cuba*. Havana: Editorial José Martí.

Bonsal, Philip W. 1971. *Cuba, Castro, and the United States*. Pittsburgh, PA: University of Pittsburgh Press.

Boscolo, Cristina. 2009. *Ọdún: Discourses, Strategies, and Power in the Yorùbá Play of Transformation*. Amsterdam: Rodopi.

Bouchet, Ceil Miller. 2016. "How Tourism Will Change Cuba." *National Geographic*, April 19, 2016. https://www.nationalgeographic.com/travel/article/how-tourism-will-change-cuba.

Boyle, Kevin, and Juliet Sheen, eds. (1997) 2003. *Freedom of Religion and Belief: A World Report*. New York: Routledge.

Brandon, George. 1983. *The Dead Sell Memories: An Anthropological Study of Santeria in New York City*. New Brunswick, NJ: Rutgers University Press.

———. 1991. "The Uses of Plants in Healing in an Afro-Cuban Religion, Santeria." *Journal of Black Studies* 22 (1): 55–76.

———. 1993. *Santería from Africa to the New World: The Dead Sell Memories*. Bloomington: Indiana University Press.

Bridgland, Fred. 2017. *The War for Africa: Twelve Months That Transformed a Continent*. Havertown, PA: Casemate Publishers.

Bright, Jake. 2015. "Meet 'Nollywood': The Second Largest Movie Industry in the World." *Fortune*, June 24, 2015. https://fortune.com/2015/06/24/nollywood-movie-industry/.

Brooklyn, Cassandra. 2021. "Dial-Up Still Exists: How Cubans Make Island Internet Work for Them." *Ars Technica*, February 10, 2021. https://arstechnica.com/information-technology/2021/02/how-cubans-make-island-internet-work-for-them/.

brown, adrienne maree. 2019. *Pleasure Activism: The Politics of Feeling Good*. Edinburgh, UK: AK Press.

Brown, David H. 2003. *Santeria Enthroned: Art, Ritual, and Innovation in an Afro-Cuban Religion*. Chicago: University of Chicago Press.

———. 2004. "Santería in Cuba." In *African Folklore: An Encyclopedia*, edited by Philip M. Peek and Kwesi Yankah. New York: Routledge.

Butler, Melvin L. 2019. *Island Gospel: Pentecostal Music and Identity in Jamaica and the United States*. Urbana: University of Illinois Press.

Cabrera, Lydia. 1957. *Anagó: Vocabulario lucumí (El Yoruba que se habla en Cuba)*. Havana: Ediciones C.R.

———. (1954) 1993. *El monte: Notas sobre las religions, la magia, las supersticiones y el folklore de los negros criollos y del pueblo de Cuba*. Havana: Editorial Letras Cubanas.

Cardenal, Ernesto. 1974. *In Cuba*. Translated by D. Walsh. New York: New Directions.

Carter-Ényì, A. 2018. "Hooked on Sol-Fa: The Do-Re-Mi Heuristic for Yorùbá Speech Tones." *Africa* 88 (2): 267–90.

Carwile, Christey. 2017. " 'The Clave Comes Home': Salsa Dance and Pan-African Identity in Ghana." *African Studies Review* 60 (2): 183–207.

Cassells, Elsada Diana. 2016. "Cuba: Still Punching above Its Weight." In *Diplomatic Strategies of Nations in the Global South: The Search for Leadership*, 319–44. New York: Palgrave Macmillan.

Castellanos, Jorge, and Isabel Castellanos. 1992. *Cultura afrocubana*, vol. 2, *El negro en Cuba, 1945–1959*. Miami: Ediciones Universal.

Castro Figueroa, Abel R. 2012. *Quo Vadis, Cuba? Religión y revolución*. Bloomington, IN: Palibrio.

Cave, Damien. 2012. "Easing Path Out of Country, Cuba Is Dropping Exit Visas." *New York Times*, October 16, 2012. https://www.nytimes.com/2012/10/17/world/americas/cuba-lifts -much-reviled-rule-the-exit-visa.html.

Chatelain, Daniel. 2003. "Tambours batas: Entretiens avec trois bataleros cubains." In *Percussion*, no. 12 (May): 24–33.

ChiefDayo. 2014. "The First Araba of the United States of America and Diaspora." December 13, 2014. http://arabaifatemple.org/the-first-araba-of-the-united-states-of-america-and -diaspora/. URL no longer active.

Chor, Ives. 2016. "Microtiming and Rhythmic Structure in Clave-Based Music: A Quantitative Study." In *Musical Rhythm in the Age of Digital Reproduction*, edited by Anne Danielsen, 37–50. New York: Routledge.

Clark, Juan. 1992. *Cuba: Mito y realidad*. Miami: Saeta Ediciones.

Clark, Mary Ann. 2007. *Santeria: Correcting the Myths and Uncovering the Realities of a Growing Religion*. Westport, CT: Praeger.

Clarke, Kamari Maxine. 2004. *Mapping Yorùbá Networks: Power and Agency in the Making of Transnational Communities*. Durham, NC: Duke University Press.

———. 2006. "Yorùbá Aesthetics and Trans-Atlantic Imaginaries." In *African and Diaspora Aesthetics*, edited by Sarah Nuttall, 290–315. Durham, NC: Duke University Press.

Clealand, Danielle Pilar. 2017. *The Power of Race in Cuba: Racial Ideology and Black Consciousness during the Revolution*. New York: Oxford University Press.

Colantonio, Andrea, and Robert B. Potter. 2006. *Urban Tourism and Development in the Socialist State: Havana during the Special Period*. Hampshire, UK: Ashgate.

Conner, Randy P., with David Hatfield Sparks. 2004. *Queering Creole Spiritual Traditions: Lesbian, Gay, Bisexual, and Transgender Participation in African-Inspired Traditions in the Americas*. New York: Harrington Park Press.

Corporate Affairs Commission. 2016. "CAC Public Search." Nigeria, Federal Ministry of Commerce and Tourism. https://search.cac.gov.ng/home.

Corzo, Gabino La Rosa. 2003. *Runaway Slave Settlements in Cuba*. Translated by Mary Todd. Chapel Hill: University of North Carolina Press.

Cox, Harvey. 1987. "Introduction by Harvey Cox." In *Fidel and Religion: Castro Talks on Revolution and Religion with Frei Betto*, by Frei Betto, 11–27. New York: Simon and Schuster.

Dada, Babatunji O. 2015. "Metricism In Yorùbá Wórò Rhythm." *Ejotmas: Ekpoma Journal of Theatre and Media Arts* 5 (1–2): 26–40.

Daniel, Yvonne. 1995. *Rumba: Dance and Social Change in Contemporary Cuba*. Bloomington: Indiana University Press.

Danielsen, Anne. 2006. *Presence and Pleasure: The Funk Grooves of James Brown and Parliament*. Middleton, CT: Wesleyan University Press.

DarkRaven66675. 2013. "Primer Festival Internacional Egúngún en Argentina—1/2." Online video clip. YouTube, February 26, 2013. https://www.youtube.com/watch?v=Mwh8YtWbLEs.

Dauda, Muritala, Mohammad Zaki Bin Ahmad, and Mohammad Faisol Keling. 2017. "Nigeria's Role and Its Peacekeeping Challenges in Africa: An Assessment." *European Journal of Social Sciences Studies* 2 (3): 46–71.

Dave, Nomi. 2019. *Music, Politics, and Pleasure in Guinea.* Chicago: University of Chicago Press.

Davies, Shelagh, Viktória G. Papp, and Christella Antoni. 2015. "Voice and Communication Change for Gender Nonconforming Individuals: Giving Voice to the Person Inside." *International Journal of Transgenderism* 16 (3): 117–59.

De Ferrari, Guillermina. 2014. *Community and Culture in Post-Soviet Cuba.* New York: Routledge.

De la Fuente, Alejandro. 2001. *A Nation for All: Race, Inequality, and Politics in Twentieth-Century Cuba.* Chapel Hill: University of North Carolina Press.

De La Torres, Miguel A. 2004. *Santeria: The Beliefs and Rituals of a Growing Religion in America.* Grand Rapids, MI: Wm. B. Eerdmans.

Delgado, Kevin M. 2009. "Spiritual Capital: Foreign Patronage and the Trafficking of Santería." In *Cuban in the Special Period: Culture and Ideology in the 1990s,* edited by Hernandez-Reguant, 51–66. New York: Palgrave Macmillan.

Dennett, R. E. 1916. "The Ogboni and Other Secret Societies in Nigeria." *Journal of the Royal African Society* 16 (61): 16–29.

Denzer, LaRay. 1994. "Yoruba Women: A Historiographical Study." *International Journal of African Historical Studies* 27 (1): 1–39.

Deschamps Chapeaux, Pedro. 1968. "Cabildos: Solo para esclavos." *Cuba: Revista Mensual* (Havana) año 7, no. 69 (January): 50–51.

Diawara, Manthia. 2018. "Édouard Glissant's Worldmentality." *Nka* 1 (42–43): 20–27.

Díaz, Juan Diego. 2016. "Tabom Voices: A History of the Ghanaian Afro-Brazilian Community in Their Own Words." Brazilian Embassy in Ghana, Tabom Heritage Project, Accra: Legend.

———. 2020. "The Musical Experience of Diasporas: The Return of a Ghanaian Tabom Master Drummer to Bahia." *Latin American Music Review* 41 (2): 131–66.

———. 2021. *Africanness in Action: Essentialism and Musical Imaginations of Africa in Brazil.* New York: Oxford University Press.

Dodson, Jualynne E. 2008. *Sacred Spaces and Religious Traditions in Oriente Cuba.* Albuquerque: University of New Mexico Press.

Dowd, Robert Alfred. 2015. *Christianity, Islam and Liberal Democracy: Lessons from Sub-Saharan Africa.* New York: Oxford University Press.

Drewal, Henry J. 1978. "The Arts of Egungun among Yoruba People." *African Arts* 11 (3): 18–98.

———. 2016. "Ifá: Visual and Sensorial Aspects." In *Ifá Divination, Knowledge, Power, and Performance,* edited by Jacob K. Olupona and Rowland O. Abiodun, 325–39. Bloomington: Indiana University Press.

Drewal, Margaret Thompson. 1992. *Yoruba Ritual: Performers, Play, Agency.* Bloomington: Indiana University Press.

———. 2003. "Improvisation as Participatory Performance: Egungun Masked Dancers in the Yoruba Tradition." In *Taken by Surprise: A Dance Improvisation Reader,* edited by Ann Cooper Albright and David Gere. Middletown, CT: Wesleyan University Press.

Dundun Ensemble of Adjarra, Benin. 1996. *The World's Musical Traditions,* vol. 8, *Yoruba Drums from Benin, West Africa.* Washington, DC: Smithsonian Folkways Recordings.

Durojaye, Cecilia. 2019. "Born a Musician: The Making of a Dundun Drummer among the Yoruba People of Nigeria." *Journal of Arts and Humanities* 8: 43–55.

Durojaye, Cecilia, Kristina L. Knowles, K. Jakob Patten, Mordecai J. Garcia, and Michael K. McBeath. 2021. "When Music Speaks: An Acoustic Study of the Speech Surrogacy of the Nigerian Dùndún Talking Drum." *Frontiers in Communication* 6: 1–17.

Eades, D. S. 1980. *The Yoruba Today*. Cambridge: Cambridge University Press.

EcuRed. "Instituto de planificación física." Accessed April 12, 2017. https://www.ecured.cu /Instituto_de_Planificaci%C3%B3n_F%C3%ADsica.

Edemodu, Austin. 2002. "Odyssey of an American Female Babalawo." *Eledá* blog, October 27. http://eleda.org/blog/2002/10/27/the-guardian-conscience-nurtured-by-truth/.

Edwards, Brent Hayes. 2003. *The Practice of Diaspora: Literature, Translation, and the Rise of Black Internationalism*. Cambridge, MA: Harvard University Press.

Edwards, Gary, and John Mason. 1998. *Black Gods: Oriṣa Studies in the New World*. New York: Yoruba Theological Archministry.

Edwards, Nadi. 2005. "Diaspora, Difference, and Black Internationalisms." *Small Axe* 9 (1): 120–28.

Ẹlẹ́buìbọn, Ifáyẹmí. 1999. *Ìyẹrẹ̀ Ifá: Tonal Poetry, the Voice of Ifá: An Exposition of Yorùbá Divinational Chants*. San Bernardino, CA: Ile Orunmila Communications.

Eledá.org. 2003. "D'Haifa Title Taken." March 13, 2003. http://eleda.org/blog/2003/03/13/dhaifa -title-taken/.

Eli Rodríguez, Victoria. 1997. *Instrumentos de la música folclórico-popular de Cuba*. Vol. 1. Havana: Centro de Investigación y Desarrollo de la Música Cubana.

Eme, Cecilia Amaoge, and Ebele Deborah Uba. 2016. "A Contrastive Study of the Phonology of Igbo and Yoruba." *UJAH: Unizik Journal of Arts and Humanities* 17 (1): 65–84.

Entralgo, Armando, and David González. 1991. "Cuban and Africa: Thirty Years of Solidarity." In *Cuban Foreign Policy Confronts a New International Order*, edited by J. Erisman and J. Kirk, 93–105. Boulder, CO: Lynn Rienner.

Esquenazi Pérez, Martha. 2001. *Del areíto y otros sones*. Havana: Editorial Letras Cubanas.

Estes, R. 1991. *The Behavior Guide to African Mammals, Including Hoofed Mammals, Carnivores, Primates*. Los Angeles: University of California Press.

Euba, Akin. 1990. *Yoruba Drumming: The Dùndún Tradition*. Bareuth, Germany: Eckhard Breitinger, Bayreuth University; Lagos, Nigeria: Elekoto Music Centre, University of Lagos.

———. 1994. "Drumming for the Egungun: The Poet-Musician in Yoruba Masquerade Theater." In *The Yoruba Artist*, edited by Rowland Abiodun, Henry J. Drewal, and John Pemberton III, 161–70. Washington, DC: Smithsonian Institution.

Euba, Titiola. 1985. "The Ooni of Ife's Crown and the Concept of Divine Head." *Nigeria Magazine* 53 (1): 1–18.

Fabian, Johannes. 1983. *Time and the Other: How Anthropology Makes Its Object*. New York: Columbia University Press.

Fabunmi, Chief M. A. 1969. *Ife Shrines*. Ife, Nigeria: University of Ife Press.

Fagborun, J. G. 1994. *The Yoruba Koiné: Its History and Linguistic Innovations*. Munich: Lincom Europa.

Falola, Toyin, ed. 2013. *Èṣù: Yoruba God, Power, and the Imaginative Frontiers*. Durham, NC: Carolina Academic Press.

Familusi, O. O. 2012. "African Culture and the Status of Women: The Yoruba Example." *Journal of Pan African Studies* 5 (1): 299–313.

Fatoba, Femi. 2005. "Healing Energies in Yoruba Ifa Religion." In *Rhythmus und Heilung: Transzendierende Kräfte in Wort, Musik und Bewegung*, edited by Esther Messmer-Hirt and Lilo Roost Vischer, 128–34. Münster, Germany: Lit.

Fatunmbi, Awo Fa'lokun. 1992–93. "The Concept of Male and Female Polarity in Ifa Divination and Ritual." *Journal of Caribbean Studies* 9 (1–2): 67–85.

Fatunmise, Chief Fagbemileke. 2013. *Iyamí Osoronga: Divine Femininity*. Bloomington, IN: Xlibris.

Feinberg, Richard E., and Richard S. Newfamer. 2016. *Tourism in Cuba: Riding the Wave toward Sustainable Prosperity*. Washington, DC: Latin America Initiative at Brookings, Kimberly Green Latin American and Caribbean Center.

Feld, Steven. (1982) 2012. *Sound and Sentiment: Birds, Weeping, Poetics, and Song in Kaluli Expression*. Durham, NC: Duke University Press.

———. 1996. "Waterfalls of Song: An Acoustemology of Place Resounding in Bosavi, Papua New Guinea." In *Senses of Place*, edited by Steven Feld and Keith Basso, 91–135. Santa Fe, NM: School of American Research Press.

———. 2017. "On Post-Ethnomusicology Alternatives: Acoustemology." In *Perspectives on a 21st-Century Comparative Musicology: Ethnomusicology or Transcultural Musicology?*, edited by Francesco Giannattasio and Giovanni Giuriati, 82–98. Udine, Italy: NOTA.

Fernández, Mirta. 2003. "Asociación Cultural Yoruba de Cuba. Conocer mejor nuestras raíces". *La Jiribilla* 11 (134). http://www.lajiribilla.cu/2003/n134_11/134_05.html.

———. 2010. "Las mujeres penetran en Ifá" [Women penetrate in Ifá]. *El Caiman Barbudo*, June 4, 2017. http://miradademujer.mex.tl/frameset.php?url5/130358_La-Mujer-en-IFA.html.

Fernandez, Nadine T. 2010. *Revolutionizing Romance: Interracial Couples in Contemporary Cuba*. New Brunswick, NJ: Rutgers University Press.

Fernández Olmos, Margarite. 2007. "Spirited Identities: Creole Religions, Creole/U.S. Latina Literature, and the Initiated Reader." In *Contemporary U.S. Latino/a Literary Criticism*, edited by Lyn Di Iorio Sandín and Richard Pérez, 63–92. New York: Palgrave Macmillan.

Fernández Robaina, Tomás. 1996. "Cuban Sexual Values and African Religious Beliefs." Appendix A in *Machos, Maricones, and Gays: Cuba and Homosexuality*, edited by Ian Lumsden. Philadelphia, PA: Temple University Press.

———. 1994. *Hablen paleros y santeros*. Havana: Editorial de Ciencias Sociales.

Fiddian-Qasmiyeh, Elena. 2015. *South-South Educational Migration, Humanitarianism, and Development: Views from the Caribbean, North Africa, and the Middle East*. New York: Routledge.

Figarola, Joel James. 2006. *La brujería Cubana: El Palo Monte: Aproximación al Pensamiento Abstracto de la Cubanía*. Santiago de Cuba, Cuba: Editorial Oriente.

Frith, Simon. 1988. *Music for Pleasure: Essays in the Sociology of Pop*. New York: Routledge.

Freyre, Frank Argoe. 2006. *Fulgencio Batista: From Revolutionary to Strongman*. New Brunswick, NJ: Rutgers University Press.

Friedhoff, A. J., M. Alpert, and R. L. Kurtzberg. 1962. "An Effect of Emotion on Voice." *Nature* 193: 357–58.

Frigerio, Alejandro. 2004. "Re-africanization in Secondary Religious Diasporas: Constructing a World Religion." *Civilisations* 51: 39–60.

Foucault, Michael. 1972. *The Archeology of Knowledge*. Translated by A. M. Sheridan Smith. New York: Pantheon.

Fox, A. A. 2004. *Real Country: Music and Language in Working-Class Culture*. Durham, NC: Duke University Press.

Gandonu, Ajato. 2011. "Nigeria's 250 Ethnic Groups: Realities and Assumptions." In *Perspectives on Ethnicity*, edited by Regina E. Holloman and Sergbei A. Arutiunov. Berlin: De Gruyter Mouton.

Garcia, David F. 2017. *Listening for Africa: Freedom, Modernity, and the Logic of Black Music's African Origins*. Durham, NC: Duke University Press.

García Basulto, Sol. 2016. "Cineasta acusa la religión yoruba en Cuba de 'machista e ignorante.'" October 29. https://www.14ymedio.com/nacional/religion_yoruba-Cuba-Noel_Rodriguez _Portuondo-Iyanifa_0_2099190066.html.

George, Edward. 2005. *The Cuban Intervention in Angola, 1965–1991: From Che Guevara to Cuito Cuanavale*. New York: Frank Kass.

Gjelten, Tom. 2008. *Bacardi and the Long Fight for Cuba: The Biography of a Cause*. New York: Viking.

Glissant, Édouard. 1997. *Poetics of Relation*. Translated by Betsy Wing. Ann Arbor: University of Michigan Press.

Godfried, Eugene. 2006. "CARLOTA: Lukumí/Yoruba Woman Fighter for Liberation Massacred in Matanzas, Cuba, in 1844." AfroCubaWeb. Accessed January 2, 2023. https://www .afrocubaweb.com/carlota.htm.

Gómez-Barris, Macarena. 2017. *The Extractive Zone: Social Ecologies and Decolonial Perspectives*. Durham, NC: Duke University Press.

González-Wippler, Migene. 1994. *Santería: The Religion, Faith, Rites, Magic*. St. Paul, MN: Llewellyn Worldwide.

Granma. 2015. "Cuban Medical Brigade Arrives in Nepal." *Granma*, May 13. https://en.granma .cu/mundo/2015-05-13/cuban-medical-brigade-arrives-in-nepal.

Grills, Cheryl, Wade W. Nobles, and Christopher Hill. 2018. "African, Black, Neither or Both? Models and Strategies Developed and Implemented by the Association of Black Psychologists." *Journal of Black Psychology* 44 (8): 791–826.

Guanche, Jesús. 1983. *Procesos etnoculturales de Cuba*. Havana: Letras Cubanas.

Guilbault, Jocelyne. 2010. "Music, Politics, and Pleasure: Live Soca in Trinidad." *Small Axe* 14 (1 [31]): 16–29.

———. 2019. "Party Music, Affect and the Politics of Modernity." *Journal of World Popular Music* 6 (2): 173–92.

Gupta, Girish. 2013. "Havana Scraps Exit Visas, but Most Cubans Won't Be Going Abroad." *Christian Science Monitor*, January 14, 2013. https://www.csmonitor.com/World/Americas /2013/0114/Havana-scraps-exit-visas-but-most-Cubans-won-t-be-going-abroad.

Hagedorn, Katherine J. 2001. *Divine Utterances: The Performance of Afro-Cuban Santería*. Washington, DC: Smithsonian Institution Press.

———. 2014. "Resorting to Spiritual Tourism: Sacred Spectacle in Afro-Cuban Regla de Ocha." In *Sun, Sound, and Sand: Music Tourism in the Circum-Caribbean*, edited by Timothy Rommen and Daniel Neely. Oxford: Oxford University Press.

Hall, Stuart. 1980. "Race, Articulation, and Societies Structured in Dominance." In *Sociological Theories: Race and Colonialism*, 16–60. Paris: UNESCO.

Hallgren, Roland. 1995. *The Vital Force: A Study of Àṣẹ in the Traditional and Neo-Traditional Culture of the Yoruba People*. Lund, Sweden: Department of History of Religions, University of Lund.

Hamilton, Andrew. 2011. "Cubans Hail a Private Property Revolution." *The Guardian*, November 5. https://www.theguardian.com/world/2011/nov/06/cubans-can-sell-homes-home-raul -fidel-castro.

Hamilton, Carrie. 2012. *Sexual Revolutions in Cuba: Passion, Politics, and Memory*. Chapel Hill: University of North Carolina Press.

Haraway, Donna. 2003. *The Companion Species Manifesto: Dogs, People, and Significant Otherness*. Chicago: Prickly Paradigm.

Hatzky, Christine. 2012. "Cuban's Educational Mission in Africa: The Example of Angola." In *The Capacity to Share: A Study of Cuba's International Cooperation in Educational Development*, edited by A. R. Hickling-Hudson, J. Corona-González, and R. Preston, 141–59. New York: Palgrave Macmillan.

———. 2015. *Cubans in Angola: South-South Cooperation and Transfer of Knowledge, 1976–1991*. Madison: University of Wisconsin Press.

Hearn, Adrian H. 2008. *Cuba: Religion, Social Capital, and Development*. Durham, NC: Duke University Press.

Hernandez-Reguant, Ariana. 2009. "Writing the Special Period: An Introduction." In *Cuba in the Special Period: Culture and Ideology in the 1990s*, edited by Ariana Hernandez-Reguant, 1–18. New York: Palgrave Macmillan.

Herrero Beatón, Ramiro. 2003. "El Festival del Caribe, el Cabildo Teatral Santiago y las religiones afrocubanas." *Del Caribe* 42: 113–14.

Herskovits, Melville. 1958. *The Myth of the Negro Past*. Boston: Beacon Press.

Hickling-Hudson, Anne, Jorge Corona-González, and Rosemary Preston, eds. 2012. *The Capacity to Share: A Study of Cuba's International Cooperation in Educational Development*. New York: Palgrave Macmillan.

Hill, Sam. 2020. "Black China: Africa's First Superpower Is Coming Sooner Than You Think." *Newsweek*, January 15, 2020. https://www.newsweek.com/2020/01/31/nigeria-next-superpower -1481949.html.

Holbraad, Martin. 2012. *Truth in Motion: The Recursive Anthropology of Cuban Divination*. Chicago: University of Chicago Press.

Huish, Robert. 2013. *Where No Doctor Has Gone Before: Cuba's Place in the Global Health Landscape*. Waterloo, Ontario: Wilfrid Laurier University Press.

Humboldt, Alexander von. 2011. *Political Essay on the Island of Cuba*. Edited by Vera M. Kutzinski and Ottmar Ette. Chicago: University of Chicago Press.

Hunwick, John. 1992. "An African Case Study of Political Islam: Nigeria." *ANNALS of the American Academy of Political and Social Science* 1 (November): 143–55.

Idowu, Bolaji E. 1962. *Olódùmarè: God in Yoruba Belief*. Ikeja, Nigeria: Longman.

Ifá Foundation International. 2014. "About Us." Accessed January 4, 2017. https://www.ifafoundation.org/about-us/. URL no longer active.

Ifeka, Caroline. 2009. "Titi Ikoli Revisited: Fetishism, Gender, and Power in Transitional Forest Economies of the Upper Cross River Borderlands, 1920s–1990s." In *Encounter, Transformation, and Identity: Peoples of the Western Cameroon Borderlands, 1891–2000*, edited by Ian Fowler and Verkijika G. Fanso, 151–68. New York: Berghahn Books.

Jackson, John L., Jr. 2006. *Real Black: Adventures in Racial Sincerity*. Chicago: University of Chicago Press.

Jassey, Victoria Rosemary. 2019. "Tambor Reverberations: Gender, Sexuality and Change in Cuban Batá Performance." PhD diss., Cardiff University.

Johnson, Paul Christopher. 2002. *Secrets, Gossip, and Gods: The Transformation of Brazilian Candomblé*. New York: Oxford University Press.

Joint Consultative Committee on Education. 1974. *Revised Official Orthography for the Yoruba Language*. Lagos, Nigeria: Joint Consultative Committee on Education, Federal Ministry of Education.

Jones, A. M. 1956. *Studies in African Music*. London: Oxford University Press.

Kahn, Carrie. 2022. "Cuba Hopes If It Builds New Hotels, Tourists Will Come, after a Long COVID Shutdown." *NPR*, May 24, 2022. https://www.npr.org/2022/05/22/1100587966/tour ists-are-returning-to-cuba-but-is-it-enough-for-the-islands-economy.

Karade, Baba Ifá. 1994. *The Handbook of Yoruba Religious Concepts*. York Beach, ME: Samuel Weiser.

Kelley, Robin D. G. 2002. *Freedom Dreams: The Black Radical Imagination*. Boston: Beacon.

Kelly, William. 2022. "'The People Live Practically Like Beasts': Informal Housing and Local Government in Santiago de las Vegas, Cuba, 1959–1965." *Cuban Studies* 51: 9–27.

King, Anthony. 1961. *Yoruba Sacred Music from Ekiti*. Ibadan, Nigeria: Ibadan University Press.

Kingdon, Jonathan, David Happold, Thomas Butynski, Michael Hoffmann, Meredith Happold, and Jan Kalina. 2013. *Mammals of Africa*. London: Bloomsbury Publishing.

Kirk, John M. 1989. *Between God and Party: Religion and Politics in Revolutionary Cuba*. Tampa: University of South Florida Press.

Kirk, John M., and H. Michael Erisman. 2009. *Cuban Medical Internationalism: Origins, Evolution, and Goals*. New York: Palgrave MacMillan.

Klein, Debra L. 2007. *Yorùbá Bàtá Goes Global: Artists, Culture Brokers, and Fans*. Chicago: University of Chicago Press.

———. 2015. "Being Àyàn in a Modernizing Nigeria: A Multigenerational Perspective." In *The Yorùbá God of Drumming: Transatlantic Perspectives on the Wood That Talks*, edited by Amanda Villepastour, 192–215. Jackson: University Press of Mississippi.

Konadu-Agyemang, Kwado, Baffour K. Takyi, and John Arthur, eds. 2006. *The New African Diaspora in North America: Trends, Community Building, and Adaption*. Lanham, MD: Lexington Books.

Konen, Alain. 2013. "'Ilé Tun' à La Havane: Une réinterprétation de l'ancestralité africaine et de la divination Ifá." *Ateliers d'anthropologie: Laboratoire d'ethnologie et de sociologie comparative. 38: Pratiques religieuses (afro-)cubaines*. https://ateliers.revues.org/9395.

Koser, Khalid, ed. 2003. *New African Diasporas*. London: Routledge.

Kubik, Gerhard. 1999. *Africa and the Blues*. Jackson: University of Mississippi Press.

Kumari, Ayele. 2014. *Iyanifa: Woman of Wisdom: Insights from the Priestesses of Ifa in the Ifa Orisha Tradition and Their Plight for the Divine Feminine*. Self-published.

Labott, Elise, Kevin Liptak, and Patrick O. 2017. "US Ending 'Wet Foot, Dry Foot' Policy for Cubans." *CNN*, January 13, 2017. https://www.cnn.com/2017/01/12/politics/us-to-end-wet -foot-dry-foot-policy-for-cubans/index.html.

Lachatañeré, Rómulo. 1992. *El sistema religioso de los afrocubanos*. Havana: Editorial de Ciencias Sociales.

———. 1939. "El sistema religioso de los Lucumís y otras influencias africanas en Cuba." *Estudios afrocubanos* 3 (1–4): 28–84.

Landry, Timothy R. 2015. "Vodún, Globalization, and the Creative Layering of Belief in Southern Bénin." *Journal of Religion in Africa* 45, fasc. 2: 170–99.

Langley, Lester D. 1983. *The Banana Wars: United States Intervention in the Caribbean, 1898–1934*. Lexington: University Press of Kentucky.

Laniran, Yetunde O., and George N. Clements. 2003. "Downstep and High Raising: Interacting Factors in Yoruba Tone Production." *Journal of Phonetics* 31 (2): 203–50.

Larduet Luaces, Abelardo. 2014. *Hacia una historia de la santería santiaguera y otras consideraciones*. Santiago de Cuba, Editorial del Caribe.

Leslie Santana, M. Myrta. 2019. "Las Transformistas: Performing Race and Sex in Post-Socialist Cuba." Doctoral dissertation, Harvard University, Graduate School of Arts & Sciences.

———. 2020. "Transgender 'Transformistas': Performing Race and Sex 'en las Américas.'" Conference Presentation, Society for Ethnomusicology Annual Conference (Virtual), October 31.

———. 2022. "*Transformista, Travesti, Transgénero*: Performing Sexual Subjectivity in Cuba." *Small Axe* 26 (2): 46–59.

Lewis, George E. 2008. *A Power Stronger Than Itself: The AACM and American Experimental Music*. Chicago: University of Chicago Press.

Lievesley, Geraldine. 2004. *The Cuban Revolution: Past, Present, and Future Perspectives*. New York: Palgrave Macmillan.

Lindfors, Bernth. 1977. *Forms of Folklore in Africa: Narrative, Poetic, Gnomic, Dramatic*. Austin: University of Texas Press.

Lock, Graham. 1999. *Blutopia: Visions of the Future and Revisions of the Past in the Work of Sun Ra, Duke Ellington, and Anthony Braxton*. Durham, NC: Duke University Press.

López, Kathleen M. 2013. *Chinese Cubans: A Transnational History*. Chapel Hill: University of North Carolina Press.

López Segrera, F. 1988. *Cuba: Política Extranjera y Revolución (1959–1988)*. Havana: Instituto Superior de Relaciones Internacionales.

López Valdés, Rafael L. 2002. *Africanos de Cuba*. San Juan, Puerto Rico: Centro de Estudios Avanzados de Puerto Rico y el Caribe, con la colaboración del Instituto de Cultura Puertorriqueña.

———. 1980. "El complejo mitológico de los jimaguas en la santería de Cuba." *Islas* 66 (May–August): 93–126.

———. 1998. "Notas para el estudio etnohistórico de los esclavos lucumí de Cuba." In *Estudios afro-cubanos: Selección de lecturas*, edited by Lázara Menéndez, 311–47. Havana: Facultad de Arte y Letras. Universidad de la Habana. Editorial Universitaria Félix Varela.

Lumsden, Ian. 1996. *Machos, Maricones, and Gays: Cuba and Homosexuality*. Philadelphia, PA: Temple University Press.

Lundgren, Silje. 2013. "'Mami, You're So Hot!' Negotiating Hierarchies of Masculinity through Piropos in Contemporary Havana." *Stockholm Review of Latin American Studies* 9: 5–20.

Machado Tineo, Alexander. 2013. "Iyanifá: aproximación a una jerarquía femenina en el Ifaísmo Cubano de hoy." MA thesis, Instituto Superior de Arte, Havana, Cuba, Departamento de Estudios Cubanos.

Madan, Marcelo. 2021. *Afrocuban Osain Treaty*. Self-published, Madan Orunmila Edition Publishing.

Maliki, Anthony. 2018. "Nigeria as a Nation of Influence." *Interpreter*, January 11, 2018. Lowy Institute. https://www.lowyinstitute.org/the-interpreter/nigeria-nation-influence.

Marcus, Sara, Karen Tongson, Paula Harper, Kimberly Mack, Eric Weisbard, and Simon Zagorski-Thomas. 2021. "Remote Intimacy: Popular Music Conversations in the COVID Era." *Journal of Popular Music Studies* 33 (1): 11–28.

Marcuzzi, Michael David. 2005. *A Historical Study of the Ascendant Role of Bàtá Drumming in Cuban Òrìsà Worship*. PhD diss., York University, Toronto.

———. 2006. "The Ipanodu Ceremony and the History of Orisa Worship in Nigeria and Cuba." In *ORISA: Yoruba Gods and Spiritual Identity in Africa and the Diaspora*, edited by Toyin Falola and Ann Geneva, 183–208. Austin: University of Texas at Austin.

————. 2011. "Writing on the Wall: Some Speculations on Islamic Talismans, Catholic Prayers, and the Preparation of Cuban Bata Drums for Orisha Worship." *Black Music Research Journal* 31 (2): 209–27.

Martín Barbero, Jesús. 1993. *Communication, Culture and Hegemony: From the Media to Mediations.* Translated by Elizabeth Fox and Robert A. White. London: SAGE Publications.

Martínez Betancourt, Julio Ismael. 2013. *Yerberos en La Habana.* Colección La Fuente Viva, No. 40. Havana: Fundación Fernando Ortiz.

————. 2014. "Apuntes históricos y antropológicos sobre nuevas fraternidades de Ifá en Cuba." Presented paper at the 34th Festival del Caribe, Santiago de Cuba, July 3–10.

————. 2015. "Ilú Iyá: Tambores nigerianos de reciente introducción en Cuba." Presentation, "Festival de Caribe: Fiesta del Fuego 35." Santiago de Cuba, July 6, 2015.

————. 2016. "Sacerdocio de Egúngún: Introducción y expansión por Cuba." Presentation, "Comité Cubano Proyecto 'La ruta del esclavo.'" Jardín Botánico Nacional, Havana.

Martínez Betancourt, Julio Ismael, and Carmen Corral Barrero. 2017. "Reciente introducción de tambores nigerianos a Cuba: el caso de los Ilú Ifá." *Clave: Revista Cubana de Música* 19 (1): 52–57.

Martínez Betancourt, Julio Ismael, and Enrique Rafael Orozco Rubio. 2016. "Cronología de la expansión del Ifá Tradicional Nigeriano por la región oriental de Cuba." In *Del Caribe*, vol. 64. Santiago de Cuba: Casa del Caribe.

Matory, J. Lorand. (1994) 2005. *Sex and the Empire That Is No More: Gender and the Politics of Metaphor in Oyo Yoruba Religion.* New York: Berghahn Books.

————. 1999. "The English Professors of Brazil: On the Diasporic Roots of the Yorùbá Nation." *Comparative Studies in Society and History* 41:72–103.

————. 2005. *Black Atlantic Religion.* Princeton, NJ: Princeton University Press.

————. 1986. "Vessels of Power: The Dialectical Symbolism of Power in Yoruba Religion and Polity-Part Two." MA thesis, University of Chicago, Department of Anthropology.

McClelland, E. M. 1982. *The Cult of Ifá among the Yoruba.* London: Ethnographica.

McDonnell, Patrick. 1990a. "Cuban Spy Attempts to Defect, Is Rejected as Risk to U.S. Security." *Los Angeles Times*, November 15, 1990. https://articles.latimes.com/1990-11-15/news/mn-6026_1_cuban-defector.

————. 1990b "Cuban Spy Seeking Asylum Is Freed from Jail." *Los Angeles Times*, November 9, 1990. https://articles.latimes.com/1990-11-09/local/me-3997_1_cuban-spy.

McGarrity, Gayle L. 1992. "Race, Culture, and Social Change in Contemporary Cuba." In *Cuba in Transition: Crisis and Transformation*, edited by Sandor Halebsky and John M. Kirk, 193–206. Boulder, CO: Westview Press.

McIntyre, Chris. 2015. *Namibia.* 5th ed. Guilford, CT: Globe Pequot Press.

McKenzie, Peter Rutherford. 1997. *Hail Orisha!: A Phenomenology of a West African Religion in the Mid-Nineteenth Century.* Leiden: Koninkÿke Brill.

Menéndez, Lázara. 1995. "¿Un cake para Obatalá?!" *Temas* 4 (October–December): 38–51.

————. 2002. *Rodar el coco: proceso de cambio en la santería.* Havana: Fundación Fernando Ortiz.

Miller, Ivor L. 2000. "A Secret Society Goes Public: The Relationship between Abakuá and Cuban Popular Culture." *African Studies Review* 43 (1): 161–88.

————. 2005. "Cuban Abakuá Chants: Examining New Linguistic and Historical Evidence for the African Diaspora." *African Studies Review* 48 (1): 23–58.

————. 2009. *Voice of the Leopard: African Secret Societies and Cuba.* Jackson: University Press of Mississippi.

Millet, José. 2000. "El foco de la santería santiaguera." *Del Caribe* 32: 110–19.

———. 1999. "Muerterismo o regla muertera." *Revista de Folklore de Fundación Joaquín Díaz* 19b (228): 208–16.

———. 2018. *Regla Konga Palo Mayombe en Santiago de Cuba: Y recuperación de la memoria de los musundis.* N.p.: Ediciones de la Fundación Casa de Caribe.

———. 1998. *Tierra tiembla: Arte ritual Afrocubano.* Translated by Desmond Joyce. Pamplona, Spain: Fundación Eugenio Granell.

Millet, José, and Rafael Brea. 1989. *Grupos folklóricos de Santiago de Cuba.* Santiago de Cuba: Editorial Oriente.

Ministerio de Educación. 1971. *Memorias: Congreso nacional de educación y cultura.* Havana: Ministerio de Educación.

Moore, Robin D. 1997. *Nationalizing Blackness: Afrocubanismo and Artistic Revolution in Havana, 1920–1940.* Pittsburgh, PA: University of Pittsburgh Press.

———. 2004. "Revolution and Religion: Yoruba Sacred Music in Socialist Cuba." In *The Yoruba Diaspora in the Atlantic World*, edited by Matt D. Childs and Toyin Falola, 260–90. Bloomington: Indiana University Press.

———. 2006. *Music and Revolution: Cultural Change in Socialist Cuba.* Berkeley: University of California Press.

Moore, Robin, and Elizabeth Sayre. 2006. "An Afro-Cuban Bata Piece for Obatala, King of the White Cloth." In *Analytical Studies in World Music*, edited by Michael Tenzer, 120–60. Oxford: Oxford University Press.

Morad, Moshe. 2014. *Fiesta de diez pesos: Music and Gay Identity and Special Period Cuba.* Surrey, UK: Ashgate.

Moreno, Isidro. 1999. "Festive Rituals, Religious Associations, and Ethnic Reaffirmation of Black Andalusians: Antecedents of the Black Confraternities and Cabildos in the Americas." In *Muteba Rahier, Representations of Blackness and the Performance of Identities*, 3–17. London: Bergin and Garvey Press.

Muñoz, José Esteban. 1999. *Disidentifications: Queers of Color and the Performance of Politics.* Minneapolis: University of Minnesota Press.

———. 2009. *Cruising Utopia: The Then and There of Queer Futurity.* New York: New York University Press.

Murchison, Gayle. 2018. "Let's Flip It! Quare Emancipations: Black Queer Traditions, Afrofuturisms, Janelle Monáe to Labelle." *Women and Music: A Journal of Gender and Culture* 22: 79–90.

Murrell, Nathaniel Samuel. 2010. *Afro-Caribbean Religions: An Introduction to Their Historical, Cultural, and Sacred Traditions.* Philadelphia, PA: Temple University Press.

Mwakikagile, Godfrey. 2002. "Nigeria." In *Nigeria: Current Issues and Historical Background*, edited by Martin P. Mathews, 17–50. New York: Nova Science Publishers.

National Insight News. "Ooni Congratulates the New Araba Agbaye." *National Insight News*, September 6, 2018. https://nationalinsightnews.com/ooni-congratulates-the-new-araba-agbaye/.

Neill, Ben. 2002. "Pleasure Beats: Rhythm and the Aesthetics of Current Electronic Music." *Leonardo Music Journal* 12:3–6.

Nichols, Michelle. 2015. "U.N. Appeals for Help for Boko Haram Displaced; Nigeria a No-Show." *Reuters*, September 25, 2015. https://www.reuters.com/article/us-un-assembly-boko-haram-aid/u-n-appeals-for-help-for-boko-haram-displaced-nigeria-a-no-show-idUSKCN0RP2IF20150925.

Nicoll, Ruaridh. 2022. "Can Cuba's Tourism Adapt to Survive after COVID Devastated the Industry?" *The Guardian*, May 6, 2022. https://www.theguardian.com/world/2022/may/06/cuba -tourism-recovery-pandemic.

Nketia, J. H. Kwabena. 1963. *African Music in Ghana*. Evanston, IL: Northwestern University Press.

Nowak, R. M. 1999. *Walker's Mammals of the World*. 6th ed. Baltimore, MD: Johns Hopkins University Press.

Nwosu, Nereus I. 1993. "The Dynamics of Nigeria's Decolonization Policy in Africa." *Transafrican Journal of History* 22:74–86.

O'Brien, David M. 2004. *Animal Sacrifice and Religious Freedom: Church of the Lukumi Babalu Aye v. City of Hialeah*. Lawrence: University Press of Kansas.

Ochoa, Todd. 2010. *Society of the Dead: Quita Manaquita and Palo Praise in Cuba*. Berkeley: University of California Press.

Ochoa Gautier, Ana María. 2014. *Aurality: Listening & Knowledge in Nineteenth-Century Colombia*. Durham, NC: Duke University Press.

———. 2006. "Sonic Transculturation, Epistemologies of Purification and the Aural Public Sphere in Latin America." *Social Identities* 12 (6): 803–825.

Odùgbemi, Ifáshade. 2007. *Ifá ìwé odú mímo: Libro sagrado de Ifá*. Madrid: Nuevos Escritores.

Offiah, Chivuzo A. J. 2017. "Globalization and the Culture/Creative Industries: An Assessment of Nigeria's Position in the Global Space." *IOSR Journal of Humanities and Social Science* 22 (1): 11–23.

Ogunleye, Foluke. 2007. *Theatre in Nigeria: Different Faces*. Ibadan, Nigeria: Humanities Publishers, University of Ibadan.

Okpewho, Isidore, and Nkiru Nzegwu, eds. 2009. *The New African Diaspora*. Bloomington: Indiana University Press.

Oládémo, Oyèrónké. 2022. *Women in Yoruba Religions*. New York: New York University Press.

Oladipo, Olusegun. 2002. *The Third Way in African Philosophy: Essays in Honour of Kwasi Wiredu*. Ibadan, Nigeria: Hope Publications.

Olajubu, Chief Oludare, and J. R. O. Ojo. 1977. "Some Aspects of Oyo Yoruba Masquerades." *Africa* 27 (3): 253–75.

Olajubu, Oyeronke. 2003. *Women in the Yoruba Religious Sphere*. Albany: State University of New York Press.

———. 2004. "Seeing through a Woman's Eye: Yoruba Religious Tradition and Gender Relations." *Journal of Feminist Studies in Religion* 20 (1): 41–60.

Ologundudu, Adedayo. 2009. "Ifá: Yorùbá Spirit of Wisdom, Knowledge and Truthfulness." *Orin Orisa. Yoruba Traditional Songs of Praises for Orisa*. Brooklyn, NY: Center for Spoken Words. CD/MP3.

Ológundúdú, Dayò. 2009. *The Cradle of Yoruba Culture*. New York: Center for Spoken Words.

Olorunnisola, Funmilola, and Demola Akinbami. 1992. *The Royal Eagle of the Yoruba*. Ibadan, Nigeria: Bookcraft.

Olson, Christa J., and René Agustín De los Santos. 2015. "Expanding the Idea of América." *Rhetoric Society Quarterly* 45 (3): 193–98.

Olson, David. 2008. "Priestess Promotes Orisa Religion." *Monterey Herald*, March 22, 2008. https://www.montereyherald.com/2008/03/22/priestess-promotes-orisa-religion/.

Olúmúyìwá, Tèmítópé. 2013. "Yoruba Writing: Standards and Trends." *Journal of Arts and Humanities* 2 (1): 40–51.

Olupona, Jacob K. 2011. *City of 201 Gods: Ilé-Ifè in Time, Space, and the Imagination*. Berkeley: University of California Press.

Olupona, Jacob K., and Rowland O. Abiodun, eds. 2016. *Ifá Divination, Knowledge, Power, and Performance*. Bloomington: Indiana University Press.

Olupona, Jacob K., and Terry Rey, eds. 2008. *Òrìṣà devotion as World Religion: The Globalization of Yorùbá Religious Culture*. Madison: University of Wisconsin Press.

Omidire, Félix Ayoh'. 2014. "Petrodollar, Bolivarianism, and the Re-Yorubanization of Santería in Chávez's Socialist Venezuela." In *Translantic Caribbean: Dialogues of People, Practices, Ideas*, edited by Ingrid Kummels, Claudia Rauhut, Stefan Rinke, and Birte Timm, 201–23. Bielefeld, Germany: transcript Verlag.

Omojola, Bode. 2011. "Ọ̀ṣun Òṣogbo: Power, Song and Performance in a Yoruba Festival." 20th Celebratory Edition, *Ethnomusicology Forum* 20 (1): 79–106.

———. 2014. *Yorùbá Music in the 20th Century: Identity, Agency, and Performance Practice*. Rochester, NY: University of Rochester Press.

Omosule, Segun. 2007. "Artistic Undercurrents of Performance: A Study of *Egungun* Costumes in Ode Irele." *Lagos Papers in English Studies*, vol. 2, 82–88.

Origunwa, Obafemi. n.d. "Odunfa Oakland 2016 Ifá Festival." Accessed April 14, 2017. https://www.obafemio.com/odunfa.html.

Orishada. 2013. "Araba Agbaye." 2013. Accessed April 13, 2017. http://orishada.com/wordpress/?page_id=12. URL no longer active.

Orozco Rubio, Enrique. 2015a. "Egbe Iran Atele Ilogbon Odugbemi. Misión: Desarrollar investigaciones y prácticas religiosas que permitan solidificar el sistema teológico legado por. . . ." [Details the history and mission of Ẹgbé Irán Átele Ilogbon Odugbemi in Santiago de Cuba]. Facebook, July 19, 2015. Accessed January 13, 2016. https://www.facebook.com/odugbemisantiagodecuba/posts/1005574406128298.

———. 2015b. "Ìyámi Òsòròngá: Myth and Reality (*Ìyámi Òsòròngá: Mito y Realiad*)." Presentation, "Festival de Caribe: Fiesta del Fuego 35." Santiago de Cuba, July 7.

———. 2022. "El empoderamiento de la mujer en el ifaismo cubano. ¿Moda o necesidad?" Presentation, "Festival del Caribe: Curso taller de religiosidad popular 2022." Santiago de Cuba, July 7.

Ortiz, Fernando. (1906) 1973. *Los negros brujos*. Miami: Ediciones Universal.

———. (1920) 1960. *La Antigua fiesta afrocubana del "día de reyes."* Havana: Ministerio de Relaciones Exteriories, Departamento de Asuntos Culturales, División de Publicaciones. Originally published in *Revista Bimestre Cubana* 15 (1): 5–26.

———. 1921. "Los cabildos afrocubanos." *Revista Bimestre Cubana* 26: 5–39.

———. (1950) 2001. *La africanía de la música folklórica cubana*. Havana: Editorial Letras Cubanas.

———. 1954. *Los instrumentos de la música afrocubana*. Vol. 4. Havana: Cárdenas y Cia.

———. 1994. *Los tambores batá de los yoruba* (Colección Raíces). Havana: Publicigraf.

Oshisada, Victor. 2014. "Nigeria: The 2014 Diary—January–March." *The Guardian*, November 30, 2014. https://allafrica.com/stories/201412041743.html.

Osundare, Niyi. 2008. "The Real Meaning of Adunni Olorisa (1915–2009) Celebrating the Late Susanne Wenger and Her Fellow Catalysts." *Présence Africaine*, nouvelle série, no. 178 (2e semestre): 108–12.

Otero, Solimar. 2010. *Afro-Cuban Diasporas in the Atlantic World*. Rochester, NY: University of Rochester Press.

Ovalle, David. 2014. "As Santería Grows and Evolves, the Increasing Focus on Africa Opens Rifts among the Sects." *Miami Herald*, March 28, 2014. https://www.miamiherald.com/news/local /community/miami-dade/article1962047.html.

Oyelami, Muraina. 1989. *Yoruba Dundun Music: A New Notation with Basic Exercises & Five Yoruba Drum Repertoires*. Lagos, Nigeria: Iwalewa.

Oyěwùmí, Oyèrónkẹ́. 2006. *What Gender Is Motherhood? Changing Yorùbá Ideals of Power, Procreation, and Identity in the Age of Modernity*. New York: Palgrave Macmillan.

Padilla Pérez, Maybell. 2006. "Sacerdotisas y brujas." *Revista Digital Consenso desde Cuba* 6 (1): 1–3.

Palmié, Stephan. 2002. *Wizards and Scientists: Explorations in Afro-Cuban Modernity and Tradition*. Durham, NC: Duke University Press.

———. 2008. "On Predications of Africanity." In *Africas of the Americas: Beyond the Search for Origins in the Study of Afro-Atlantic Religions*, edited by Stephan Palmié, 1–37. Leiden, Netherlands: Brill.

———. 2013. *The Cooking of History: How Not to Study Afro-Cuban Religion*. Chicago: University of Chicago Press.

Partido Comunista de Cuba. 1976. "Plataforma programática del Partido Comunista de Cuba." Departamento de Orientación Revolucionaria del Comité Central del Partido Comunista de Cuba. Havana, Cuba.

Paulding, Ben. 2017. "Meter, Feel, and Phrasing in West African Bell Patterns: The Example of Asante Kete from Ghana." *African Music: Journal of the International Library of African Music* 10 (3): 62–78.

Pear, Robert. 1989. "Cuban General and Three Others Executed for Sending Drugs to U.S." *New York Times*, July 14, 1989. https://www.nytimes.com/1989/07/14/world/cuban-general-and -three-others-executed-for-sending-drugs-to-us.html.

Peel, J. D. Y. 1989. "The Cultural Work of Yoruba Ethnogenesis." In *History and Ethnicity*, edited by Elizabeth Tonkin, Maryon MacDonald, and Malcolm Chapman, 189–215. London: Routledge.

———. 2000. *Religious Encounter and the Making of the Yoruba*. Bloomington: Indiana University Press.

———. 2016. *Christianity, Islam, and the Orişa Religion: Three Traditions in Comparison and Interaction*. Oakland: University of California Press.

Peñalosa, David. 2009. *The Clave Matrix—Afro-Cuban Rhythm: Its Principles and African Origins*. Redway, CA: Bembe Books.

Perez, Louis A., Jr. 1986. *Cuba under the Platt Amendment, 1902–1934*. Pittsburgh, PA: University of Pittsburgh Press.

Perna, Vincenzo. 2005. *Timba: The Sound of the Cuban Crisis*. London: Routledge.

Peters, Christabelle. 2012. *Cuban Identity and the Angolan Experience*. New York: Palgrave Macmillan.

Peters, Philip. 2012. *Cuba's Entrepreneurs: Foundation of a New Private Sector*. Arlington, VA: Lexington Institute.

Pinn, Anthony B. 1998. *Varieties of African-American Religious Experience*. Minneapolis, MN: Augsburg Fortress Publishers.

Polack, Peter. 2013. *The Last Hot Battle of the Cold War: South Africa vs. Cuba in the Angolan Civil War*. Havertown, PA: Casemate Publishers.

Porcello, Thomas, Louise Meintjes, Ana Maria Ochoa, and David W. Samuels. 2010. "The Reorganization of the Sensory World." *Annual Review of Anthropology* 39 (1): 51–66.

Pouymiró, Nagybe Madariaga. 2015a. "La menstruación, bendición o maldición de Enrique Orozco Rubio." Conference presentation, Fiesta del Fuego. Santiago de Cuba, June 6..

———. 2015b. *Ritmos nuevos para los Tambores Bata: Por el derecho de igualdad de género.* Self-published.

Price, Richard, and Sally Price. 2003. *The Root of Roots: or, How Afro-American Anthropology Got Its Start.* Chicago: Prickly Paradigm; Bristol, UK: University Presses Marketing.

Probst, Peter. 2004. "Vital Politics: History and Heritage in Osogbo, Nigeria." In *Between Resistance and Expansion: Explorations of Local Vitality in Africa.* New Brunswick, NJ: Transaction Publishers.

———. 2011. *Osogbo and the Art of Heritage: Monuments, Deities, and Money.* Bloomington: Indiana University Press.

Pryor, Andrea. 1999. "The House of Añá: Women and Batá." *CBMR Digest* 12 (2): 6–8.

Radio Encyclopedia. 2013. "Female Percussionists Defend Legitimacy of Their Music in Cuba." Havana, Cuba. https://www.radioenciclopedia.cu/cultural-news/news/female-percussionists -defend-legitimacy-of-their-music-in-cuba-20130708/.

Ramos, Miguel, 2000. "The Empire Beats On: Oyo, Bata Drums and Hegemony in Nineteenth-Century Cuba." PhD diss., Florida International University, Miami. *ProQuest ETD Collection for FIU.* AAI1399164. https://digitalcommons.fiu.edu/dissertations/AAI1399164.

Rancière, Jacques. (2004) 2009. *Aesthetics and Its Discontents.* Cambridge: Polity Press.

Rauhut, Claudia. 2014. "The Reconstruction of Yoruba and Lukumí in Cuban Santería." In *Translantic Caribbean: Dialogues of People, Practices, Ideas,* edited by Ingrid Kummels, Claudia Rauhut, Stefan Rinke, and Birte Timm, 181–200. Bielefeld, Germany: transcript Verlag.

Raynolds, Laura B., and Joanna K. Uhry. 2010. "The Invented Spellings of Non-Spanish Phonemes by Spanish–English Bilingual and English Monolingual Kindergarteners." *Reading and Writing* 23 (5): 495–513.

Redacción Internacional. 2014. "Aplauso mundial por acercamiento entre Cuba y Estados Unidos." *Granma,* December 18, 2014. https://www.granma.cu/mundo/2014-12-18/aplauso-mundial -por-acercamiento-entre-cuba-y-estados-unidos.

República de Cuba / Republic of Cuba. Constitución Política de 1976 (Political Constitution of 1976). Accessed February 2, 2016. https://pdba.georgetown.edu/Constitutions/Cuba/cuba 1976.html#mozTocId644806.

Richards, David. 1994. *Masks of Difference: Cultural Representations in Literature, Anthropology, and Art.* Cambridge: Cambridge University Press.

Richman, K. E. 2008. "A More Powerful Sorcerer: Conversion, Capital, and Haitian Transnational Migration." *Nieuwe West—Indische Gids* 82 (1): 3–45.

Richmond, M. 1991. "Exporting the Education Revolution: The Cuban Project to Become a World Education Power." In *Cuban Foreign Policy Confronts a New International Order,* edited by H. M. Erisman and J. M. Kirk, 167–79. Boulder, CO: Lynne Rienner.

Rodriguez, Andrea. 2017. "Cuba Sees Explosion in Internet Access as Ties with US Grow." January 14, 2017. https://phys.org/news/2017-01-cuba-explosion-internet-access-ties.html.

Rodríguez Portuondo, Noel, dir. 2016. *Ìyánifá: La necesaria evolución.* 2016. Aşé Recordings. Film.

Roland, Kaifa. 2011. *Cuban Color in Tourism and La Lucha.* New York: Oxford University Press.

Rollefson, J. Griffith. 2008. "The 'Robot Voodoo Power' Thesis: Afrofuturism and Anti-Anti-Essentialism from Sun Ra to Kool Keith." *Black Music Research Journal* 28 (1): 83–109.

Romeu, Jorge Luis. 2013. "Cuban Freemasons in the Development of Civil Society in Political Opening." In *Handbook of Contemporary Cuba: Economy, Politics, Civil Society, and Globalization*, edited by Mauricio A. Font, 278–90. New York: Taylor & Francis.

Rommen, Timothy. 2007. *"Mek Some Noise": Gospel Music and the Ethics of Style in Trinidad*. Berkeley: University of California Press.

Roots and Rooted: For Those That Love Traditional African Religion. 2010. "Interview with Awo Owolabi, Son of the Araba." July 14, 2010. https://www.rootsandrooted.org/index quepeq1399.html. URL no longer active.

Rose, Tricia. 1994. *Black Noise: Rap Music and Black Culture in Contemporary America*. Middleton, CT: Wesleyan University Press.

Rose Marketing. 2016. "Rose Unveils the New Cuban Consumer Survey at Their Presentation in Havana." September 23, 2016. http://www.rose.ru/news/2465/. URL no longer active.

Rossbach de Olmos, Lioba. 2014. "Cruces y entrecruzamientos en los caminos de los orichas: Tradiciones en conflicto." *INDIANA* (Instituto Ibero-Americano en Berlín) 31: 9–107.

Routon, Kenneth. 2010. *Hidden Powers of the State in the Cuban Imagination*. Gainesville: University of Florida Press.

Rowe, D. 1995. *Popular Cultures: Rock Music, Sport and the Politics of Pleasure*. London: SAGE Publications.

Roy, Joaquín. 2009. *The Cuban Revolution (1959–2009): Relations with Spain, the European Union, and the United States*. New York: Palgrave Macmillan.

Rubiera Castillo, Daisy. 2020. "Women in Santería or Regla de Ocha: Gender, Myth, and Reality." In *Afrocubanas: History, Thought, and Cultural Practices*, edited by Devyn Spence Benson, Daisy Rubiera Castillo, and Inés María Martiatu Terry, 91–112. London: Rowman and Littlefield International.

Ruskin, Jesse. 2010. " 'Talking Drums' on Rural and Global Stages." *UCLA African Studies Center* (blog), February 1, 2010. https://international.ucla.edu/africa/article/113707.

Sachs, Jeffrey D. 2012. "Nigeria Hurtles into a Tense Crossroad." *New York Times*, January 10, 2012. https://www.nytimes.com/2012/01/11/opinion/nigeria-hurtles-into-a-tense-crossroad .html.

Sáenz Coopat, Carmen María. 1997. "Tambores dundún." In *Instrumentos de la música folclórico-popular de Cuba*, vol. 2, edited by V. Rodríguez, A. Casanova Oliva, J. Guanche Pérez, Z. Ramos Venereo, C. Sáenz Coopat, L. Vilar Alvarez, and M. Vinueza González, 357–62. Havana: Editorial de Ciencias Sociales.

Salehi-Nejad, Alireza. 2011. *The Third World: Country or People?* London: Titan.

Samuel, Kayode M. 2008/2009. "Instrumental Technology of Dundun of the Yoruba." *Nigerian Art Reflections* 8:47–65.

———. 2014. "Male Attitudes to Female Dùndún Drumming in Western Nigeria." *Nigerian Field* 79, parts 1 and 2: 25–40.

———. 2021. "The Language of Gángan, A Yorùbá Talking Drum." *Frontiers in Communication* 6: 1–14.

Sanger, David E. 2022. "Biden Administration Lifting Some Trump-Era Restrictions on Cuba." *New York Times*, May 16, 2022. https://www.nytimes.com/2022/05/16/us/politics/biden-cuba -policy.html.

Santa Cruz, Miguel, Gustavo Díaz, Juan González, Cándido Martínez, Domingo Hernández, Alberto Yenkins and group, Marcus Portillo Domínguez and group, et al. (1957) 2003. *Havana & Matanzas, Cuba, ca. 1957: Batá, Bembé, and Palo Songs from the Historic Recordings of Lydia Cabrera and Josefina Tarafa*. Compact disc. Washington, DC: Smithsonian Folkways Records.

Santo, Diana Espírito. 2015. *Developing the Dead: Mediumship and Selfhood in Cuban Espiritismo*. Gainesville: University Press of Florida.

Sawyer, Mark. 2006. *Racial Politics in Post-Revolutionary Cuba*. Cambridge: Cambridge University Press.

Sayre, Elizabeth. 2000. "Cuban Batá Drumming and Women Musicians: An Open Question." *Center for Black Music Research Digest* 13 (1): 12–15.

Scarpaci, Joseph L. 2005. *Plazas and Barrios: Heritage Tourism and Globalization in the Latin American Centro Histórico*. Tucson: University of Arizona Press.

———. 2006. "Environmental Planning and Heritage Tourism in Cuba during the Special Period: Challenges and Opportunities." In *Environmental Planning in the Caribbean*, edited by Jonathan Pugh and Janet Henshall Momsen, 85–104. New York: Routledge.

Schieffelin, B., and R. Doucet. 1994. "The 'Real' Haitian Creole: Ideology, Metalinguistics, and Orthographic Choice." *American Ethnologist* 21 (1): 176–200.

Seremetakis, Nadia. 1994. *The Senses Still: Perception and Memory as Material Culture in Modernity*. Chicago: University of Chicago Press.

Schweitzer, Kenneth. 2013. *The Artistry of Afro-Cuban Batá Drumming: Aesthetics, Transmission, Bonding, and Creativity*. Jackson: University Press of Mississippi.

Scott, David. 1999. Preface to "The Archeology of Black Memory: An Interview with Robert A. Hill." *Small Axe* 5: 82.

Serazio, Michael. 2016. "Guerrilla Marketing: How Cubans Work Around a National Ban on Advertising." *The Atlantic*, March 21, 2016. https://www.theatlantic.com/business/archive /2016/03/how-do-cubans-do-business-in-a-country-that-bans-ads/474507/.

Sexteto Habanero. (1928) 1995. "Dónde estás corazón." Written by Martinez Serrano. *Sexteto Habanero 1926–1931*. Recorded in New York and Havana, Cuba, 1926–1931. Compact disc. Crawley, England: Harlequin.

Shain, Richard M. 2018. *Roots and Reverse: Senegalese Afro-Cuban Music and Tropical Cosmopolitanism*. Middletown, CT: Wesleyan University Press.

Sharma, Devika, and Frederik Tygstrup, eds. 2015. *Structures of Feeling: Affectivity and the Study of Culture*. Berlin: De Gruyter.

Shepherd, Verene. 2006. *Engendering History: Caribbean Women in Historical Perspective*. London: Ian Randle.

Simoni, Valerio. 2016. *Tourism and Informal Encounters in Cuba*. New York: Berghahn.

Simpson, George Eaton. 1962. "The Shango Cult in Nigeria and in Trinidad." *American Anthropologist* 64 (6): 1204–19.

Sklar, Robert L. 1963. *Nigerian Political Parties: Power in an Emergent African Nation*. Princeton, NJ: Princeton University Press.

Smith, Christen Anne. 2016. "Towards a Black Feminist Model of Black Atlantic Liberation: Remembering Beatriz Nascimento." *Meridians* 14 (2): 71–87.

Smith, Robert S. 1988. *Kingdoms of the Yoruba*. Madison: University of Wisconsin Press.

Spiro, Michael, and Justin Hill. 2017. *Underneath the Sacred Rhythms: Orú del Igbodú (Oro Seco)*. Published by the authors.

Soares, Kristie. 2020. "Dancing with Death: Celia Cruz's Azúcar and Queer of Color Survival." Counterpoints Lecture, American Music Research Center, University of Colorado, Boulder (Virtual Presentation), November 2, 2020.

Soyinka, Wole. 1976. *Myth, Literature, and the African World*. Cambridge: Cambridge University Press.

Spencer, Leland G., IV. 2015. "Introduction: Centering Transgender Studies and Gender Identity in Communication Scholarship." In *Transgender Communication Studies: Histories, Trends, and Trajectories*, edited by Leland G. Spencer and Jamie C. Capuzza, 9–22. Lanham, MD: Lexington Books.

Steingo, Gavin. 2016. *Kwaito's Promise: Music and the Aesthetics of Freedom in South Africa*. Chicago: University of Chicago Press.

Stoller, Paul. 1989. *The Taste of Ethnographic Things: The Senses in Anthropology*. Philadelphia: University of Pennsylvania Press.

Stoner, K. Lynn. 1991. *From the House to the Streets: The Cuban Woman's Movement for Legal Reform, 1898–1940*. Durham, NC: Duke University Press.

Strongman, Robert. 2019. *Queering Black Atlantic Religions: Transcorporeality in Candomblé, Santería, and Vodou*. Durham, NC: Duke University Press.

Sublette, Ned. 2004. *Cuba and Its Music: From the First Drums to the Mambo*. Chicago: Chicago Review Press.

———. 2016. "Ancient Text Messages: Batá Drums in a Changing World." Audio blog post. Afropop Worldwide. February 11, 2016.

Taleb, Nassim Nicholas. 2012. *Antifragile: Things That Gain from Disorder*. New York: Random House.

Tallotte, William. 2018. "Improvisation as Devotion: *Nāgasvaram* Music and Ritual Communication in Hindu Temple Festival Processions." *Ethnomusicology Forum* 27 (1): 88–108.

Telles, Edward E. 2004. *Race in Another America: The Significance of Skin Color in Brazil*. Princeton, NJ: Princeton University Press.

Thabiti Willis, John. 2017. *Masquerading Politics: Kinship, Gender, and Ethnicity in a Yoruba Town*. Bloomington: Indiana University Press.

Thornton, Brendan Jamal. 2016. *Negotiating Respect: Pentecostalism, Masculinity, and the Politics of Spiritual Authority in the Dominican Republic*. Gainesville: University Press of Florida.

Tongson, Karen. 2011. *Relocations: Queer Suburban Imaginaries*. New York: New York University Press.

Torres, Eli. 2016. "Oloye Ifanla Italeke." http://ORISAIFA.COM/OLOYE.HTML. URL no longer active.

Torres Zayas, Ramón. 2010. *Relación barrio-juego abakuá en la ciudad de la Habana*. Havana: Fundación Fernando Ortiz.

Truax, B. 2001. *Acoustic Communication*. Westport: Ablex.

UN DESA (United Nations Department of Economic and Social Affairs). 2017. "World Population Projected to Reach 9.8 Billion in 2050, and 11.2 Billion in 2100." June 21, 2017. New York. https://www.un.org/development/desa/en/news/population/world-population-prospects-2017.html.

UPI Archives. 1990. "Government Blocks Release of Cuban Agent." UPI, November 10, 1990. https://www.upi.com/Archives/1990/11/10/Government-blocks-release-of-Cuban-agent/3610658213200/.

US Embassy in Cuba. "U.S. Embassy Havana." Accessed November 26, 2020. https://cu.usembassy.gov/embassy/havana/.

Van Der Meer, Tony. 2017. "Spiritual Journeys: A Study of Ifá /Òrìṣà Practitioners in the United States Initiated in Nigeria." PhD diss., Antioch University, Leadership and Change Program. https://aura.antioch.edu/etds/337.

Vaughan, Umi. 2012. *Rebel Dance, Renegade Stance: Timba Music and Black Identity in Cuba*. Ann Arbor: University of Michigan Press.

Vaughan, Umi, and Carlos Aldama. 2012. *Carlos Aldama's Life in Batá: Cuba, Diaspora, and the Drum*. Bloomington: Indiana University Press.

Vázquez Montalbán, Manuel. 1998. *Y Dios entró en La Habana*. Madrid, Spain: El País/Aguilar.

Vega, Martin Moreno. 2000. *The Altar of My Soul: The Living Traditions of Santeria*. Westminster, MD: Ballantine Books.

Vélez, María Teresa. 2000. *Drumming for the Gods: The Life and Times of Felipe García Villamil, Palero, Santero, and Abakuá*. Philadelphia: Temple University Press.

Verger, Pierre. 1952. "Le culte des vodun d'Abomey aurait-il été apporté à Saint-Louis de Maranhon par la mère du roi Ghèzo?" In *Les afro-américains*, 157–60. [Mémoires de l'IFAN, 27]. Dakar, Senegal: IFAN.

Viera, William Bravo. 2015. *Templo de Ifá de Cuba: Información actualizada*. Text document. Author's private collection.

Villepastour, Amanda. 2010. *Ancient Text Messages of the Yoruba Bàtá Drum: Cracking the Code*. Farnham, UK: Ashgate.

———. 2013. "Amelia Pedroso: The Voice of a Cuban Priestess Leading from the Inside." In *Women Singers in Global Contexts: Music, Biography, Identity*, edited by Ruth Hellier and Ellen Koskoff, 54–72. Urbana: University of Illinois Press.

———. 2015a. "Anthropomorphizing Ayan in Transatlantic Gender Narratives." In *The Yorùbá God of Drumming: Transatlantic Perspectives on the Wood That Talks*, edited by Amanda Villepastour, 125–46. Jackson: University Press of Mississippi.

———, ed. 2015b. *The Yorùbá God of Drumming: Transatlantic Perspectives on the Wood That Talks*. Jackson: University Press of Mississippi.

———. 2020. "The Cuban Lexicon Lucumí and African Language Yorùbá: Musical and Historical Connections." In *Handbook of the Changing World Language Map*, edited by Stanley D. Brunn and Roland Kehrei, 2575–602. Cham, Switzerland: Springer.

———. 2021. "The Legacy of Ortiz's Yorubization of Lucumí: Translation as Transculturation." *HAU: Journal of Ethnographic Theory* 11 (1): 153–73.

Vincent, Amanda. 2006. "Bata Conversations: Guardianship and Entitlement Narratives about the Bata in Nigeria and Cuba." PhD diss., School of Oriental and African Studies (SOAS), University of London.

Virani, Vivek. 2022. "From Satsaṅg to Stage: Negotiating Aesthetic Theologies and Aspirational Subjectivities in a North Indian Bhajan Competition." *Ethnomusicology* 66 (1): 106–37.

Viveiros de Castro, Eduardo. (2004) 2019. "Exchanging Perspectives: The Transformation of Objects into Subjects in Amerindian Ontologies." *Common Knowledge* 25 (1–3): 21–42.

Warden, Nolan. 2006. "Cajón Pa' Los Muertos: Transculturation and Emergent Tradition in Afro-Cuban Ritual Drumming and Song." MA thesis, Ethnomusicology, Tufts University.

Weinstein, Norman C. 1993. *A Night in Tunisia: Imaginings of Africa in Jazz*. New York: Limited Editions.

Whalman, Maude Southwell. 2001. "African Charm Traditions Remembered in the Arts of the Americas." In *Self-Taught Art: The Culture and Aesthetics of American Vernacular Art*, edited by Charles Russel, 146–65. Jackson: University Press of Mississippi.

Whitefield, Mimi. 2016. "Cubans Don't Make Much, but It's More Than State Salaries Indicate." *Miami Herald*, July 12, 2016. https://www.miamiherald.com/news/nation-world/world/americas/cuba/article89133407.html.

The White House. 2014. "Statement by the President on Cuba Policy Changes." Office of the Press Secretary. December 17, 2014. https://obamawhitehouse.archives.gov/the-press-office /2014/12/17/statement-president-cuba-policy-changes.

Wiart, Cristophe. 2006. *Medicinal Plants of the Asia-Pacific: Drugs for the Future?* Hackensack, NJ: World Scientific Publishing.

Williams, Dan. 1987. "Duped CIA, 'Double Agents' Claim: U.S.-Cuban Tensions Rise as Spying Charges Spiral." *Los Angeles Times*, July 26, 1987. https://www.latimes.com/archives/la-xpm -1987-07-26-mn-1227-story.html.

Williams, Raymond. 1977. *Marxism and Literature*. Oxford: Oxford University Press.

Wirtz, Kristina. 2007a. "Divining the Past: The Linguistic Reconstruction of 'African' Roots in Diasporic Ritual Registers and Songs." *Journal of Religion in Africa* 37:242–74.

———. 2007b. "How Diasporic Religious Communities Remember: Learning to Speak the 'Tongue of the Oricha' in Cuban Santería." *American Ethnologist* 34 (1): 108–26.

———. 2014. *Performing Afro-Cuba: Image, Voice, Spectacle in the Making of Race and History*. Chicago: University of Chicago Press.

———. 2016. "The Living, the Dead, and the Immanent Dialogue across Chronotopes." *HAU: Journal of Ethnographic Theory* 6 (1): 343–69.

Wolfe, Cary. 2009. *What Is Posthumanism?* Minneapolis: University of Minnesota Press.

Wong, Deborah. 2019. *Louder and Faster: Pain, Joy, and the Body Politic in Asian American Taiko*. Berkeley: University of California Press.

Yái, Ọlábíyí Babalọlá. 2001. "Yoruba Religion and Globalization: Some Reflections." *Cuadernos Digitales* 15 (October): 1–21.

Yavas, M. 2006. *Applied English Phonology*. Malden, MA: Blackwell Publishing.

Yoruba Cultural Association of Cuba (ACYC). (2004) 2013. "Respuesta del Consejo de Sacerdotes Mayores de Ifá de la República de Cuba y de los 1621 Miembros Babalawos de la Asociación Cultural Yoruba de Cuba, a la descabellada actitud de algunos Babalawos que dicen haber iniciado a ciertas mujeres en Culto a Ifá: Anexo 1." In "Iyanifá: aproximación a una jerarquía femenina en el Ifaísmo Cubano de hoy." Alexander Machado Tineo. Master's thesis, Instituto Superior de Arte, Departamento de Estudios Cubanos.

Zeuske, Michael Max P. 2007. "Cuba." In *Encyclopedia of the Middle Passage*, edited by Toyin Falola and Amanda Warnock, 121–23. Westport, CT: Greenwood Press.

Zimman, Lal. 2018. "Transgender Voices: Insights on Identity, Embodiment, and the Gender of the Voice." *Language and Linguistics Compass* 12 (8): e12284.

Index

Page numbers in italics refer to figures.

www.ingramcontent.com/pod-product-compliance
Lightning Source LLC
Chambersburg PA
CBHW032128020426
42334CB00016B/1087